Quantum Computing Experimentation with Amazon Braket

Explore Amazon Braket quantum computing to solve combinatorial optimization problems

Alex Khan

BIRMINGHAM—MUMBAI

Quantum Computing Experimentation with Amazon Braket

Group Product Manager: Pavan Ramchandani
Publishing Product Manager: Kushal Dave
Senior Editor: Keagan Carneiro
Content Development Editor: Adrija Mitra
Technical Editor: Saurabh Kadave
Copy Editor: Safis Editing
Project Coordinator: Rashika Ba
Proofreader: Safis Editing
Indexer: Tejal Daruwale Soni
Production Designer: Jyoti Chauhan
Marketing Coordinator: Sonakshi Bubbar

First published: July 2022

Production reference: 1290722

Published by Packt Publishing Ltd.
Livery Place
35 Livery Street
Birmingham
B3 2PB, UK.

978-1-80056-526-5

www.packt.com

To my family and friends who have suffered through my crazy ideas and tangents; believe it or not, it is you who inspire me to take risks and be myself.

To the authors, researchers, and entrepreneurs in quantum computing who have taken the time to share their wisdom and stories with the rest of us.

And, to you, my reader, since you are curious and taking a chance. It is my hope that this book will help to clarify some aspects of a complicated discipline.

– Alex Khan

Foreword

It is truly an honor to receive a request to write a foreword for a book like this, in this particular space, at this specific time in history, and by a colleague whom I believe will make significant contributions to this industry during his tenure. That book is *Quantum Computing Experimentation with Amazon Braket*, the space is quantum computing, the time in history is the infancy of an advanced technology that realistically expects the change the world, and my colleague is Alex Khan.

Alex and I got involved with quantum computing at roughly the same time, and with connections and collaborations with other esteemed colleagues in the domain, such as Dr. Keeper Lane Sharkey, we all began our journey in this space, making contributions where our respective talents best positioned us to: Alex in the quantum start-up, education, and consultancy space; Keeper in the quantum chemistry space; and I brought quantum computing to a fortune-five health company with 350,000 global employees and continue to lead the quantum efforts there.

It's not surprising to see contributions by industry leaders such as Alex manifested in books of this nature and undergirded by quantum vendors such as AWS, who bring significant and diverse computational capabilities to the table. The fusion of these two actors in the wild brings a richness to both the educational process and the process of developing valued industry skills, resulting in a far better outcome for the individual, and this is likely to be a key training model in the quantum space moving forward.

The book's focus is as the title suggests: it's a journey to explore and experiment with quantum computing using the Amazon Braket experience. This is appealing to both the neophyte and the experienced practitioner, as the latter will procure a solid tactical vendor education through a digestible and methodical pedagogy, and the former will get that plus an introduction to quantum basics as well. Readers will explore advanced topics in the later chapters, which is the ultimate commission of the book: to show real-world applications.

The book begins with the mechanics and specifics of the AWS platform, which is both necessary and wise since AWS brings an "infrastructure as code" approach to quantum computing, in addition to being the only vendor to make multiple quantum hardware architectures available under one cost-effective platform. This is important to industries in the wild seeking to get into quantum because experimentation now becomes an OpEx (operational expenditure) as opposed to a CapEx (capital expenditure), and that significantly lowers the entry price to quantum experimentation and increases the potential for senior leadership buy-in. Practitioners developing quantum capabilities on that framework will have more highly valued skill sets in the marketplace because of the exposure to multiple hardware platforms, as each platform brings something unique and different to the table when it comes to solving problems.

This book also provides a solid introduction to and overview of the two different quantum architectures (gate-based and annealing) and how to use them. The differences between the architectural variants within the gate-based architectures are significant, but nuanced. The differences between the annealing and the gate-based architectures are significant and glaring. The practitioner who gets hands-on experience in comparing and contrasting these two significantly different architectures and how they relate to specific use cases will have developed valuable capabilities. To this end, the book provides a solid journey through the D-Wave, OQC, IonQ, and Rigetti quantum architectures.

This book does a great job of weaving together specific use cases with general quantum education in the flow of its content. That's a non-trivial task since the annealing architecture is so different than the gate-based architectures, and the ways of conceptualizing the problems (and solutions) vary significantly between any architecture being used, particularly at the algorithm level.

This book spends a decent amount of time on advanced subjects such as QAOA, QUBO, and hybrid algorithms, doing a solid job of laying out the use cases under consideration and how the various architectures would be used to address those subjects at a tactical level. This approach is particularly helpful when addressing the single versus multiple objective optimization use case as it highlights the differences between the annealing approach and the gate-based approach, something that's found in later chapters.

The quantum computing space is following a very similar maturation trajectory to the classical computing space in that it begins in the lab and ends in the hands of the consumer. We call that the producer/consumer difference. The producers make the technology, and the consumers use it to solve real problems in the wild. The consumers can only make proper use of the technology when both it and their understanding of how to effectively use it reach a certain level of maturity. The time between when producers mature the technology enough for consumers to effectively engage it can be viewed as eras, and certain seminal events have to occur before computation moves from one era to another. The classical illustration of one of those seminal events of this is when Dennis Ritchie invented C and UNIX, which enabled classical computing to move out from the labs and into the hands of the consumer.

While we are all still firmly in the producer era of the quantum adventure, we can (and should) expect a series of tactical improvements (or small victories) that help move the maturity of the whole just a little bit forward, and when added up over time, can move the overall industry's maturity a great deal.

I think this book is one of those victories; it educates, inspires, and motivates quantum practitioners of the consumer stripe to enrich and broaden their experience in the quantum space, and that has great value to that type of individual who'll make the greatest impact in the wild when fully enabled with mature tools.

Matthew R. Versaggi, MS, MBA – Optum Technology / United Health Care

- *Senior Director of Artificial Intelligence and Cognitive Technology*
- *Distinguished Engineer*
- *Academy of Technology Appointee*

Contributor: O'Reilly Report: State of Healthcare Technology

- *Quantum Computing and Healthcare*
- *Cognitive Technology and Healthcare*

Minneapolis, MN, 2022

Reviews

"Informative, interesting, understandable, practical, comprehensive, thorough, effective – just excellent!"
– *Terrill Frantz, Professor at Harrisburg University of Science and Technology, USA*

"Alex has done wonders by blending storytelling techniques with a crisp and clear explanation of the technical aspects of a complex quantum technology. Every element of the technological advances that service providers achieved inside Amazon Braket is well chronicled. On top of that, every piece of code is written in an optimized and self-explanatory manner. The managerial aspects of using quantum computers to solve real-life problems are also discussed, which will help users properly evaluate the tool. Overall, this book is a fantastic treasure trove to get you started on quantum computing, and on Amazon Braket in particular." – *Anshul Saxena, Christ University - India*

"*Quantum Computing Experimentation with Amazon Braket* is an essential resource for businesses and developers preparing for how quantum computers will impact their respective industries. Alex provides practical examples of familiar optimization problems accompanied by easy-to-understand coding guides for multiple available systems on Amazon Braket. Comforting hints, links to additional resources, and pre-execution cost estimation methods bring necessary clarity in what is a new frontier for many readers." – *Mike Heiner, Information Systems Professional*

"An easily digestible guide for quantum-based cloud computing. Khan leverages Amazon Braket to take complex topics and simplify them for those interested in quantum computing. Readers familiar with AWS will recognize parallels between existing cloud services, while those familiar with quantum will be exposed to cloud fundamentals through a guided journey." – *Zia K. Mohammad, Senior Product Manager, AWS Quantum*

"Alex Khan's book provides a detailed step-by-step insight into Amazon's quantum computing environment. The book is very insightful to both novices and experienced quantum computing software developers, with an examination into all the options available in Amazon Braket. Well done, Alex!" – *John P. Cummings, Quantum Computing Engineer*

"Well done! I thought the book was very well laid out and contained thoughtful code and explanations of how to solve optimization problems using Braket. Overall, I think this book will be very helpful to a wide variety of people, especially AWS users who want to experiment with QC. Congratulations!" – *Salvatore Certo, Quantum Computing Technical Manager*

Contributors

About the author

Alex Khan is an advisor, entrepreneur, and educator in quantum computing. He is the CEO of ZebraKet, an Ontario-based quantum start-up in supply chain optimization and currently heads QuantFi/Quantescence USA operations, leading an effort to bring a high-end quantum emulator to market. Alex has been working in quantum computing since 2018 and was the CPO at Chicago Quantum, where he co-authored papers on portfolio optimization using D-Wave. He continues to be an advisor at QuSecure. As a corporate faculty, he teaches undergraduate to graduate level courses in quantum computing at Harrisburg University. He has participated in multiple hackathons, advised on a research paper on optimized lockdown schedule during COVID evolution using quantum annealing, developed solutions for VR game optimization and NLP using D-Wave, and has presented introductory topics in quantum computing at quantum meetups, including using D-Wave and IonQ through Amazon Braket. Alex has over 20 years of experience providing IT solutions, developing products, and managing large IT initiatives in the healthcare and insurance industry. He is an engineering/physics dual major and received his BSME from Purdue University, MSME from KSU, MBA with Health Sector Management from Duke University, and a certificate in quantum computing from MIT|xPro.

I would like to thank Michael Brett, whose support allowed me to experiment with Amazon Braket, eventually making this book possible. I am grateful to the Packt Publishing team, who trusted me to bring a unique book into the quantum computing ecosystem and have helped and guided me at every step. I am also indebted to the technical reviewers, who over the year have diligently given me very constructive feedback leading to many improvements.

About the reviewers

Rakshit Jain is a certified IBM Associate Quantum Developer who is very passionate about operating systems, quantum computing, and cyber security (white hat, obviously). He's currently in the penultimate year of his studies at The Hong Kong Polytechnic University, where he leads the Google Developer Student Club as the Vice-President. Driven by curiosity, he experiments with (and breaks) any bleeding edge technology he can get his hands on. When he's not writing scripts, he is DJing at events or climbing mountains.

Gopal Mahadevan is an optimization software engineer/quantum algorithms researcher and consultant to financial institutions, to help them apply quantum and quantum-inspired solutions to solve their computationally intractable problems and prepare for (inevitable) quantum disruption. He recently completed a master's degree in Quantum Computing Technologies and is an IBM Certified Associate Quantum Developer (Qiskit).

Table of Contents

Preface

Section 1: Getting Started with Amazon Braket

1

Setting Up Amazon Braket

Technical requirements	4	Shutting down the notebook service in Braket	18
The overall Amazon Braket landscape	4	Remote access to Amazon Braket using Boto3	19
Creating an AWS account	5		
Starting the Amazon Braket service	8	Validating if SDK installation is working	22
Configuring the AWS S3 service	12		
Working with the notebook service	13	Signing in to the AWS account	22
Starting the notebook service in Braket	13	Summary	23
Using notebooks and examples in Braket	15	Further reading	23

2

Braket Devices Explained

Annealing-based quantum devices	26	Amazon Braket simulators	36
Introducing D-Wave quantum devices	27	Simulators executing on a local device	37
		Simulators executing on Amazon resources	37
Gate-based quantum devices	31		
An overview of IonQ's quantum device	32	Summary	38
Introducing Rigetti quantum devices	34	Further reading	38
Oxford Quantum Circuits	35		

3

User Setup, Tasks, and Understanding Device Costs

Technical requirements	39	Finding your tasks and results	51
Setting up user groups and users	40	Understanding device costs and billing	55
Creating a user group	41	QPU versus simulator devices	56
Setting up users	43	Viewing your charges	58
Creating a policy for users	45	Summary	60
Running test code	49	Further reading	60

4

Writing Your First Amazon Braket Code Sample

Technical requirements	61	Putting together a simple quantum circuit example	73
Finding active devices	62		
Assigning a device	64	Representing a binary value using a quantum circuit	74
Using the local simulator	64	Running a circuit on the Amazon simulator	77
Using Amazon simulators or quantum devices	65	Actual cost of using the Amazon simulator	80
Estimating the cost of the device	66	Summary	80
Creating a simple quantum circuit	72	Further reading	81
		Concluding Section 1	81

Section 2: Building Blocks for Real-World Use Cases

5

Using a Quantum Annealer – Developing a QUBO Function and Applying Constraints

Technical requirement	86	Quantum annealing	88
Solving optimization problems	86	Quadratic Unconstrained Binary Optimization (QUBO) problems	89
Simulated annealing	87		

A simple conceptual model for D-Wave   90

A QUBO example using three variables
and ExactSolver()   92

Running the three-variable problem on
D-Wave annealer   94

A party optimization example   98

A team selection example   101

A simple process for solving problems
using D-Wave   102

Reviewing data   103

Representing the problem in graph form   104

Summarizing the problem   104

The traditional formulation   105

A tool to visualize the energy landscape   108

A simple penalty function to implement
the constraint   111

Running the problem on classical
and quantum solvers   115

Summary   119

Further reading   119

6

Using Gate-Based Quantum Computers – Qubits and Quantum Circuits

Technical requirements   122

What is a quantum circuit?   122

Understanding the basics of a qubit   123

Using matrix mathematics   126

Using matrix mathematics to represent
single-qubit gates   127

Using quantum gates in a quantum circuit   134

**Single-qubit gate rotation
example – the Bloch Clock   138**

Representing the hour of the day using θ 139

Representing the minutes and seconds using φ 139

**Building multiple qubit
quantum circuits   141**

Three-qubit circuit example   143

**Example inspired by the Google
Supremacy experiment   153**

The actual Google experiment   153

Circuit implementation on Amazon Braket   154

Execution results for a single 7x2 circuit   156

Summary   174

Further reading   174

7

Using Gate Quantum Computers – Basic Quantum Algorithms

Technical requirements   178

What is a quantum Oracle?   178

**Observing the effect of amplitude
amplification   179**

Grover's operator using unitary matrices   180

Grover's search algorithm using
quantum circuits   185

Repetitions of the Grover diffuser operator   189

Using Grover's algorithm in searches   190

Working with phases   190

Translating between the Computational
basis and the Fourier basis   194

Adding phase information to a qubit   196
How the phase adder circuit is used in
quantum circuits   200

Using Quantum Fourier Transform
and its inverse   204
Adding numbers using the phase adder   206

Summary   207
Further reading   208

8

Using Hybrid Algorithms – Optimization Using Gate-Based Quantum Computers

Technical requirements   210
Representing a binary quadratic
function using a phase adder   210
Introduction to QAOA concepts   220
Experimentally validating
QAOA concepts   224

Fine-tuning parameters for QAOA   230
Implementing QAOA for
optimization   236
Summary   239
Further reading   240

9

Running QAOA on Simulators and Amazon Braket Devices

Technical requirements   242
Further QAOA considerations   242
Full QAOA hybrid algorithm using
a classical parameter optimizer   242
Multiple-step parameter optimization
in QAOA   251

Benchmarking QAOA on Amazon
Braket devices   253

Optimizing an 11x11 matrix   253
Optimizing a 34x34 matrix   258
Optimizing a 38x38 sparse matrix   262

Summary of results   268
Summary   269
Further reading   269
Concluding section 2   270

Section 3: Real-World Use Cases

10

Amazon Braket Hybrid Jobs, PennyLane, and other Braket Features

Technical requirement   276
Utilizing Amazon Braket Hybrid Jobs 276
Permissions   277
Using Amazon Braket Hybrid Jobs   278

A QAOA example using Amazon
Braket Hybrid Jobs   281
Job Control Code   282
Job Source Module   286

Xanadu PennyLane   288
Calling Amazon Braket devices from
PennyLane   288

Using PennyLane within Amazon Braket
Hybrid Jobs   289
Xanadu Borealis   289
IBM Qiskit   289
Other Amazon Braket
Hybrid Jobs features   290
Controlling the region of the environment   290
Hardware configuration   290
Multiple parallel device execution   290
Debugging failed jobs   290
Containers   291

Summary   292
Further reading   292

11

Single-Objective Optimization Use Case

Technical requirements   296
Introduction to the knapsack problem 296
Visualizing the knapsack problem   297
QUBO formulation for the
knapsack problem   302
Implementing the knapsack QUBO in code 305
Stitching the QUBO matrices together   313

Getting results from different
QUBO samplers   316
Using the probabilistic sampler   317

Running the knapsack problem on
a D-Wave device   326
Running the knapsack problem
on Amazon Braket simulator SV1   328
Running the knapsack optimization problem
on a Rigetti Aspen 11 device   331
Running on a Rigetti Aspen M-1 device   332

A process for solving constrained
optimization problems   333
Summary   334
Further reading   335

12

Multi-Objective Optimization Use Case

Technical requirements	**338**	Evaluating the optimal values using the D-Wave annealer	353
Looking into a mock inventory management problem	**338**	**Determining a better global solution**	**359**
Setting up the multi-objective problem	338	Evaluating with the classical probabilistic solver	361
Evaluating the best product mix based on scenario A	341	Evaluating the best solution using D-Wave	365
Determining the conflict based on the opposing objectives	**347**	**Summary**	**375**
		Further reading	**375**
Evaluating the results with the probabilistic solver	347	**Concluding section 3**	**377**

Appendix – Knapsack BQM Derivation

Index

Other Books You May Enjoy

Preface

Thank you for showing interest in this book, *Quantum Computing Experimentation Using Amazon Braket*. This is a niche topic; however, over the last few years, quantum computing has received considerable attention from governments who want to win the quantum race, investors who have poured massive amounts of money into quantum computing start-ups, and early adopters who are seeing it as a potential strategic advantage in the future. Accessing quantum computers through Amazon Braket is useful and important for several reasons. In the case of many quantum computing devices, either direct access is not possible or requires contract negotiations or minimum monthly payments. Amazon Braket removes all these issues by providing a relatively easy-to-learn integrated platform with pay-per-use access to popular quantum computing hardware.

The goal of this book is to help the reader gradually understand key concepts in quantum computing and get comfortable with experimenting with quantum circuits and practical optimization use cases through the Amazon Braket platform. We will also cover quantum annealing and get familiar with how to convert an optimization problem into a format or structure to run on a quantum annealer and gate-based quantum computer.

Reasons to get into Amazon Braket

- Like some other platforms, Amazon Braket provides quantum circuit designers convenient access to a number of quantum computing devices through one framework. In the past, we had to use different SDKs and methods to access each device.

- You might have an application that utilizes elastic compute resources, such as EC2, and want to extend that application to quantum computing in the future. Amazon Braket allows you to build extensions to your existing code that uses other Amazon services.

- Amazon Braket contains some exclusive simulators, such as TN1, SV1, and DM1.

- The Amazon Braket pay-per-use model can be useful when experimenting with and scaling quantum device usage.

There is a personal reason I have chosen to write this book. I have been teaching quantum computing and have had the opportunity to explain quantum computing concepts to many students. I want to share basic concepts with you that I hope will give you a practical understanding of how to eventually tackle business use cases through quantum computing by the end of this book.

Who this book is for

This book is for the following people:

- Students who have already taken some introductory quantum computing courses and are ready to learn how to use both quantum annealing and gate-based quantum computing for optimization problems in real-world use cases

- Industry professionals and technologists such as systems analysts, business analysts, architects, and developers who want to be introduced to practical skills in using quantum computers through Amazon Braket for practical optimization use cases

- Entrepreneurs who want to create a quantum start-up and want to experience some of the tools and capabilities quantum computing has to offer

- Vice-presidents of IT, CIOs, vice-presidents of architecture, chief architects, solution architects, actuarial fellows, and other practitioners and professionals who want to evaluate quantum computing for future strategic advantage and to differentiate their companies

- Companies already utilizing other AWS capabilities, such as Lambda and EC2, who want to expand to quantum computing within the AWS platform

What this book covers

Chapter 1, Setting Up Amazon Braket, gives you the basic information to get started with Amazon Braket and get familiar with the components on the platform that you will be interacting with and using.

Chapter 2, Braket Devices Explained, goes beyond just listing the devices that are available. You will be introduced to the architecture and use of the quantum computing systems that are available in the Amazon Braket service.

Chapter 3, User Setup, Tasks, and Understanding Device Costs, is more applicable for the system administrator, or the root user. However, you will also get an understanding of what is available and will be able to have informed conversations with the systems administrator.

Chapter 4, Writing Your First Amazon Braket Code Sample, gets you started with some basic code in Amazon Braket that determines information about the quantum devices or simulators and explains how to use them through code and determine some of their properties and costs.

Chapter 5, Using a Quantum Annealer – Developing a QUBO Function and Applying Constraints, covers quantum annealing and how the D-Wave quantum annealer works. This method is quite different from gate quantum computers, and this chapter will introduce you to the basic structure in which information is prepared to send to the D-Wave quantum annealer.

Chapter 6, Using Gate-Based Quantum Computers – Qubits and Quantum Circuits, starts with a simple introduction of the Qubit and the matrix representation of quantum gates and goes over simple quantum circuits using Amazon Braket code. In all cases, attempts are made to show the process of scaling a circuit to utilize Amazon Braket quantum devices and simulators.

Chapter 7, Using Gate Quantum Computers – Basic Quantum Algorithms, goes over the concept of an Oracle in a quantum circuit and introduce a few basic quantum algorithms, including Amplitude Amplification. The concept of a phase adder is introduced leading to the detailed development of the Quantum Fourier Transform circuit.

Chapter 8, Using Hybrid Algorithms – Optimization Using Gate-Based Quantum Computers, develops the binary quadratic function using a phase adder and introduces the concept of amplifying the probability of finding the minimum value through the Quantum Approximate Optimization Algorithm. The fine-tuning of parameters and the implementation of the algorithm are shown in detail.

Chapter 9, Running QAOA on Simulators and Amazon Braket Devices, explores advanced considerations in the implementation of QAOA and the evaluation of the performance of this algorithm on various Amazon Braket devices.

Chapter 10, Amazon Braket Hybrid Jobs, PennyLane, and Other Braket Features, explains how to set up a more efficient hybrid algorithm through the implementation of QAOA using Amazon Hybrid Jobs. The chapter briefly introduces the integration of PennyLane and other features in Amazon Braket.

Chapter 11, Single Objective Optimization Use Case, covers an example of implementing the knapsack problem on both quantum annealing and gate-based quantum computers through mapping this real-world use case into a binary quadratic model.

Chapter 12, Multi-Objective Optimization Use Case, shows you how to find solutions to real-world use cases that have conflicting objectives using the D-Wave quantum annealer.

Appendix – Knapsack BQM Derivation, contains a detailed derivation of converting the knapsack problem into an equivalent quadratic unconstrained binary optimization problem. This is a critical technique for using quantum computers for real-world optimization problems.

To get the most out of this book

The majority of the development can be done within the Amazon Braket Notebooks environment. However, the book will go over setting up the Amazon Braket SDK and Boto 3 so that the reader can run code remotely. It is expected the user is familiar with Jupyter Notebook and Python 3. This book only shows screenshots and steps in the Microsoft Windows environment.

Software/Hardware covered in the book	OS Requirements
Python and Jupyter Notebook	Windows
Amazon Braket SDK and Boto3	Windows
D-Wave Ocean SDK	Windows

Before getting started, please ensure you have working installations of Python and Jupyter Notebook. This can be done by installing the latest version of Anaconda from `anaconda.org`*. Also, you will need to be comfortable creating a new environment either using Anaconda Navigator or directly from Anaconda Prompt.*

What should you know before starting this book?

A basic awareness of quantum computing is helpful before reading this book. I have written this book for someone who has already taken some introductory quantum computing courses. Having said that, I will be going over all the necessary concepts and building blocks at a simple-to-understand and gradual pace to progress to optimization use cases using both quantum annealing and gate-based quantum computing.

Download the example code files

You can download the example code files for this book from GitHub at `https://github.com/PacktPublishing/Quantum-Computing-Experimentation-with-Amazon-Braket`. In case there's an update to the code, it will be updated on the existing GitHub repository.

We also have other code bundles from our rich catalog of books and videos available at `https://github.com/PacktPublishing/`. Check them out!

Download the color images

We also provide a PDF file that has color images of the screenshots/diagrams used in this book. You can download it here: `https://packt.link/4tYx3`.

Conventions used

There are a number of text conventions used throughout this book.

`Code in text`: Indicates code words in text, database table names, folder names, filenames, file extensions, pathnames, dummy URLs, user input, and Twitter handles. Here is an example: "Replace `amazon-braket-Your-Bucket-Name` with the bucket instance name and `Your-Folder-Name` with the folder name you created in the S3 bucket instance. Keep the quotes."

A block of code is set as follows:

```
device_name_list=[]
for device in device_list:
device_name_list.append(device.name)
print('Valid device names: ',device_name_list)
```

Output generated by the code is set as follows:

Output

```
Valid device names: ['Advantage_system4.1', 'Advantage_ system6.1',
'Aspen-M-1', 'DW_2000Q_6', 'IonQ Device', 'SV1', 'TN1', 'dm1']]
```

When we wish to draw your attention to a particular part of a code block, the relevant lines or items are set in bold:

```
[default]
exten => s,1,Dial(Zap/1|30)
exten => s,2,Voicemail(u100)
exten => s,102,Voicemail(b100)
exten => i,1,Voicemail(s0)
```

Any command-line input or output is written as follows:

```
pip install jupyterlab
pip install notebook
```

Bold: Indicates a new term, an important word, or words that you see onscreen. For example, words in menus or dialog boxes appear in the text like this. Here is an example: "Now select the **Access keys** section and then click on **Create new Access Key** to create a unique security key."

Italics: Indicates references to figures, tables, or chapters in the book along with any term that would be in quotes. Here is an example: "While the service is running, it incurs a small charge, which is covered in *Chapter 3, User Setup, Tasks, and Understanding Device Costs.*"

> **Tips or important notes**
> Appear like this.

Get in touch

Feedback from our readers is always welcome.

General feedback: If you have questions about any aspect of this book, mention the book title in the subject of your message and email us at customercare@packtpub.com.

Errata: Although we have taken every care to ensure the accuracy of our content, mistakes do happen. If you have found a mistake in this book, we would be grateful if you would report this to us. Please visit www.packtpub.com/support/errata, selecting your book, clicking on the Errata Submission Form link, and entering the details.

Piracy: If you come across any illegal copies of our works in any form on the Internet, we would be grateful if you would provide us with the location address or website name. Please contact us at copyright@packt.com with a link to the material.

If you are interested in becoming an author: If there is a topic that you have expertise in and you are interested in either writing or contributing to a book, please visit authors.packtpub.com.

Share Your Thoughts

Once you've read *Quantum Computing Experimentation with Amazon Braket*, we'd love to hear your thoughts! Scan the QR code below to go straight to the Amazon review page for this book and share your feedback.

https://packt.link/r/1800565267

Your review is important to us and the tech community and will help us make sure we're delivering excellent quality content.

Introduction

In the last few years, the discussion of quantum computers has escaped from the research universities and labs into the mainstream. This is an excellent development. As a physics-engineering dual major who has spent most of his career implementing cutting-edge technology in medium-sized organizations, I got excited when I heard about quantum computing and the D-Wave Leap program in 2018. In 2019, I shifted my career to quantum computing and jumped in with both feet. I found the concepts, achievements, and the whole discipline fascinating. This discipline called upon so much of my past background in mathematics, materials, entropy, quantum mechanics, and so on. A lot of the scientific work in bringing quantum computing out of the laboratory and onto the cloud was accomplished by D-Wave Systems, Inc., and IBM. Now, people like me could jump in and start using these systems. We were told the drive was towards commercializing the technology, using quantum computers in real-world use cases, creating a quantum workforce, making the technology accessible to non-PhDs, and seeking public investment. I started working with other companies to learn and develop an appreciation of the technology and later created my own start-up in quantum computing. I have learned from many in the industry, and hope I contributed to the learning of others. Over the last three years, I have learned some lessons and had some times when the fog cleared, and I have gained some insights. In this book, I hope to bring those insights to you in the simplest way possible.

Each chapter is laid out with a set of experiments using the quantum computing devices available in Amazon Braket. Each chapter builds on the last chapter's code or experiments. The code steps have been simplified and, in many cases, after the basics of the theory, equation, or code have been covered, that portion is wrapped in a function for later use. Thus, the reader can continue to gain an understanding of the type of results achieved with the theory and code explained in an efficient manner.

I have tried to write all my own functions and minimize the use of libraries outside of Amazon Braket, Python, NumPy, and Matplotlib. In this regard, I was forced to write my own function to visualize the single-qubit Bloch sphere. My goal was to give the reader all the code in the most accessible format using very simple Python functions. I have also not tried to make the code efficient or fast as I believe it takes away from the readability and accessibility of the code from non-developers. Jupyter Notebook has become a common tool for explaining and testing code. Therefore, I have provided all the code in Jupyter Notebook, except one module which required a Python file. I hope that this will allow those who are somewhat familiar with programming or have learned programming in college to understand the basic structure required for quantum computing. If you are an experienced developer, please feel free to make your own enhancements.

I have also had to exclude many topics that one might expect to be in a standard book on quantum computing and did not want to repeat or duplicate content that is already described in detail in other books. Please check the references in the *Further reading* section at the end of each chapter.

This book might almost seem like a tour through the quantum computing landscape. However, I try not to drop the reader into the many topics of quantum computing, from machine learning to cryptography to simulations. This book will blaze a trail that leads to optimization. I go over how quantum gates are unitary matrices and show how quantum circuits are a combination of matrix multiplications. I show various quantum circuits and give the user ample experiments to gain an intuition for more complicated quantum algorithms, such as the **Quantum Fourier Transform** (**QFT**) and **Quantum Approximate Optimization Algorithm** (**QAOA**). I also show how a **binary quadratic model** (**BQM**) can be solved on both the quantum annealer by D-Wave and on gate quantum computers using QAOA. I, however, do not cover some of the commonly discussed quantum algorithms, such as Simons, Deutsch–Jozsa, Bernstein-Vazirani, Shor's, and the **Variational Quantum Eigensolver** (**VQE**). There are several reasons for this. Firstly, these are covered at length in various introductory quantum computing books and the Qiskit textbook online. Secondly, even though these algorithms show unique and interesting properties of quantum circuits and even indicate quantum advantage, my focus was to build on the necessary areas of quantum computing to get to optimization use cases. As such, I had to make considerable compromises in scope.

When you run the code, your results will most likely differ from mine. This is because quantum computers are probabilistic and even if the probability profile or distribution is the same, the act of limited sampling and noise will produce varying results. For example, if we both have unbiased coins that are supposed to theoretically produce 50% heads and 50% tails, that does not mean that you will get the same sequence or count of heads versus tails as I would if we sample a few times.

Quantum computing is a rapidly evolving field with large investments and a massive amount of development. Every day something new and interesting comes up, and the Amazon Braket team has been enhancing and adding features to the platform. As such, systems are being improved and old systems are being replaced on Amazon Braket on a regular basis. During the writing of this book, Rigetti Aspen-11 (38 qubits) was replaced by M-1 (80 qubits) for a period and Oxford Quantum Circuits **Lucy** was added. D-Wave Advantage 1.0 was replaced by Advantage 4.1 and 6.1. In addition, these devices can be turned off for maintenance. Therefore, I suggest you check on the currently available devices, use the book to familiarize yourself with the technology, make appropriate code changes to use the latest devices available, and re-run the code to evaluate the new capabilities.

Getting the best results from the current devices requires considerable knowledge of the technology, settings, and even the research. There are advanced techniques and native gates that leverage this knowledge and can produce better results than I have shown in this book. My goal has been to introduce you to the basic methods and concepts that you should be aware of, and I have not used advanced techniques. For this reason, your results from this book will likely be inferior to results from advanced libraries, benchmark studies, and technical research papers.

I have had discussions with other educators regarding what should be included in such a book and what should not. We have debated how various concepts in quantum computing should be described so that it makes things easy for readers who are new to the industry but is not misleading about the technology. I will admit that some of my simplifications might not be mathematically or scientifically 100% accurate nor use the standard or technical quantum computing terminology used by PhDs in the field. I have done this to minimize the volume of new terms that you have to get familiar with, as well as the syntax and notation that becomes a hurdle in just getting a view of the landscape. I will encourage the reader to seek out other books and literature if they decide to dig deeper into this subject and realize that there will be some re-learning of concepts from the ground up. However, I have still exposed you to some important linear algebra concepts, Kronecker product, matrix multiplication, simple Dirac notation, and mathematical equations related to describing binary quadratic models. I would consider this treatment the minimum to understand the concepts.

The results in this book cannot be used to benchmark the performance of one quantum computer against another or with classical computers. Firstly, none of the algorithms have been optimized for the hardware, and secondly, each quantum device has different characteristics that require specific adjustments for that device. For example, IonQ uses specific gate operations, which are slightly different from Rigetti's quantum processor. In addition, specific gate rotations have fewer errors than others. Single-qubit and two-qubit gate operations have different levels of errors depending on the qubit and qubit pairs they are applied to. This requires experts in that quantum computer to suggest optimal techniques to achieve a specific result. Finally, there is a lot of research going into finding specific theoretical and actual advantages of using quantum computers. An advantage in one part of the algorithm can easily vanish if another part of the algorithm scales poorly. I have not attempted to review the quantum computer fidelity, single and two-qubit gate errors, or mathematical scaling to optimize the execution of the circuits. These topics are well outside the scope of this book.

In the end, however, I hope I have been able to bring out the key essence of using quantum computers for optimization problems. Quantum computing can become a full career for some, just as information technology became a career for many no matter what subject they studied in college. To purchase new quantum computing technology, to put it to practical use, to extract competitive advantage, to innovate, to communicate ideas with different departments on how to bring this technology into everyday use, or to tease out use cases where it could improve existing processes, it is important to have a hands-on appreciation of what is involved. This book aims to provide you with this kind of knowledge and is only a start, but I am glad you have taken that step.

I thank you for purchasing this book, and hope that you enjoy it.

– Alex Khan

Section 1:
Getting Started
with Amazon Braket

In this first section, you will learn how to get started in Amazon Braket, set up the environment, review devices and their costs, and start Jupyter Notebook within the console. We will look at some Amazon Braket examples. You will learn how the various components in the Amazon Braket environment work, and what to watch out for. This includes how to find example notebooks, list of tasks submitted and where to find the results. We will cover some administrative tasks as well to ensure you understand how to set up user permissions and where to find billing and utilization information. You will learn how to set up a remote connection to Amazon Braket, and you will learn how to switch devices in the code and walk through the process in a starter application that incorporates key Braket API functions.

This section contains the following chapters:

- *Chapter 1, Setting Up Amazon Braket*

- *Chapter 2, Braket Devices Explained*

- *Chapter 3, User Setup, Tasks, and Understanding Device Costs*

- *Chapter 4, Writing Your First Amazon Braket Code Sample*

1
Setting Up Amazon Braket

Amazon Braket is a new offering on the AWS platform that started in August 2020. The service allows users to experiment with various quantum processors and simulators. Users are able to program their quantum circuits or develop their optimization problems and submit them to various quantum devices in Amazon Braket. These devices include various **quantum processing units (QPUs)**, quantum simulators, and the D-Wave **quantum annealer**.

Before we can get started with Amazon Braket, it is necessary to take a few steps. Typically, these steps would be done by a system administrator; however, if you are setting up your own account, it will be helpful to follow along. As a system administrator, you will need to create a root account, set up the users, and enable and configure their access to the Amazon Braket service through permission policies.

This chapter will begin with signing into AWS and starting the Amazon Braket service. First, we will go over the key components of Amazon Braket that you should be familiar with. Then, we will review how to set up remote access with Amazon Braket. This is necessary for users who will not be entering the AWS console and will instead be executing jobs from their local development environment.

Both users and administrators should be aware of the options, setup process, and devices available in Amazon Braket, which will make the setup more appropriate for both administrative and user needs.

In this chapter, we'll cover the following topics:

- The overall Amazon Braket landscape
- Creating an AWS account as an administrator
- Starting the Amazon Braket service
- Configuring the AWS S3 service
- Working with the notebook service in Braket
- Remote access to Amazon Braket using Boto3
- Validating if SDK installation is working
- Signing into the AWS account as a user

Technical requirements

The source code for this chapter can be found in the following GitHub repository:

`https://github.com/PacktPublishing/Quantum-Computing-Experimentation-with-Amazon-Braket/tree/main/Chapter01`

The overall Amazon Braket landscape

The overall setup in Amazon Braket is shown in *Figure 1.1*. The middle section shows the components within AWS. On the left-hand side, you can see the optional local system (remote user environment), and on the right-hand side, you can see the quantum devices that are accessible through Amazon Braket as of May 2022.

> **Note: Amazon Braket Changes**
>
> New devices are being added and outdated devices are being removed from the Amazon Braket service on a regular basis. Please refer to the devices section in Amazon Braket for information about the latest devices, and watch out for notifications of any changes to the Amazon Braket service.

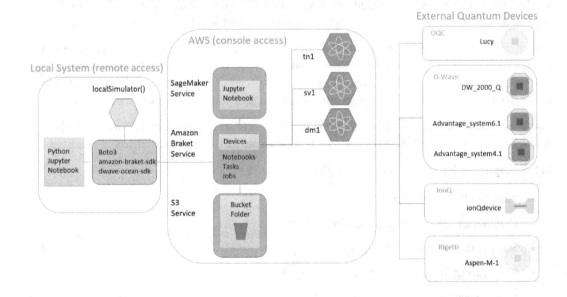

Figure 1.1 – The components of Amazon Braket as of May 14, 2022

Next, let's create our AWS account!

Creating an AWS account

This section is for setting up a root account in AWS by a system administrator. We will go over the fundamental steps needed to set up an AWS account and start the Amazon Braket service.

To set up a new AWS Braket account, perform the following steps:

1. Navigate to `http://aws.amazon.com/braket`.

   This will give you more information about Amazon Braket before you sign up.

2. Now, you can click on **Get Started with Amazon Braket**.

   Alternatively, you click on **Sign In to the Console**. In either case, you should see the following screen:

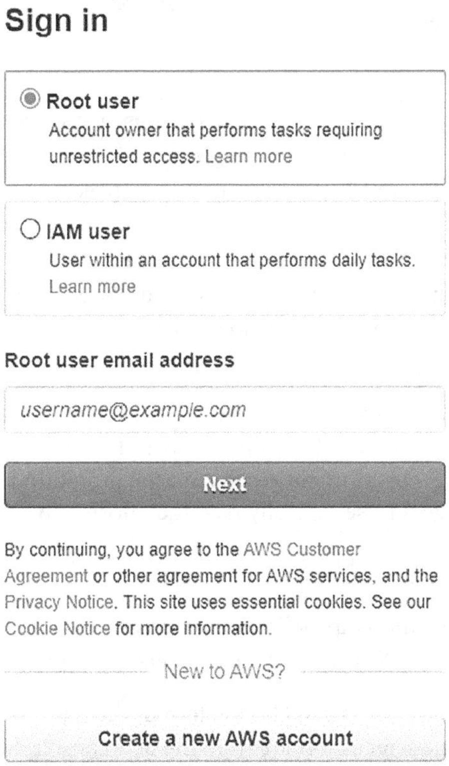

Sign in

⦿ **Root user**
Account owner that performs tasks requiring unrestricted access. Learn more

○ **IAM user**
User within an account that performs daily tasks. Learn more

Root user email address

username@example.com

Next

By continuing, you agree to the AWS Customer Agreement or other agreement for AWS services, and the Privacy Notice. This site uses essential cookies. See our Cookie Notice for more information.

——————— New to AWS? ———————

Create a new AWS account

Figure 1.2 – The console's sign-in screen

3. Select **Create a new AWS account**.

4. The following dialog box will appear:

Explore Free Tier products with a new AWS account.

To learn more, visit aws.amazon.com/free.

Sign up for AWS

Root user email address
Used for account recovery and some administrative functions

AWS account name
Choose a name for your account. You can change this name in your account settings after you sign up.

Verify email address

OR

Sign in to an existing AWS account

Figure 1.3 – The Sign up for AWS screen

5. Now you can sign up with a new account. There will be five steps, and you will be asked to add your credit card information and select the level of the account. This varies from the basic account, which has no monthly charge, to an enterprise version.

> **Note: When Are Charges Incurred?**
> You will be billed for services that you have turned on and are running or if you submit any job to a quantum device. New users might receive special promotional free tier services and free monthly simulator usage. Please carefully read the information on the screen as you set up your account.

More information regarding account setup, policies, charges, and the billing of quantum device usage will be explained in *Chapter 3, User Setup, Tasks, and Understanding Device Costs*.

After you have created your account and signed back into your account, you should be able to see your AWS console. In this chapter, the screenshots are from the new console version, where you can click on the **Switch to the New Console Home** option. Your console might not have any items in **Recently visited services**. However, as you navigate to these services, they will be added to the list as follows:

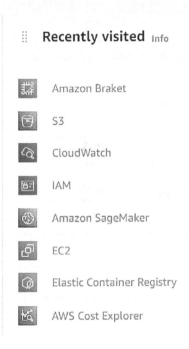

Figure 1.4 – The AWS Management Console services list

Note that you can always return to this console by clicking on the AWS logo in the upper-left corner of the screen:

Figure 1.5 – Using the AWS logo to return to the console Home

Alternatively, if you have logged out, you can also return by typing `http://console.aws.amazon.com/` into your browser window.

You have now created your new AWS account. In the next section, we will go over how to start the Amazon Braket service.

Starting the Amazon Braket service

The Amazon Braket service provides users with an integrated platform from which they can write their code, submit jobs to quantum devices, and view any results that are returned. Depending on how the administrator decides to set up user accounts, the users may or may not have access to the console and might only access the Braket service using code running on their own local computer. This additional step will be covered in the **Remote access to Amazon Braket using Boto3** section.

If this is the first time you are accessing Amazon Braket, let's get the service started:

1. Now that you are on the AWS Management Console interface, you can click on or locate the Amazon Braket service. After clicking on the **Amazon Braket** link, you will see the **Getting started with Amazon Braket** page, as shown in *Figure 1.6*:

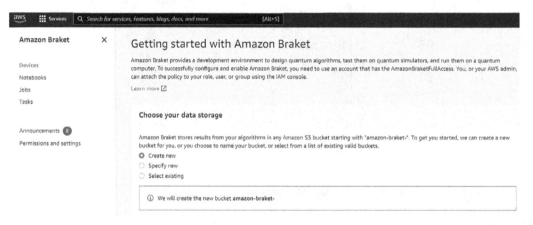

Figure 1.6 – Getting started with Amazon Braket

2. From this screen, you can create new data storage where your job data will be stored. A bucket is a file storage location created by the Amazon S3 (or storage) service. This is where the results of your quantum compute jobs are stored by Amazon Braket.

    The ID portion of the bucket name in *Figure 1.6* has been removed, but you will see your own unique ID. You can keep this name or specify a new one, as described in the following two options:

    *   **Create New** should already be selected. This will generate a new S3 bucket instance with the name created by default.

- Additionally, you can click on the **Specify New** button to give the bucket a customized name. Please bear in mind that the bucket name has to be unique to Amazon and must start with `amazon-braket-`. Please write down the name, as you will need this later.

3. Next, we review the permissions and continue:

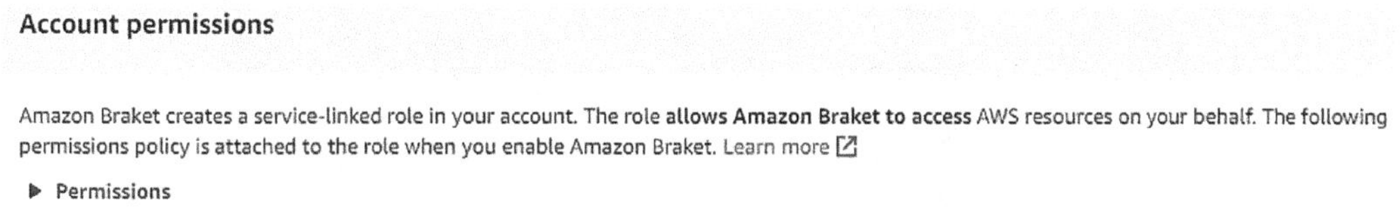

Account permissions

Amazon Braket creates a service-linked role in your account. The role allows **Amazon Braket to access** AWS resources on your behalf. The following permissions policy is attached to the role when you enable Amazon Braket. Learn more ☑

▶ Permissions

Figure 1.7 – Account permissions

4. Then, we can accept the **Terms & conditions** section by clicking on the checkbox:

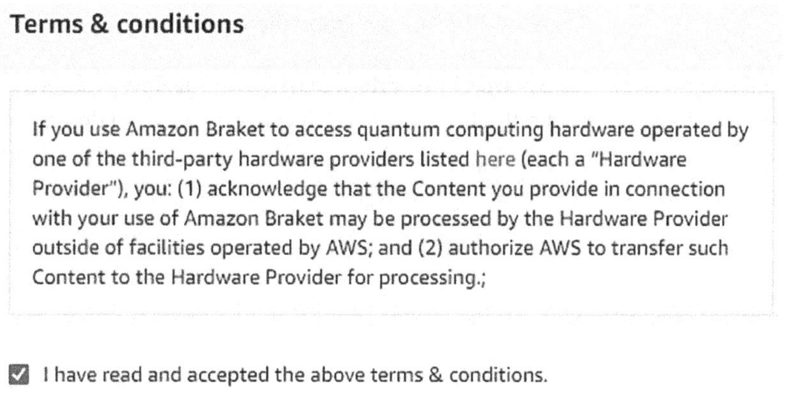

Terms & conditions

> If you use Amazon Braket to access quantum computing hardware operated by one of the third-party hardware providers listed here (each a "Hardware Provider"), you: (1) acknowledge that the Content you provide in connection with your use of Amazon Braket may be processed by the Hardware Provider outside of facilities operated by AWS; and (2) authorize AWS to transfer such Content to the Hardware Provider for processing.;

☑ I have read and accepted the above terms & conditions.

Figure 1.8 – Terms & conditions

5. Now, click on **Enable Amazon Braket**. There are no charges for enabling the Amazon Braket service.

You should now see a screen with the Amazon Braket menu on the left-hand side, as shown in *Figure 1.9*:

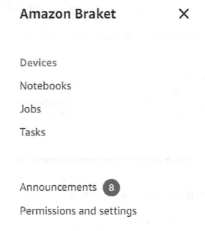

Figure 1.9 – The Amazon Braket menu

Additionally, you will see the Amazon Braket devices that are available, as shown in *Figure 1.10*. The following screenshot only shows the QPU devices. If you scroll down, you will also see the simulators:

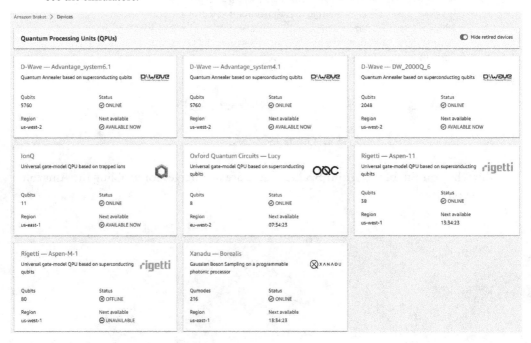

Figure 1.10 – The QPU devices available in Amazon Braket (as of July 2022)

We will go into more detail about the devices in *Chapter 2, Braket Devices Explained*.

6. Now if you click on **Notebooks** from the menu. You will see the following screen with an empty list of notebooks:

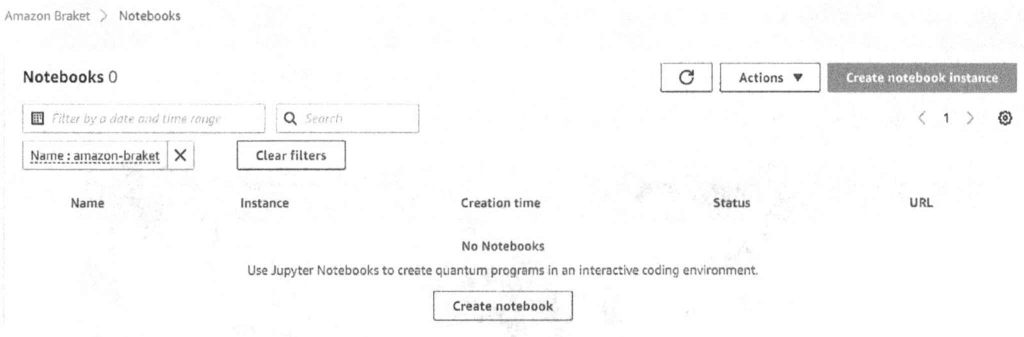

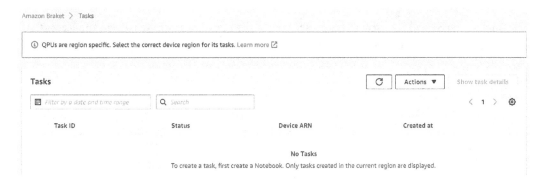

Figure 1.11 – Notebook instances

We will come back to this later in the *Working with the notebook service* section.

7. If you click on **Tasks** in the left-hand menu, you will see the following screen with an empty list of tasks:

Figure 1.12 – The list of tasks submitted to quantum devices

We still have a few more items to review and set up before we can use AWS Braket.

After the Amazon Braket service has been started, we can review the key components within the service. These include the devices, the notebook instances, and the job list.

Now we need to further review the S3 storage service and create any folders for the user to use.

Configuring the AWS S3 service

When the Amazon Braket account was created, it automatically created a bucket in the S3 service. In the previous section, you might have also decided to rename the default bucket with a different name. Let's go back to the S3 service and complete the setup:

1. Select the **AWS logo** button from the upper-left corner of the screen.
2. Then, find the **S3** service link by searching in the search box at the top of the screen:

Figure 1.13 – Searching for the S3 service

3. Clicking on S3 will take you to the S3 service. In the future, you will see this in the **Recently visited services** section of the AWS Management Console interface:

Figure 1.14 – Bucket assigned to Amazon Braket

You will see your bucket name listed with its unique ID or the name you assigned, along with your region.

4. Click on the **amazon-braket-[id]** bucket name to open the details screen:

Figure 1.15 – The Amazon Braket bucket details

5. Now, create a new folder using the **Create folder** button. The folder is the location where the job files are stored. Additionally, you can let your users know the folder they will be sending their jobs to. How you organize the folders is up to you. You can also skip this step and not assign folder names. In this case, users can send jobs with any folder name and the S3 bucket service will create a new folder if it does not already exist.

6. Enter a folder name. Then, click on the **Create Folder** button.

> **Note: Saving the Bucket and Folder Names**
>
> It is helpful to copy and paste the bucket name and the folder name in a notepad file, as you will need them later.

We have reviewed the S3 service and decided on the folder structure for our users. Additionally, we have saved the bucket and folder names since we will need to give this information to the users.

In the next section, we will review the notebook service. This section is useful for users who are going to access the AWS console and use Jupyter Notebook or JupyterLab from within Amazon Braket.

> **Note: Jupyter Notebook**
>
> Jupyter Notebook allows users to review existing code examples to run on Amazon Braket, or they can create their own code and save it. In the next section, we will review the notebook service that is available within Amazon Braket. After that, we will look at how to set up a remote instance of Jupyter Notebook and use with the Amazon Braket service.

Working with the notebook service

Amazon Braket provides Jupyter Notebook and JupyterLab within the notebook section. For those not familiar with programming in Python, Jupyter Notebook provides an easy-to-use interface where you can clearly identify code and rich text sections to explain your code clearly.

Some users will find using Braket notebooks easy to use as they are integrated with the Braket service and do not require the creation of an environment and loading of software libraries to get started. Additionally, the notebooks include Amazon Braket code examples for those who are already familiar with Python and quantum computing.

Starting the notebook service in Braket

The administrator must decide whether users are going to access the notebooks from within AWS Braket or only submit jobs using the remote method via Boto3. Amazon Braket examples are available when the Jupyter Notebook or JupyterLab is created. These notebooks can also be found on GitHub at `https://github.com/aws/amazon-braket-examples`.

> **Note: Notebooks and SageMaker**
>
> It is helpful to know that the notebooks in Amazon Braket are part of the SageMaker service. Even though we will not go into SageMaker, the notebooks created in Amazon Braket are also visible in the SageMaker service.

If users are given permission to enter the AWS console and access Amazon Braket and its components, then care must be given in terms of how the permissions are set up and which policies are utilized. More details on policies and permissions are given in *Chapter 3, User Setup, Tasks, and Understanding Device Costs*.

> **Note: When Do You Not Need to Start the Notebook Instance?**
>
> If you are going to access Amazon Braket from your own local computer instance of Jupyter Notebook or Python, then you do not need to create or start a notebook instance. You should also review the section on **Remote access to Amazon Braket using Boto3**.

For now, let's assume the administrator intends that the users will access Jupyter Notebook from within the AWS console. In this case, the following steps will get the notebook instance started:

1. Click on the **Notebooks** menu item on the left-hand side.

2. You should see an empty list of notebooks, as shown in *Figure 1.11*.

3. Click on the **Create notebook instance** button:

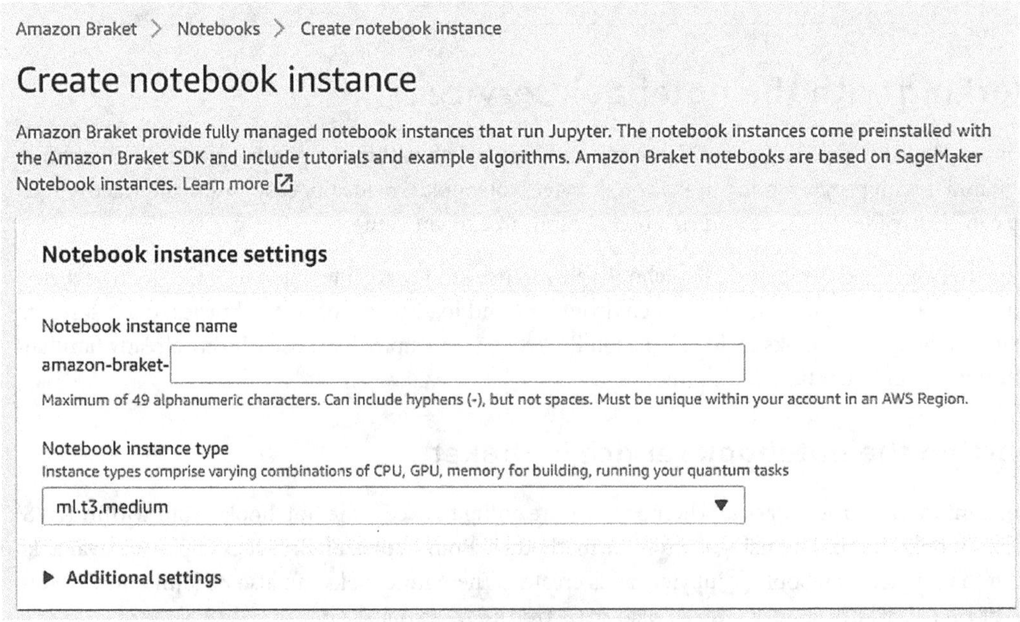

Amazon Braket > Notebooks > Create notebook instance

Create notebook instance

Amazon Braket provide fully managed notebook instances that run Jupyter. The notebook instances come preinstalled with the Amazon Braket SDK and include tutorials and example algorithms. Amazon Braket notebooks are based on SageMaker Notebook instances. Learn more ☑

Notebook instance settings

Notebook instance name

amazon-braket-[   ]

Maximum of 49 alphanumeric characters. Can include hyphens (-), but not spaces. Must be unique within your account in an AWS Region.

Notebook instance type
Instance types comprise varying combinations of CPU, GPU, memory for building, running your quantum tasks

[ml.t3.medium   ▼]

▶ **Additional settings**

Figure 1.16 – Create notebook instance window

This will open a screen where you can give your notebook instance a name.

4. You can modify the permissions and encryption as needed. This is an advanced topic and beyond the scope of this book. *Chapter 3, User Setup, Tasks, and Understanding Device Costs*, will also cover instructions on permissions and policies; however, for now, you can continue with these steps.

5. Click on the **Create notebook instance** button.

    Now you will see your notebook in the list.

6. You can click on the radio button on the left-hand side of the notebook and then click on the **Actions** drop-down menu and select **Start**:

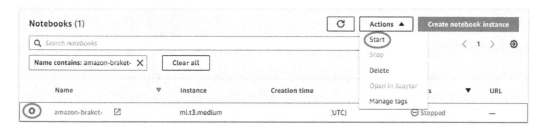

Figure 1.17 – Starting the notebook instance

It will take a few minutes for Amazon to bring up the notebook service. During this time, the status will be **Pending**, and you can click on the **refresh** button to update the status.

After the service is up, the status will go to **InService**.

This section covered steps on how to start the Amazon Braket notebook service. In the next section, we will look at how to open the notebooks and use them.

Using notebooks and examples in Braket

After the notebook service has been started, the user can begin to use the notebooks. From the **Notebooks** menu, you can see your notebook instance. Notice that it is **InService** and there are **Actions** available:

Figure 1.18 – The actions available when the notebook instance is running

Now you can use the link under **URL** to navigate to the notebooks. Alternatively, go to **Actions** and then select **Open in Jupyter**:

1. Clicking on **Open in Jupyter** will open the following screen, which should be familiar to Jupyter Notebook users:

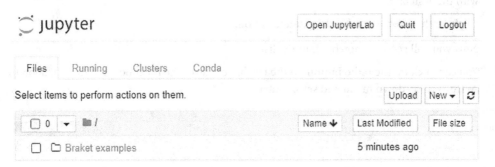

Figure 1.19 – Jupyter Notebook with the Braket examples folder

2. The **Open JupyterLab** button at the top of the Jupyter Notebook window will open the following JupyterLab screen:

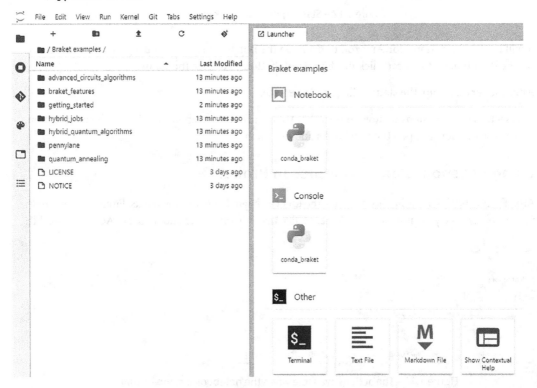

Figure 1.20 – JupyterLab starting at the Braket examples folder

3. Now you can double-click on the **Braket examples** folder and navigate to an example that you would like to review.

4. Next, you can navigate to various notebooks either through Jupyter Notebook or JupyterLab. However, the first ones to check out are in the /braket_examples/getting_started folder. Please follow the steps in the notebooks to execute each line and try them out.

5. Some sample notebooks will require your S3 bucket and folder name. Typically, these examples will execute the code on an Amazon Braket device. In such cases, you will find two lines that need to be updated. Please enter the S3 bucket name and folder name that you created earlier:

```
# Please enter the S3 bucket you created during
onboarding in the code below
my_bucket = "amazon-braket-Your-Bucket-Name" # the name
of the bucket
my_prefix = "Your-Folder-Name" # the name of the folder
in the bucket
```

6. Replace amazon-braket-Your-Bucket-Name with the bucket instance name and Your-Folder-Name with the folder name you created in the S3 bucket instance. Keep the quotes.

Note: Cost Warning

Before running code on a quantum device, please read *Chapter 3, User Setup, Tasks, and Understanding Device Costs*, and the section on device costs. You could incur substantial costs by accidentally running a large job on an expensive quantum device.

---

7. To shut down the lab, ensure you have saved all your updates. Click on **File** and then click on the **Shutdown** button, which is at the bottom of the list. Then, click on **Shutdown** again. You will get the following message:

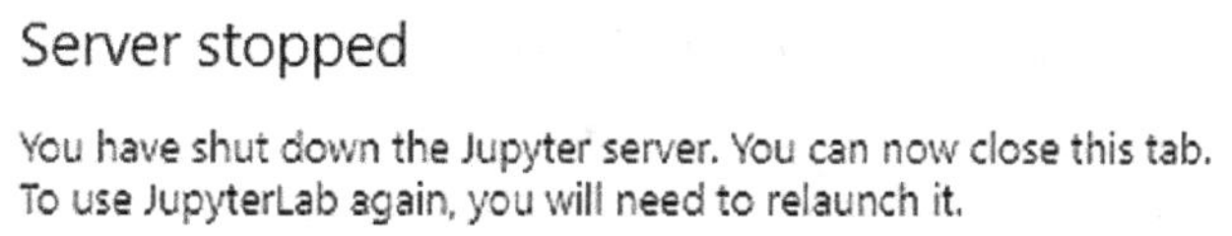

Server stopped

You have shut down the Jupyter server. You can now close this tab.
To use JupyterLab again, you will need to relaunch it.

Figure 1.21 – The JupyterLab shutdown message

8.   To shut down the Jupyter Notebook, ensure you have saved your notebooks. Then, click on the **Quit** button in the upper-right corner. You will get the following message:

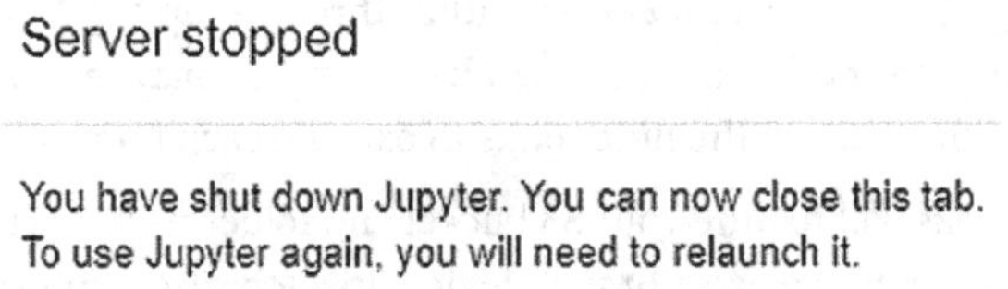

Server stopped

You have shut down Jupyter. You can now close this tab.
To use Jupyter again, you will need to relaunch it.

Figure 1.22 – The Jupyter Notebook shutdown message

In this section, you reviewed how to open the Jupyter Notebook or JupyterLab and use an example notebook from the Braket examples. You will need to update two lines in the notebook code for it to send the output files to the correct bucket and folder. You also looked at how to shut down the notebook and lab.

If your users have access to the AWS console and work in the same folder structure as the JupyterLab and S3 bucket, you will need to organize the folder structure properly for their use and ensure the users cannot accidentally shut down the Braket Notebook service. In *Chapter 3, User Setup, Tasks, and Understanding Device Costs*, we will cover the permissions and policies to ensure users have access to the appropriate functions.

In the next section, we will review the procedure for shutting down the Amazon Braket notebook service.

Shutting down the notebook service in Braket

In this section, we will review the procedure for shutting down the Amazon Braket notebook service. While the service is running, it incurs a small charge, which is covered in *Chapter 3, User Setup, Tasks, and Understanding Device Costs*. However, it is necessary to keep the service running if users are allowed to work together in Jupyter Notebooks or Jupyter Lab without losing their changes.

Different notebooks can be created for different projects or teams.

> **Note: Losing Data Warning**
>
> If you **Stop** the notebook instance of the notebook service, you will lose all of your changes.
>
> When you **Start** the notebook instance, it will refresh the original Braket examples and clear any previously stored information.
>
> While the notebook service is running, you will incur a small charge, which can add up if you keep the notebook service running without ever shutting it down. However, this will allow all your changes to be retained as long as you save your Jupyter files and close the Jupyter notebooks and Jupyter labs properly.

To shut down the notebook service, you will need to click on the radio button next to the notebook instance name. Then, navigate to **Actions** and **Stop** the service:

Figure 1.23 – Shutting down the Braket notebook service; please read
the Losing Data warning before proceeding with this step

The service will show a status of **Stopping** as Amazon turns down the service. Finally, the service will be **stopped**, and there will be no charges incurred from the SageMaker service.

In this section, you also reviewed that you can stop the Amazon Braket notebook service. This will clear all the changes that you might have made or your users might have made to their notebooks.

In the next section, we will go over how to allow users to submit jobs from their own installation of Jupyter Notebook on their local computer. This is necessary if, as the administrator, you decide that users will not have access to the AWS console. Or even if they do have access to the console, they will also be able to connect to Amazon Braket remotely and manage their code instances locally on their computers.

Remote access to Amazon Braket using Boto3

Users that want to access Amazon Braket from their local Jupyter Notebook will need to set up Boto3 and the Braket and D-Wave SDK. Additionally, they will need to have credentials to use remote access when their user account has been created; alternatively, that setting can be turned on later too.

For the root user, this is the procedure for creating the security credential to access Braket remotely. Please perform this procedure with caution. Amazon does not recommend remote access for a root account. However, the root user may set up this access to test the connection and also become familiar with the procedure that will be required for other users. Let's continue:

1. Before setting up the remote connection to Amazon Braket, you will need to create your security key. In order to do this, click on your username in the upper-right corner of the screen to open the drop-down menu and click on **My Security Credentials**:

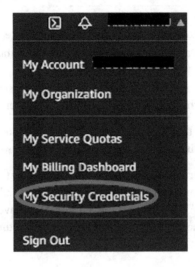

Figure 1.24 – The My Security Credentials menu

2. Now select the **Access keys** section and then click on **Create new Access Key** to create a unique security key.

    A unique security key and an access key will be created. You should copy and paste them both into the notepad file along with the bucket name and the folder name. Keep this file secure. The values of these keys will be needed in the next part.

3. The final items needed are the regions of the device you will be using. There are only two values:

    ```
    us-east-1
    us-west-1
    ```

4. Download and install the latest version of Anaconda from https://www.anaconda.com/products/distribution. Using your Anaconda installation, open Anaconda Navigator and create a new environment for Braket. Ensure you add Jupyter Lab and Jupyter Notebook to it.

You can also create the environment using command-line arguments from the Anaconda console:

```
conda env list
conda create Braket
conda activate Braket
```

If you did not add Jupyter Notebook or Jupyter Lab through Anaconda Navigator, then you can use the following command line to install the Jupyter lab and Jupyter notebook from the Anaconda console:

```
pip install jupyterlab
pip install notebook
```

5. Now you can install the following SDK using these `pip` commands in your Anaconda console:

```
pip install dwave-ocean-sdk
pip install boto3
pip install amazon-braket-sdk
```

6. Now we need to set up the `config` file with all the correct information for the local Jupyter Notebook to connect to your AWS account and execute the device code through the SDK. In File Explorer, go to your user account folder. This will be under the `C:/Users/[your account name]` folder. Over here, create a folder called `.aws`.

7. Next, open up Notepad and create the following entries:

```
[default]
region = us-east-1
#region = us-west-1
aws_access_key_id=ThIsIsmYAceSSKeyID
aws_secret_access_key=THisISAWsSECrEtACCEsskEY
```

8. Save this file with the name of `config` in the `.aws` folder.

Note: Config file and returning to Jupyter Notebook

Config file format: The config file has no extension and there are no quotes around the keys.

Returning to use the Jupyter Notebook: When you return to use the Jupyter notebooks, you will open your Anaconda console and then retype `conda activate Braket` followed by `Jupyter Notebook`.

In this section, you learned how to install the necessary SDK to ensure a remote user can connect to the Amazon Braket service and send tasks to a device. In the next section we will validate the installation is working.

Validating if SDK installation is working

In this section, we will execute the test code found on the GitHub repo for this chapter. We will only ensure the Amazon Braket SDK is installed properly and working. More details on the Amazon devices will be covered in *Chapter 2, Braket Devices Explained*, and we will set up the appropriate permissions to run a remote connection between Amazon Braket and a remote Jupyter notebook session in *Chapter 3, User Setup, Tasks, and Understanding Device Costs*. Let's verify that the SDK is installed properly:

1. Open your Anaconda Prompt application.
2. Activate your **Braket** environment. Your prompt should already say (base). Type the command following the prompt as shown here:

    ```
    (base) Conda activate Braket
    ```

3. Start your Jupyter Notebook session using the following command:

    ```
    (Braket) Jupyter Notebook
    ```

4. After your Notebook session starts, navigate to the GitHub repository of the book, select the Chapter 1 folder, and then open the Sample Braket Install Test.ipynb file.
5. Now you should run one line of code from the following snippets at a time using the **Run** button. Let's start with loading the libraries:

    ```
    from braket.circuits import Circuit
    from braket.devices import LocalSimulator
    ```

    If there is no error, then the SDK has been installed properly. You may stop here or also execute the following two lines in the code to ensure there are no errors.

The next section is only information relevant for users who are going to have access to the AWS console and will sign in to the console to access Amazon Braket, the notebooks, jobs, and other services that are allowed.

Signing in to the AWS account

If you are not the administrator and have been assigned an AWS account with console access, then you can go directly to the AWS website, log in to your account, and start using the Amazon Braket service:

1. Navigate to the Amazon Braket website by typing https://aws.amazon.com.
2. From the main menu, select **Sign in to Console**.
3. Now, you can click on **IAM user** and fill in the information provided by your system administrator. You will need the account ID or account alias and the initial password to sign in. If you are authorized to change the password, then you will be able to change the initial password.

This section demonstrated how to log in to the AWS console as a user. The administrator will have to provide the necessary information to the user that will be generated during the setup of the user in the IAM management section. This will be covered in *Chapter 3, User Setup, Tasks, and Understanding Device Costs*.

Summary

This chapter covered the main components of the Amazon Braket service. We went over how to create an AWS account, which, for our purpose, was the root account. Then, we started the Amazon Braket service and configured the S3 service with the appropriate directory file(s). Following this, we started the Braket notebook service for users that will be signing into the AWS console and using the Amazon Braket instance of the notebooks and examples. Additionally, we reviewed the changes needed on a notebook so that it can send job information to the correct folder. We also discussed the pros and cons of keeping the notebook instance open versus shutting down the notebook service. We discussed how to enable users to gain access to the Amazon Braket service remotely through their local computer installation of Jupyter Notebook. Finally, we also showed how users can sign in to Amazon Braket through their console access.

This is a very basic level of information to get the Amazon Braket service set up and ready to use. However, there is more information that is needed for the administrator and users to utilize Braket safely and properly.

In the next chapter, we will cover the different devices that are available in Amazon Braket. We will look at the companies that provide these devices, some history of the devices, and the device architecture. This information will be relevant to how the devices should be used for quantum computing and for the type of use cases they can solve.

Further reading

More information can be found using the following resources:

- More general information regarding Amazon Braket is available at `https://aws.amazon.com/braket/`.

- Please check out the various tabs, including **Features**, **Pricing**, **FAQs**, and **Getting Started**, that can be found at `https://aws.amazon.com/braket/getting-started`.

2
Braket Devices Explained

This chapter will go over the various devices that are currently (as of May 2022) available within Amazon Braket. It is very important to clarify upfront that these are all considerably different devices in their technology and purpose. The devices are organized under **quantum processing units** (**QPUs**) and simulators.

This chapter will go over important details of each quantum processor and simulator. We will review each device's architecture since this will be relevant to how we use that device. We will also review the costs of using the devices. Because Amazon Braket is an evolving technology, it is important to refer to the Amazon Braket service for current information; however, these chapters will discuss more general topics to orient the reader.

Amazon Braket includes QPUs and simulators. Within the QPU category, there are a number of devices that can be separated into **quantum annealing** and **gate-based quantum computing**. D-Wave is the only company that currently provides quantum annealers, while IonQ, Rigetti, and **Oxford Quantum Circuits** (**OQC**) provide gate-based quantum processing devices.

Amazon Braket also provides three quantum **simulators** for gate-based quantum computing. These simulate the changing quantum state using classical calculations on classical **central processing units** (**CPUs**). In the section on simulators, we will discuss the use and importance of these devices.

It might be helpful to revisit the overall setup of AWS Braket from *Chapter 1, Setting Up Amazon Braket*. You can see a diagrammatic representation of this here:

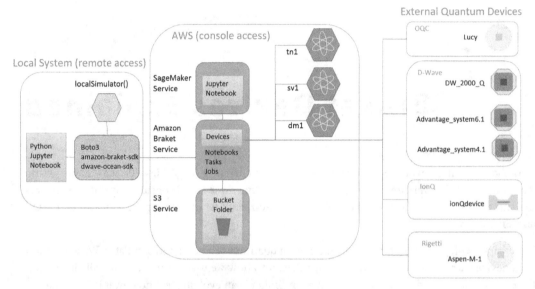

Figure 2.1 – High-level components and devices in Amazon Braket

These are the topics we will be covering in the chapter:

- Annealing-based quantum devices
- Gate-based quantum devices
- Amazon Braket simulators

Let's start by reviewing annealing-based devices that are available in Amazon Braket.

Annealing-based quantum devices

Quantum annealing is a process to solve optimization problems, based on the idea of simulated annealing. Quantum annealing is used to solve a class of problems that are called **Ising** or **quadratic unconstrained binary optimization** (**QUBO**). Simply put, these are problems that have a sum based on binary variables and products of pairs of the same variables along with coefficients on each term, and the goal is to find a combination of values that will provide the minimum sum. We will return to this in *Chapter 5, Using Quantum Annealers – Developing a QUBO Function and Using Constraints*. For now, it is important to realize that Amazon Braket provides D-Wave devices that use quantum annealing as a method to solve specific optimization problems, and these are inherently different from gate-based quantum computers.

Introducing D-Wave quantum devices

D-Wave Systems Inc., a privately held company, was created based on the concept of quantum annealing in 1999 in Burnaby, **British Columbia** (**BC**), Canada. The original idea was published by Tadashi Kadowaki and Hidetoshi Nishimori in 1998. Later, a team of scientists and engineers was able to use existing semiconductor technology and leverage superconducting materials, including research on a component called a **Josephson junction,** to create basic units of quantum data called **qubits**. This led to the creation of the D-Wave company in 1999, and over time, considerable research has been done and many engineering challenges have been overcome.

D-Wave devices can leverage various quantum mechanical properties, including magnetic spin interactions between qubits, entangling qubits together, and creating an annealing schedule to induce the type of random fluctuations needed, augmented with a **quantum tunneling** effect, to produce the desired results and thus solve optimization problems by finding the lowest energy. However, it is not guaranteed that D-Wave devices will always find the lowest energy value (the minimum). The primary reason for this is due to the dynamics of energy levels, from the beginning annealing cycle to the end. At the beginning of the annealing cycle, the energy levels represent an equal probability of applying one of two binary values to each variable. This equal superposition state is shown by E_0 to E_4 at time t_0 in *Figure 2.2*. Later in the annealing cycle, problem parameters are added to the system—these are coefficient terms in the problem and will change the values of the energy levels. If done properly, the system remains at the lowest energy level; however, the gap in energy between the lowest and next energy level can become quite small. This is because the difference in discrete energy values when dealing with hundreds or thousands of variables can also become very small. At certain points in the annealing schedule, the gap can become less than random fluctuations of the state of the quantum device, causing the qubit to jump to a higher energy value.

You can see a diagrammatic representation of the process here:

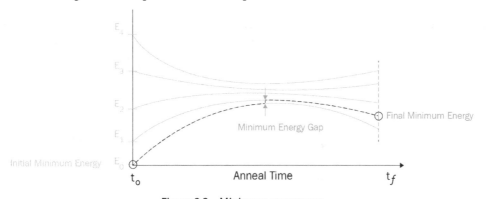

Figure 2.2 – Minimum energy gap

Thus, for this reason, D-Wave quantum processors are called annealers or annealing quantum computers. Systems that would achieve the precise evolution of quantum states, holding minimum values and reaching the global minimum every time would be considered an "adiabatic" quantum computer.

Nevertheless, D-Wave systems do a great job in sampling, using quantum tunneling to provide a quantum advantage in certain unique problem configurations and typically finding the minimum energy value in the landscape, given enough **sampling**. Sampling is the number of times the same problem is rerun on the device. It is also called the number of **shots**. By sampling many times, we are assured that the annealer will find many low energy values and also the global minimum in the landscape. In addition to increasing the sampling, we can also slow down the annealing time and modify other parameters to increase the likelihood of finding the global minimum.

More details of how quantum annealing works, along with an explanation of local and global minima and how this quantum annealer is leveraged to solve real-world problems, will be discussed in *Chapter 5, Using Quantum Annealers – Developing a QUBO Function and Applying Constraints*, and later in *Chapter 11, Single Objective Optimization Use Case*, and *Chapter 12, Multi-Objective Optimization Use Case*.

Now that you have a bit of historical background on D-Wave, it is important to note that the D-Wave 2000Q device and the newer D-Wave Advantage model are very reliable, sophisticated, and useful tools for solving optimization problems. In the rest of this section, we will go over some details of the architecture of the two devices.

D-Wave 2000Q

D-Wave 2000Q was produced in January 2017, and its architecture is called the Chimera, with 2,048 qubits arranged in groups of eight. As shown in the following diagram, the qubits are represented by rectangles. These rectangles represent a loop called a **superconducting quantum interference device (SQUID)** through which a superconducting current flows. There are four qubits arranged with the longer side of the rectangle lying horizontally, and four more qubits arranged with the longer side of the rectangle displayed vertically. The region where one of these SQUID loops overlaps with the other SQUID loop is where one qubit interacts with the other qubit. This is how one qubit is coupled with the other qubit. The circulating current creates a magnetic field, and these fields interact with each other:

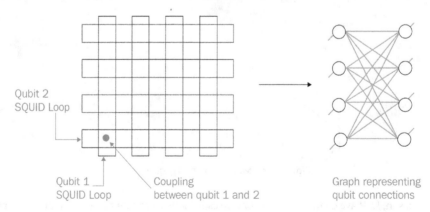

Figure 2.3 – D-Wave 2000Q qubit architecture

One qubit is thus connected to four others within the group and to one more qubit contained in another similar group. This way, the groups of eight qubits are interconnected with other groups.

In practice, we have to convert our real-world problems into a graphical representation. If this representation is having relationships from one vertex (or node) to all others, then it is a fully connected graph. Let's see how D-Wave embeds a fully connected graph problem onto its Chimera architecture. The following screenshot shows a fully connected graph with 20 vertices:

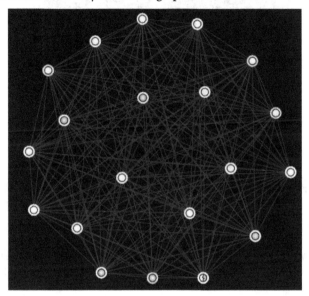

Figure 2.4 – Fully connected problem graph with 20 vertices (nodes)

As we will see later, we will convert our problems into a graphical representation, as with the one shown in *Figure 2.4*. However, before sending the problem to the hardware, an *embedding* function is used to find the ideal way to map the vertices in the problem graph to the appropriate hardware qubits. Similarly, connections between the vertices are mapped to connections between the qubits.

Since there are limited connections between qubits in the hardware, during this embedding phase, one vertex in the problem is represented by multiple qubits in a chain. This allows the connectivity of all the qubits in the chain, to be used as the connections needed in the problem graph. An example of this is shown in *Figure 2.5*, where a 7-qubit chain is identified as representing one vertex in the problem. In other words, we use up many of the available qubits to embed a single vertex, node, or variable of the problem.

Thus, in a fully connected problem where each of the variables has a relationship with every other variable in the problem, D-Wave 2000Q can use up all its 2,048 qubits at around 65 variables.

You can see a visual representation of this here:

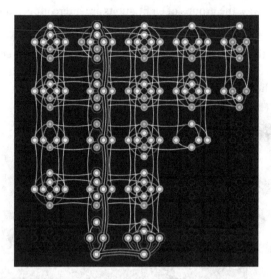

Figure 2.5 – D-Wave 2000Q architecture showing one vertex (or variable) embedded on a 7-qubit chain

D-Wave Advantage

In September 2020, D-Wave Advantage became available, with 5,640 qubits. The D-Wave Advantage system is based on the Pegasus architecture with higher connectivity between qubits, as shown in the following screenshot:

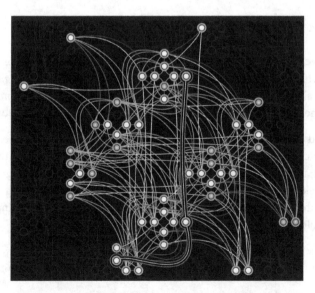

Figure 2.6 – D-Wave Advantage Pegasus architecture with a single variable using 3 qubits

With 5,640 qubits and higher connectivity between qubits, D-Wave Advantage can handle a fully connected graph problem with approximately 134 vertices.

The following table shows the device name used when jobs are submitted to D-Wave (as of May 2022):

Name	Device	Qubits
D-Wave Advantage 6.1	`AwsDevice('arn:aws:braket:::device/qpu/d-wave/Advantage_system6')`	5640
D-Wave Advantage 4.1	`AwsDevice('arn:aws:braket:::device/qpu/d-wave/Advantage_system4')`	5640
D-Wave 2000Q	`AwsDevice('arn:aws:braket:::device/qpu/d-wave/DW_2000Q_6')`	2048

Table 2.1

For more information about D-Wave please check out `https://www.dwavesys.com/`.

We have completed our introduction to D-Wave, an annealing computer available in Amazon Braket. Now, we will switch gears and discuss gate-based quantum computers.

Gate-based quantum devices

In most cases, when we talk about quantum computers, we are discussing **gate-based** quantum computers. These are devices that leverage quantum properties of **superposition**, **entanglement**, and **parallelism** and use what is called gate operations to convert the initial state of the quantum bits, or **qubits**, into a final state. They are also sometimes called analog quantum computers since these gate operations are basically microwave or laser pulses being used to change the quantum information stored on the qubit. Similar pulses are used to manipulate this quantum information in specific ways by a set of gates. We can think of a gate as a function that changes the value of the qubit. We will learn more about how these quantum computers work in *Chapter 6, Using Gate-Based Quantum Computers – Qubits and Quantum Circuits*. As previously mentioned, Amazon Braket provides gate-based quantum devices from IonQ, Rigetti, and OQC.

Now, we will look at IonQ's ion trap device provided in Amazon Braket.

An overview of IonQ's quantum device

IonQ has had an interesting journey, appreciated by those who have spent many years waiting for this technology to become a reality and to be able to access this ion trap through Amazon Braket in 2020.

The story of IonQ started in the **National Bureau of Standards** (later renamed the **National Institute of Standards and Technology** (**NIST**)) in 1945 when the Cesium clock was invented by Isidor Rabi. An actual ion trap with the ability to hold ions in a magnetic field was invented in 1960 by Wolfgang Paul. The NIST team, under Dave Wineland's *Ion Storage Group*, continues to improve on the atomic clock.

Taking an idea proposed by Ignacio Cirac and Peter Zoller in 1994 that a **controlled-NOT** (**cNOT**) operation is possible between two ions, Chris Monroe, working to build a better atomic clock at Dave Wineland's *Ion Storage Group* and not realizing that he was building a new field of quantum computing, showed in 1995 that such a CNOT operation and resulting entanglement is possible in an ion trap.

Between 2000 and 2007, Chris Monroe and David Wineland showed various engineering and architectural improvements in their ion trap, shuttling atomic ions through a complex ion-trap chip and architecture for a large-scale ion-trap computer. This work continued as Chris Monroe joined the University of Maryland in 2007 and then worked with Duke University professor Jungsang Kim on scaling the ion trap in 2013. The two together formed IonQ in 2015, and Chris Monroe became the **chief executive officer** (**CEO**) in 2018. In 2020, IonQ was made available in Amazon Braket as an 11-qubit fully entangled quantum computer with a lower error rate than any other device available in the market. In October 2021, IonQ went public under the CEO Peter Chapman.

Ion traps hold ions in a vacuum and use the Ytterbium ion's outer shell electron movement from its lower to higher energy level through laser pulses as the qubit. The same lasers generating entangled photons can entangle two ions as well. Overall, this system with actual quantized energy values and suspension in a vacuum helps to create a quantum computer that can entangle every qubit with every other qubit and reduce noise from the surroundings, as depicted in the following diagram:

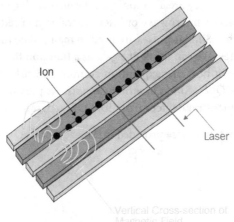

Figure 2.7 – Linear ion trap

The IonQ device allows researchers—and now you—to run a quantum circuit on a quantum computer that is 11 positively charged ions of ytterbium *(171Yb+)* after one of the electrons has been removed from the outer shell. Even though the ions are arranged linearly, it is the pair of entangled laser pulses that entangle pairs of ions together, and it is the lasers that through their tuned pulses cause gate operations on the qubits. Therefore, a practical graph of the qubit arrangement is a fully connected graph, as shown here:

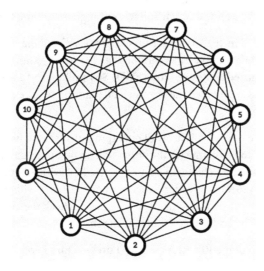

Figure 2.8 – IonQ qubit connectivity graph

The final item to keep in mind is gate operations that are allowed on an IonQ device. These include x, y, z, rx, ry, rz, h, cnot, s, si, t, ti, v, vi, xx, yy, zz, swap, and i. A more detailed explanation of these will be given in *Chapter 5, Using Quantum Annealers – Developing a QUBO Function and Using Constraints*.

In the following table, you can view IonQ device information:

Name	Device	Qubits
IonQ device	AwsDevice('arn:aws:braket:::device/qpu/ionq/ionQdevice')	11

Table 2.2

For more information please refer to material provided at https://ionq.com/best-practices.

In this section, we discussed IonQ as a representative of an ion trap quantum computer. Now, we will switch gears to Rigetti quantum devices, which are made from superconducting qubits.

Introducing Rigetti quantum devices

Chad Rigetti completed his Ph.D. at Yale University in 2009 with a thesis titled *Quantum Gates for Superconducting Qubits*. Reading it, you can see the very basic operations of all the gates and procedures to engineer quantum circuits with Josephson junctions, charge qubits, flux qubits, and phase qubits, and a combination of these parts to create and fabricate superconducting qubits. The paper goes over the details of the mathematics behind quantum computing and single and two-gate operations (CNOT gate), the Bloch sphere, entanglement, and noise.

Rigetti Computing was founded in 2013 as a start-up under the Y Combinator incubator and received a series of funding as it tested its 3-qubit superconducting chip using aluminum circuits on a silicon wafer. In 2016, it received **United States dollars (USD)** $64 million in funding and was testing an 8-qubit chip the next year; it also provided the Forest cloud platform to access its quantum computing devices from the cloud.

The company has continued to offer a wide array of quantum processors to users for a fee. Their initial offerings included the ability to *book* time on the chip and run quantum circuits on up to 36 qubits. As of this writing both the Aspen-11 chip with 38 and Aspen-M-1 with 80 qubits have been available in Amazon Braket at different times. In order to accommodate this, I will go over both systems so that the reader is familiar with the two systems. However, please check the available device and make the necessary adjustments to the code when you are using this book.

You can view a representation of the Rigetti Aspen-M-1 architecture here:

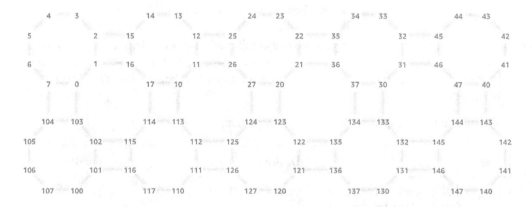

Figure 2.9 – Rigetti Aspen-M-1 architecture

Since—in the case of Rigetti devices—there are limited connections between qubits, to create the most efficient circuit, we need to be aware of the connectivity between qubits. Even when two qubits are not connected, the system will **transpile** or translate the desired circuit by moving the state to a qubit that has connectivity and then running a two-qubit operation, and then returning the states. This is done by using swap gates. The process does add to the depth of the final circuit and thus can also add to the noise and loss of coherence of the circuit. It is helpful when creating a circuit for such devices with limited connectivity to optimize the circuit so that it minimizes swap operations. Ideally, the circuit designed will be close to the circuit that is transpiled.

The Aspen-M-1 device has 80 qubits and allows the following gate operations:

cz, xy, ccnot, cnot, cphaseshift, cphaseshift00, cphaseshift01, cphaseshift10, cswap, h, i, iswap, phaseshift, pswap, rx, ry, rz, s, si, swap, t, ti, x, y, z

A detailed explanation of these will be given in *Chapter 6, Using Gate-Based Quantum Computers – Qubits and Quantum Circuits.*

The following table provides Rigetti device information:

Name	Device	Qubits
Aspen-11	AwsDevice('arn:aws:braket:::device/qpu/rigetti/ Aspen-11')	38
Aspen-M-1	AwsDevice('arn:aws:braket:::device/qpu/rigetti/ Aspen-M-1')	80

Table 2.3

More information on the Rigetti devices can be found at https://qcs.rigetti.com/qpus.

Oxford Quantum Circuits

We have discussed both annealing and gate quantum computing devices. Since the **Oxford Quantum Circuits (OQC)** Lucy 8-qubit device is a recent addition at the time of this writing, it will not be covered in this book. It is available in the **eu-west-2** region. Please feel free to run 8 qubit or less gate-based quantum circuits on this device in later chapters if you are interested and have the device available in your region. More information can be found at https://oxfordquantumcircuits.com/ technology.

Now, we will look at the simulators that are available on Amazon Braket.

Amazon Braket simulators

Amazon Braket now provides five simulators that allow quantum developers to create their ideal circuit to meet their application or business use case without worrying about qubit connectivity. Two of these simulators are run on the local computer, while three are special simulators created to model quantum circuits and are run on Amazon's hardware. In the following table, you can see that there are various qubit limits on each. You can pick the appropriate simulator based on the number of qubits desired and whether you want to simulate noise or not:

Name	Device	Qubits
Free local simulators		

Local state vector simulator	`LocalSimulator()`
	
	 `LocalSimulator("default")`
	
	 `LocalSimulator(backend="default")`
	
	 `LocalSimulator(backend="braket_sv")`
	
	 Note: These are all the same device
		25

Local density matrix simulator	`LocalSimulator(backend="braket_dm")`	12
Simulators using Amazon Braket resources		
Tensor Network Simulator TN1	`AwsDevice('arn:aws:braket:::device/quantum-simulator/amazon/tn1')`	50
Density Matrix Simulator DM1	`AwsDevice('arn:aws:braket:::device/quantum-simulator/amazon/dm1')`	17
State Vector Simulator SV1	`AwsDevice('arn:aws:braket:::device/quantum-simulator/amazon/sv1')`	34

Table 2.4 – Braket simulator device information

Chapter 8, Using Hybrid Algorithms – Optimization Using Gate Based Quantum Computers, will go into more detail about these simulators, the kind of results they provide, and limitations on the type of circuit, gate depth, and time of execution.

However, here is a brief description of the role each will play in the execution of your circuit.

Simulators executing on a local device

Two local simulators execute on your local device through the SDK, as detailed next.

Local state vector simulator

A **state vector** simulator basically does the linear algebra by taking the state of each qubit vector and performing **inner products** or **tensor products** on one or many qubits as necessary to derive the final state vector of the system. This is purely a mathematically intensive process and therefore is limited by the memory capacity of the system to track all elements of the final system, which can be as large as $2^n \times 2^n$, where n is the number of qubits.

Local density matrix simulator

A **density matrix** describes the quantum state of any physical system and is able to represent mixed states. State vector simulators only represent pure states; however, when a system decoheres or has errors, it is entangled with some *other* system that cannot be defined, so the mixed state becomes the *best* representation of the system with errors. A density matrix simulator thus represents a simulation of a quantum computer with errors. Noise is introduced using gate noise operations such as a bit flip (where a 0 is changed to a 1 or vice versa), or **depolarizing** errors, where a **Pauli** gate (X, Y, or Z) is applied. Noise can also be applied to specific gates and qubits. Since this simulator runs on your local device, it is limited to 12 qubits. We will not be covering density matrix simulators in this book.

Simulators executing on Amazon resources

Three simulators run on Amazon resources, as detailed next.

State vector simulator (SV1)

SV1 is a state vector simulator using Amazon resources and can simulate up to 34 qubits of a dense circuit. Large circuits can take considerable time to run, and there is a time limit of 6 hours on SV1. You can consider this as a brute-force method that runs through every scenario and keeps track of all possible states. Its runtime increases linearly with the number of gates, and exponentially with the number of qubits.

Density matrix simulator (DM1)

This density matrix simulator is operated using Amazon resources and can simulate up to 17 qubits. It has an operational time limit of 6 hours. It also scales linearly with the number of gate operations and exponentially with the number of qubits. We will not be covering density matrix simulators in this book.

Tensor network simulator (TN1)

TN1 is a special simulator that uses Amazon TensorFlow resources. It can simulate up to 50 qubits. However, it works better for sparse circuits and circuits that represent special structures such as the **quantum Fourier transform** (**QFT**) circuit. We will work our way up to this type of circuit in *Chapter 6, Using Gate-Based Quantum Computers – Qubits and Quantum Circuits*, and *Chapter 7, Using Gate Quantum Computers – Basic Quantum Algorithms*. It first evaluates the circuit in the "rehearsal phase", where it evaluates an optimal execution and time-estimates the circuit's runtime. If the time estimate is within the limit of 6 hours, then it will perform the execution of the circuit in what is called the "contraction phase."

Summary

In this chapter, we have covered all the external and internal quantum computing devices currently available in Amazon Braket. This chapter showed the breadth of technology that is available through Amazon Braket since each type of device relies upon many years of development with different qubit and quantum computing technologies. The growing number of internal quantum simulators also present different methods of simulating the evolution of quantum states.

The next chapter, *Chapter 3, User Setup, Tasks, and Understanding Device Costs*, will dive into more details about the Amazon Braket service. We will go over where a user can find the execution status of the tasks submitted to different devices and it is also critical for a system administrator who is setting up users, security, and access to the devices. The next chapter will also cover the billing section of Amazon Braket.

If you are a user who wants to quickly execute a simple circuit on a local simulator that will not cost anything, then you can skip to *Chapter 4, Writing Your First Amazon Braket Code Sample*, where we will introduce our first Braket code example.

Further reading

This section includes various links that can be referenced to get more information on the topics covered in this chapter:

- These links provide general Amazon Braket information:

  - https://aws.amazon.com/braket/

  - https://aws.amazon.com/braket/faqs/

- These links provide more information about devices:

  - https://docs.aws.amazon.com/braket/latest/developerguide/braket-devices.html

  - https://aws.amazon.com/braket/quantum-computers/

3

User Setup, Tasks, and Understanding Device Costs

In *Chapter 1*, *Setting Up Amazon Braket*, we covered the basic setup of AWS Braket and details on starting the Braket service and notebooks. We also looked at the devices that are available in Amazon Braket in detail in *Chapter 2*, *Braket Devices Explained*.

In this chapter, we will go further into some critical administrative and reference information. We will set up the user groups and the users with the desired security access using permissions policies. We will review the Amazon Braket task list, which is a list of tasks submitted by users to the Amazon Braket devices, and consider how to find your results if they are not in the task list. Finally, we'll look at the cost of the different devices and how to find the billing summary.

The topics we will cover in this chapter are the following:

- Setting up user groups and users
- Creating policies for users
- Running test code
- Finding your tasks and results
- Understanding device costs and billing

Technical requirements

The JSON configuration files used in this chapter are available at https://github.com/PacktPublishing/Quantum-Computing-Experimentation-with-Amazon-Braket/tree/main/Chapter03.

Setting up user groups and users

It is prudent to set up users with appropriate permissions to limit user access and ensure a safe experience. As an administrator, you want to ensure the users cannot access functionality they do not need. However, if you wish to proceed using Amazon Braket as a single root user, you can skip to the *Running test code* section.

There are many options and features, and all of them can be controlled by creating policies or modifying an existing policy. We will go over only two examples, so that you become comfortable with the minimum required process. Any further policy changes should be done by an expert AWS administrator.

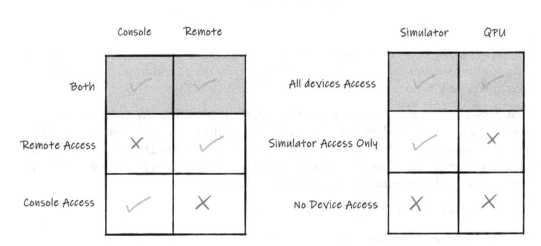

Figure 3.1 – Sample scenario of deciding between two security options

The first choice to make is whether users will be accessing the Amazon Braket notebooks from within the AWS Console or will be accessing the devices remotely through their own local Jupyter notebooks. Another choice is whether the user's device access will be restricted. For example, users may only be allowed to use their local CPU for processing, which will not incur a cost and thus they don't have Amazon Braket device access. Alternatively, the user may be given access to Amazon Braket simulators but not the external **Quantum Processor Unit** (**QPU**) devices, which can be more expensive. Lastly, access can be given to all devices.

In most cases, we can group different users into a user group. This way, we do not need to set access permissions for every single user individually. In the next section, we will create a user group and then set permissions to that group.

Creating a user group

In order to create a new user group, let's work through the following steps:

1. First, we need to navigate to the **Identify and Access Management (IAM)** service. To do this, search for IAM in the AWS Console search bar.

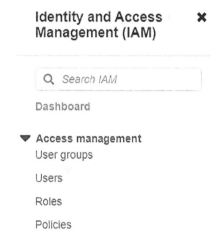

Figure 3.2 – Identity and Access Management (IAM) function menu

2. The IAM screen has a number of options on the left side, however, we will only use a few of them. For now, select **User groups**.

3. This will show the **User groups** screen. Now click on **Create group**.

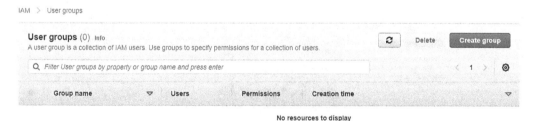

Figure 3.3 – User groups screen

4. On the **Create user group** screen, we have a few options. Let's go through them one by one. First, we need to give the group a name – I have entered `Remote_Users`. These will be users that will submit their jobs remotely and will not have access to the AWS Console.

Figure 3.4 – Entering the user group name

5. In the **Attach permissions policies** search field, enter `Braket`. This will show one or two policies. Select **AmazonBraketFullAccess** by clicking on the checkbox.

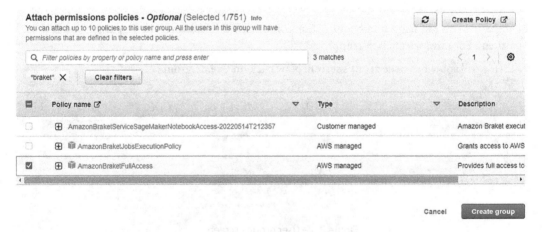

Figure 3.5 – Attach policies to user group

6. Next, click on **Create group.**

Setting up users

We have already set up a user group, so now we will add users to this group to give them remote access only:

1. From the **IAM** menu, select **Users**.

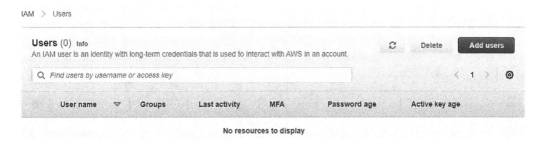

Figure 3.6 – User entry screen

2. On the **Users** screen, click on **Add users**.

3. Create a *username* that the user will use to log in. Also, now you can select whether the user will have remote access, AWS Console access, or both, as shown in *Figure 3.1*. To specify this, click the appropriate checkboxes for remote access (**Access key – Programatic access**) and for AWS Console access (**Password – AWS Management Console access**).

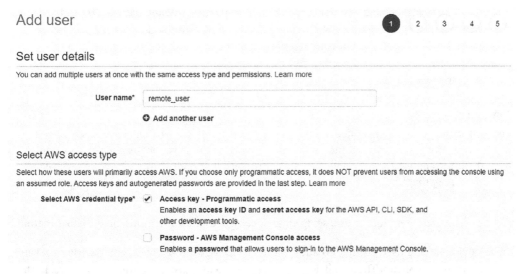

Figure 3.7 – Enter the username and select the type of access

4. Click on the **Next: Permissions** button at the bottom of the screen.

5. On the **Set permissions** screen, check the group the user needs to be added to. We will select the **Remote_Users** group that we created earlier.

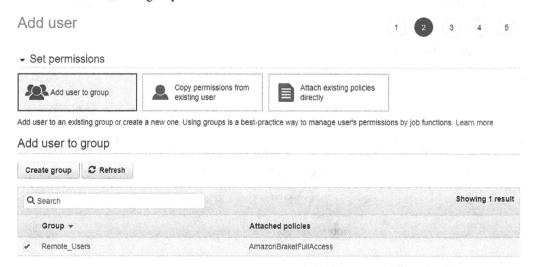

Figure 3.8 – Add the user to a group

6. Now you can click on the **Next: Tags** button at the bottom of the screen, then click on the **Next: Review** button, and finally, the **Create user** button.

    Since we have just created a remote user, the user will have both an *access key ID* and a *security access key* automatically generated at this point. You should now either download the keys by clicking on the **Download .csv** button, or copy both the access key ID and security access key. You will need to give this information to the user so that they can enter it in their *config file*.

Note: Keys Warning

The security access key is generated uniquely at this step. If it is lost, you will have to regenerate it. Please ensure you download the `.csv` file containing the keys for the user or copy and paste the information. The user will enter this information in their config file, as we reviewed in *Chapter 1, Setting Up Amazon Braket*.

---

7. The preliminary steps for the user setup are now complete and you can click on the **Close** button.

We have now created a user group and added users to that group. Now we can decide to set up permissions through policies. These policies can be applied to user groups or individual users. In the next section, we will go over how to create these policies.

Creating a policy for users

We will now create two simple policies so that we can restrict access to the Braket simulators and external QPUs based on a user allowance.

To start with, we will create a new policy called `No_Device_Access` that restricts access to all Braket devices. In other words, this will prevent access to the Braket simulators SV1, TN1, and DM1, along with the external QPUs. However, the user can still use local simulators, which do not incur a cost:

1. From the main **Identity and Access Management (IAM)** menu, select **Policies**. You can also filter to see only the Braket policies.

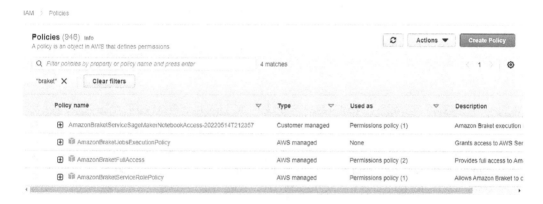

Figure 3.9 – Policy list

2. Now click on **Create Policy**.

3. Next, click on the **JSON** tab and paste the following script, which can be found on the GitHub repository for this chapter in the `no_device_access_policy.json` file:

```
{
        "Version": "2012-10-17",
        "Statement": [
            {
                "Sid": "VisualEditor0",
                "Effect": "Deny",
                "Action": [
                    "braket:GetQuantumTask",
                    "braket:CreateQuantumTask",
                    "braket:CancelQuantumTask"
                ],
```

```
                "Resource": "arn:aws:braket::[add account
                               id]:device/*"
        },
        {

            "Sid": "VisualEditor1",
            "Effect": "Deny",
            "Action": [
                "braket:GetDevice",
                "braket:SearchDevices",
                "braket:SearchQuantumTasks"
            ],
            "Resource": "arn:aws:braket::[add account
                           id]:device/*"

        }
    ]
}
```

Notice there are two places where you must replace [add account id] with your *account ID*. This can be found on the top-right corner of the screen by clicking on your account name and then copying account_id.

Note: Error warning

There will be two error messages stating the ARN Region is missing, which can be ignored.

---

4. Click on **Next: Tags**, then **Next: Review**, and then enter No_Amazon_Braket_Device_ Access for the name of the policy.

5. Finally, click on **Create Policy**.

You should now be able to find the policy in the search field by typing in the name of the policy.

We can repeat the same process to create a policy to restrict access to any QPU device. The policy can be found on the GitHub repository for this chapter in the no_qpu_access_policy.json file. We can call this No_Amazon_Braket_QPU_Access and it will allow access only to the Braket simulators (and, of course, the free local simulators). In order to apply this policy, enter the following **JSON** code in *step 3* of the preceding exercise:

```json
{
    "Version": "2012-10-17",
    "Statement": [
        {
            "Effect": "Deny",
            "Action": [
                "braket:CreateQuantumTask",
                "braket:CancelQuantumTask",
                "braket:GetQuantumTask",
                "braket:SearchQuantumTasks",
                "braket:GetDevice",
                "braket:SearchDevices"
            ],
            "Resource": [
                "arn:aws:braket::[add account id]:
                device/qpu/*"
            ]
        }
    ]
}
```

Notice again that you must replace [add account id] with your *account ID*.

We now have two policies that we can add individually to users or apply to an entire user group. Let's add one of the policies that we just worked on to the user group we created earlier:

1. Select **User groups**.
2. Simply click on the user group that you created.
3. Select the **Permissions** tab.

4.   Click on the **Add permissions** button and then select **Attach Policies**:

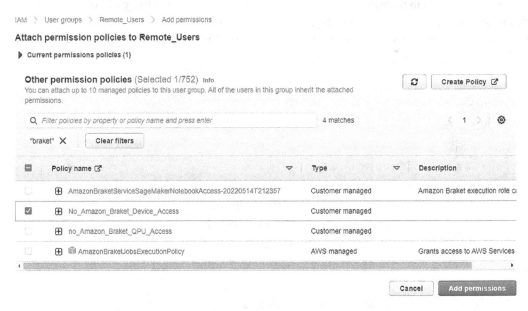

Figure 3.10 – User group permissions policies

5.   Search for the No_Amazon_Braket_Device_Access policy if it is not already visible.

6.   Check the **No_Amazon_Braket_Device_Access** checkbox and then click on the **Add permissions** button all the way at the bottom of the screen.

All users in this group will now inherit this policy and will not be able to access or send jobs to the Amazon Braket simulators SV1, TN1 or DN1, nor external QPUs.

You have now seen how to create your own policy and apply it at the user-group level. You can also copy and modify existing policies and attach policies to an individual user. You will also be able to decide whether the user has remote access, AWS Console access, or both. This completes the administrative setup.

In the next section, we will run the test code to ensure that the Boto3 setup from *Chapter 1, Setting Up Amazon Braket* and the permissions set up in this chapter are working properly.

Running test code

In this section, we will execute the test code found on the GitHub repository for this chapter. If you have set up the user with remote access and have completed all the steps in *Chapter 1, Setting Up Amazon Braket*, to set up a remote development environment using Anaconda, and you have installed the Amazon Braket SDK along with Boto3, then you are ready to start the test. You should have set up the config file and added the access keys for the user account with the appropriate access permissions as shown in the last section. So, let's get started with the code:

1. Open your Anaconda Prompt application. You should see the default environment (base) at the beginning. Please continue typing after that.

2. Activate your Braket environment using the following command:

    ```
    (base) conda activate Braket
    ```

3. Start your Jupyter Notebook session using the following command:

    ```
    (Braket) Jupyter Notebook
    ```

4. After your Notebook session starts, navigate to the downloaded code for this book, select the Chapter 3 folder, and then open the Sample Braket Test.ipynb file.

5. Now you should run one line of code from the following snippets at a time using the **Run** button. Let's start with loading the libraries:

    ```python
    from braket.aws import AwsDevice, AwsQuantumTask
    from braket.circuits import Circuit
    from braket.devices import LocalSimulator
    ```

6. Set the number of shots for the Amazon Braket device. This is the number of times the device will repeat the quantum circuit to get probabilistic results. Remember that quantum computers produce only one set of results per shot. So, in order to get an accurate representation of the probability profile, we have to repeat the experiment many times:

    ```python
    # Set the number of shots
    n_shots = 10
    ```

7. Now we set the device to the SV1 simulator:

    ```python
    # Use SV1 device
    device = AwsDevice("arn:aws:braket:::device/
                        quantum-simulator/amazon/sv1")
    ```

8. The next line has the key parameters that the user needs to edit. In the following code, make sure to replace [bucket Name] with the bucket name you created in S3. You can replace [Folder Name] with the folder you created in *Chapter 1*, *Setting Up Amazon Braket*, or type in any folder name and this task result will be stored in that folder:

```
# Set the S3 bucket and folder name
my_bucket = "[bucket Name]"
my_prefix = "[Folder Name]"
s3_folder = (my_bucket, my_prefix)
```

9. The next line will create the quantum circuit. You do not need to know what this means yet:

```
# Define the quantum circuit
circ = Circuit().h(0).cnot(0, 1)
print(circ)
```

10. Now send the circuit to the SV1 simulator for execution:

```
# Run the circuit
result = device.run(circ, s3_folder, shots =
                    n_shots).result()
counts = result.measurement_counts
print(counts)
```

Output:

```
Counter({'00': 6, '11': 4})
```

If you see the results as shown here, it means you were successfully able to remotely execute the code from your local device on the Amazon Braket service and the SV1 simulator.

What if you got errors during the preceding steps? Firstly, if you had set the user policy to **No_Amazon_Braket_Device_Access**, and got a message similar to AccessDeniedException: An error occurred (AccessDeniedException) when calling the GetDevice operation:..., this means the policy rightly prevented you from accessing any device on Amazon Braket. You should delete the policy and replace it with the **No_Amazon_Braket_QPU_Access** policy, then restart the Jupyter Notebook kernel, and run the code again.

If there are other errors, then please review *Chapter 1*, *Setting Up Amazon Braket*, to ensure you have all the components installed correctly and the config file has the correct access keys and Region specified. If the code worked all the way, then you know everything has been set up correctly. You also have results saved in your S3 folder from this execution.

In the next section, we will review where user tasks and results are stored. This can be helpful if the user cannot retrieve their data using their code and wants to look at the task status or retrieve `task_id` to pull the results later. It can also be helpful if the user has Console access and wants to find their results or `result_id` to pull the results later using the code.

Finding your tasks and results

In this section, we will examine where you can view the various tasks sent to the quantum and simulator devices and how to retrieve the results. Before proceeding, please make sure you have submitted some tasks using the test code either through a root account, or through a user account that has been given access to the Console, otherwise you will not be able to see the tasks. You can go back as the system administrator and give Console access to the user by selecting **IAM**, **Users**, security credentials, and then assign a Console password.

After this is done, let's go back into the Console to view the results:

1. In the **Amazon Braket** service, click on the **Tasks** menu item. You can see a list of tasks, their statuses, the device they were run on, and the time of creation. Users that have access to the AWS Console can also use this method to view their tasks. The tasks in the following example were run on the SV1 simulator:

Figure 3.11 – Tasks list

2. Click on the task id link. This will show the details of the task.

Figure 3.12 – Task details

3.   Now click on the link of the task at the bottom left under **S3**. The results of the task are available in the `results.json` file.

Objects (1)

Objects are the fundamental entities stored in Amazon S3. You can use Amazon S3 inventory ⤢ to get a list of all objects in your bucket. For others to access your objects, you'll need to explicitly grant them permissions. Learn more ⤢

☐	Name ▲	Type ▽	Last modified ▽	Size ▽	Storage class ▽
☐	📄 results.json	json	May 21, 2021, 15:32:21 (UTC-04:00)	50.8 KB	Standard

Figure 3.13 – Results file

4.   You can now select the `results.json` file and download it to your computer.

Let us review the `results.json` file section by section.

The actual circuit sent was a simple Hadamard represented by "h" on qubit 0, and then a control NOT gate from qubit 0 to qubit 1 represented by "cnot". This information is found in the `instructions` section. The number of shots used was 1,000 on the SV1 simulator.

The following file was generated with 1,000 shots; however, only two are displayed and the rest have been truncated. The measurements are shown in the `measurements` section of the file and were done on qubits 0 and 1. The measurement results from this file are read programmatically to produce the histogram results of the quantum measurement:

```
{
    "braketSchemaHeader": {
        "name":
            "braket.task_result.gate_model_task_result",
        "version": "1"
    },
    "measurements": [
        [
            1,
            1
        ],
```

```
...998 entries truncated...
        [
            1,
            1
        ]
    ],
    "measuredQubits": [
        0,
        1
    ],
    "taskMetadata": {
        "braketSchemaHeader": {
            "name": "braket.task_result.task_metadata",
            "version": "1"
        },
```

The account and task ids are also in the file, however we have removed them in this example:

```
    "id": "arn:aws:braket:us-east-1:
            [account id]:quantum-task/[task id]",
```

The number of shots is identified as 1000, along with the device the task was run on – in this case, the sv1 simulator:

```
    "shots": 1000,
    "deviceId": "arn:aws:braket:::device/
                quantum-simulator/amazon/sv1",
    "deviceParameters": {
        "braketSchemaHeader": {
            "name": "braket.device_schema.simulators.
              gate_model_simulator_device_parameters",
            "version": "1"
        },
        "paradigmParameters": {
            "braketSchemaHeader": {
                "name": "braket.device_schema.
                  gate_model_parameters",
```

```
                "version": "1"
            },
            "qubitCount": 2,
            "disableQubitRewiring": false
        }
    },
    "createdAt": "2021-05-21T19:32:17.837Z",
    "endedAt": "2021-05-21T19:32:20.027Z",
    "status": "COMPLETED"
},
"additionalMetadata": {
    "action": {
        "braketSchemaHeader": {
            "name": "braket.ir.jaqcd.program",
            "version": "1"
        },
```

The circuit sent is shown in the `instructions` section as follows. The Hadamard gate is represented by "h" on qubit 0, and the control NOT gate from qubit 0 to qubit 1 is represented by "cnot":

```
        "instructions": [
            {
                "target": 0,
                "type": "h"
            },
            {
                "control": 0,
                "target": 1,
                "type": "cnot"
            }
        ],
        "results": [],
        "basis_rotation_instructions": []
    },
```

```
        "simulatorMetadata": {
            "braketSchemaHeader": {
                "name":
                    "braket.task_result.simulator_metadata",
                "version": "1"
            },
            "executionDuration": 113
        }
    }
}
```

> **Note: Finding All Your Results**
>
> If there are no tasks, but you know you ran the tasks on a quantum device, you have two options:
>
> 1. Check your Region. If your Region in the Console is different from the device Region, you will not see your results. You can change your Region to the Region of the device to see the specific device results.
>
> 2. You can go to the S3 service, which will show you the buckets you or your users created, and you can find the results of the tasks sent to the devices in those folders.

Now that we are familiar with how the administrator and users can access their tasks and results, in the next section, we will examine how the devices available in Amazon Braket are priced.

Understanding device costs and billing

We will now look at the very important topic of device costs. We will look at the published device costs and then also explore how to estimate the cost of a QPU or simulator device based on the number of *shots* the device is used for. The number of shots is the number of times the circuit will be recreated, run, and the end results measured by the device. Since quantum systems have probabilistic results, this process requires multiple shots to get the probability distribution of all the possible results.

QPU versus simulator devices

QPU devices are charged a fee per task and then there is a per shot charge. The number of qubits you measure at the end of your circuit will, to some extent, determine the number of shots.

Hardware Provider	QPU family	Per-task price	Per-shot price
D-Wave	2000Q	$0.30000	$0.00019
D-Wave	Advantage	$0.30000	$0.00019
IonQ	IonQ device	$0.30000	$0.01000
OQC	Lucy	$0.30000	$0.00035
Rigetti	Aspen-11	$0.30000	$0.00035
Rigetti	M-1	$0.30000	$0.00035

Figure 3.14 – Cost of QPU devices available in Amazon Braket (these prices are correct as of May 2022; check the current prices at https://aws.amazon.com/braket/pricing/)

In order to limit the number of measurements, I am going to use a heuristic. For example, if you are measuring two qubits in equal superposition, you can have up to four different values with equal probability. Here, it would be sufficient to do 100 shots. In other words, we should see each value approximately 25 times. Of course, you could also do more shots to get a more accurate probability profile. On the other hand, if you were measuring 10 qubits in equal superposition, then there is a possibility of 210 values or 1,024 different values when measured in the Z basis. The Z basis is the default basis in which all measurements will be done. If you would like to have the possibility of observing the probability of each of these values, I would recommend 1,024x25= 25,600 shots at a minimum. Typically, we do not measure a circuit where all the qubits are in equal superposition. In most quantum algorithms, there is an expectation of a few states with high probability. In the following plot, the diagonal line can be considered a conservative minimum without a good understanding of the specific function of the quantum circuit.

Keeping in mind what we just discussed, bear in mind that each device has a "maximum" number of shots that are allowed. For example, for IonQ, the maximum number of shots is 10,000. This allows you to determine the adequate number of shots to use, however, the actual number will depend on the precision needed and will be based on the number of possible high-probability states in the output based on the quantum circuit itself.

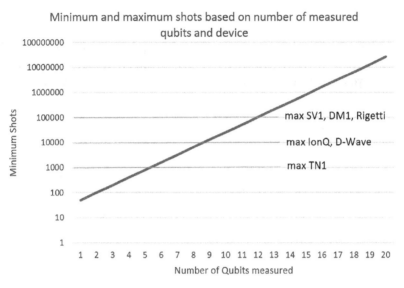

Figure 3.15 – Approximate minimum (diagonal line) and maximum (horizontal line) shots per device based on the number of qubits measured (x axis) – note that the y axis is logarithmic

The simulator devices, on the other hand, are charged by the actual time utilized. To get an accurate assessment of the cost of the circuit, it is necessary to run the circuit and then calculate the cost. This will be explained further in *Chapter 4, Writing Your First Amazon Braket Code Sample*, where the first Amazon Braket sample code will show how to estimate the cost of the circuit. However, keep in mind that based on the number of qubits in the circuit, the number of gates used, the number of qubits measured, and the number of shots, the amount of time the simulator will run changes. For very large circuits, it is possible for simulators to run for 10 minutes or more.

Simulator	cost per minute($)
sv1	$ 0.075
tn1	$ 0.275
dm1	$ 0.075

Figure 3.16 – Cost of Amazon Braket simulator devices (correct as of May 2022 – for updated values, check https://aws.amazon.com/braket/pricing/ and click on the Simulator tab)

> **Note: Price Changes**
>
> These costs are based on the published costs as of this writing. Amazon may change the costs at any time. To get the current costs, please refer to the devices in Amazon Braket and check their costs.

Viewing your charges

In order to view your monthly charges, you can use the **Billing** service. Initially, you will have zero costs, however, as time goes on and you use the system more and more, the billing dashboard will be more useful to view your month-to-date spend.

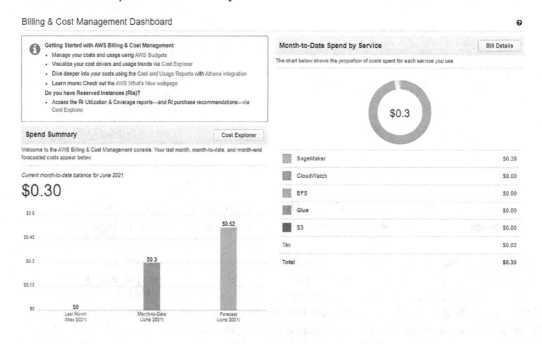

Figure 3.17 – Amazon Billing service screen

More details of the costs can be found by clicking on the **Cost Explorer** button. If you have been using Amazon Braket for a while, Cost Explorer can allow you to look at monthly costs and drill down into services. You can also find Cost Explorer by searching for `AWS Cost Explorer` in the search bar.

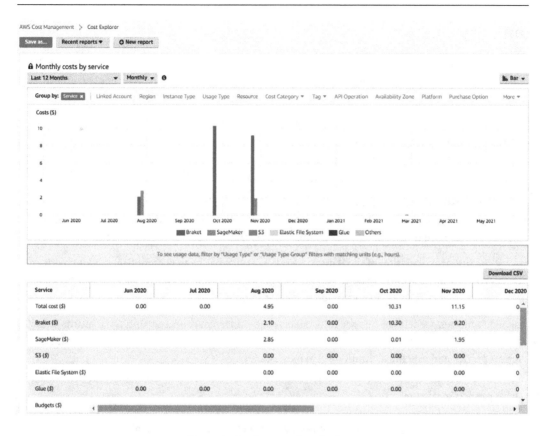

Figure 3.18 – Amazon Cost Explorer

> **Note: Notebook Costs**
>
> The cost to run Notebook instances will show under the SageMaker service. A typical medium Notebook service with 5 GB of volume will cost $0.05 per hour after the Free Tier allowance has expired.

This cost information and the tools discussed here will allow the administrator to monitor costs, decide which services should be allowed, and allocate budgets in AWS. Many advanced monitoring and budget features are available in AWS Billing and can be explored by the administrator within AWS.

Summary

We have looked at how to add users to an AWS account. We showed how the administrator, or the root user, will create user groups, and then add users to the group. We covered a simple scenario of configuring user access either through the AWS Console or remotely. We also created policies for restricting access to certain devices.

We ran sample code to ensure our remote connection to Amazon Braket was working and the user policy was created properly. We looked at where user tasks can be monitored and where the results are stored.

Finally, we reviewed the costs of using Amazon Braket. These include the cost of sending jobs to quantum devices and are based on the number of shots. We also reviewed the costs of quantum simulators and showed how to view costs in the AWS Billing service and Cost Explorer.

Now that the initial explanation of the Amazon Braket service has been accomplished, along with an explanation of the devices and the administrative tasks to access and set permissions to the Amazon Braket service, we are ready to dive into our first code sample.

In the next chapter, we will go deeper into measuring device costs and setting up a rudimentary quantum circuit so we can execute it on a simulator and understand the basic steps to determine device properties and execute a circuit on Amazon Braket.

Further reading

- More information on user setup and policy management can be found at the following links:

    - https://docs.aws.amazon.com/IAM/latest/UserGuide/id.html

    - https://docs.aws.amazon.com/IAM/latest/UserGuide/access_policies_create.html

    - https://docs.aws.amazon.com/IAM/latest/UserGuide/access.html

- More information on pricing can be found here: https://docs.aws.amazon.com/braket/latest/developerguide/braket-pricing.html

- More information on billing can be found at the following links:

    - https://docs.aws.amazon.com/awsaccountbilling/latest/aboutv2/billing-what-is.html

    - https://docs.aws.amazon.com/account-billing/index.html

4

Writing Your First Amazon Braket Code Sample

In this chapter, we will go over some very basic code to get started in Amazon Braket. We will create a very simple quantum circuit to represent a binary number on a quantum register. This will demonstrate the basics of how to set up a quantum circuit and then measure it on a quantum device. We will spend some time understanding how to access the devices through the code and estimating the cost of running a quantum circuit on a device. Then, we will create the quantum circuit and run it. Finally, we can get a more accurate picture of the cost of execution. In this chapter, we will only use two simple quantum gates; however, we will use them somewhat classically, so a deep explanation of the complex nature of quantum states and gate operations will not be needed.

In this chapter, we will cover the following key topics:

- Finding active devices
- Assigning a device
- Cost estimation
- Creating a simple quantum circuit
- Running a circuit on a simulator device
- Actual simulator costs

Technical requirements

The source code for this chapter can be found in the following GitHub repository:

`https://github.com/PacktPublishing/Quantum-Computing-Experimentation-with-Amazon-Braket/tree/main/Chapter04`

Finding active devices

In the previous chapters, we discussed the devices that are available in Amazon Braket. Here, we will look at how to access the device information through code. This will become necessary as new devices are added.

> **Note: Amazon Braket Device Availability**
>
> Carefully evaluate the devices present when you purchase this book and run this code. New devices might have been added, and some devices might have been turned off. Also, depending on the region in which you set up your config file, you might see different devices.

To do this, perform the following steps:

1. The following code retrieves active devices in Amazon Braket in the form of a list. The following output has been formatted to be easier to read:

```
from braket.aws import AwsDevice
device_list=AwsDevice.get_devices(statuses=['ONLINE'])
print(device_list)
```

Output:

```
[Device('name': Advantage_system4.1, 'arn':
arn:aws:braket:::device/qpu/d-wave/Advantage_system4),

Device('name': Advantage_system6.1, 'arn': arn:aws:braket:us-
west-2::device/qpu/d-wave/Advantage_system6),

Device('name': Aspen-M-1, 'arn': arn:aws:braket:us-west-
1::device/qpu/rigetti/Aspen-M-1),

Device('name': DW_2000Q_6, 'arn': arn:aws:braket:::device/
qpu/d-wave/DW_2000Q_6),

Device('name': IonQ Device, 'arn': arn:aws:braket:::device/
qpu/ionq/ionQdevice),

Device('name': SV1, 'arn': arn:aws:braket:::device/quantum-
simulator/amazon/sv1),

Device('name': TN1, 'arn': arn:aws:braket:::device/quantum-
simulator/amazon/tn1),

Device('name': dm1, 'arn': arn:aws:braket:::device/quantum-
simulator/amazon/dm1)]
```

The device name and **Amazon Resource Name (ARN)** are returned. This long string contains information about whether the device is a QPU or a simulator, along with the device manufacturer and the QPU name.

2. We can simply store the device names in a list so that we can assign a device with the name. The names are case sensitive:

```
device_name_list=[]
for device in device_list:
    device_name_list.append(device.name)
print('Valid device names: ',device_name_list)
```

Output:

```
Valid device names:  ['Advantage_system4.1', 'Advantage_
system6.1', 'Aspen-M-1', 'DW_2000Q_6', 'IonQ Device', 'SV1',
'TN1', 'dm1']]
```

3. A helpful function that can be used to quickly get the list of available devices is as follows:

```
def available_devices():
    from braket.aws import AwsDevice
    device_list=AwsDevice.get_devices(statuses=['ONLINE'])
    device_name_list=[]
    for device in device_list:
        device_name_list.append(device.name)
    #print('Valid device names: ',device_name_list)
    return(device_name_list)
```

4. Once the function has been executed, we should get the names of all the available devices:

```
available_devices()
```

Output:

```
['Advantage_system4.1',
 'Advantage_system6.1',
 'Aspen-M-1',
 'DW_2000Q_6',
 'IonQ Device',
 'SV1',
 'TN1',
 'dm1']
```

Since the devices are regularly upgraded, please run this function and make appropriate changes as you progress through this book. In the next section, we can use this information to assign a device that you want to work with.

Assigning a device

We can assign various devices available in Amazon Braket, however, each device uses different resources. The *local simulator* uses the local computer resources to execute the circuit if using a remote connection. The Amazon Braket simulators *TN1* and *SV1* use Amazon resources. External quantum devices such those available from D-Wave, IonQ, or Rigetti use compute time on the quantum hardware housed at the respective facilities of these providers in Barnaby, Maryland, or California respectively.

Each type of device has a limit in terms of the number of qubits, the amount of circuit information it can handle, and in some cases, the *depth of the circuit* that it can execute. The **circuit depth** can be thought of as the number of columns of gate after the circuit has been converted into its low-level transpiled version. This is the version where all the gates on each qubit are packed together, as much as is feasible, using *native* gate operations on the hardware. Native gate operations are the basic gates that the gate-based quantum computer can execute on its **Quantum Processing Unit (QPU)**. Other more complex gate operations are *converted* or *transpiled* into these native gates.

Using the local simulator

Before a circuit can be executed on a device, we need to assign the device. First, let's see how to assign the local simulator. The local simulator can handle up to 25 qubits without noise, or up to 12 qubits with noise, and its execution will depend upon the memory and filesystem limitations of the computer it is run on.

The local simulator (without noise) is assigned using either of the following functions. The first is as follows:

```
device = LocalSimulator()
```

Alternatively, you can use the following:

```
device = LocalSimulator(backend="braket_sv")
```

The `LocalSimulator()` function uses the Braket **state vector simulator**. Since quantum computing produces probabilistic answers, the state vector simulator calculates all the **exact** probabilities of the final state. The actual values produced in the final measured results reflect these *probabilities*, and the accuracy of this increases with the number of shots. For example, if we know that the probability of getting each side of dice is 1/6, then as we increase the number of times we roll a dice, the more accurately the results will reflect this probability.

Using Amazon simulators or quantum devices

We will now assign Amazon simulators or external quantum devices for use. Here is an example of how to assign a device using the `arn` value:

1. This is the typical way of assigning a device for use:

   ```
   rigetti = AwsDevice("arn:aws:braket:us-west-1::device/
   qpu/rigetti/Aspen-M-1") print(rigetti)
   ```

   Output:

   ```
   Device('name': Aspen-M-1, 'arn': arn:aws:braket:us-west-
   1::device/qpu/rigetti/Aspen-M-1)
   ```

2. Rather than providing the full `arn` value, the following function only requires the device name to set the device. Here, `Name` refers to the device name as returned by the `available_devices()` function:

   ```
   device=AwsDevice.get_devices(names=Name)
   ```

   For example, if you're using the *SV1* device, it will be as follows:

   ```
   sv1=AwsDevice.get_devices(names='SV1')
   print(sv1)
   ```

   Output:

   ```
   [Device('name': SV1, 'arn': arn:aws:braket:::device/quantum-
   simulator/amazon/sv1)]
   ```

   > **Note: Device Name**
   > The device name is case-sensitive.

3. The `set_device(Name)` function can be helpful as a reusable function to set the device, based on the name. In this case, the full `arn` value is not necessary:

   ```
   def set_device(Name):
       device_list=AwsDevice.get_devices(names=Name)
       if len(device_list)==1:
           device=device_list[0]
           print(device)
           return(device)
       else:
           print('No device found')
           print('use name from list',
                   available_devices())
   ```

4. In the case of a wrong name, an error message with available device names will be given:

```
device=set_device('svi')
```

Output:

```
No device found
```

```
use name from list ['Advantage_system1.1', 'Aspen-9',
'DW_2000Q_6', 'IonQ Device', 'SV1', 'TN1', 'dm1']
```

Now that we know various ways and options in which to assign a device in Amazon Braket, in the next section, let's find the cost of the device.

Estimating the cost of the device

The following code shows how to estimate the cost of the different devices. Because we assigned the device in the last section, we can further use the device to determine the cost. The `estimate_cost` function has the appropriate calculations to estimate the cost of the device that is passed through along with the number of shots. The default number of shots is `1000`.

Let's get started! Perform the following steps:

1. The following function calculates the costs of the simulators on a cost per minute basis, while the cost of the quantum devices is calculated based on the QPU rate and the number of shots. Note that this function is making some assumptions about the `cost_per_task` amount, and the available QPUs and simulators. Please update these in the code if `cost_per_task` has changed in the Amazon Braket pricing table:

```
def estimate_cost(device,num_shots=1000):
    #device=set_device(Name)
    cost_per_task=0.30
    Name=device.name
    if Name in ['SV1','TN1','dm1']:
        price_per_min=
            device.properties.service.deviceCost.price
        unit=device.properties.service.deviceCost.unit
        print('simulator cost per ',unit,': $',
                price_per_min)
        print('total cost cannot be estimated')
    elif Name in['Advantage_system6.1',
        'Advantage_system4.1','DW_2000Q_6',
        'Aspen-M-1','IonQ Device']:
```

```
            price_per_shot=
                device.properties.service.deviceCost.price
            unit=device.properties.service.deviceCost.unit
            print('device cost per ',unit,': $',
                    price_per_shot)
            print('total cost for {} shots is
                    ${:.2f}'.format(num_shots,
                    cost_per_task+num_shots*price_per_shot))
        else:
            print('device not found')
            print('use name from list',
                    available_devices())
```

We use the preceding function with the SV1 device. Since the cost of the SV1 device is based on the time of execution, it is not possible to estimate the actual cost prior to execution. We will see how to calculate the actual costs after execution later in this chapter.

2. The next line of code shows the result of adding SV1, a simulator, to the `estimate_cost` function:

```
device_name='SV1'
device=set_device(device_name)
estimate_cost(device)
```

Output:

```
Device('name': SV1, 'arn': arn:aws:braket:::device/quantum-
simulator/amazon/sv1)

simulator cost per   minute : $ 0.075

total cost cannot be estimated
```

Since we picked a simulator, the device cost is dependent on the execution time, so this cannot be accurately calculated. Please try using different device names to see what results you get for the simulators versus the QPUs.

The following function can help you to more accurately estimate the cost based on the number of measured qubits. For this equation, we will use a heuristic that, for each possible state in the output of our quantum device, we should measure at least 25 times. The number of possible states in the output is 2^n, where n is the number of measured qubits.

$$minimum\ number\ of\ shots\ suggested = 25 \times 2^{measured\ qubits}$$

This provides the minimum number of shots based on the number of qubits that are being measured. You can update this equation, as desired, according to your own preference.

3. As the number of qubits increases, each device reaches its maximum number of shots limit. If the number of recommended shots is greater than the maximum number of shots of the device, the maximum number of shots is returned by the following function:

```
def estimate_cost_measured_qubits(device,measured_
qubits):
    #device=set_device(Name)
    min_shots_per_variable=25
    max_shots=device.properties.service.shotsRange[1]
    print('max shots:', max_shots)
    num_shots=
      min_shots_per_variable*2**measured_qubits
    if num_shots>max_shots:
        num_shots=max_shots
        print('for {} measured qubits the maximum
                allowed shots: {:,}'.format(
                measured_qubits,num_shots))
    else:
        print('for {} measured qubits the number of
                shots recommended: {:,}'.format(
                measured_qubits,num_shots))
    estimate_cost(device,num_shots)
```

4. For example, let's determine the cost of using IonQ with a circuit where we will measure 5 qubits:

```
device=set_device('IonQ Device')
estimate_cost_measured_qubits(device, 5)
```

Output:

```
Device('name': IonQ Device, 'arn': arn:aws:braket:::device/
qpu/ionq/ionQdevice)

max shots: 10000

for 5 measured qubits the number of shots recommended: 800

device cost per  shot : $ 0.01

total cost for 800 shots is $8.30
```

5. The next block includes the code to give the cost estimate for each of the devices based on the maximum number of allowed shots and the maximum number of qubits. Therefore, for now, in the case of the Rigetti and IonQ devices, the maximum number of qubits has been hardcoded in this function. When you create your circuit, the number you should use is the actual number of qubits you are using. Also, keep in mind the simulators do not give a cost upfront, as the cost is estimate at the end of the execution based on the time to solution. Now, let's look at each of the three categories of devices separately:

- The costs for the simulators can be found using the following code:

```
for Name in ['SV1','TN1','dm1']:
    device=set_device(Name)
    qubit_count =
        device.properties.paradigm.qubitCount
    estimate_cost_measured_qubits(device, qubit_count)
    print('---')
```

Output:

```
Device('name': SV1, 'arn': arn:aws:braket:::device/quantum-simulator/amazon/sv1)

max shots: 100000

for 34 measured qubits the maximum allowed shots: 100,000

simulator cost per  minute : $ 0.075

total cost cannot be estimated

---

Device('name': TN1, 'arn': arn:aws:braket:::device/quantum-simulator/amazon/tn1)

max shots: 1000

for 50 measured qubits the maximum allowed shots: 1,000

simulator cost per  minute : $ 0.275

total cost cannot be estimated

---

Device('name': dm1, 'arn': arn:aws:braket:::device/quantum-simulator/amazon/dm1)

max shots: 100000

for 17 measured qubits the maximum allowed shots: 100,000
```

```
simulator cost per  minute : $ 0.075

total cost cannot be estimated

---
```

- The costs for the D-Wave devices can be found using the following code:

```
for Name in ['Advantage_system6.1',
  'Advantage_system4.1','DW_2000Q_6']:
    device=set_device(Name)
    qubit_count =
      device.properties.provider.qubitCount
    estimate_cost_measured_qubits(device, qubit_count)
    print('---')
```

Output:

```
Device('name': Advantage_system6.1, 'arn': arn:aws:braket:us-
west-2::device/qpu/d-wave/Advantage_system6)

max shots: 10000

for 5760 measured qubits the maximum allowed shots: 10,000

device cost per  shot : $ 0.00019

total cost for 10000 shots is $2.20

---

Device('name': Advantage_system4.1, 'arn':
arn:aws:braket:::device/qpu/d-wave/Advantage_system4)

max shots: 10000

for 5760 measured qubits the maximum allowed shots: 10,000

device cost per  shot : $ 0.00019

total cost for 10000 shots is $2.20

---

Device('name': DW_2000Q_6, 'arn': arn:aws:braket:::device/
qpu/d-wave/DW_2000Q_6)

max shots: 10000

for 2048 measured qubits the maximum allowed shots: 10,000

device cost per  shot : $ 0.00019

total cost for 10000 shots is $2.20

--- +
```

- The costs for the Rigetti and IonQ devices can be found using the following code:

```
for Name in ['Aspen-9','IonQ Device']:
    device=set_device(Name)
    if Name=='Aspen-9':
        qubit_count=31
    elif Name=='IonQ Device':
        qubit_count=11
    estimate_cost_measured_qubits(device, qubit_count)
    print('---')
```

Output:

```
Device('name': Aspen-M-1, 'arn': arn:aws:braket:us-west-
1::device/qpu/rigetti/Aspen-M-1)

max shots: 100000

for 2048 measured qubits the maximum allowed shots: 100,000

device cost per  shot : $ 0.00035

total cost for 100000 shots is $35.30

---

Device('name': IonQ Device, 'arn': arn:aws:braket:::device/
qpu/ionq/ionQdevice)

max shots: 10000

for 11 measured qubits the maximum allowed shots: 10,000

device cost per  shot : $ 0.01

total cost for 10000 shots is $100.30
```

As you can see, the device costs vary considerably. However, you can modify this function for your own needs and execute it prior to running a quantum circuit on a device based on the number of shots and the number of qubits measured.

6. Since we could not estimate the cost of the simulators in advance, it is possible to calculate the cost after execution with the help of the following method, which returns the duration of the execution:

```
results.additional_metadata.simulatorMetadata.
executionDuration
```

In this case, we would execute the quantum circuit on the device and then multiply the result of the preceding method by the cost per minute.

You have now experimented with some simple Braket functions to find the device name, assign a device and estimate its costs. In the case of simulators, we could not estimate the cost in advance, so we will come back to this after we have created a simple circuit and visualized that circuit in the following section.

In the next section, we will create a simple quantum circuit and execute it on a quantum simulator.

Creating a simple quantum circuit

Now we are ready to create a simple quantum circuit in Amazon Braket.

When creating a quantum circuit in Braket, it should be noted that the circuit expands as different qubits are identified. *Figure 4.1* shows the quantum circuit we are creating:

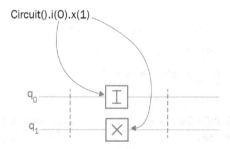

Figure 4.1 – Visualizing a simple circuit in Amazon Braket

The circuit starts with a state of $|0\rangle$ on each qubit. In this chapter, please do not worry about the | and the ⟩ brackets around the numbers. We will review this later in *Chapter 6, Using Gate-Based Quantum Computers - Qubits and Quantum Circuits*. We will only use two very simple quantum gates. For our purposes right now, the **X** gate will also refer to as a **NOT** gate. The **X** gate will change the $|0\rangle$ state into a $|1\rangle$ state and vice versa. Additionally, we will use the identity gate, **I**, which leaves the original $|0\rangle$ value as is. If the $|1\rangle$ state was preceded by the identity gate, **I**, then that value would not change either.

For now, we will treat the circuit as dealing with classical values only. Therefore, we will use **0** for the $|0\rangle$ state and **1** for the $|1\rangle$ state.

In the following code, we will start by loading the appropriate Amazon Braket libraries along with `matplotlib`:

```
from braket.circuits import Circuit, Gate, Observable
from braket.devices import LocalSimulator
from braket.aws import AwsDevice
import matplotlib.pyplot as plt
%matplotlib inline
```

Now, we can begin the creation of our first quantum circuit by using the `Circuit()` function. In the following example, `bits` is assigned a quantum circuit with the identity gate I on qubit **0** and the **X** gate on qubit **1**:

```
bits = Circuit().i(0).x(1)
print(bits)
```

Output:

```
T  :  |0|

q0  :  -I-

q1  :  -X-

T  :  |0|
```

This simple quantum circuit can be read as having started with the **00** register and, after running through the two gates, **I** and **X**, together, results in the register containing a value of **01**:

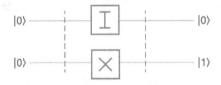

Figure 4.2 – A simple circuit using the I and X gates to produce 01

We have created a very basic quantum circuit. Now, we can implement this for any number, **N**, in the next section.

Putting together a simple quantum circuit example

Below is the full code that is needed to assign the local simulator device and then run the `bits` circuit on the local simulator device with 1,000 shots.

The results are returned to the `counts` variable. The results are printed and then plotted:

```
device = LocalSimulator()
result = device.run(bits, shots=1000).result()
counts = result.measurement_counts
print(counts)
plt.bar(counts.keys(), counts.values());
plt.xlabel('states');
plt.ylabel('counts');
```

Output:

```
Counter({'01': 1000})
```

The following diagram shows the histogram plot of the probabilities of the results:

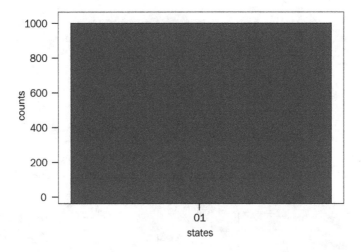

Figure 4.3 – Results showing 01 as the only resulting state; all 1,000 shots have the same answer

The results are probabilistic. However, since we only converted 00 into 01, the results are always 01. This is the only state that is produced on this simulator since the $|01\rangle$ state has a 100% probability of being in the answer.

Representing a binary value using a quantum circuit

Now we can create a simple function that takes a decimal number and converts it into a quantum state that represents the binary value of the number.

In the following function, first, we get the binary value of the number and then create a quantum circuit that has the same number of qubits as the length of the binary value representing the number. Next, we represent the binary number as a quantum state. In the case of a zero in the binary number we will place the **I** gate and for a one in the binary number we will place the **X** gate. Please note that the **X** gate will convert the original state of |0⟩ into a |1⟩ state and the **I** gate does not change the state so leaves the original state of |0⟩ as is. Let us now review the code:

```
def build_binary_circ(N):
    binary_num=bin(N)[2:]
    num_qubits=len(binary_num)
    print(binary_num)
    binary_circuit=Circuit()
    position=0
    for bit in binary_num:
        #print(bit)
        if bit=='0':
            binary_circuit.i(position)
        else:
            binary_circuit.x(position)
        position+=1
    return(binary_circuit)
```

Now we can run the function. In the following example, we use the number 6, which has been converted into the binary value of **110**. The function is then used to put an **X** gate on qubit **0**, an **X** gate on qubit **1**, and an **I** identity gate on qubit **2**:

```
binary_circuit=build_binary_circ(6)
print(binary_circuit)
```

Output:

```
110
T  : |0|

q0 : -X-

q1 : -X-

q2 : -I-

T  : |0|
```

The preceding output is a representation of the quantum circuit.

Next, we use `LocalSimulator()` function as the device and run the circuit generated by the `build_binary_circ()` function:

```
device = LocalSimulator()
result = device.run(binary_circuit, shots=1000).result()
counts = result.measurement_counts
print(counts)
```

Output:

```
Counter({'110': 1000})
```

Again, the output is based on the probabilities, which are 100% for the one answer of 110. We get the correct value, which is the binary representation of 6.

Now we will plot the bar chart to show the same result within a plot:

```
plt.bar(counts.keys(), counts.values());
plt.xlabel('states');
plt.ylabel('counts');
```

As expected, the following plot only has one value of **110** represented for all 1,000 results:

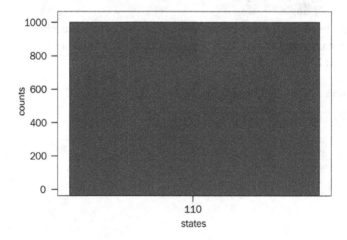

Figure 4.4 – Results showing 110 encoded in the quantum circuit

We have created a simple quantum circuit and executed it on the local simulator. In the next section, we will take this one step further by executing the same circuit on an Amazon Braket simulator.

Running a circuit on the Amazon simulator

Now we have a circuit that we can run on a simulator. However, before we can run on the simulator device, we need to set the Amazon S3 bucket information. This will tell Braket where to save the resulting json output file. Then, we will create a simple function that will run the circuit on the desired device and plot the results. If you are interested in using the Amazon Braket console to check that your task has appeared in the task list, and also find the resulting output file in your S3 folder, please review *Chapter 3, User Setup, Tasks, and Understanding Device Costs*.

Let's get started! Perform the following steps:

1. First, you will have to use your appropriate Amazon Braket S3 bucket name along with the folder where the results should be stored. Remember to replace the values in the appropriate places in the following code:

    ```
    # Enter the S3 bucket you created during onboarding in
    the code below
    my_bucket = "amazon-braket-[your bucket]" # the name of
    the bucket
    my_prefix = "[your folder]" # the name of the folder in
    the bucket
    s3_folder = (my_bucket, my_prefix)
    ```

2. Now, let's create a run_circuit() function that will take device, circuit, shots, and s3_folder, execute the circuit on the device, and return the results:

    ```
    def run_circuit(device, circuit, shots, s3_folder):
        import matplotlib.pyplot as plt
        %matplotlib inline
        result = device.run(binary_circuit, shots=shots,
            s3_destination_folder=s3_folder).result()
        counts = result.measurement_counts
        print(counts)
        plt.bar(counts.keys(), counts.values());
        plt.xlabel('states');
        plt.ylabel('counts');
        return(result)
    ```

3. The next function is used to determine the actual simulator cost. This takes the actual time of execution of the circuit and calculates the cost based on the rate:

```
def actual_simulator_cost(device, result):
        price_per_min=
          device.properties.service.deviceCost.price
        price_per_ms=price_per_min/60/1000
        unit=device.properties.service.deviceCost.unit
        duration_ms=result.additional_metadata
          .simulatorMetadata.executionDuration
        if unit=='minute':
            print('simulator cost per ',unit,': $',
                    price_per_min)
            print('total execution time: ',
                    duration_ms, "ms")
            print('total cost estimated:
                    $',duration_ms*price_per_ms)
```

4. Now we are ready to execute the three functions that we have created. Let's use the `build_binary_circ()` function to build a circuit that represents the number **2,896** in binary on a quantum register, run the circuit to evaluate the end state, and then get the cost for a sample run on SV1.

This first section creates the circuit to represent the binary number, as demonstrated earlier:

```
N=2896
qubit_count=len(bin(N))-2
print('qubit count: ', qubit_count)
binary_circuit=build_binary_circ(N)
print(binary_circuit)
```

Output:

```
qubit count:  12
101101010000
T   : |0|
q0  : -X-
q1  : -I-
q2  : -X-
q3  : -X-
```

```
q4   : -I-
q5   : -X-
q6   : -I-
q7   : -X-
q8   : -I-
q9   : -I-
q10  : -I-
q11  : -I-
T    : |0|
```

5. Now we can set the device to the Amazon Braket simulator, *SV1*. Then, we can run the cost estimation function that also shows the number of shots we should run based on the number of qubits measured.

    We already know there is only one valid state in the result. Knowing this information, we can substantially reduce the number of shots on this simulator.

    We use the estimate_cost_measured_qubits() function to estimate the cost for SV1:

    ```
    device=set_device('SV1')
    estimate_cost_measured_qubits(device, qubit_count)
    ```

    Output:

    ```
    Device('name': SV1, 'arn': arn:aws:braket:::device/quantum-
    simulator/amazon/sv1)

    max shots: 100000

    for 12 measured qubits the maximum allowed shots: 100,000

    simulator cost per  minute : $ 0.075

    total cost cannot be estimated
    ```

6. In this case, and especially since we are using a simulator and understand there is only one valid state, we will only use *10* shots when we run the circuit. A new run_circuit() function is created to easily run a quantum circuit and plot the results.

    Here is the code of the execution of the circuit, the raw results, and the resulting histogram. You can see that the same binary number is returned for all *10* shots:

    ```
    result=run_circuit(device, binary_circuit, 10, s3_folder)
    ```

Output:

```
Counter({'101101010000': 10})
```

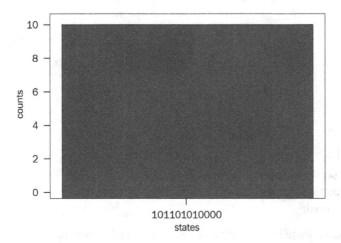

Figure 4.5 – Results showing 101101010000 encoded in the quantum circuit

Actual cost of using the Amazon simulator

Finally, we can get the actual cost of executing this circuit on the simulator by running the `actual_simulator_cost()` function:

```
actual_simulator_cost(device, result)
```

Output:

```
simulator cost per minute : $ 0.075
```

```
total execution time: 3 ms
```

```
total cost estimated: $ 3.7500000000000005e-06
```

Now, we have an accurate representation of the costs that will be incurred when we run a circuit on an Amazon Braket simulator.

Summary

In this chapter, we showed the basics of writing code in Amazon Braket by creating a simple quantum circuit, executing it on an Amazon Braket device, and displaying the probabilistic results.

We started by using the Amazon Braket functions to find the appropriate device and then got cost estimates for using that device based on the number of shots. Then, we created a simple circuit to display a binary number on a quantum register using the `LocalSimulator()` function. Finally, we ran that circuit on the SV1 simulator and got an accurate value for the cost of execution.

Further reading

In this chapter, we used a few functions to get the properties of the devices. The following two resources offer more details on how to determine other device properties and device capabilities:

- For more information on Amazon Braket Python Schemas, please visit `https://amazon-braket-schemas-python.readthedocs.io/en/latest/index.html`.

- For more information on the parameters that are used when calling devices, please visit `https://amazon-braket-sdk-python.readthedocs.io/en/stable/_apidoc/braket.aws.aws_device.html`.

- Detailed information on tracking pricing: `https://docs.aws.amazon.com/braket/latest/developerguide/braket-pricing.html`

Concluding Section 1

We now end *Section 1*. We have gone over the basics of Amazon Braket and its components.

In *Chapter 1, Setting up Amazon Braket*, we reviewed how to get started with Amazon Braket and its various components.

In *Chapter 2, Braket Devices Explained*, we looked at the devices that are available on Amazon Braket.

In *Chapter 3, User Setup, Tasks, and Understanding Device Costs*, we went into more detail about the user administration, including the user group setup and permissions, and we explained the cost structure of the devices.

In this chapter, we wrote a simple quantum circuit and executed it on the local and Amazon Braket SV1 simulators.

In *Section 2*, we will go over the mathematical and quantum concepts that are necessary to start using the quantum annealer, gate quantum computers, and hybrid circuits, which use both classical code and quantum computers. These building blocks and fundamentals will be necessary to gain an understanding of how quantum annealers are used and how quantum circuits are created. We will start by showing how D-Wave's quantum annealer performs optimization using some simple use cases. Next we will start a journey towards doing the same using gate quantum computers. In *Chapter 6, Using Gate-Based Quantum Computers - Qubits and Quantum Circuits*, we will switch to understanding quantum gates based on linear algebra, and how those gates are used to create quantum circuits. We will then create simple quantum circuits and expand our understanding of circuits that represent Monte Carlo and then can be used to increase the probability of finding the global minimum of an objective function. This will lead us to developing the gate-based equivalent of an optimization algorithm which is called **Quantum Approximate Optimization Alogrithm** or **QAOA**. By *Chapter 9, Running QAOA on Simulators and Amazon Braket Devices* will try more elaborate use cases using this hybrid method and compare results with the D-Wave quantum annealer. This journey will require considerable patience as it includes a lot of details in how these algorithms are developed and considerable execution and experimentation to demonstrate the type of results returned by our current quantum computing devices and how to interpret and improve on those results. Let's get started with the next section.

This fundamental understanding of circuits will then be used when we solve real-world use cases in *Section 3*.

Section 2: Building Blocks for Real-World Use Cases

This section discusses the foundational elements and algorithms to solve real-world problems using quantum computers. Since optimization problems on the D-Wave annealer use a different method than gate-based quantum computers, this section shows the nuances of each method. We will review how quantum annealing finds the optimal solution and develops the hybrid algorithm for gate-based quantum computers that is used for optimization. You will see how a problem can be structured to be submitted to both the annealer and to a gate-based quantum computer. By the end of this section, you will be familiar with both options and will be able to decide when to pick different devices thanks to your familiarity with the techniques needed to use each type of device.

This section contains the following chapters:

- *Chapter 5, Using a Quantum Annealer – Developing a QUBO Function and Applying Constraints*
- *Chapter 6, Using Gate-Based Quantum Computers – Qubits and Quantum Circuits*
- *Chapter 7, Using Gate Quantum Computers – Basic Quantum Algorithms*
- *Chapter 8, Using Hybrid Algorithms – Optimization Using Gate-Based Quantum Computers*
- *Chapter 9, Running QAOA on Simulators and Amazon Braket Devices*

5

Using a Quantum Annealer – Developing a QUBO Function and Applying Constraints

In this chapter, we will switch gears from learning about the Amazon Braket service to diving into the programming and basic information needed to solve a real-world problem on a quantum annealer or, more specifically, one of the D-Wave devices available on Amazon Braket.

We will review the concept of quantum annealing, followed by solving a small three-variable problem using D-Wave. Next, we will extend the number of variables and introduce a very simple way to visualize quadratic problems through a party optimization problem. After this, we will use a team selection example to introduce some critical tools, including how to visualize an energy landscape and how to constrain the number of items selected in a solution.

The key sections are as follows:

- Solving optimization problems
- Simulated annealing versus quantum annealing
- Basics of **Quadratic Unconstrained Binary optimization (QUBO)**
- A **QUBO** example using three variables
- A party optimization example
- A team selection example

Technical requirement

You can find the code for this chapter under the following GitHub repository:

`https://github.com/PacktPublishing/Quantum-Computing-Experimentation-with-Amazon-Braket/tree/main/Chapter05`

Solving optimization problems

Those familiar with solving machine learning or optimization problems will know that there are algorithms that are frequently used to find the global optimum (minimum or maximum) value of a function. The function is typically called the `objective` function and has many variables and produces a multidimensional landscape, such as a mountain range, with high and low elevations.

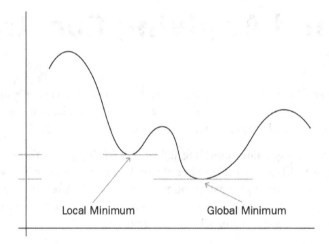

Figure 5.1 – Local minimum versus global minimum

Typical methods used to find the global optimum include **gradient descent**, **simulated annealing**, or various **genetic algorithms**. Even though these are successful and fast algorithms, there is a chance that while searching a large landscape produced by a function with many variables, these algorithms often settle on a minimum (or maximum) that is not the global optimum value but a local optimum. These algorithms use random starting points and probabilistic behavior in moving around a landscape, with the intention of sampling many sections of the landscape to move toward the optimum.

Simulated annealing

Simulated annealing uses a unique technique conceptually based on the real process of annealing. Annealing is a process of heating metals, holding the temperature for a set time, applying additives, and then allowing them to cool to create alloys. It was specifically used to create swords. While hot, the metal allows the additives to disperse, giving it the desired properties. These can include increased strength, a sharper edge, or making a sword less brittle and more flexible in some places, and harder in others. Then, the metal is cooled slowly or rapidly (quenched) to fix the additives in place. This is referred to as the **annealing cycle**.

In the case of a simulated annealing algorithm, the *temperature* is simulated by the extent of random changes to the variables to allow a higher amount of sampling of the landscape. Every time the variables are changed, the energy value of the objective function is measured (please refer to *Figure 5.2*). The similarity to annealing is that this temperature (or the extent of random changes) is adjusted from hot to cold on a desired temperature schedule. This allows the algorithm to sample more parts of the landscape early in the annealing cycle and then narrow in on smaller regions as the temperature is cooled. This is helpful if another valley might be deeper at this initial stage. As the algorithm progresses, the temperature or the randomness is reduced so that the sampling then begins to fixate on the valley it has found and moves down to the minimum. The fact that annealing starts with larger jumps in the beginning when hot and then shorter jumps when cool typically allows the algorithm to jump out of local minimums initially, but then it settles into the minimums of the deeper valleys. The lowest energy value of all the samples then becomes the solution.

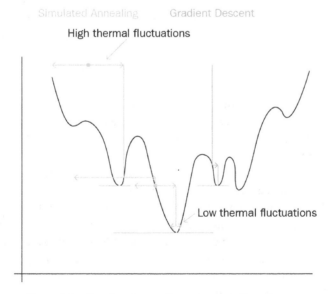

Figure 5.2 – Simulated annealing versus gradient descent

With the correct temperature schedule and number of samples, the technique can jump at the right time and not get stuck in local minimums. Of course, with a very complicated landscape, with many deceptively deep valleys that do not contain the global minimum or landscapes with flat plateau regions, it is possible to still not achieve the goal.

Quantum annealing

This is where the Japanese researchers *Tadashi Kadowaki* and *Hidetoshi Nishimori*, from the *Tokyo Institute of Technology*, come in. In a milestone paper, *Quantum Annealing in Transverse Ising Model*, they proposed that a quantum annealing process could be created where the quantum device would use a very interesting property in quantum mechanics called **quantum tunneling**. This property appears in quantum mechanics when, for example, a particle is trapped in an energy well or cavity. In this case, based on another rule of quantum mechanics called **Heisenberg's uncertainty principle**, it is not possible to know both the location and momentum of a particle with a specific amount of precision. For a particle in a progressively tighter cavity, it would be possible to know its location and then eventually, if it cannot move, its momentum. In other words, in a very tight cavity, a particle should have zero velocity and a precisely known position. Quantum mechanics breaks the particle free of its trap and probabilistically appears outside the cavity. This meets Heisenberg's uncertainty principle, since the position of the particle becomes probabilistically *spread out*. This allows a quantum particle to jump barriers that, in our classical world, is not possible. It is this very property we need to *jump* out of or *tunnel* through energy barriers if another cavity close to it might lead to a lower value. In the case of quantum annealing, as we saw in *Chapter 2, Braket Devices Explained*, the qubits start in an initialized energy configuration with the system in the ground state. During the annealing process, the problem coefficients are applied to the qubit **bias** and **coupling** terms. We will cover this in detail later in the code; however, for now, this basically changes the energy of each state over the annealing time, as shown in the left plot in *Figure 5.3*. As the energy landscape changes, initial high-thermal energy allows the system to continue to find and settle in the lowest energy location. Quantum tunneling effects play a role in allowing the system to jump past energy barriers to lower energy states through this whole process, as shown by the curved arrows in the right plot. In the right plot, as time progresses, the ground state changes from 000 to 001 and then 101. As the annealing cycle evolves, the gap between the lowest energy value and the next energy value can become quite small, and sometimes even less than the thermal noise of the qubits. This can cause the state to jump from the lowest energy to the higher energy, which we don't want. If the process is run slow enough and the temperature is reduced, the tunneling effects can continue to keep the system in its lowest energy past this gap. Finally, the qubits are measured and the ground state is determined. As you can see in *Figure 5.3*, there are many places where a quantum annealer might jump to the next higher level or not tunnel to stay in the ground energy. A system that would always reach the ground state would be called an **Adiabatic** system. This is one reason we sample using many shots and get many different solutions. In the ideal case, we find the ground energy as well.

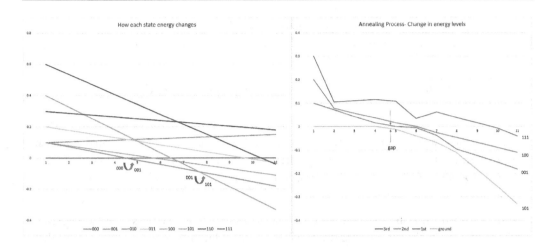

Figure 5.3 – The quantum annealing process, showing the change
of the energy levels through the annealing cycle

In a quantum annealer, the magnetic moments are represented by a +1 or -1 state (called the **Ising** states or **spin** states). However, we will only use the QUBO model with 0 and 1 in this book. The magnetic fields (or flux) in the qubits interact with each other and utilize the quantum tunneling effect to switch out of the local minimum toward a lower energy state, leading toward the global minimum. This is what gives a quantum annealer its strength.

We will now move to how we can use the properties of a quantum annealer to solve **combinatorial optimization** problems. These are problems where two variables affect each other. More specifically, we will deal with quadratic optimization problems where pairs of variables have some defined interaction. More clearly, these are problems where there are no more than two variable interactions. We will learn more about this in the next section.

Quadratic Unconstrained Binary Optimization (QUBO) problems

We will now focus on understanding what kind of problems are solved by a quantum annealer and how a problem is mapped onto the annealer. This process is the same for any solver that can solve QUBO problems. These are a special class of problems where you have binary variables and the relationship between them is no more than quadratic. In other words, you can have the product of two variables but not three variables, and you can have the square of the variables but not the cube or higher. In addition, the variables can only have the values of 0 or 1 (binary) or +1 or -1 (spin).

You can see the following equation as a representation of a QUBO problem. When solving this type of problem, we are trying to minimize the cost function shown in *equation 5.1*.

$$minimize \sum_{i=0}^{N-1} a_i x_i + \sum_{i<j}^{N-1} a_{ij} x_i x_j \quad where \ x \in \{0,1\} \ eq(5.1)$$

This equation can be written in many forms; however, I will use this format so that I can distinguish between the linear terms on the left and the quadratic terms on the right. The equation shows that we are trying to minimize the value of the energy (or cost) as we apply the binary value of 0 or 1 to the x_i or x_j variables, where i and j are in the range 0 to N-1.

Let's write this out for an example, where N=3. This means we have three variables, x_0, x_1, and x_2. Each variable has a linear coefficient, a_0, a_1, and a_2 respectively. In addition, we have quadratic terms that are the products of two variables (for example, $x_0 x_1$). For each of these quadratic terms, there will also be a coefficient, which in this case will be a_{01}.

$$minimize \ (\ a_0 x_0 + a_1 x_1 + a_2 x_2 + a_{01} x_0 x_1 + a_{02} x_0 x_2 + a_{12} x_1 x_2 \ ) \ eq.(5.2)$$

There are now three linear terms and three quadratic terms. To find the minimum of this cost function, we can randomly try either 0 or 1 for various values of x and then evaluate the result. After trying all combinations, we will find the set of values of x that produce the minimum value for the overall equation. We can then report which x value was a 0 and which was a 1. This would be a brute-force way of finding the minimum.

For very large problems, it is not practical to try out every combination of values of x being 0 or 1; therefore, with many variables (where N is large), we can use a randomized method, where we randomly try out different values for all the x values. This would be a **Monte Carlo** method, which is basically a random sampling method.

D-Wave's annealer tries to solve this type of equation and finds the minimum value of the cost function through quantum annealing.

A simple conceptual model for D-Wave

Let's now spend a bit of time discussing how different values of x can be found for this type of cost function using D-Wave or other QUBO solvers.

First, let's look at the behavior of magnets. In *Figure 5.4*, you can see that, in the case of magnets, a north pole attracts a south pole and vice versa. If the magnets are close together, the attractive force is strong, and if they are further apart, the attractive force is weak. We will call this the coupling force between the magnets. If you flip the magnet, then they will repel each other and will want to return to a lower energy configuration by trying to flip over. Again, depending on how close the magnets are, the coupling force that wants the magnets to flip can be small or large.

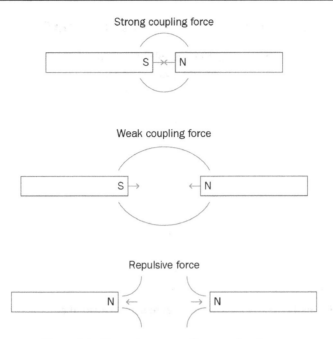

Figure 5.4 – Magnets representing coupling terms

D-Wave uses a quantum property called **entanglement** with which it can couple the pair-wise behavior between any two given qubits. By entangling all the qubits required in this way, based on the hardware architecture, the problem can be mapped on the annealer. In this case, by changing the coupling strength, we can control the strength by which a pair of qubits will end up with the same value or a different value. We do not need to know the details of quantum entanglement, or how this is accomplished, but for our purposes, it is important to know that a large positive coefficient will force the two pair-wise variables to have the same binary value of 00 or 11, and a large negative coefficient will force the two variables to have an opposite binary value – in this case, 01 or 10. The strength of the value or the absolute value of the coefficient controls how strongly the two values "must" be the same or opposite. Also, if the coefficient is zero, then there is no relationship between the two pairs of variables; thus, they are independent and can both be either 0 or 1 without impacting each other.

A QUBO example using three variables and ExactSolver()

Let's make this concept more concrete with the example of the three variables. But before we start, we will represent the relationship between each of the values on a grid.

	a_0	a_1	a_2
a_0	-0.5		
a_1	0.5	1.0	
a_2	-0.25	0.25	-0.75

Figure 5.5 – Coefficients showing both linear terms and quadratic interaction terms

We can now see that some values are negative and some are positive. The negative values contribute to a "lower" cost, while the positive values contribute to a "higher" cost. In the grid in *Figure 5.5*, you can see, for example, the values of a_0 = **-0.5**, a_1 = **1.0**, and a_2 = **-0.75**. These are the linear coefficients on x_0, x_1, and x_2 respectively. On the other hand, the coupling values, or the influence of one x variable on the other, are also found in the table. The coupling terms are thus a_{01} = **0.5**, a_{02} = **-0.25** and a_{12} = **0.25**. We do not need to fill all the values in the table, as it would be repetitive. The coupling strength between x_0 and x_1 is the same as that between x_1 and x_0. There is only one link in the pair-wise coupling.

These relationships can also be represented in the form of a graph with nodes (or vertices) and links (or edges), as shown in the following figure:

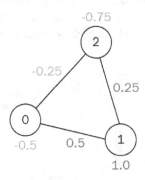

Figure 5.6 – Coefficients represented on a graph

These relationships are all we need to find the binary values of x_0 to x_2, which will minimize the cost function. Let's write out the full equation with the coefficients now:

$$minimize\ (-0.5x_0 + x_1 - 0.75x_2 + 0.5x_0x_1 - 0.25x_0x_2 + 0.25x_1x_2)\ eq.\ (5.3)$$

Please make sure to compare the coefficients in *equation 5.2* with the values in *equation 5.3*. We can use various methods to solve this and find the values of x_0, x_1, and x_2 that will minimize this cost function, but in our case, we will first use D-Wave's ExactSolver() function and then, in the next section, we will solve the same problem using D-Wave's DW2000Q quantum annealer. Let us start by using the ExactSolver() function:

1. We will need to import dimod as the only library at this time:

    ```
    import dimod
    ```

2. Let's define the binary quadratic model in dictionary form.

    First, we will create the dictionary of linear terms. The a_0, a_1, and a_2 linear coefficients are associated with the x_0, x_1, and x_2 variables:

    ```
    linear={('x0'):-0.5, ('x1'):1.0, ('x2'):-0.75}
    print(linear)
    ```

    Output:

    ```
    {'x0': -0.5, 'x1': 1.0, 'x2': -0.75}
    ```

    Next, we insert the quadratic terms using the appropriate coefficients. The a_{01}, a_{02}, and a_{12} quadratic coefficients are the coupling terms between the pair of x_0x_1, x_0x_2, and x_1x_2 variables.

    ```
    quadratic={('x0','x1'):0.5, ('x0','x2'):-0.25,
                ('x1','x2'):0.25}
    print(quadratic)
    ```

    Output:

    ```
    {('x0', 'x1'): 0.5, ('x0', 'x2'): -0.25, ('x1', 'x2'): 0.25}
    ```

    Now, we can use the BinaryQuadraticModel dimod function to combine these two linear and quadratic terms and also identify the variables ($x_0...x_2$) as Binary. Remember that we want x_0 to x_2 to be either 0 or 1:

    ```
    vartype = dimod.BINARY
    bqm = dimod.BinaryQuadraticModel(linear, quadratic,
                                     vartype)
    ```

3. We are now ready to execute this cost function on the `dimod` local classical solver function, `ExactSolver()`, that will accurately produce all the appropriate cost values for the different combinations of x values as 0 or 1. The solution is then sorted with the lowest cost shown first:

```
sampler = dimod.ExactSolver()
response = sampler.sample(bqm)
print(response)
```

Output:

```
  x0 x1 x2 energy num_oc.
6  1  0  1   -1.5      1
7  0  0  1   -0.75     1
1  1  0  0   -0.5      1
0  0  0  0    0.0      1
5  1  1  1    0.25     1
4  0  1  1    0.5      1
2  1  1  0    1.0      1
3  0  1  0    1.0      1
['BINARY', 8 rows, 8 samples, 3 variables]
```

The first column is a sequence number and can be ignored for this brute-force solver.

The first row of the results shows that the lowest cost solution has a value of -1.5 and requires x_0=1, x_1=0, and x_2=1. The next lowest energy of -0.75 is found when only x_2=1, while x_0 and x_1 are 0.

We have seen how to create a binary quadratic model of a cost function of three variables using a dictionary in Python and then found the minimum of that cost function using the `ExactSolver()` solver, which is available in D-Wave through Amazon Braket.

In the next section, we will set up code to find the minimum value of this cost function using the D-Wave quantum annealer.

Running the three-variable problem on D-Wave annealer

In this section, we will set up the D-Wave annealer as a solver and then execute the binary quadratic model on the **DW_2000Q_6** device.

Let's get started:

1. Please enter your appropriate bucket name and your folder name in the following code block:

```
# Enter the S3 bucket you created during onboarding in
the code below
my_bucket = "amazon-braket-[your bucket]" # the name of
the bucket
my_prefix = "[your folder]" # the name of the folder in
the bucket
s3_folder = (my_bucket, my_prefix)
```

2. We will import the additional libraries needed from Amazon Braket to designate the D-Wave sampler to perform the embedding and then run the solver through Amazon Braket:

```
from braket.aws import AwsDevice
from braket.ocean_plugin import BraketSampler,
BraketDWaveSampler
from dwave.system.composites import EmbeddingComposite
```

3. Next, you can pick the appropriate D-Wave device to use. Since Amazon Braket devices are always being enhanced, please run the `available_devices()` function to ensure that you have an updated list of devices, and make appropriate corrections in the next code block.

4. We will designate `DW_2000Q_6` as the device and then use the `BraketDWaveSampler` function to set up the sampler and the `EmbeddingComposite` function to map the variables to the lattice of qubits on D-Wave 2000Q. We also find some properties of the device and print them out:

```
DWave_device='DW_2000Q_6' #if using 2000Q
# DWave_device='Advantage_system6.1' #if using advantage
6.1
# DWave_device='Advantage_system4.1' #if using advantage
4.1

# Please run available_devices() to validate the latest
QPU available and edit the above list
device =AwsDevice.get_devices(names=DWave_device)[0]
sampler = BraketDWaveSampler(s3_folder,device.arn)
sampler = EmbeddingComposite(sampler)
max_shots=device.properties.service.shotsRange[1]
print('Number of qubits: ',
```

```
                   device.properties.provider.qubitCount)
    print('Number of couplers',
              len(device.properties.provider.couplers))
    print('Shots max {:,}'.format(max_shots) )
```

Output:

```
Number of qubits:   2048
Number of couplers 5974
Shots max 10,000
```

5. The following code allows us to estimate the number of shots that are desired for the three variables and the price of using the device on Amazon Braket:

```
#Estimate cost:
variables=3
shots=25*2**variables
if shots>max_shots:
    shots=max_shots
price_per_shot=
   device.properties.service.deviceCost.price
print('Recommended shots', shots)
print('Estimated cost
         ${:.2f}'.format(0.3+price_per_shot*shots))
```

Output:

```
Recommended shots 200
Estimated cost $0.34
```

6. We do not need to set chainstrength with such a small number of variables; the embedding will use one qubit per variable, so there will be no *chain* of qubits that represent one variable.

    Finally, we run the D-Wave sampler using the binary quadratic model of our problem cost function, and the required shots:

```
#chainstrength = 1
response = sampler.sample(bqm, num_reads=shots)
print(response)
```

Output:

```
x0 x1 x2 energy num_oc. chain_.
 0  1  0   1    -1.5     200      0.0
['BINARY', 1 rows, 200 samples, 3 variables]
```

The solution shows that D-Wave finds x_0=1, x_1=0, and x_2=1 is the best solution, with the lowest cost value of -1.5. Note that D-Wave found this for all 200 shots. This clearly shows that D-Wave was efficiently able to find this lowest energy value from the problem.

We will now recap what we have learned from the results. If we go back to the grid in *Figure 5.5*, we can see the contributions of the cost from each linear and quadratic term. Each number (or coefficient) supplies a positive or negative cost if it is selected based on the binary variables.

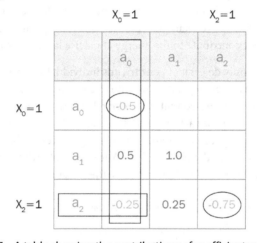

Figure 5.7 – A table showing the contributions of coefficients where x_i=1

The way to look at this is that since x_0 and x_2 have a value of 1 in the solution, then their linear and quadratic coefficients will contribute to the final cost. Based on the table in *Figure 5.7*, you can see that there are two linear contributions, a_0=-0.5 and a_2=-0.75 (ovals), which equate to where x_i is 1, and one quadratic contribution at a_0a_2 (where the rectangles overlap), which means we have a single quadratic contribution of -0.25. The sum of these three contributions is -1.75, which is indeed the lowest value we can attain from this problem. Any other combination will add contributions that will have a higher cost value. Thus, the optimal solution is x_0=1, x_1=0, and, x_2=1.

We can also represent the binary values of 0 and 1 as off and on, or in and out. Therefore, we want to set up our problem in such a way that the result tells us something about the condition of the optimal selection. When converting your real-world problem, think of your variables, and determine whether they can be defined as binary. An example could be that you have many hubs that a flight will go to. If the hub is on the flight path, it has a value of 1, and if the flight does not go to the hub, its value is 0.

So far, we have reviewed what quantum annealing is and gone over a very simple example of how to embed an objective function on a quantum annealer using a quadratic binary optimization formulation. We solved a three-variable binary optimization problem on a brute-force solver and then we solved the same problem on a D-Wave quantum annealer device. We have a lot more to learn about embedding real-world problems on D-Wave, visualizing the landscape, and adding constraints. We will now start with a party optimization example.

A party optimization example

In this example, imagine that you are throwing a party and inviting five friends. We will give them unique names from Alice to Frank, as shown in *Figure 5.8*. You have made an estimate of how much each of your friends contributes to the energy of a party. These are the *linear* or *diagonal* terms in the table in *Figure 5.8*. Your values are from -1 (a negative contribution to the party) to +1 (a maximum positive contribution to the party). For example, Alice has the most positive contribution to a party of 0.5, while Eve who does not contribute to the energy at parties has a value of -1.

Now, you also realize that not only do each of your friends individually contribute to a party's energy but their energy contribution changes, depending on who else is at the party with them. You are feeling quite sophisticated for having determined that *pair-wise* relationships or *quadratic* relationships are important in this case. You recall how each pair of friends contribute to the energy of a party when they are present together. Again, your values are from -1 (negative contribution to the party) to +1 (maximum positive contribution to the party). Thus, Alice and Bob, when together, have the most positive impact at 1.0, while Alice and Eve together have the worst effect on a party at -1.

	Alice	Bob	Charlie	David	Eve	Frank
Alice	0.5					
Bob	1	0				
Charlie	0.5	0.25	-0.25			
David	-0.5	-1	0	-0.5		
Eve	-1	-1	0.25	0.5	-1	
Frank	0.25	-0.25	0	0.5	-0.5	-0.5

Figure 5.8 – The friends' contribution to a party

Now that you have this information, you want to optimize and find which friends would be the optimal guests at a party with the most energy contribution. You are only going to invite these friends.

Download the party example code from the GitHub site along with the `Friends.csv` file. Let's look at the steps needed to solve this problem. Since we only have a few friends, we can run this through `ExactSolver()`:

1. First, let's import the necessary libraries:

    ```
    import pandas as pd
    import dimod
    ```

2. Then, we load the `friends.csv` file into a matrix, T. Note that we only have values in the lower-left corner:

    ```
    file_name='friends.csv'
    Temp = pd.read_csv(file_name, ).values
    T=Temp[:,1:]
    print(T)
    ```

    Output:

    ```
    [[0.5 nan nan nan nan nan]
     [1.0 0.0 nan nan nan nan]
     [0.5 0.25 -0.25 nan nan nan]
     [-0.5 -1.0 0.0 -0.5 nan nan]
     [-1.0 -1.0 0.25 0.5 -1.0 nan]
     [0.25 -0.25 0.0 0.5 -0.5 -0.5]]
    ```

3. Next, we extract the names:

    ```
    dim=len(T[0])
    Names=['']*dim
    for i in range(dim):
        Names[i]=Temp[i,0]
    print(Names)
    ```

    Output:

    ```
    ['Alice', 'Bob', 'Charlie', 'David', 'Eve', 'Frank']
    ```

4. We are now going to create the linear and quadratic terms for the binary quadratic model. Note that we change the sign on the T matrix, since the coefficients represent maximizing the energy, but in our solvers, we always minimize. First, we will view the linear terms:

```
linear={Names[i]:-T[i][i] for i in range(dim)}
quadratic={(Names[i],Names[j]):-T[i][j] for i in
          range(dim) for j in range(dim) if i>j}
print(linear)
```

Output:

```
{'Alice': -0.5, 'Bob': -0.0, 'Charlie': 0.25, 'David': 0.5,
'Eve': 1.0, 'Frank': 0.5}
```

Next, we can also view the quadratic terms:

```
print(quadratic)
```

Output:

```
{('Bob', 'Alice'): -1.0, ('Charlie', 'Alice'): -0.5,
('Charlie', 'Bob'): -0.25, ('David', 'Alice'): 0.5, ('David',
'Bob'): 1.0, ('David', 'Charlie'): -0.0, ('Eve', 'Alice'):
1.0, ('Eve', 'Bob'): 1.0, ('Eve', 'Charlie'): -0.25, ('Eve',
'David'): -0.5, ('Frank', 'Alice'): -0.25, ('Frank', 'Bob'):
0.25, ('Frank', 'Charlie'): -0.0, ('Frank', 'David'): -0.5,
('Frank', 'Eve'): 0.5}
```

5. Now that we have our linear and quadratic terms, we will create the **binary quadratic model (BQM)** and send it to the ExactSolver() function. We only show some of the best results:

```
vartype = dimod.BINARY
bqm = dimod.BinaryQuadraticModel(linear, quadratic,
                                 vartype)
sampler = dimod.ExactSolver()
response = sampler.sample(bqm)
print(response)
```

Output:

Alice	Bob	Charlie	David	Eve	Frank	energy	num_oc.
5	1	1	1	0	0	0	-2.0	1
2	1	1	0	0	0	0	-1.5	1
58	1	1	1	0	0	1	-1.5	1
61	1	1	0	0	0	1	-1.0	1
6	1	0	1	0	0	0	-0.75	1
1	1	0	0	0	0	0	-0.5	1
57	1	0	1	0	0	1	-0.5	1
62	1	0	0	0	0	1	-0.25	1

The best value is the first row and shows that the best energy for the overall party would be if you invite Alice, Bob and Charlie. The value of the energy is +2.0, after changing the sign.

Can you validate that this is the optimal solution? Was the answer obvious just from looking at the linear and quadratic terms? Can you run **BQM** on one of the Amazon Braket D-Wave devices and see whether you get the same results?

In the next section, we will look at a more complicated example.

A team selection example

In this example, imagine your manager, the **Vice President** (**VP**), just heard about the new capability of quantum computers to solve optimization problems. The VP has been wanting to build a team with key resources in the company based on the following:

- Their individual ratings conducted by the managers
- The ratings given by their peers who worked best together

The values have been averaged over a few years, and the rating given by employee 1 to employee 2 is separate from the ratings given by employee 2 to employee 1 and are usually the same, but in some cases, they are off by 1. The 100 employee names are not disclosed. The ratings go from 0 to 5, with 5 being the highest rating. The VP is looking for a way to incorporate the data to identify 10 key individuals for a special group project where the team score is highest, based on both the manager scores and the pair-wise employee-employee score. The VP also wants you to consider the manager score to have the same weight as each employee-employee pair-wise score; however, they would like to be able to control the ratio. The last statement the VP makes before leaving is, "I want to know the combination of 10 employees that have the highest score as a team and not necessarily those who got the highest total scores individually."

First of all, let's look at the last statement. Is there a difference? To understand combinatorial optimization, it is important to grasp the difference between summing up the total individual scores received by the 10 employees, and also adding the pair-wise scores of all the 10 employees selected into the team.

A simple process for solving problems using D-Wave

It is always a good idea to first understand a problem and try to solve it using the current traditional formulation before progressing to converting the problem into a QUBO. This way, you will understand the problem and the assumptions or trade-offs being made when deriving the QUBO. It also gives a good way to benchmark the results. After deriving the QUBO, we solve the problem classically. I have included a tool to visualize the energy landscape, which we will discuss soon. This tool allows you to see where the minimum of the landscape is and what results to expect from a classical QUBO solver, such as a simulated annealer. After we are convinced that we have the correct formulation and the QUBO is producing good results, we can progress to solving it on a quantum annealing device. This also prevents unnecessary waste of money by using a quantum device before we are ready.

After running our first few tests on a quantum device, if we find that the results are not adequate or the energy values are not low enough, we might need to adjust the parameters available to us in the quantum annealing solver (D-Wave 2000Q or D-Wave Advantage).

The preceding steps have been summarized as follows in *Figure 5.9*. We will follow these steps as we progress through this example.

Step 1:	Step 2:	Step 3:
A. Fully understand the traditional formulation and goal	A. Understand how to translate the traditional formulation into a QUBO	A. Solve the matrix using Classical solvers or Simulated Annealing
B. Create the traditional formulation and find a solution	B. Present the data as a matrix	B. Convert the matrix into a Binary Quadratic Model and solve using Quantum Annealing devices
	C. Add appropriate constraints or penalty	C. Validate results by checking with original formulation
	D. Visualize the landscape	D. Improve results of Quantum devices by modifying embedding and parameters

Figure 5.9 – The steps to solving QUBO problems on D-Wave

Reviewing data

To fully understand the problem as in **Step 1 (A)** of *Figure 5.9*, let's look at the data file and produce a heat map. A heat map of the data is reproduced in *Figure 5.10*. The diagonal terms are the ratings given by the employee's manager and seem to generally be higher than the ratings given by one employee for another. Also, note that this is not symmetric. In other words, the values on one side of the blue diagonal do not always match the other side, as can be noted clearly by the red values that are only on the lower-left triangle but not in the upper-right triangle.

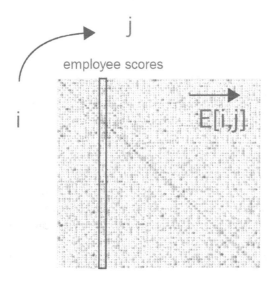

Figure 5.10 – A heat map of the employee score data

The blue arrow indicates that employee i gives a score to employee j. The vertical line represents all the scores given to employee j. The faint blue diagonal line is the score given by the manager to the employee (where i=j). In this example, E[i,j] is not equal to E[j,i], and we will show how this is handled in the next section.

Representing the problem in graph form

We can now represent the problem in the form of a graph and put in some sample values to understand how the scores are represented, as shown in *Figure 5.11*.

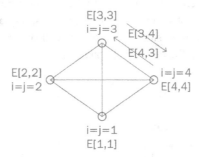

Figure 5.11 – Showing four manager-employee scores on a graph
and one pair of employee-employee scores

This is only a partial representation of the whole problem, but it shows some key elements and how they are going to be implemented in code. One thing to note is that since the score given by employee i to employee j is not the same as that given by employee j to employee i, we have a relationship between elements that depends on direction, and this is represented by the two arrows. These two values can be handled by most solvers; however, the D-Wave quantum annealer can only have one relationship between variables or employees in this case, so in order to solve this on D-Wave, we will have to "add" the two E[i,j] and E[j,i] values together and then implement them in D-Wave's quadratic terms.

Summarizing the problem

Just to get started with the code, we can write down some of the key points from the problem and how we will start formulating them with arrays in Python. These points are jotted down in *Figure 5.12*.

1. Total employees 100, (i=0...i=99)
2. E[i,j] not always equal to E[j.i] (except when i=j)
3. E[i,j] is the score by employee i given to employee j when i is not equal to j, and is the score given by manager to employee when i=j (eg, E[i,i])
4. E[i,j] values range from 0 to +5
5. Final Team employee count constrain to 10
6. If final team has employees 1,9 then the total team score is E[1,1]+E[9,9]+E[1,9]+e[9,1]
7. Team Score = Sum ((manager - employee terms) + (employee - employee terms))
8. Goal: Maximize Team score
9. Assume weight of manage - employee value = employee - employee value

(Note "-" refers to " to" and is not the negative sign as used above).

Figure 5.12 – A summary of the key concepts in the problem

Now, we have completed **Step 1 (A)** in *Figure 5.9* and have a good understanding of the problem.

The traditional formulation

We are ready to start running through the process in the code. We will go to **Step 1 (B)** in *Figure 5.9*, where we want to first create the traditional formulation in the code:

1. Copy matrix from the file:

```
import pandas as pd
E = pd.read_csv("employees.csv", header=None ).values
if (len(E[0])==len(E[1])):
  dim=len(E)
  print(dim)
```

Output:

100

Note that the full matrix is stored in E.

2. Now, we want to create the traditional formulation. As was stated in the problem, the VP gives a hint on what the traditional formulation is: "…not necessarily *those who got the highest total scores* from other employees." Assuming this is the traditional way the VP has evaluated employees, let's find the employees with the top scores, based on ratings from other employees and the manager. Thus, we just need to add up an employee's scores, which is equivalent to summing up the column (as shown as the purple vertical rectangle in *Figure 5.10*.

3. After the employee scores are added and sorted, we find the top 10 employees. Please review the code in the chapter's GitHub repository. The output is as follows:

```
Employee/score

12 173

92 172

28 169

16 169

65 167

14 167

59 165

23 165

2 165

85 164
```

We also create a smaller matrix, Top_E, of only the scores of these 10 employees. The team score is calculated as the sum of the smaller matrix of all the manager-employee scores and the employee-employee scores from this subset. The results are sorted by the employee number and the output is as follows:

```
New Employee Team [ 2 12 14 16 23 28 59 65 85 92]
[[5.  1.  2.  1.  3.  1.  1.  3.  3.  1.]
 [1.  3.  3.  1.  1.  4.  1.  3.  1.  2.]
 [2.  3.  3.  2.  1.  1.  3.  1.  1.  2.]
 [1.  1.  2.  3.  2.  2.  1.  1.  2.  5.]
 [3.  1.  1.  2.  3.  1.  2.  1.  1.  1.]
 [1.  4.  1.  2.  1.  3.  2.  1.  3.  1.]
 [1.  1.  3.  1.  2.  2.  3.  1.  2.  2.]
 [3.  3.  1.  1.  1.  1.  1.  3.  2.  1.]
 [3.  1.  1.  2.  1.  3.  2.  2.  3.  1.]
 [1.  2.  2.  5.  1.  1.  2.  1.  1.  4.]]
```

This team's total score based on this smaller matrix is found to be 189.0. Do you think that this team score is the highest of any other 10-member team? This is the question we are really asking, so let's continue to answer this question.

4. It is time to start looking at this problem beyond the traditional way and think about how to convert this into a binary quadratic problem, as stated in **Step 2 (A)** in *Figure 5.9*.

In the employee.csv file, the diagonal terms, E[i,i], represent the linear coefficients for the manager-employee score, and the non-diagonal terms, E[i,j], represent the quadratic relationships between pair-wise employees (employee-employee). We can see that it is a binary problem, since we are looking for employees selected into the team or not selected into the team, thus $e_i = 0$ if not selected and $e_i=1$ if selected. Since we want to minimize the energy, we add negative signs to the E matrix. We also know we must add a constraint or penalty so that we only get 10 employees in the answer.

$$min \left[\sum_{i}^{N-1} -E[i,i]e_i + \sum_{i \neq j}^{N-1} -E[i,j]\, e_i e_j \right] \quad eq.\,(5.4)$$

$$where\; e_i \in \{0,1\} \quad eq.\,(5.5)$$

$$with\; constraint: \sum_{i}^{N-1} e_i = 10 \quad eq.\,(5.6)$$

5. As shown in **Step 2 (B)** in *Figure 5.9*, we need to convert the data to a standard matrix; however, since the data is already presented to us in the form of a matrix, this step is complete.

6. In the following code, we send the -Top_E matrix to the simulated annealer:

```
import neal
import dimod
Nsampler = neal.SimulatedAnnealingSampler()
QDWaveSA = dimod.BinaryQuadraticModel(
  -Top_E, dimod.BINARY)
SAresponse = Nsampler.sample(QDWaveSA)
for Ssample in SAresponse.data():
    print( Ssample)
```

Output:

```
Sample(sample={0: 1, 1: 1, 2: 1, 3: 1, 4: 1, 5: 1, 6: 1, 7:
1, 8: 1, 9: 1}, energy=-189.0, num_occurrences=1)
```

We get an energy value of -189. This is the equivalent of the sum we found in *Step 3*.

7. Now, let's repeat this step for the full matrix, -E:

```
Nsampler = neal.SimulatedAnnealingSampler()
QDWaveSA = dimod.BinaryQuadraticModel(-E,
                            dimod.BINARY)
SAresponse = Nsampler.sample(QDWaveSA)
for Ssample in SAresponse.data():
    print( Ssample)
```

Output:

```
Sample(sample={0: 1, 1: 1, 2: 1, 3: 1, 4: 1, 5: 1, 6: 1, 7:
1, 8: 1, 9: 1, 10: 1, 11: 1, 12: 1, 13: 1, 14: 1, 15: 1, 16:
1, 17: 1, 18: 1, 19: 1, 20: 1, 21: 1, 22: 1, 23: 1, 24: 1,
25: 1, 26: 1, 27: 1, 28: 1, 29: 1, 30: 1, 31: 1, 32: 1, 33:
1, 34: 1, 35: 1, 36: 1, 37: 1, 38: 1, 39: 1, 40: 1, 41: 1,
42: 1, 43: 1, 44: 1, 45: 1, 46: 1, 47: 1, 48: 1, 49: 1, 50:
1, 51: 1, 52: 1, 53: 1, 54: 1, 55: 1, 56: 1, 57: 1, 58: 1,
59: 1, 60: 1, 61: 1, 62: 1, 63: 1, 64: 1, 65: 1, 66: 1, 67:
1, 68: 1, 69: 1, 70: 1, 71: 1, 72: 1, 73: 1, 74: 1, 75: 1,
76: 1, 77: 1, 78: 1, 79: 1, 80: 1, 81: 1, 82: 1, 83: 1, 84:
1, 85: 1, 86: 1, 87: 1, 88: 1, 89: 1, 90: 1, 91: 1, 92: 1,
93: 1, 94: 1, 95: 1, 96: 1, 97: 1, 98: 1, 99: 1}, energy=-
15304.0, num_occurrences=1)
```

Here, we get a score of -15,304.0. This represents all the employees. So we really have not found the top 10 employees using this method.

What does this tell us? It is not obvious, but a simulated annealer or any other solver is finding the minimum energy, and since every employee adds to the negative energy in either -Top_E or -E, the best solution is to add up all the employees and give the total energy of the matrix. This would not be the case if there were scores of negative values. For example, if the scores ranged from -5 to +5, then it is possible that the solvers would pick the positive values (in the negative matrix, -E) that would penalize some of the employees and reduce the number of employees in the answer. Somehow, we have to penalize the total matrix so that only 10 employees are picked in the answer. We are coming to this soon, but first, we need to visualize the landscape.

I find it helpful to visualize the landscape using a probabilistic solver. This will show you what your landscape looks like and what answers to expect. We will review this tool in the next section.

A tool to visualize the energy landscape

It is not practical to visualize a multidimensional energy landscape; however, we can organize the energy landscape based on the number of values in the solution. For example, if we have a 100-variable problem, that would mean we are dealing with 100 dimensions, and it would not be practical to visualize the landscape. However, what if we could calculate every solution with one value in it? There are 100 such solutions in a 100-variable problem. We can determine the energy of each of the 1-value solutions and plot those, and then we can look at all the 2-value solutions as combinations out of the total 100 variables. This gives us 4,950 different energy values. This way, we can tell how the energies change based on the number of solutions, or the count, and whether there is a pattern where the energies increase, decrease, or have a minimum somewhere in between.

Figure 5.13 shows an example of different landscapes plotted this way. These plots can easily tell whether the minimum will be where no value is selected (the middle plot in the bottom row), or when almost all values are selected (the right-most plot in the middle row). You can also see that some landscapes are quite complicated, and the minimum can be in a wide range of values. If we do more sampling, we will see the landscape more clearly.

The key point to note is that by using this tool, you can understand whether the landscape will give the expected results. For example, if you have a landscape where the minimum has a large count in the solution and you are expecting to have only a few values in your result, then you might have to add a constraint to change the landscape from the plot shown on the right in the bottom row to the one shown on the right on the top row.

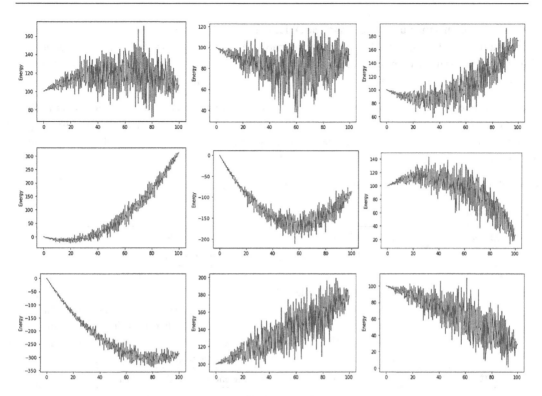

Figure 5.13 – Sample energy landscapes, with the x axis representing
the number of values selected in the solution (the count)

When we run the visualization tool, `ProbabilisticSampler()`, on the `-E` matrix, we get the plot shown in *Figure 5.14*. The sample code for this function is included in the GitHub repository of this chapter.

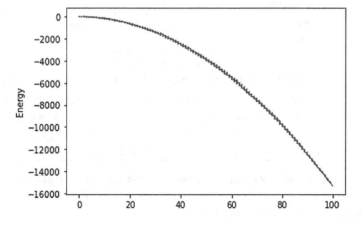

Figure 5.14 – A visualization of the energy landscape

The x axis represents the number of binary variables in the solution that had a +1 value, or the count in the solution. In this case, it is the count of the employees in the solution. The y axis is the energy. You can see that as more employees are selected for the team, the more negative the energy becomes. If this was sent to a quantum annealer, we would just get all the employees in the solution.

It should be easy to realize at this point that sending this to a quantum annealer will not help in any way; it will just give a solution where all the e_i variables are equal to 1. We must find a way to bring the minimum of the landscape to where the count or the number of employees selected in the solution equals 10.

`ProbabilisticSampler()` can be used with the following parameter list:

Parameter list:

Parameter	Explanation
Q	The full non-symmetric matrix that we want to visualize
plot_limit	The amount of times to sample at each count value. Please note that this probabilistic sampler will sample the same amount per count. In some cases, this will be more than the possible values, but in most cases, it will be much lower than all the possible values at that count. This allows you to sample the landscape with a low number, for quick visualization and then increase sampling and narrow the limits for better results.
offset=0	Offset value default = 0. This is the energy added to all the result in the end.
min_limit=0	The minimum number of values in the solution (count) to start with – default = 0
max_limit=0	The maximum number of values in the solution (count) to end with; the default is the maximum number.

Return values:

Return value	Explanation
min_list	A list of elements in the last solution. This is an array of the index values that were in the solution.
e_min	The lowest energy found in the sampling. Note that this is not always the actual lowest energy of the landscape. Results improve as the plot limit is increased.
comb_list	A list of all possible combinations for the count range. This value can be used to evaluate the percentage of sampling performed. For example, if your plot limit was 100, and the value in comb_list is 10,000, then you only sampled 1% of all possible values for that count.

You can now use this tool to visualize your matrix before sending it to a QUBO solver (a simulated annealer or D-Wave's quantum annealer). In the next section, we will look at how to convert this landscape to the required count or number of employees in the solution.

A simple penalty function to implement the constraint

Now, we move to **Step 2 (C)** in *Figure 5.9*. Let's look at the penalty term we need for the constraint in *equation 5.6*. We make it more generic by replacing the number 10 with the M variable and rewriting, as shown here:

$$Constraint: \left(\sum_i^{N-1} e_i \right) = M \quad eq. (5.7)$$

This penalty can be converted into the following equation:

$$Penalty = S \left(\sum_i^{N-1} e_i - M \right)^2 \quad eq. (5.8)$$

This is basically an equation of the **y=(x-c)²** form. If you plot this equation for different values of x, you will find it is a parabola with the minimum, where x=c. We use this to add the penalty – that is, employees=10 – to the QUBO. We introduce a multiplier, S, for the strength of this penalty, so it is effective on the rest of the QUBO.

It turns out that expanding *equation 5.8* leads to the following equation:

$$S \left[\sum_i^{N-1} (1 - 2 \cdot M) e_i + \sum_{i \neq j}^{N-1} e_i e_j + M^2 \right] \quad eq. (5.9)$$

Here, M² is going to be an **offset** that we will add to the result of the QUBO. Note that, except for the offset, *equation 5.9* is in the same form as our QUBO, with linear and quadratic terms. Thus, we can now add this to our QUBO formulation:

$$min \left\{ \sum_i^{N-1} -E[i,i] e_i + \sum_{i \neq j}^{N-1} -E[i,j] e_i e_j + S \left(\sum_i^{N-1} (1 - 20) e_i + \sum_{i \neq j}^{N-1} e_i e_j \right) \right\} \quad eq. (5.10)$$

$$where \; e_i \in \{0,1\} \; and \; offset = 100$$

Now that we understand the QUBO and the penalty function, let's use this information to modify the original matrix, E, to the C matrix by adding the penalty matrix, P. Note that we implement S as the strength variable. To get the correct result, we will pick the value of 90:

1. The following code shows how we create the P penalty matrix:

```
# The constraint matrix
size=dim
max_count=10
strength=90
#strength=1
P=np.ones((size,size))
for i in range(size):
  for j in range(size):
   if i==j:
     P[i,i]=strength*(1-2*max_count)
   else:
     P[i,j]=strength
offset=(max_count)**2
```

2. Now, we need to add Penalty to the original -E matrix:

```
C=P-E
```

3. We now visualize the landscape by running the ProbabilisticSampler() function again:

```
min_list, e_min, comb_list=
ProbabilisticSampler(C,1000,offset, 5, 15)
```

Output:

```
Best found: [2, 16, 25, 43, 44, 51, 65, 69, 77, 87]
count: 10
Energy: -9103.0
Solutions Sampled: 11000
```

The plot will show that the minimum is now close to 10, based on the strength of the penalty term used. We also find a valid solution with a count of 10. If it is not, we might need to adjust strength of the penalty.

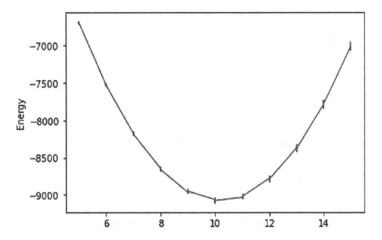

Figure 5.15 – The modified matrix with the minimum at 10 employees

We can change the minimum and maximum count values to zoom in or out on the energy landscape. This meets our objective for **Step 2 (D)** in *Figure 5.9*.

4. Since we know where to focus our search, we can increase the sample count and look for more solutions where the count is 10. This takes a while to run:

```
min_list, e_min, comb_list=
    ProbabilisticSampler(C,100000,offset, 10, 10)
```

Output:

```
Best found:  [16, 18, 19, 34, 36, 56, 65, 69, 84, 92]
```

```
count: 10
```

```
Energy: -9126.0
```

```
Solutions Sampled: 100000
```

The plot shows a broad range of values at the single count of 10.

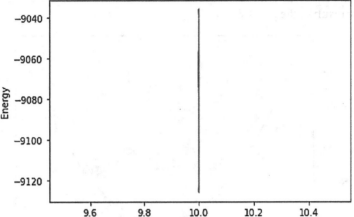

Figure 5.16 – The energy range at the count of 10 with higher sampling

Note that we do not want to use the energy from the plot or a constrained model because it includes the penalty terms and thus does not represent the score. To get that, we need to take the employee numbers in the solution and calculate the score using the original E matrix.

5. The following code is used to find the team score of the best solution found in the last step, based on the ratings from others within this team. We use the values from the original E matrix:

```
Top_e_PS=min_list
# Team score from the original Employee score matrix,
using the employee index numbers
team_score=0
for i in (Top_e_PS):
 for j in (Top_e_PS):
 team_score+=E[i,j]
print("Employees", Top_e_PS, "Team Score:",team_score)
```

Output:

```
Employees [16, 18, 19, 34, 36, 56, 65, 69, 84, 92] Team
Score: 226.0
```

This score is better than the score found using the traditional method.

Running the problem on classical and quantum solvers

Now that we have sampled the landscape and ensured that the solution is at the correct number of employees, we can proceed with running the modified matrix on the classical simulated annealer and the quantum annealing devices.

Let's get started:

1. We can now run the modified C matrix on the simulated annealer, as stated in **Step 3 (A)** in *Figure 5.9*, using the following code:

```
# print qubits with value 1
best=0
team_score=0
for sample, energy, n_occurences in SAresponse.data():
        sample_list=[]
        for i in range(dim):
            #sample_str.append(str(sample['a'+str(a)]))
            if sample[i]==1:
                sample_list.append(i)
        for i in (sample_list):
            for j in (sample_list):
                team_score+=E[i,j]
        if best==0:
            Top_e_DW=sample_list
            best_DWave_val='best Simulated
                Annealer:'+str(sample_list)+'
                team_score:'+str(team_score)+'
        best=1
        print(sample_list, team_score, len(sample_list),
            n_occurences)
        #break #comment out break to see all values
print(best_DWave_val)
```

Output:

```
[0, 1, 4, 19, 23, 45, 47, 59, 78, 95] 194.0 10 1
```

```
best Simulated Annealer:[0, 1, 4, 19, 23, 45, 47, 59, 78, 95]
team_score:194.0 count:10 occurrences:
```

```
1
```

Note that the score here is better than the traditional but not as good as `ProbabiliticSolver()`. This should also indicate the complexity of finding good results from all the possible results of total possible solutions.

2. Now, we will run the C matrix on the D-Wave quantum annealer. Since we have more than 64 fully connected variables, we will need to use one of the Advantage devices. Please ensure that you have edited the code to include the latest D-Wave devices:

```
# Please ensure you are using the latest available D-Wave
devices on Amazon Braket
# DWave_device='DW_2000Q_6' #if using 2000Q
#DWave_device='Advantage_system6.1'
#if using advantage
DWave_device='Advantage_system4.1' #if using Advantage

device =AwsDevice.get_devices(names=DWave_device)[0]
sampler = BraketDWaveSampler(s3_folder,device.arn)
sampler = EmbeddingComposite(sampler)
max_shots=device.properties.service.shotsRange[1]
print('Number of qubits: ',
      device.properties.provider.qubitCount)
print('Number of couplers',
      len(device.properties.provider.couplers))
print('Shots max {:,}'.format(max_shots) )
```

Output:

```
Number of qubits:  5760
```

```
Number of couplers: 37440
```

```
Shots max 10,000
```

3. For D-Wave, we need to convert the matrix into the binary quadratic model and complete **Step 3 (B)** in *Figure 5.9*. The code to create the binary quadratic model **BQM** to run on the D-Wave device is shown as follows. The full code to select the D-Wave device is available in the GitHub repository of the chapter.

Please note carefully that we are adding the two terms C[i,j] and C[j,i] together in the quadratic terms of the BQM, since we can only have one value. Most other solvers can handle a matrix and use both sides of it:

```
linear={i:C[i][i] for i in range(dim)}
quadratic={(i,j):C[i][j]+C[j][i] for i in range(dim)
    for j in range(dim) if i>j}
vartype = dimod.BINARY
bqm = dimod.BinaryQuadraticModel(linear, quadratic,
                                    vartype)
shots=shots
chain_strength = 1.3
response = sampler.sample(bqm, num_reads=shots,
    chain_strength=chain_strength)
```

The output is stored in `response`; however, we will use the following code to reformat the output and use the original E matrix to calculate the score, as mentioned in **Step 3 (C)** in *Figure 5.9*:

```
# print team info
best=0
team_score=0
for sample, energy, n_occurences, chain_break_freq in
response.data():
    sample_list=[]
    for i in range(dim):
        #sample_str.append(str(sample['a'+str(a)]))
        if sample[i]==1:
            sample_list.append(i)
    for i in (sample_list):
        for j in (sample_list):
            team_score+=E[i,j]
    if best==0:
        Top_e_DW=sample_list
        best_DWave_val='best D-Wave:
        '+str(sample_list)+' team_score:
        '+str(team_score)+' count:'+ str(len(sample_
list)) +' occurences:'+str(n_occurences)
        best=1
```

```
        print(sample_list, team_score, len(sample_list),
            n_occurences)
        break #comment out break to see all values
  print(best_DWave_val)
```

Output:

```
[12, 13, 14, 25, 46, 51, 65, 70, 80, 81] 196.0 10 1

best D-Wave:[12, 13, 14, 25, 46, 51, 65, 70, 80, 81] team_
score:196.0 count:10 occurrences:1
```

In this particular case, with the number of samples at the maximum value of 10,000, we got the best team score of 196.0. This is better than the simulated annealer; however, it appears the probabilistic sampler found the best value. Keep in mind that D-Wave is looking for one value in 1,267,650,600,228,229,401,496,703,205,375.

4. Typically, at this stage, you will have some initial values that are sometimes not as good as you would expect. **Step 3 (D)** in *Figure 5.9* involves ensuring that you are using the hardware appropriately and getting the most out of the quantum annealer. More adjustments can be made to the penalty strength, annealing_time, and chain_strength. Note that we already used the maximum num_reads (or shots), so that cannot be increased. In addition, there are various embedding tools provided by D-Wave; however, this is not going to be covered in this book.

5. All the various results are presented as follows for comparison:

```
Summary of Results:

Traditional method

employees:[2, 12, 14, 16, 23, 28, 59, 65, 85, 92] team_score:
189 count:10

Probabilistic Solver

employees: [16, 18, 19, 34, 36, 56, 65, 69, 84, 92] team_
score: 226.0 count:10

Simulated Annealer

employees:[0, 1, 4, 19, 23, 45, 47, 59, 78, 95] team_
score:194.0 count:10

D-Wave Advantage (Paid)

employees: [12, 13, 14, 25, 46, 51, 65, 70, 80, 81] Team
Score: 196.0 count:10
```

The best value found on D-Wave has a team score of 196.

After ensuring that we have the correct landscape and have implemented the penalty function correctly, with the right strength to move the minimum of the energy landscape to a count of 10 employees, we ran the matrix through the simulated annealer and then the D-Wave quantum annealer. The results shown are after tweaking some of the parameters; however, it might be possible to find better solutions. We then presented a comparison of the solutions using traditional method, probabilistic sampler, the simulated annealer, and the D-Wave quantum annealer.

Summary

In this chapter, we have run through a lot of material to understand how to solve problems on a quantum annealer such as D-Wave. We solved several simple problems to get a flavor of how to think about solving real-world optimization problems. We started with a simple three-node graph problem and then expanded that to a party optimization problem. Finally, we went over some critical steps in solving QUBO problems using a team selection example. We progressed through the example in three steps and utilized a visualization tool for the QUBO energy landscape, and also learned how to add a simple constraint on the number of variables in the solution. Then, we reviewed and compared solutions through the traditional method, the probabilistic sampler, the simulated annealer, and the D-Wave Advantage system.

In the next chapter, we will switch gears and return to gate quantum computing devices. We will start discussing qubits and their properties and show the basics of solving simple problems, using quantum algorithms on gate quantum computers.

Our goal in the next few chapters will be to reach the same point as we did in this chapter – that is, being able to solve a simple optimization problem on a gate-based quantum computer, and learn how to formulate problems and write algorithms on gate quantum computers. We will also observe the potential strengths and current limitations of these types of quantum processers.

Further reading

- The original paper on quantum annealing:

  `https://arxiv.org/abs/cond-mat/9804280`

- Details on quantum tunneling:

  `https://arxiv.org/pdf/1411.4036.pdf`

- Details on D-Wave:

  `https://docs.dwavesys.com/docs/latest/doc_physical_properties.html`

6

Using Gate-Based Quantum Computers – Qubits and Quantum Circuits

In the previous chapter, we learned how to find the minimum of an energy function using a quantum annealer. This is a single-purpose solver, where any problem that can be converted into a QUBO can be solved on a D-Wave quantum annealer or other QUBO solvers. In this chapter, we will move to a more general class of quantum computers that are intended to solve any kind of mathematical problem. It would be accurate to say that a classical computer that allows any kind of calculation through a basic set of logical gates is a universal computer. Similarly, a quantum computer that allows the use of a set of logical gates that, in combination, can be used to solve any kind of mathematical problem, would be called a **Universal Quantum Computer**. This chapter deals with the general set of quantum computers that we often hear about, which is referred to as universal or gate-based quantum computers. These utilize a combination of gates or a quantum circuit to solve some specific problem.

Since the audience of this book is someone who's new to Amazon Braket but somewhat familiar with the basic elements of quantum computing, such as qubits or quantum gates, we will learn how to implement matrix mathematics and equivalent gates on Amazon Braket. This will include a brief discussion about what a qubit is and how it is represented using a Bloch sphere. These concepts will be implemented in a practical way using Amazon Braket's `Circuit()` function, where we will experiment with a circuit inspired by the Google Supremacy experiment.

In this chapter, we will cover the following topics:

- What is a quantum circuit?

- Understanding the basics of a qubit

- Single-qubit gate rotation example – the Bloch Clock

- Building multiple qubit quantum circuits

- Example inspired by the Google Supremacy experiment

Technical requirements

The source code for this chapter is available in the following GitHub repository:

```
https://github.com/PacktPublishing/Quantum-Computing-Experimentation-
with-Amazon-Braket/tree/main/Chapter06
```

The concepts of vectors, orthogonality, identity matrix, matrix multiplication, tensor product, and the equations shown in this chapter come from linear algebra and trigonometry, so it might be helpful to review those concepts as needed. There are several excellent books on this subject and two are included in the *Further reading* section if you wish to dive deeper into the mathematics of quantum computing.

What is a quantum circuit?

Quantum circuits are needed to "program" or tell a quantum computer what to do. These programs are dramatically different from most code that we are familiar with, but we still use Python or other languages to assemble the circuit before giving it to the quantum computer to execute. The execution itself involves transpiling or converting the instructions into a simpler set of logical gate operations and then, finally, into laser or microwave signals that are sent to individual qubits.

In this section, we will cover the basics of qubit representation and matrix mathematics as a foundation for understanding quantum gates. Next, we will look at a basic set of quantum gates and how to put them in a quantum circuit. Then, we will look at multiple qubit circuits and how to do the equivalent matrix multiplication to get the same results as that produced from a quantum circuit.

Finally, we will create a special circuit inspired by the Google Supremacy experiment. There, we will alternatively combine a set of randomly selected single-qubit gates and then entangle random pairs of qubits using a two-qubit gate. We will also execute this on real quantum devices to verify the results, and then compare the speed and accuracy of the results from simulators and the Rigetti and IonQ quantum devices.

Understanding the basics of a qubit

A qubit is dramatically different from a classical bit because it stores more information than the single binary value that a classical bit can store. A quantum bit can be pictured as a sphere with a vector pointing at any point on that sphere. The top of the sphere is the zero-state, shown as $|0\rangle$, while the bottom of the sphere is the one-state, shown as $|1\rangle$. These two states can be represented in matrix form as follows:

$$|0\rangle = \begin{bmatrix} 1 \\ 0 \end{bmatrix} \; and \; |1\rangle = \begin{bmatrix} 0 \\ 1 \end{bmatrix} \quad eq.\,6.1$$

However, we said that a qubit represents all the points on a sphere, called a Bloch sphere. So, these states can be represented as a combination of two state vectors:

$$|v\rangle = \alpha_0 |0\rangle + \alpha_1 |1\rangle = \begin{bmatrix} \alpha_0 \\ \alpha_1 \end{bmatrix} \quad eq.\,6.2$$

Here, α_0 and α_1 are complex numbers.

Since α_0 and α_1 are complex numbers, they include both a real component and an imaginary phase component. We will represent this as a rotation about the vertical z-axis of the Bloch sphere:

$$A = a + b\,e^{i\gamma} \quad eq.\,6.3$$

Here, γ is an angle of rotation (or the phase angle) in radians from 0 to 2π, and from trigonometry the relationship between α_0 and α_1 is given by:

$$\alpha_0{}^2 + \alpha_1{}^2 = 1 \quad eq.\,6.4$$

This is necessary to ensure the vector's length is always 1.

Note that the vector, $|v\rangle$, is a resulting vector, which is the superposition of two complex numbers, α_0 and α_1, that represent the two orthogonal states, $|0\rangle$ and $|1\rangle$. **Orthogonality** usually refers to two vectors that are perpendicular to each other:

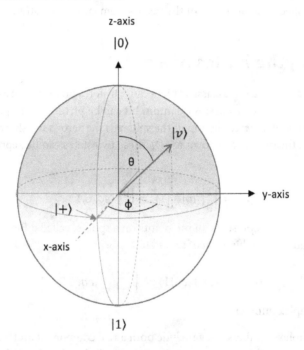

Figure 6.1 – A Bloch sphere is used to represent one Qubit

We will show the representation of the qubit as a Bloch sphere initially for one qubit. Note that two or more qubits cannot be accurately represented using a Bloch sphere, so we will not use it for more than one qubit.

Now, let's look at some qubit states both in matrix and Bloch sphere form:

1. First, let's learn how to implement the $|0\rangle$ state using the `arr_0` matrix:

```
Import numpy as np
arr_0=np.array([[1+0j],[0+0j]])
```

2. We can represent this array as a Bloch sphere by using the `draw_bloch()` function, which is available in the Jupyter notebook for this chapter:

    ```
    draw_bloch(arr_0)
    ```

    In this case, the state vector is pointing to the top of the Bloch sphere (or to the North pole), as shown here:

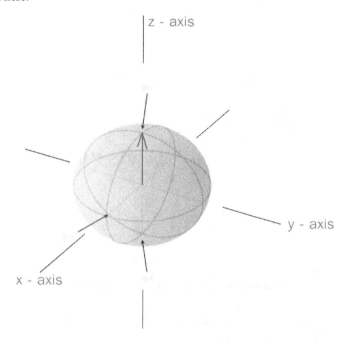

Figure 6.2 – Bloch sphere showing the state of |0⟩

3. You can run the same procedure for the |1⟩ state by creating the `arr_1` matrix:

    ```
    Arr_1=np.array([[0+0j],[1+0j]])
    draw_bloch(arr_1)
    ```

This is what the Bloch sphere will look like at this point:

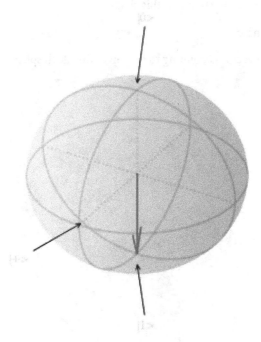

Figure 6.3 – Bloch sphere showing the state of|1⟩

Now, let's learn how a qubit state can be manipulated using gates. Gates can also be represented by specific matrices. Now, let's review these matrices and use them to change the state of the qubit.

Using matrix mathematics

To understand the way gate operations work on quantum computers, it is important to understand two key ways of performing matrix mathematics. The first is to use regular matrix multiplication, which can be implemented in Python code using the @ symbol. The other is a tensor product of two matrices, which can be implemented in Python using the NumPy kron() function and is represented by the ⊗ symbol.

When an operator acts on a qubit state, we use matrix multiplication. Typically, we call this matrix a **unitary operator** because the matrices that can perform gate operations must meet the criteria that they are unitary and do not change the size of the vector from a length of 1. Though not critical for our purpose, in linear algebra, by definition, this means that the matrix multiplied by its Adjoint (Transpose Complex Conjugate) must result in an identity matrix.

Using matrix mathematics to represent single-qubit gates

In this section, we are going to define some unitary operators and show their behavior as they act on a single-qubit state:

1. We will start with the simplest one, which is the identity operator. This is similar to multiplying a number by 1. We should get the same result that we started with. Let's multiply the $|0\rangle$ matrix with the identity matrix, which is represented by the matrix multiplication shown in the following equation. Note that the operator is on the left of the $|0\rangle$ state, which has been represented in matrix form, and that the result is the same matrix:

$$\begin{bmatrix} 1 & 0 \\ 0 & 1 \end{bmatrix}\begin{bmatrix} 1 \\ 0 \end{bmatrix} = \begin{bmatrix} 1 \\ 0 \end{bmatrix} \qquad eq.\,6.5$$

2. First, let's create the identify matrix as `arr_i`:

```
# I operator
arr_i=np.array([[1,0],[0,1]])
```

3. Now, we must "apply" the identity operator to the $|0\rangle$ state matrix. Note that the operator is on the left of the state it is affecting and that we use the matrix multiplication symbol, @:

```
draw_bloch(arr_i @ arr_0)
```

Output:

Matrix:

```
[[1.+0.j]
 [0.+0.j]]
```

The initial matrix did not change.

4. Now, we must define the NOT operator, which is also known as the X gate or the Pauli X operator, in the `arr_x` array. This is similar to the NOT operation in classical gates, where it will convert a 0 into a 1 and vice versa. In this case, the X Operator will represent the x gate and will convert the $|0\rangle$ state into a $|1\rangle$ state and vice versa:

```
# x operator
arr_x=np.array([[0,1],[1,0]])
```

5. Now, let's apply this operator to the $|0\rangle$ state:

    ```
    draw_bloch(arr_x @ arr_0)
    ```

    Output:

    ```
    Matrix:
    [[0.+0.j]
     [1.+0.j]]
    ```

    Notice that the state has changed to the $|1\rangle$ state. This is also represented by the vector pointing to the South pole on the Bloch sphere, as shown in the following diagram:

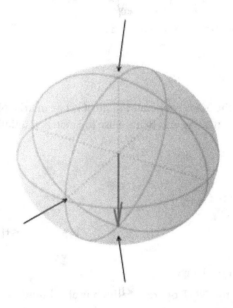

Figure 6.4 – Bloch sphere showing the $|1\rangle$ state

6. For completeness, let's also define some other more commonly used gates in their unitary matrix form:

    ```
    # y operator
    arr_y=np.array([[0,-1j],[1j,0]])
    # z operator
    arr_z=np.array([[1,0],[0,-1]])
    # h operator
    arr_h=(1/np.sqrt(2))*(np.array([[1, 1],[1, -1]]))
    # t operator
    ```

```
arr_t=np.array([[1,0],[0,np.exp(1j*np.pi/4)]])
# s operator
arr_s=np.array([[1,0],[0,np.exp(1j*np.pi/2)]])
```

The y operator rotates the vector similar to the x operator, only the rotation is around the Y-axis. This becomes more apparent when the initial vector does not start at the |0⟩ state. The z operator rotates the qubit state by π radians around the Z-axis. First, we would need to move the initial state away from |0⟩ to see any effect of this. The h operator (which also represents the Hadamard gate) rotates the state from the |0⟩ state to the |+⟩ state, which is on the front of the Bloch sphere on the X-axis, as shown in *Figure 6.1*.

7.   Now, let's rotate the qubit state from the |0⟩ state to the |+⟩ state using the h operator.

This is equivalent to the following matrix multiplication:

$$\frac{1}{\sqrt{2}}\begin{bmatrix} 1 & 1 \\ 1 & -1 \end{bmatrix}\begin{bmatrix} 1 \\ 0 \end{bmatrix} = \frac{1}{\sqrt{2}}\begin{bmatrix} 1 \\ 1 \end{bmatrix} \qquad eq.\,6.6$$

8.   Now, we will repeat the same process in code and also draw the Bloch sphere:

```
draw_bloch(arr_h @ arr_0)
```

Output:

Matrix:

[[0.70710678+0.j]

 [0.70710678+0.j]]

The fraction shows that the final state is as follows:

$$\begin{bmatrix} \alpha_0 \\ \alpha_1 \end{bmatrix} = \begin{bmatrix} \dfrac{1}{\sqrt{2}} \\ \dfrac{1}{\sqrt{2}} \end{bmatrix} \qquad eq.\,6.7$$

This is a superposition state where the qubit has an equal probability of becoming a 0 or a 1 when measured. The probability is α^2, so the probability of |0⟩ is 0.5 and the probability of |1⟩ is 0.5.

The vector, as represented on the Bloch sphere, is at the equator of the X-axis. This location is called the |+⟩ state:

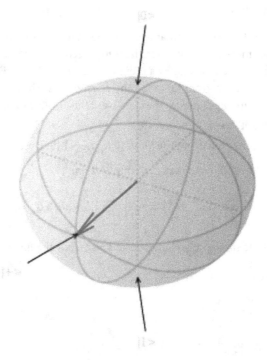

Figure 6.5 – Bloch sphere representing the qubit at the |+⟩ state

9. For clarity, let's visualize the h operator's effect on the quantum state of the qubit. This operator, as mentioned earlier, is also called the Hadamard gate and provides a rotation around the X, Y, and Z-axes simultaneously. It is hard to visualize this, but the following diagram may help. We discussed the z operator and the x (or NOT) operator. The Hadamard gate is equivalent to a rotation with the axis halfway between the Z and X-axes:

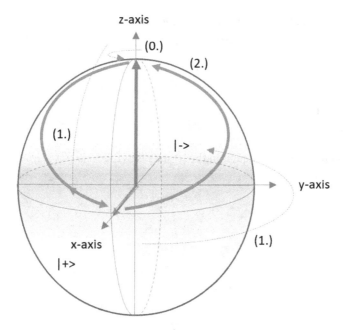

Figure 6.6 – Effect of using the Hadamard gate

In the preceding diagram, we applied the Hadamard gate twice:

- (1.) Starting at the $|0\rangle$ state, the Hadamard moves the qubit to the $|+\rangle$ state.

- (2.) Starting at the $|+\rangle$ state, the Hadamard moves the qubit back to the $|0\rangle$ state.

10. Now, let's re-prepare the plus state and store it in the `arr_plus` variable:

```
arr_plus=arr_h @ arr_0
print(arr_plus)
```

Output:

```
[[0.70710678+0.j]
 [0.70710678+0.j]]
```

11. Now, let's use the `arr_z` matrix, which represents the Pauli-Z matrix. This is also represented by the z gate and is a π rotation around the Z-axis. We can use this to rotate the qubit from the $|+\rangle$ state to the $|-\rangle$ state. This is equivalent to matrix multiplication:

$$\begin{bmatrix} 1 & 0 \\ 0 & -1 \end{bmatrix} \frac{1}{\sqrt{2}} \begin{bmatrix} 1 \\ 1 \end{bmatrix} = \frac{1}{\sqrt{2}} \begin{bmatrix} 1 \\ -1 \end{bmatrix} \qquad eq.\,6.8$$

The same process can be represented with the following code:

```
arr_minus=draw_bloch(arr_z @ arr_plus)
```

Output:

```
Matrix:
[[ 0.70710678+0.j]
 [-0.70710678+0.j]]
```

The Bloch sphere showing the qubit in the |-⟩ state is as follows:

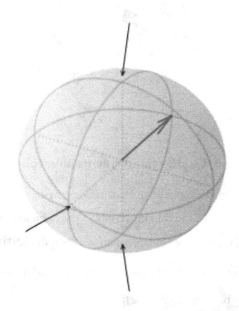

Figure 6.7 – Bloch sphere showing the qubit state of |-⟩

12. Our final example will be to rotate the qubit vector π/4 degrees using the t gate or the `arr_t` matrix. This is equivalent to the following matrix multiplication:

$$\begin{bmatrix} 1 & 0 \\ 0 & e^{i\frac{\pi}{4}} \end{bmatrix} \frac{1}{\sqrt{2}} \begin{bmatrix} 1 \\ -1 \end{bmatrix} = \begin{bmatrix} \frac{1}{\sqrt{2}} \\ -\frac{1}{2} - \frac{1}{2}i \end{bmatrix} \qquad eq.\,6.9$$

Note the following:

$$e^{i\frac{\pi}{4}} = \cos\left(\frac{\pi}{4}\right) + \sin\left(\frac{\pi}{4}\right)i = \frac{1}{\sqrt{2}} + \frac{1}{\sqrt{2}}i \qquad eq.\,6.10$$

The same process can be done with the following code:

```
arr_r=draw_bloch(arr_t @ arr_minus)
```

Output:

```
Matrix:
[[ 0.70710678+0.j ]
 [-0.5         -0.5j]]
```

The final position on the qubit vector is on the equator of the Bloch sphere rotated $\pi/4$ from the $|-\rangle$ state or rotated at an angle of $5/8\ \pi$ from the $|+\rangle$ state, as shown here:

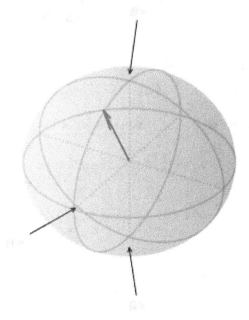

Figure 6.8 – Bloch sphere showing the final state with a z-rotation angle of $\varphi = (5/8)\ \pi$

At this point, we have studied the behavior of one qubit with some simple rotations of the vector representing the qubit. We used the Bloch sphere to visualize the state vector of the qubit and also looked at the equivalent mathematical representation of the rotations using their equivalent unitary matrices.

Now, let's build the same single-qubit rotations using the Amazon Braket `Circuit()` function and their equivalent quantum gates.

Using quantum gates in a quantum circuit

In the previous section, we worked with a single qubit, performed various operations on that single-qubit using matrix multiplication, and showed the results on a Bloch sphere. Now, let's look at the same process using quantum gates using the Amazon Braket `Circuit()` function. We will use the custom `draw_circuit()` function, which will allow you to submit a **single-qubit** quantum circuit that will display the quantum circuit diagram, show the results after executing it using the `LocalSimulator()`, and display a Bloch sphere.

Let's get started:

1. The `draw_circuit()` function is provided in this chapter's code. We will use this here to make drawing and executing the single gate circuits easier. The following is the relevant code:

    ```
    def draw_circuit(circ):
        circ=circ.state_vector()
        print(circ)
        device = LocalSimulator()
        result = device.run(circ).result()
        arr_r=np.array(
            [[result.values[0][0]], [result.values[0][1]]])
        draw_bloch(arr_r)
    ```

2. We can run the identity gate on the 0th qubit by using `i(0)`. This will leave the original qubit state of $|0\rangle$ unchanged:

    ```
    circ=Circuit().i(0)
    draw_circuit(circ)
    ```

    Output:

    ```
    T   :  |0|
    q0  :  -I-
    T   :  |0|
    Matrix:
    [[1.+0.j]
     [0.+0.j]]
    ```

    As you can see, the circuit is represented in the first three lines and that after q0, we have only one gate, I. T represents the depth of the circuit. The resulting matrix shows that the state is still $|0\rangle$. The following diagram shows the resulting Bloch sphere showing the same:

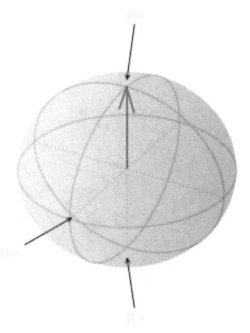

Figure 6.9 – Bloch sphere showing the |0⟩ state

3. Now that we know how some of the other unitary single-qubit gates work, let's try to bring the qubit to the |-⟩ state. We have several options, but here, we will start with a Hadamard gate, then a Z gate. Both gates will be applied to qubit 0. This provides the appropriate rotations to bring the qubit state to the |+⟩ state and then provides a π rotation around the Z-axis to bring the qubit to the |-⟩ state:

```
circ=Circuit().h(0).z(0)
draw_circuit(circ)
```

Output:

```
T   :  |0|1|
q0  :  -H-Z-
T   :  |0|1|
Matrix:
[[ 0.70710678+0.j]
 [-0.70710678+0.j]]
```

The qubit is now at the |-⟩ state. The Bloch sphere should also confirm this:

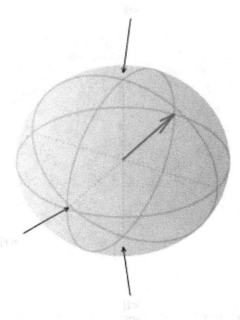

Figure 6.10 – Bloch sphere showing the |-⟩ state

4. Starting at the |0⟩ state, we can also try applying a Hadamard with a T gate, which is a π/4 rotation around the Z-axis:

```
circ=Circuit().h(0).t(0)
draw_circuit(circ)
```

Output:

```
T   :  |0|1|
q0  :  -H-T-
T   :  |0|1|
Matrix:
[[0.70710678+0.j ]
 [0.5       +0.5j]]
```

The Bloch sphere shows the qubit state as follows:

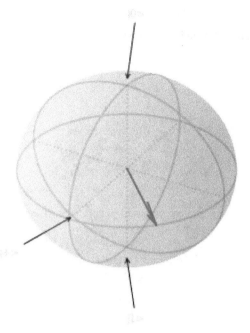

Figure 6.11 – Bloch sphere after starting at |0⟩ and applying an H and a T gate

5. Now, let's look at the effect of the circuit by starting at the |0⟩ state and then applying the X, H, and S gates. The S gate is a π/2 rotation around the Z-axis. So, in this case, we move to the |1⟩ state due to the X gate, then the |-⟩ state because of the Hadamard, and then a π/2 degree rotation around the Z-axis (around the equator) to the |-i⟩ state. This is equivalent to the following matrix multiplication:

$$\begin{bmatrix} 1 & 0 \\ 0 & i \end{bmatrix} \frac{1}{\sqrt{2}} \begin{bmatrix} 1 & 1 \\ 1 & -1 \end{bmatrix} \begin{bmatrix} 0 & 1 \\ 1 & 0 \end{bmatrix} \begin{bmatrix} 1 \\ 0 \end{bmatrix} = \frac{1}{\sqrt{2}} \begin{bmatrix} 1 \\ -i \end{bmatrix} \qquad eq.\,6.11$$

The equivalent circuit can be set up with the following code:

```
circ=Circuit().x(0).h(0).s(0)
draw_circuit(circ)
```

Output:

```
T   : |0|1|2|
q0 : -X-H-S-
T   : |0|1|2|
Matrix:
```

```
[[0.70710678+0.j         0.]
 [0.        -0.70710678j]]
```

The Bloch sphere representation is as follows:

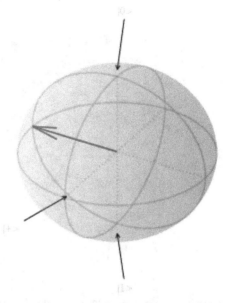

Figure 6.12 – Bloch sphere in the |-i⟩ state

Most of the gates we have used so far had predefined rotations around the X or Z-axis. We can also apply specific angle rotations to the qubit around any of the three axes. We will look at the rotation functions using an example in the next section.

Single-qubit gate rotation example – the Bloch Clock

We can apply specific rotations around each axis using the rx(q,θ), ry(q,θ), or rz(q,φ) gates. Here, q is the qubit number, and θ and φ are the rotation angles in radians. Thus, any value from 0 to 2π or 0 to -2π will fully rotate the vector around that axis back to the starting point. Any multiples will cause multiple rotations.

To try out two new gates **RY** and **RZ**, represented by the following functions, ry() and rz(), we will encode the time of the day in the Bloch sphere. Looking back at *Figure 6.1*, we will use the rotation around the Y-axis or the θ angle to represent the hour of the day and the φ angle to represent the minutes.

Representing the hour of the day using θ

Thus, through the day, the qubit vector will spiral down from the |0⟩ state, representing midnight, to the equator, which will be at noon, and then continue to spiral down to the |1⟩ state toward midnight again. The top of the hour (:00) will be represented with a phase of π degrees. Thus, we will use the ry(θ) gate to rotate the qubit vector in the -y direction to represent the top of the hour. Thus, θ represents a fraction of the 24 hours through the day.

Representing the minutes and seconds using φ

To represent the clockwise rotation of the minutes and seconds around the Z-axis, we will rotate the φ angle in the reverse direction using the rz() gate, starting at π degrees. The bloch_clock() code is as follows:

```
def bloch_clock():
    from time import gmtime
    import datetime
    import numpy as np
    time=gmtime()
    #set to EDT
    HR=time.tm_hour-4
    if HR<0:
        HR=HR+24
    MIN=time.tm_min
    SEC=time.tm_sec
    print''HR'',HR,''MIN'',MIN,''SEC'', SEC,''ED'')
    circ=Circuit().ry(0,-(HR+MIN/60
        +SEC/3600)*np.pi/24).rz(0,-(MIN+SEC/60)*2*np.pi/60)
    draw_circuit(circ)
```

Output:

```
HR: 11 MIN: 35 SEC: 30 EDT
T  : |    0    |    1    |


q0 : -Ry(-1.52)-Rz(-3.72)-
```

```
T  :  |    0    |    1    |
```

Additional result types: StateVector

Matrix:

```
[[-0.20612405+0.69586314j]
 [ 0.19539087+0.65962852j]]
```

For 11:35:30, the Bloch Clock shows the following output:

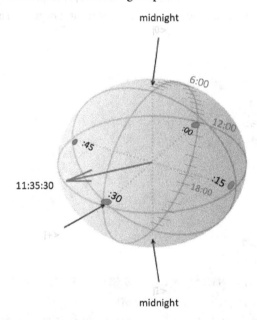

Figure 6.13–- Bloch Clock showing 11:35:30

You can get your own time on the Bloch sphere by running `bloch_clock()`. Please adjust the hour to your time zone by adjusting the constant in the `HR=time.tm_hour-4` line.

We are now going to start dealing with multiple qubits. It is not practical to show a multiple qubit state space using a Bloch sphere, even though there are different ways to split the information into phase diagrams or show partial information on a single sphere. In any case, next, we will focus on using larger matrices that represent more qubits and also show how matrix multiplication can easily be represented by using gates on a quantum circuit.

Building multiple qubit quantum circuits

In this section, we will build the matrix math for a full circuit that contains multiple qubits and then show how the results match the output from a quantum gate circuit. So far, we have used matrix multiplication and the @ symbol to multiply the original state with a series of matrices that represent unitary operators or quantum gates on one qubit. When we are dealing with multiple qubits, the vector space of each will have to be multiplied together using the tensor product, which is typically represented by the ⊗ symbol. We will use the NumPy `kron()` function to calculate this:

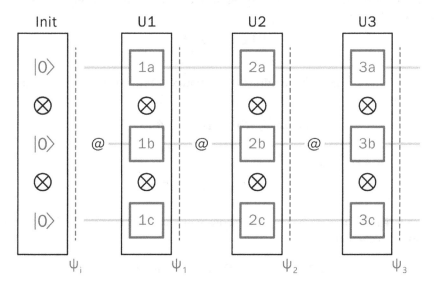

Figure 6.14 – Matrix multiplication of a quantum gate circuit

The preceding diagram shows a sample quantum circuit with various gates (squares) each representing a 2x2 matrix. The initial state on each qubit is going to be the $|0\rangle$ state. To represent this quantum circuit using matrix multiplication, we can use the tensor product between each of the gates to create a unitary matrix that represents a column of gates. Thus, to create U1, we need the tensor product between 1a, 1b, and 1c. To get the ψ_2 state, we need to apply the unitary matrix, U1, to the prior state, ψ_1, using matrix multiplication. Each subsequent column of gates is applied the same way to the previous state, or they can be multiplied together as a single unitary and then applied once to the initial state to get the final state of the circuit. Let's build the matrix math of this circuit step by step:

1. Let's start with the tensor product of the initial state, (ψ_i), of the qubits. Since we have three qubits, this will be as follows:

$$\psi_i = |0\rangle \otimes |0\rangle \otimes |0\rangle \quad eq. 6.12$$

For n qubits, we could write the following general expression:

$$|0^{\otimes n}\rangle \quad eq.\,6.13$$

2. The next unitary will be given by the following equation:

$$U1 = 1a \otimes 1b \otimes 1c \quad eq.\,6.14$$

3. The next state, ψ_1, is given by multiplying the matrix of the initial state, I, with U1. Thus, we get the following:

$$\psi_1 = U1 \,@\, \psi_i\, I \quad eq.\,6.15$$

4. The next state, ψ_2, is given by multiplying the matrix of the state ψ_1 with U2. Thus, we get the following:

$$U2 = 2a \otimes 2b \otimes 2c \quad eq.\,6.16$$

We also get the following:

$$\psi_2 = U2 \,@\, \psi_1 \quad eq.\,6.17$$

5. Finally, the ψ_3 state is given by multiplying the matrix of the state, ψ_2, with U3. Thus, we get the following equation:

$$U3 = 3a \otimes 3b \otimes 3c \quad eq.\,6.18$$

We also get the following equation:

$$\psi_3 = U3 \,@\, \psi_2 \quad eq.\,6.19$$

6. As mentioned earlier, we can also combine all the gate operations into a single unitary matrix and then apply that to the initial state. Thus, another way to represent ψ_3 would be as follows:

$$\psi_3 = U3 \,@\, U2 \,@\, U1 \,@\, |0^{\otimes 3}\rangle \quad eq.\,6.20$$

This can also be expanded for clarity:

$$\psi_3 = (3a \otimes 3b \otimes 3c) \,@\, (2a \otimes 2b \otimes 2c) \,@\, (1a \otimes 1b \otimes 1c) \,@\, |0^{\otimes 3}\rangle \quad eq.\,6.21$$

Having looked at the general process of matrix multiplication to represent a quantum circuit, in the next section, we will use this process to get the final state of a specific circuit with single-qubit and two-qubit gates. You should keep in mind that to ensure each unitary has the correct size, any missing gates can be filled with the I identity matrix. Technically, in an actual quantum circuit, gates will be stacked to the left to eliminate any gaps, unless this is prevented due to a multiple qubit gate.

Three-qubit circuit example

We will now use what we have learned to create a slightly more complicated quantum circuit on three qubits. The diagram below shows this sample circuit with four unitary gate operations on the three qubits. The first and last operation has all Hadamard gates, while U2 has single qubit gates, and U3 has a CNOT gate with an Identity gate. We have looked at all these steps already, but now we will put it together to get the final state of this quantum circuit through both matrix multiplication and then finally using quantum gates.

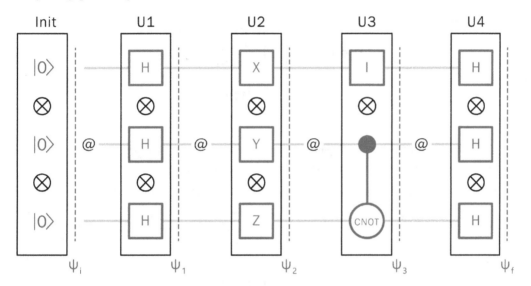

Figure 6.15 – Sample circuit to create

Now, let's use this information to learn how to calculate the end state matrix for a set of gates in a three-qubit quantum circuit, as shown in the preceding diagram:

1. Starting with the bottom two qubit states of|0⟩ and then adding the third top qubit state of |0⟩, we must use the NumPy kron() function twice:

```
arr_psi_i=np.kron(arr_0,np.kron(arr_0, arr_0))
print(arr_psi_i)
```

Output:

```
[[1.+0.j]
 [0.+0.j]
 [0.+0.j]
 [0.+0.j]
```

```
[0.+0.j]

[0.+0.j]

[0.+0.j]

[0.+0.j]]
```

The equivalent matrix representation involves the tensor product of the three matrices:

$$\begin{bmatrix} 1 \\ 0 \end{bmatrix} \otimes \begin{bmatrix} 1 \\ 0 \end{bmatrix} \otimes \begin{bmatrix} 1 \\ 0 \end{bmatrix} = \begin{bmatrix} 1 \\ 0 \\ 0 \\ 0 \\ 0 \\ 0 \\ 0 \\ 0 \end{bmatrix} = \begin{bmatrix} 1 \ |000\rangle \\ 0 \ |001\rangle \\ 0 \ |010\rangle \\ 0 \ |011\rangle \\ 0 \ |100\rangle \\ 0 \ |101\rangle \\ 0 \ |110\rangle \\ 0 \ |111\rangle \end{bmatrix} \qquad eq.\,6.22$$

2. Now, let's add Hadamards or **H**-gate, which is represented by the $\frac{1}{\sqrt{2}}\begin{bmatrix} 1 & 1 \\ 1 & -1 \end{bmatrix}$ matrix, to all the qubits. This will bring them to an equal superposition state.

Thus, the first unitary matrix will be the tensor product of three Hadamard gates:

```
arr_U1=np.kron(arr_h,np.kron(arr_h, arr_h))
print(arr_U1)
```

Output:

```
[[ 0.35355339   0.35355339   0.35355339   0.35355339   0.35355339
0.35355339   0.35355339   0.35355339]

 [ 0.35355339 -0.35355339   0.35355339 -0.35355339   0.35355339
-0.35355339   0.35355339 -0.35355339]

 [ 0.35355339   0.35355339 -0.35355339 -0.35355339   0.35355339
0.35355339  -0.35355339 -0.35355339]

 [ 0.35355339 -0.35355339 -0.35355339   0.35355339   0.35355339
-0.35355339  -0.35355339   0.35355339]

 [ 0.35355339   0.35355339   0.35355339   0.35355339 -0.35355339
-0.35355339  -0.35355339 -0.35355339]

 [ 0.35355339 -0.35355339   0.35355339 -0.35355339 -0.35355339
0.35355339  -0.35355339   0.35355339]

 [ 0.35355339   0.35355339 -0.35355339 -0.35355339 -0.35355339
-0.35355339   0.35355339   0.35355339]

 [ 0.35355339 -0.35355339 -0.35355339   0.35355339 -0.35355339
0.35355339   0.35355339 -0.35355339]]
```

3. To get the state, we need to look at the effect the `arr_U1` unitary matrix has on the initial state, `arr_psi_i`. This is given by the following matrix multiplication:

$$\psi_1 = \left[\frac{1}{\sqrt{2}}\begin{bmatrix}1 & 1\\1 & -1\end{bmatrix} \otimes \frac{1}{\sqrt{2}}\begin{bmatrix}1 & 1\\1 & -1\end{bmatrix} \otimes \frac{1}{\sqrt{2}}\begin{bmatrix}1 & 1\\1 & -1\end{bmatrix}\right] @ \begin{bmatrix}1\\0\\0\\0\\0\\0\\0\\0\end{bmatrix} = \begin{bmatrix}1/\sqrt{8}\,|000\rangle\\1/\sqrt{8}\,|001\rangle\\1/\sqrt{8}\,|010\rangle\\1/\sqrt{8}\,|011\rangle\\1/\sqrt{8}\,|100\rangle\\1/\sqrt{8}\,|101\rangle\\1/\sqrt{8}\,|110\rangle\\1/\sqrt{8}\,|111\rangle\end{bmatrix} \qquad eq.\,6.23$$

4. To run the circuit, let's use the `LocalSimulator()` and `run_circuit_local()` functions, which can be found in the code for this chapter, to produce the results:

```
def run_circuit_local(circ):
    # This function prints the quantum circuit and
    # calculates the final state vector
    # This can be used for multiple qubits and only
    # uses the local simulator
    # The Bloch sphere is not printed
    circ=circ.state_vector()
    print(circ)
    device = LocalSimulator()
    result = device.run(circ).result()
    arr_r=np.array(result.values).T
    print(arr_r)
    return(arr_r)
```

5. Now, we can create the circuit equivalent, as shown here:

```
circ_psi_1=Circuit().h([0,1,2])
result=run_circuit_local(circ_psi_1)
```

Output:

```
T   :  |0|
q0  :  -H-
q1  :  -H-
q2  :  -H-
```

```
T   : |0|
```

```
Additional result types: StateVector
```

```
[[0.35355339+0.j]
 [0.35355339+0.j]
 [0.35355339+0.j]
 [0.35355339+0.j]
 [0.35355339+0.j]
 [0.35355339+0.j]
 [0.35355339+0.j]
 [0.35355339+0.j]]
```

6. Now, let's apply three different single-qubit gates to create a unitary, U2. Let's use gates x () $\begin{bmatrix} 0 & 1 \\ 1 & 0 \end{bmatrix}$, y () $\begin{bmatrix} 0 & -i \\ i & 0 \end{bmatrix}$, and z () $\begin{bmatrix} 1 & 0 \\ 0 & -1 \end{bmatrix}$ from the top down. The following matrix multiplication is involved:

$$\psi_2 = \left[\begin{bmatrix} 0 & 1 \\ 1 & 0 \end{bmatrix} \otimes \begin{bmatrix} 0 & -i \\ i & 0 \end{bmatrix} \otimes \begin{bmatrix} 1 & 0 \\ 0 & -1 \end{bmatrix} \right] @ \begin{bmatrix} 1/\sqrt{8}\,|000\rangle \\ 1/\sqrt{8}\,|001\rangle \\ 1/\sqrt{8}\,|010\rangle \\ 1/\sqrt{8}\,|011\rangle \\ 1/\sqrt{8}\,|100\rangle \\ 1/\sqrt{8}\,|101\rangle \\ 1/\sqrt{8}\,|110\rangle \\ 1/\sqrt{8}\,|111\rangle \end{bmatrix} = \begin{bmatrix} -1/\sqrt{8}\,i\,|000\rangle \\ 1/\sqrt{8}\,i\,|001\rangle \\ 1/\sqrt{8}\,i\,|010\rangle \\ -1/\sqrt{8}\,i\,|011\rangle \\ -1/\sqrt{8}\,i\,|100\rangle \\ 1/\sqrt{8}\,i\,|101\rangle \\ 1/\sqrt{8}\,i\,|110\rangle \\ -1/\sqrt{8}\,i\,|111\rangle \end{bmatrix} \quad eq.\,6.24$$

The matrix code to build U2 is as follows:

```
arr_U2=np.kron(arr_x,np.kron(arr_y, arr_z))
print(arr_U2)
```

Output:

```
[[ 0.+0.j  0.+0.j  0.+0.j  0.+0.j  0.+0.j  0.+0.j  0.-1.j
 0.+0.j]
 [ 0.+0.j -0.+0.j  0.+0.j  0.+0.j  0.+0.j -0.+0.j  0.+0.j
 0.+1.j]
 [ 0.+0.j  0.+0.j  0.+0.j  0.+0.j  0.+1.j  0.+0.j  0.+0.j
 0.+0.j]
 [ 0.+0.j  0.-0.j  0.+0.j -0.+0.j  0.+0.j  0.-1.j  0.+0.j
 -0.+0.j]
```

```
[ 0.+0.j   0.+0.j   0.-1.j   0.+0.j   0.+0.j   0.+0.j   0.+0.j
 0.+0.j]
[ 0.+0.j  -0.+0.j   0.+0.j   0.+1.j   0.+0.j  -0.+0.j   0.+0.j
 0.+0.j]
[ 0.+1.j   0.+0.j   0.+0.j   0.+0.j   0.+0.j   0.+0.j   0.+0.j
 0.+0.j]
[ 0.+0.j   0.-1.j   0.+0.j  -0.+0.j   0.+0.j   0.-0.j   0.+0.j
 -0.+0.j]]
```

7. The following code develops `arr_psi_2`, which will apply the U2 operator to the last state, `arr_psi_1`:

```
arr_psi_2=arr_U2 @ arr_psi_1
print(arr_psi_2)
```

Output:

```
[[0.-0.35355339j]
 [0.+0.35355339j]
 [0.+0.35355339j]
 [0.-0.35355339j]
 [0.-0.35355339j]
 [0.+0.35355339j]
 [0.+0.35355339j]
 [0.-0.35355339j]]
```

8. The following is the same process using quantum gates:

```
circ_psi_2=circ_psi_1.x(0).y(1).z(2)
result=run_circuit_local(circ_psi_2)
```

Output:

```
T   : |0|1|
q0  : -H-X-
q1  : -H-Y-
q2  : -H-Z-
T   : |0|1|

Additional result types: StateVector
[[0.-0.35355339j]
```

```
[0.+0.35355339j]
```
```
[0.+0.35355339j]
```
```
[0.-0.35355339j]
```
```
[0.-0.35355339j]
```
```
[0.+0.35355339j]
```
```
[0.+0.35355339j]
```
```
[0.-0.35355339j]]
```

As you can see, the resulting state vector from the circuit is the same as that when using matrix multiplication.

9. So far, we have only applied the Hadamard gates and single-qubit gates. As you can see, we have eight amplitudes from the three qubits. As you may recall, the number of amplitudes is 2^n where n is the number of qubits, and is one feature that gives quantum computers their advantage. We can now apply a **CX** or **CNOT** gate on two qubits with the cnot () function. This is a two-qubit gate. The following is its matrix representation. In this case, the first qubit is the control and the second qubit is the target. If the control qubit has a state of $|1\rangle$, then the second qubit will perform an X operation and flip the qubit:

$$CNOT = \begin{bmatrix} 1 & 0 & 0 & 0 \\ 0 & 1 & 0 & 0 \\ 0 & 0 & 0 & 1 \\ 0 & 0 & 1 & 0 \end{bmatrix} \qquad eq.\,6.25$$

We will simply show how a CNOT gate works in the following steps before using this gate in the circuit:

I.   First, we must create the arr_cx array as the CNOT matrix:

```
arr_cx=np.array([[1, 0, 0, 0], [0, 1, 0, 0], [0, 0, 0,
1], [0, 0, 1, 0]])
```

II.   To prove this point, let's create a state of $|10\rangle$:

```
arr_10= np.kron(arr_1, arr_0)
print(arr_10)
```

Output:

```
[[0.+0.j]
 [0.+0.j]
 [1.+0.j]
 [0.+0.j]]
```

III.   Now, we can perform the cnot () operation on arr_10 or |10):

```
arr_11= arr_cx @ arr_10
print(arr_11)
```

Output:

```
[[0.+0.j]
 [0.+0.j]
 [0.+0.j]
 [1.+0.j]]
```

Since the first qubit is in a state of |1), the second qubit will change states from |0) to |0). Thus, we will see a |11) resulting state.

10. Back to our three-qubit circuit, since we want to apply the cnot () gate on qubit 1 and 2 with the and use the identity i () gate $\begin{bmatrix} 1 & 0 \\ 0 & 1 \end{bmatrix}$ on qubit 0 so that we can create the third unitary, U3:

$$U3 = \begin{bmatrix} 1 & 0 \\ 0 & 1 \end{bmatrix} \otimes \begin{bmatrix} 1 & 0 & 0 & 0 \\ 0 & 1 & 0 & 0 \\ 0 & 0 & 0 & 1 \\ 0 & 0 & 1 & 0 \end{bmatrix} \qquad eq.\,6.26$$

The code is as follows:

```
arr_U3=np.kron(arr_i,arr_cx)
print(arr_U3)
```

Output:

```
[[1 0 0 0 0 0 0 0]
 [0 1 0 0 0 0 0 0]
 [0 0 0 1 0 0 0 0]
 [0 0 1 0 0 0 0 0]
 [0 0 0 0 1 0 0 0]
 [0 0 0 0 0 1 0 0]
 [0 0 0 0 0 0 0 1]
 [0 0 0 0 0 0 1 0]]
```

11. The final state, ψ_3, is then stored in `arr_psi_3` using the following code:

```
arr_psi_3=arr_U3 @ arr_psi_2
print(arr_psi_3)
```

Output:

```
[[0.-0.35355339j]
 [0.+0.35355339j]
 [0.-0.35355339j]
 [0.+0.35355339j]
 [0.-0.35355339j]
 [0.+0.35355339j]
 [0.-0.35355339j]
 [0.+0.35355339j]]
```

12. The same can be done using the quantum gates:

```
circ_psi_3=circ_psi_2.i(0).cnot(1,2)
result=run_circuit_local(circ_psi_3)
```

Output:

```
T   : |0|1|2|
q0 : -H-X-I-
q1 : -H-Y-C-
             |
q2 : -H-Z-X-
T   : |0|1|2|
Additional result types: StateVector
[[0.-0.35355339j]
 [0.+0.35355339j]
 [0.-0.35355339j]
 [0.+0.35355339j]
 [0.-0.35355339j]
 [0.+0.35355339j]
 [0.-0.35355339j]
 [0.+0.35355339j]]
```

13. The final step is to add Hadamard gates to each qubit again and measure the final circuit. In this case, we will just create the circuit from scratch to show how convenient it is to use gate circuits to represent all the matrix math that is happening in the background:

```
circ_psi_3=Circuit().h([0,1,2]).x(0).y(1).z(2).i(0).
cnot(1,2).h([0,1,2])
arr_psi_3=run_circuit_local(circ_psi_3)
```

Output:

```
T   :  |0|1|2|3|

q0  :  -H-X-I-H-

q1  :  -H-Y-C-H-
                 |
q2  :  -H-Z-X-H-

T   :  |0|1|2|3|
```

```
Additional result types: StateVector
[[0.-2.36158002e-17j]
 [0.-1.00000000e+00j]
 [0.-1.26316153e-34j]
 [0.-9.52420783e-18j]
 [0.+0.00000000e+00j]
 [0.+0.00000000e+00j]
 [0.+0.00000000e+00j]
 [0.+0.00000000e+00j]]
```

14. We can determine the probabilities of each state by squaring each of the amplitudes. Here, the resulting state is given by the following equation:

$$\psi_3 = \begin{bmatrix} 0\,|000\rangle \\ -i\,|001\rangle \\ 0\,|010\rangle \\ 0\,|011\rangle \\ 0\,|100\rangle \\ 0\,|101\rangle \\ 0\,|110\rangle \\ 0|111\rangle \end{bmatrix} \qquad eq.\,6.27$$

15. Below we will now repeat the process using a quantum circuit and adding the gates. This will help us avoid all the matrix multiplication we did in the previous steps. On a simulator or an error-free quantum computer, we should get 001 100% of the time:

```
circ_psi_3=Circuit().h([0,1,2]).x(0).y(1).z(2).i(0).
cnot(1,2).h([0,1,2])
device = LocalSimulator()
result = device.run(circ_psi_3, shots=1000).result()
counts = result.measurement_counts
print(counts)
# plot using Counter
plt.bar(counts.keys(), counts.values());
plt.xlabel('v'lue')'
plt.ylabel('c'unts')'
```

Output:

```
Counter({'0'1':'1000})
```

The resulting bar chart also shows the same result of getting 001 only:

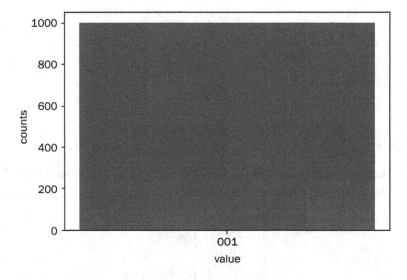

Figure 6.16 – Resulting probabilities after measuring the circuit using LocalSimulator()

With that, we have completed several steps showing how quantum gates are equivalent to specific matrices and that the structure of a quantum circuit can be simulated using a step-by-step process, which involves creating unitary matrix operators that act on the previous state vector. Initially, we looked at the process of matrix multiplication for a single-qubit example. We also saw that we can extend this process to multiple qubits, so long as we take the tensor product of each column of gates to ensure they are converted into a unitary matrix. Then, we multiplied the matrix of the initial state with the first unitary, which applies Hadamards to the three qubits to bring them into superposition. We did the same to the second state, which applies the single-qubit x, y, and z gates, and then the third, which applies an identity gate to the first qubit, followed by a two-qubit control gate or the CNOT gate on the next two qubits, which entangle the two qubits together. The final step involved adding Hadamards to all the qubits to remove the superposition, just before the circuit is measured. We started with a state of all zeros and returned with 001, which is measured 100% of the time through this circuit.

This simple circuit lays the foundation for the next section, where we will look at a modified example inspired by the Google Supremacy experiment.

Example inspired by the Google Supremacy experiment

We will apply what we have learned about gate operations to an experiment inspired by the Google Supremacy experiment. The paper titled *Quantum supremacy using a programmable superconducting processor* was published in *Nature* in October 2019. The links to this paper and the counter-claim by IBM can be found in the *Further reading* section. This is a good example to start with, as it does not require a specific quantum circuit, and can also explain, to some extent, the process used in the widely talked about experiment.

The actual Google experiment

The Google experiment used an alternating set of randomly selected single-qubit gates $(\sqrt{X}, \sqrt{Y}, \sqrt{W})$. It entangled one of a different set of interconnected qubits using a combination of iSWAP and a CrZ $(\pi/6)$ gate that had been calibrated for minimum error between that specific pair of qubits. This includes five other rotation angles that I have not shown.

The following equation shows the matrices for the aforementioned $\sqrt{X}$ and $\sqrt{Y}$ gates:

$$\sqrt{X} = \frac{1}{2}\begin{pmatrix} 1+i & 1-i \\ 1-i & 1+i \end{pmatrix} \qquad eq.\,6.28$$

The W gate is defined as $(X + Y)/\sqrt{2}$.

The two-qubit gate uses a combination of an iSWAP and CrZ(Y), where y = π /6. Other rotations for optimizing the two-qubit gate for the highest fidelity of the qubit pair interaction have not been shown here:

$$iSWAP = \begin{bmatrix} 1 & 0 & 0 & 0 \\ 0 & 0 & i & 0 \\ 0 & i & 0 & 0 \\ 0 & 0 & 0 & 1 \end{bmatrix} \; and \; CrZ(\gamma) = \begin{bmatrix} 1 & 0 & 0 & 0 \\ 0 & 1 & 0 & 0 \\ 0 & 0 & e^{-i(\frac{\gamma}{2})} & 0 \\ 0 & 0 & 0 & e^{i(\frac{\gamma}{2})} \end{bmatrix} \qquad eq.\,6.30$$

The single and multiple qubit gates were repeated r times, where r=20. Since this experiment was done on their 54-qubit Sycamore quantum processor with one qubit not functioning properly, this led to a 53-qubit system and thus 2^{53} different possible states. As we have seen, based on the matrix calculations, to simulate one step of 53 gates on 53 qubits, we must find the tensor products of 53 gates, which creates a matrix of size $2^{53}x2^{53}$. The team stated that the RAM availability in the Jülich supercomputer (with 100,000 cores and 250 terabytes) limited calculations to up to 48 qubits. Beyond that, other hybrid methods were used. The claim that was made was that with the quantum processor, these calculations, with r=20 and 1 million measurement samples, were performed in 200 seconds, while classical processors would require 50 trillion core hours and consume 1 petawatt hour of energy (estimated to take 10,000 years with a million-core supercomputer). Counterclaims were made by IBM and other teams.

Circuit implementation on Amazon Braket

For our purposes, we will create a circuit where we can randomly select single-qubit gates for each qubit, and then use the two-qubit CNOT gate to entangle qubits. We will use identity gates so that we can move the CNOT gates up and down, thus randomly entangling different sets of qubits. The following diagram shows two sample repetitions of this circuit. We will calculate the full circuit's unitary using tensor products and matrix multiplication, along with its equivalent gate circuit, and run it on the local simulator and the Amazon Braket SV1 and TN1 simulators. Finally, we will look at the performance of both the Rigetti and IonQ quantum devices:

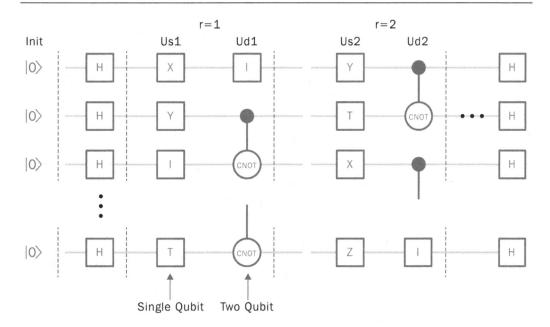

Figure 6.17 – Google Quantum supremacy-inspired circuit with alternating random
single-qubit gates (X, Y, Z, I, T) and randomly placed CNOT gates repeated r times

The function that creates the circuit and equivalent unitary for the full circuit is qc_rand() and
is provided in the code for this chapter. All you need to do is provide the number of qubits and the
number of repeats, r, in the circuit. The last parameter is a Boolean to create the unitary. This is True
by default, but if your classical processor cannot generate the unitary (around 11 or 12 qubits), set
Matrix=False.

We will start with seven qubits, q=7, and set the repeats to two, r=2. This allows us to see all the
different options with good results.

> **Note – Code Preparation**
>
> As you follow along, do not accidentally execute a run on the quantum devices (the IonQ Device
> and Aspen) unless you are willing to budget $32 and $1.42 for this configuration.
>
> Execute the available_devices() function to ensure you have the latest device names,
> adjust the code accordingly, and run experiments on the devices available at the time you
> execute the code.
>
> Please execute the estimate_cost() or estimate_cost_measured_qubits()
> function before running these devices with the appropriate number of qubits and desired number
> of shots. In the following code, I have executed these functions to give you price estimates.

At the end of this section, I will go over some insights as to which configurations do not work or give poor results. Then, you can try out different configurations at the end of this section, though note that the IonQ execution can get very expensive. It can cost up to $100 if you're executing the circuit on 11 qubits with the maximum number of suggested shots at 10,000. Executing a 32-qubit circuit on Rigetti with 100,000 shots can cost $35.00.

Execution results for a single 7x2 circuit

We will start with a small circuit with 7 qubits and repeat the alternating single and two-qubit gates twice. Since we will also apply Hadamard gates, this is a gate depth of 6. Due to the number of qubits, the circuit should work on all local devices, simulators, and quantum devices and provide good results.

> **Note – Each Run Will Generate a Different Circuit**
> Since the circuit is randomly generated, when you run the code, you will end up generating a different circuit with different results. Have fun!

Later, we will compare the results when using larger circuits.

Execution on a local device

In this section, we will review the code as we implement the circuit using matrix math and use simulators on local devices. Let's get started:

1. To create a circuit for 7 qubits and repeat the circuit twice, we must enter the following code:

```
q=7
r=2
Ufinal, g_circ=qc_rand(q,r)
```

The equation returns both the randomly generated unitary, Ufinal, and its equivalent quantum circuit, g_circ.

2. We can view this circuit by printing it:

```
print(g_circ)
```

Output:

```
T   : |0|1|2|3|4|5|
q0  : -H-X-I-X-C-H-

              |

q1  : -H-I-C-X-X-H-

              |
```

```
q2  :  -H-I-X-X-C-H-

                |

q3  :  -H-T-C-T-X-H-

                |

q4  :  -H-X-X-X-C-H-

                |

q5  :  -H-X-C-X-X-H-

                |

q6  :  -H-Z-X-Z-I-H-

T   :  |0|1|2|3|4|5|
```

Notice that the gate position, $T:0$, has the Hadamard gates, the $T:1$ position has the random single-qubit gates (X,I,T, and Z), and the $T:2$ position has the two-qubit CNOT gates. Positions $T:3$ and $T:4$ repeat with a new set of single-qubit gates and a different positioning of the CNOT gates to entangle a different set of qubits. Finally, $T:5$ has Hadamard gates on all its qubits. We can use the values of T to determine the gate depth of the circuit or use the g_circ.depth function.

3. We can also view a portion of the $2^7 \times 2^7$ unitary matrix, as follows:

```
    print(Ufinal)
```

Output:

```
[[-7.13653841e-20+2.87907611e-19j
7.13653841e-20+5.79454127e-19j

  -5.00000000e-01-5.00000000e-01j ...    7.13653841e-20-
5.79454127e-19j

    1.42730768e-19-2.89363173e-18j
0.00000000e+00+0.00000000e+00j]

 [ 7.13653841e-20-2.87907611e-19j
5.00000000e-01+5.00000000e-01j

  -7.13653841e-20-5.79454127e-19j ...
-1.80608886e-18+1.44681586e-18j

    0.00000000e+00+0.00000000e+00j
1.42730768e-19+5.75815222e-19j]

 [ 1.66335809e-18-2.02263109e-18j   7.13653841e-20-
5.79454127e-19j

    7.13653841e-20-1.44681586e-18j ...
```

```
7.13653841e-20+5.79454127e-19j

   1.42730768e-19+1.15890825e-18j
0.00000000e+00+0.00000000e+00j]

 ...

 [-7.13653841e-20+2.87907611e-19j
1.80608886e-18+1.44681586e-18j

   7.13653841e-20+5.79454127e-19j ...   5.27553581e-18-
1.44681586e-18j

   0.00000000e+00+0.00000000e+00j -1.42730768e-19-
5.75815222e-19j]
 [-8.60225200e-18+5.49207804e-18j
-7.13653841e-20+5.79454127e-19j

  -7.13653841e-20+1.44681586e-18j ... -7.13653841e-20-
5.79454127e-19j

  -1.42730768e-19-1.15890825e-18j
0.00000000e+00+0.00000000e+00j]
 [-7.13653841e-20-2.87907611e-19j   7.13653841e-20-
1.44681586e-18j

   7.13653841e-20-5.79454127e-19j ...
7.13653841e-20+1.44681586e-18j

   0.00000000e+00+0.00000000e+00j
-1.42730768e-19+5.75815222e-19j]]
```

Keep in mind that this is a 2^7 x 2^7 (128x128) matrix.

4. Now, we can apply the unitary to an array that represents the initial state of $|00000000000\rangle$. The following code is mostly printing the results by squaring each amplitude in the results to convert them from amplitudes into probability of measurements, then turning the results into a percentage for plotting:

```
n=q
x_val=[]
y_val=[]
init_arr=np.zeros((2**n,1))
init_arr[0]=1
shots=1000
result=shots*np.square(np.abs(Ufinal @ init_arr))
y_val_t=(result.T.ravel())
```

```
for i in range (len(y_val_t)):
    y_val.append(int(100*y_val_t[i]/shots))
x_val=range(2**n)
x_index=np.argsort(x_val)
for i in (x_index):
    if y_val[i]>=1:
        print(x_val[i],':', y_val[i])
plt.bar(x_val, y_val)
plt.xlabel('states');
plt.ylabel('percent');
plt.title('q='+str(n)+', r='+str(r)+
          ' Unitary Matrix Multiplication')
plt.rcParams["figure.figsize"] = (30,30)
plt.rcParams['figure.dpi'] = 150
plt.show()
```

Output:

```
6 : 49

30 : 49
```

There are a total of 128 possible states or values based on the seven qubits that are used. This circuit produces two results: one is 6 with a probability of 49% and the other is 30 with a probability of 49%. These values have been rounded, and there might be other probabilities smaller than 1% that have been ignored for our purposes:

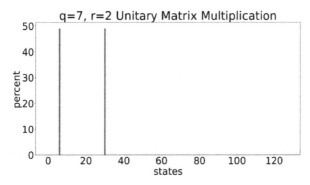

Figure 6.18 – Resulting state probabilities from matrix multiplication

5.   Now, let's convert the unitary matrix into a circuit. This can be done using a function provided in Amazon Braket called `.unitary(matrix=Unitary, targets=targets)`, where `Unitary` is the matrix being added to the circuit and `targets` is a list of all the qubits that the unitary will span. In our case, `targets=[0,1,2,3,4,5,6]`:

```
targets=[]
circ_Ufinal=Circuit()
for I in range (n):
    targets.append(i)
circ_Ufinal=circ_Ufinal.unitary(matrix=Ufinal,
                                    targets=targets)
print(circ_Ufinal)
```

Output:

```
T   :  |0|

q0  : -U-
        |

q1  : -U-
        |

q2  : -U-
        |

q3  : -U-
        |

q4  : -U-
        |

q5  : -U-
        |

q6  : -U-
T   :  |0|
```

The preceding output shows a quantum circuit built out of only one unitary matrix.

6. Now, we will see that executing this unitary circuit is equivalent to the matrix multiplication we did in *Step 4*. We will set the device as a `LocalSimulator` and then run the `circ_Ufinal` circuit using `device.run()`. Please note that in the code, we are converting the resulting counts into percentages using `y_val.append(int(100*i/shots))` and only showing values equal to or greater than 1% to keep the output constrained using `if y_val[i]>=1`:

```
device = LocalSimulator()
shots=1000
result = device.run(circ_Ufinal, shots=shots).result()
counts = result.measurement_counts

#print(counts)
x_val=[]
y_val=[]
for i in (counts.keys()):
    x_val.append(int(i,2))

for i in (counts.values()):
    y_val.append(int(100*i/shots))

x_index=np.argsort(x_val)
for i in (x_index):
    if y_val[i]>=1:
        print(x_val[i],':', y_val[i])
plt.bar(x_val, y_val, color='b')
plt.title('q='+str(n)+', r='+str(r)+
        ' Unitary on LocalSimulator')
plt.xlabel('states');
plt.ylabel('percent');
plt.rcParams["figure.figsize"] = (20,10)
plt.rcParams['figure.dpi'] = 300
plt.show()
```

Output:

```
6 : 52
30 : 47
```

Notice that the results in the output are the same two values as in *Step 4*; that is, 6 and 30. However, the percentages are a bit different due to all the other smaller probabilities being rounded:

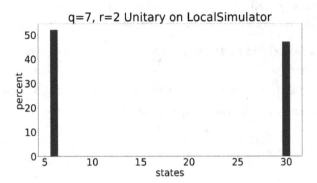

Figure 6.19 – Resulting state probabilities after using a gate circuit based on the single unitary

7. Now, we will run the gate circuit, g_circ, that was generated in *Step 1*. Here, we only show the relevant part of the circuit that gets the results. The rest of the code is similar to that in *Step 6*. The full code is available in this chapter's code repository:

```
result = device.run(g_circ, shots=shots).result()
```

Output:

6 : 48

30 : 52

Again, the two values that are in the output have approximately the same percentages they had previously:

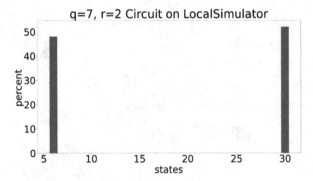

Figure 6.20 – The resulting state probabilities after using the gate quantum circuit on LocalSimulator

With that, we have evaluated the quantum circuit using matrix math and done the same on local simulators. In the next subsection, we will use the Amazon Braket simulators.

Execution on Amazon Braket simulators

In this section, we will continue running the 7 x 2 circuit on both the SV1 and TN1 Amazon Braket simulators:

1. First, we will run the same unitary circuit on the SV1 simulator. The necessary code required is shown here:

    I. The following code will assign the device to SV1 using the set_device() function that is provided in the code for this chapter. The cost for the device can be found using the estimate_cost() function provided in the code:

    ```
    device_name='SV1'
    device=set_device(device_name)
    estimate_cost(device)
    ```

    Output:

    ```
    Device('name': SV1, 'arn': arn:aws:braket:::device/quantum-
    simulator/amazon/sv1)

    simulator cost per  minute : $ 0.075

    total cost cannot be estimated
    ```

    I. Now, we can calculate the estimated number of shots using the estimate_cost_measured_qubits() function, which is provided in the code for this chapter:

    ```
    shots=estimate_cost_measured_qubits(device, n)
    ```

    Output:

    ```
    max shots: 100000

    for 7 measured qubits the number of shots recommended: 3,200

    simulator cost per  minute : $ 0.075

    total cost cannot be estimated
    ```

II.   Now, let's run the unitary circuit, `circ_Ufinal`, on SV1. Note that before executing an Amazon Braket device, ensure that you have assigned the values of `s3_folder`:

```
title='q='+str(n)+', r='+str(r)+' Unitary on '+device_
name
result=run_circuit(device, circ_Ufinal, shots, s3_folder,
title, False)
```

Output:

```
6 : 50

30 : 49
```

This results in the following chart:

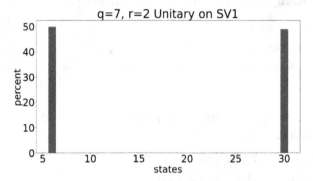

Figure 6.21 – Resulting state probabilities after using the unitary circuit on SV1

2.   We will repeat the same process using `g_circ` on SV1:

```
title='q='+str(n)+', r='+str(r)+' Gate circuit on
'+device_name
result=run_circuit(device, g_circ, shots, s3_folder,
title, False)
```

Output:

```
6 : 50

30 : 49
```

This results in the following chart:

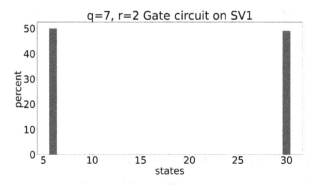

Figure 6.22 – Resulting state probabilities after using the gate circuit on SV1

3. On TN1, we can only run the gate circuit. The following is the code and output from the TN1 execution:

I.   Assign the device:

```
device_name='TN1'
device=set_device(device_name)
estimate_cost(device)
```

Output:

```
Device('name': TN1, 'arn': arn:aws:braket:::device/quantum-
simulator/amazon/tn1)
```

```
simulator cost per  minute : $ 0.275
```

```
total cost cannot be estimated
```

I.   Estimate the shots:

```
shots=estimate_cost_measured_qubits(device, n)
```

Output:

```
max shots: 1000
```

```
for 7 measured qubits the maximum allowed shots: 1,000
```

```
simulator cost per  minute : $ 0.275
```

```
total cost cannot be estimated
```

II.   Run the circuit:

```
title='q='+str(n)+', r='+str(r)+' Gate circuit on
'+device_name
result=run_circuit(device, g_circ, shots, s3_folder,
title, False)
```

Output:

```
6 : 49
```

```
30 : 50
```

The probabilities of the two states are also shown in the following bar chart:

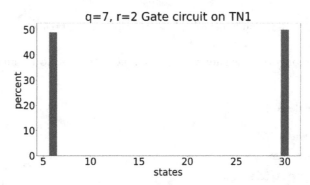

Figure 6.23 – Resulting state probabilities after using the gate circuit on TN1

So far, we have seen that all these devices practically give the same results – at least, at the current number of qubits. This was intended to drive the point that all simulators should give the same values and that those values are consistent with matrix multiplication, which we learned about in this chapter.

In the next subsection, we will execute the same circuit, g_circ, on the IonQ device, as well as on the Rigetti Aspen M-1 device.

Execution on quantum devices

So far, we have executed the random circuit on simulators. Now, we will run it on quantum devices. We have access to IonQ, which has 11 qubits, and Rigetti's Aspen M-1 quantum computer, which has 80 qubits. Of course, we will only use 7 qubits for this circuit. This process will give you a hands-on perspective regarding the performance of current quantum computers. Follow these steps:

> **Warning**
>
> Please only execute this section of the code if you are willing to be charged the cost of the quantum devices based on the number of shots submitted.

1. First, we set must the device to `IonQ Device`. Next, we must estimate the number of shots based on the number of qubits that will be measured and then we run the circuit:

    I.   Assign the device:

    ```
    device_name='IonQ Device'
    device=set_device(device_name)
    estimate_cost(device)
    ```

    Output:

    ```
    Device('name': IonQ Device, 'arn': arn:aws:braket:::device/
    qpu/ionq/ionQdevice)

    device cost per  shot : $ 0.01

    total cost for 1000 shots is $10.30
    ```

    II.   Estimate the shots:

    ```
    shots=estimate_cost_measured_qubits(device, n)
    ```

    Output:

    ```
    max shots: 10000

    for 7 measured qubits the number of shots recommended: 3,200

    device cost per  shot : $ 0.01

    total cost for 3200 shots is $32.30
    ```

    I.   Run the circuit:

    ```
    title='q='+str(n)+', r='+str(r)+
       ' Gate circuit on '+device_name
    result=run_circuit(device, g_circ, shots, s3_folder,
                     title, False)
    ```

    Output:

    ```
    0 : 1

    2 : 2

    6 : 44

    14 : 1
    ```

```
22 : 2
26 : 2
30 : 36
38 : 1
```

The following bar chart shows the results:

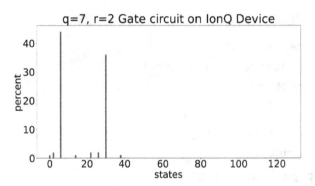

Figure 6.24 – Resulting state probabilities after running the gate circuit on the IonQ device

This is the first time we have seen other resulting values with small probabilities. It should be noted that the IonQ device has fully connected qubits and a reasonably low error rate. However, the probabilities of our two primary numbers have reduced to 44% and 36%, respectively. With more repetitions, these probabilities will reduce further due to errors arising in the execution of the gate operations.

> **Note – Using Native Gates to Improve Results**
>
> We have not used **native** gate operations for IonQ. Native gate operations are ideal for quantum computers. Single-qubit gate operations and especially two-qubit gate operations that use native gates have the least error. More information on this can be found in the *Further reading* section.

2. Now, we will repeat the same steps on the available Rigetti Aspen device. Please run the `available_devices()` function to check which Aspen device is available. As of this writing both Aspen 11 and Aspen-M-1 quantum processors have been available at different times. Since Aspen has limited connectivity between qubits, it is important to set up the circuit with the architecture in mind. This will result in fewer errors in the output.

> **Note – Aspen M-1 Connectivity**
>
> The `device.properties.dict()['paradigm']['connectivity']` function can be used to determine the connectivity between qubits.

The following code shows how to determine the Rigetti-M-1 quantum processor's connectivity and embed the quantum circuit on qubits that are connected:

I.   Assign the device:

```
device_name='Aspen-M-1'
device=set_device(device_name)
estimate_cost(device)
```

Output:

```
Device('name': Aspen-M-1, 'arn': arn:aws:braket:us-west-
1::device/qpu/rigetti/Aspen-M-1)

device cost per  shot : $ 0.00035

total cost for 1000 shots is $0.65
```

I.   Estimate the shots:

```
shots=estimate_cost_measured_qubits(device, n)
```

Output:

```
max shots: 100000

for 7 measured qubits the number of shots recommended: 3,200

device cost per  shot : $ 0.00035

total cost for 3200 shots is $1.42
```

II.   Determine the Aspen connectivity:

```
device.properties.dict()['paradigm']['connectivity']
```

Output:

```
{'fullyConnected': False,
 'connectivityGraph': {'0': ['1', '103', '7'],
  '1': ['0', '16', '2'],
  '10': ['11', '113', '17'],
  '100': ['101', '107'],
  '101': ['100', '102', '116'],
  '102': ['101', '103', '115'],
```

```
'103': ['0', '102', '104'],

...

'2': ['1', '15'],

...

'5': ['4', '6'],
'6': ['5', '7'],
'7': ['0', '6']}}
```

Based on this output, it appears that qubits 2 and 3 are not connected. The qubit connectivity appears to be as follows:

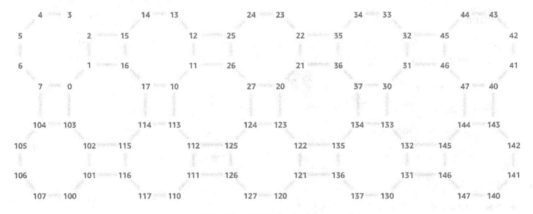

Figure 6.25 – Rigetti M-1 qubit connectivity

Since qubits 2 and 3 are not connected, the default embedding will use different qubit combinations and can result in a mapping we do not prefer. To hardcode the embedding, we will need to recreate the quantum circuit with the required qubit numbers.

III.   Rebuild the quantum circuit with the desired qubit mapping:

```
m=[10,11,12,13,14,15,16]
q=7
r=2
n=q
g_circ=Circuit().h([m[0],m[1],m[2],m[3],m[4],m[5],m[6]])
g_circ=g_circ.x(m[0]).i(m[1]).i(m[2]).t(m[3]).x(m[4]).x(m
[5]).z(m[6])
g_circ=g_circ.i(m[0]).cnot(m[1],m[2]).cnot(m[3],m[4]).
cnot(m[5],m[6])
g_circ=g_circ.x(m[0]).x(m[1]).x(m[2]).t(m[3]).x(m[4]).x(m
```

```
[5]).z(m[6])
g_circ=g_circ.cnot(m[0],m[1]).cnot(m[2],m[3]).
cnot(m[4],m[5]).i(m[6])
g_circ=g_circ.h([m[0],m[1],m[2],m[3],m[4],m[5],m[6]])
print(g_circ)
```

Output:

```
T    : |0|1|2|3|4|5|

q10 : -H-X-I-X-C-H-
                  |

q11 : -H-I-C-X-X-H-
                  |

q12 : -H-I-X-X-C-H-
                  |

q13 : -H-T-C-T-X-H-
                  |

q14 : -H-X-X-X-C-H-
                  |

q15 : -H-X-C-X-X-H-
                  |

q16 : -H-Z-X-Z-I-H-

T    : |0|1|2|3|4|5|
```

The preceding code creates the same random circuit we used on the simulators and IonQ. However, in this case, we are defining specific qubit numbers we want to use on the Rigetti Aspen M-1 device. This circuit is specifically for the Rigetti QPU as other devices do not allow us to skip qubit numbers. To enforce this embedding on the Rigetti device, we need to use the `disable_qubit_rewiring=True` parameter, as shown here:

```
result = device.run(circuit, shots=shots,
    s3_destination_folder=s3_folder,
    disable_qubit_rewiring=True).result()
```

Please review the `run_rigetti()` code to see how this is used. The rest of the code is the same as it is for `run_circuit()`. Let's proceed.

IV.   Run the circuit:

```
title='q='+str(n)+',  r='+str(r)+
  ' Gate circuit on '+device_name
result=run_rigetti(device, g_circ, shots, s3_folder,
                   title, False)
```

Output:

Device('name': Aspen-M-1, 'arn': arn:aws:braket:us-west-1::device/qpu/rigetti/Aspen-M-1)

0 : 1

2 : 2

4 : 1

6 : 11

10 : 1

14 : 4

22 : 1

24 : 1

26 : 2

30 : 11

38 : 3

46 : 2

54 : 1

58 : 1

62 : 5

70 : 1

94 : 1

98 : 1

102 : 5

110 : 2

118 : 2

120 : 1

```
122 : 1
126 : 5
```

The output values are in percent. As shown in the following chart, we have many more results showing up in the output with smaller probabilities:

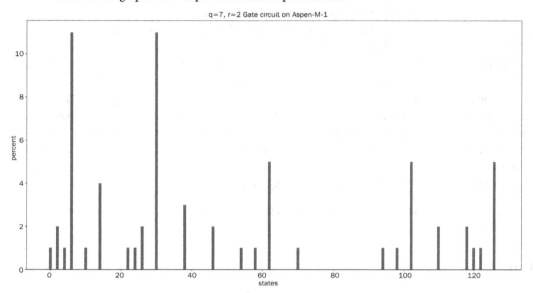

Figure 6. 26 – Resulting state probabilities after running the gate circuit on the Rigetti Aspen-M-1 device

The probability of detecting the two primary numbers, 6 and 30, is now at 11%. Any more repetitions in this circuit and we would not be able to detect the expected output. Also, if we "carelessly" placed a circuit on the Aspen architecture and didn't try to carefully optimize the circuit to qubit connections, we would see more errors.

This exercise, along with the code samples and functions, should help you create sample quantum circuits or even build an equivalent unitary matrix using tensor products and matrix multiplication. The value will come from finding real use cases that require tensor products and then determining the equivalent gate model. The simulators can provide cost-effective ways of testing considerably large circuits. The Google Supremacy experiment is a great learning opportunity. You can try using different gates with random rotations as well, such as the RX, RY, and RZ gates. Many quantum gates are in the literature, and it is also important to review the gates that are available in the quantum devices. Gates such as xx, yy, and zz are available on IonQ and provide unique and flexible unitary matrices and qubit rotations to work with.

Summary

In this chapter, we looked at the basics of quantum gates and quantum circuits. Quantum circuits provide you with a unique opportunity to practice tensor products and work with complex numbers. We worked with simple matrices and showed how unitary matrices represent quantum gates. First, we experimented with a single-qubit system and looked at an example of encoding the time on a single qubit. Then, we learned how a quantum circuit with multiple qubits can be represented by tensor products and matrix multiplication, which leads to simulated results. Amazon Braket provides its own set of simulators that can take gate circuit instructions and provide the resulting probabilities. We saw that by using Amazon Braket simulators, it is possible to simulate considerably large circuits. Even though these classical resources take time, it will be advantageous to build up your skills to solve problems with these simulators while better quantum computers are developed that have been scaled up with more qubits and are less error-prone. We took our knowledge of developing a quantum circuit to build a random circuit inspired by the Google Supremacy experiment. We compared the results between our unitary matrix and those from the Amazon local simulator, the SV1 and TN1 simulators, and the IonQ and Rigetti AspenM-1 quantum computers.

Having gone over the basics of quantum circuits, in the next chapter, we will take the next step toward quantum algorithms.

Further reading

To learn more about the topics that were covered in this chapter, take a look at the following resources:

- Mathematics of quantum computing books by Packt Publishing:

  - *Essential Mathematics for Quantum Computing*, by *Leonard S. Woody III*: https://www.packtpub.com/product/programming/9781801073141

  - *Dancing with Qubits*, by *Robert S. Sutor*: https://www.packtpub.com/product/data/9781838827366

- Amazon Braket Documentation: https://docs.aws.amazon.com/braket/latest/developerguide

- Google Supremacy papers: https://www.nature.com/articles/s41586%20019%201666%205

- Response from IBM: https://www.ibm.com/blogs/research/2019/10/on-quantum-supremacy/

- NumPy functions:

  - https://numpy.org/doc/stable/reference/generated/numpy.kron.html

  - https://numpy.org/doc/stable/reference/generated/numpy.matmul.html

- OpenQASM support in Amazon Braket:

  https://github.com/aws/amazon-braket-examples/blob/main/examples/braket_features/Getting_Started_with_OpenQASM_on_Braket.ipynb

- IonQ native gates:

  - https://ionq.com/docs/get-started-with-amazon-braket

  - https://ionq.com/docs/getting-started-with-native-gates

- Rigetti native gates and qubit connectivity:

  - https://qcs.rigetti.com/qpus

  - https://docs.aws.amazon.com/braket/latest/developerguide/braket-submit-to-qpu.html

  - https://aws.amazon.com/braket/quantum-computers/rigetti/

- Use the following code to find all supported gates:

  ```
  device.properties.dict()['action']['braket.ir.jaqcd.
  program']['supportedOperations']
  ```

- Use the following code to find native gates:

  ```
  device.properties.paradigm.nativeGateSet
  ```

- Use the following function to evaluate the connectivity:

  ```
  device.properties.dict()['paradigm']['connectivity']
  ```

- Use the following setting to disable automated embedding of the circuit on qubits:

- ```
  disable_qubit_rewiring=True
  ```
  ```

Code deep dive:

Please review the code for the following functions, which were provided as part of the code for this chapter and can be found in this book's GitHub repository:

- `qc_rand()`
- `run_circuit()`
- `run_rigetti()`

7
Using Gate Quantum Computers – Basic Quantum Algorithms

In this chapter, we'll continue exploring gate quantum computers and dive further into building some basic algorithms using gates. In the previous chapter, we introduced various gate operations and showed how quantum gates were randomly used to compare a quantum circuit with classical results in the Google supremacy experiment. However, in this chapter, we will use gates in a more meaningful way to show that certain, specific calculations can be performed on quantum computers that are dramatically different from the way calculations are performed on a classical computer. Several very famous algorithms have been developed for quantum computers over time. In this book, we will focus on only a few of these algorithms by experimenting with Amazon Braket simulators and external devices. Our goal is to develop a general intuition of how information is stored on qubits and how it can be manipulated. For examples of other quantum algorithms, as well as a deep dive into the algorithms covered here, please review the *Further reading* section.

In *Chapter 6, Using Gate-Based Quantum Computers – Qubits and Quantum Circuits*, we introduced the Bloch sphere and showed how the qubit vector was defined by its angle from the vertical z-axis, as well as its angle around the equator, which is measured from the $|+\rangle$ state. The former can be used to calculate probability amplitudes and thus the probability of measuring qubit states, while the latter represents a phase angle. We also covered how a Hadamard gate or operator moves the qubit vector from the $|0\rangle$ state, which is on the z-axis, to the $|+\rangle$ state at the equator, after which we can rotate the vector along the equator using various gates that produce a z rotation and introduce phase information. This chapter will deal with information along the z-axis, also known as the Computational basis, and phase information, which we will refer to as the Fourier basis.

The ability to increase the probability of measuring a state is known as **amplitude amplification**. It is a key component of **Grover's algorithm**, which is used to *bring out* the values we are searching for that are stored in a circuit. This is called an **Oracle**.

We will also learn how to move information between the Computational basis and the Fourier basis using a quantum algorithm called the **Quantum Fourier Transform** (**QFT**). The QFT and its inverse are used frequently in quantum computing and are key components of Shor's algorithm, which leverages QFT. We will also see how QFT is used in addition, by *adding* to the phase information of a set of qubits.

In this chapter, we will cover the following topics:

- What is a quantum Oracle?
- Observing the effect of amplitude amplification
- Working with phases

Technical requirements

The source code for this chapter can be found in this book's GitHub repository at `https://github.com/PacktPublishing/Quantum-Computing-Experimentation-with-Amazon-Braket/tree/main/Chapter07`.

What is a quantum Oracle?

In a classical computer, information is stored in memory or a database. Typically, when we perform operations, the data is copied from its storage location to the CPU so that the operation can be performed. If we are searching for a value in a string, an array, or a database, this operation must read the memory and decide whether we have found a match or not. All this happens very fast and under layers of software that instruct the computer to perform the action in the most efficient manner at the processor level.

If we are going to search for a number in a database, or if we are going to determine which bits in memory are a 0 versus a 1, then at the lowest system level, the data must be read in groups of bits from memory and compared. At the time of writing, there is no equivalent to **random-access memory** (**RAM**) or **read-only memory** (**ROM**), nor a database that can store information for a long time so that it can be accessed as needed. The simple circuits we created in the previous chapters started with a quantum register with all the qubits initialized to a $|0\rangle$ state. Then, we added gates to implement the operations. If we wanted the qubit to start in a $|1\rangle$ state, we would use an X gate and switch the value of the qubit to a $|1\rangle$ state. This, in effect, is a way to bring data into a quantum register. What if we wanted to simulate a function that returns a specific value, or a conditional clause that returns specific values based on the input states? Since we can't fully implement RAM, ROM, a database, or a function, we must add it to the circuit as a sort of black box with the *answer* already programmed. This is called the **Oracle**. Then, we operate on the Oracle, assuming that, in the future, it will represent a futuristic quantum memory of sorts, where all the values are stored in a long-term superposition. Then, based on the algorithm, we can perform our operation and reveal the answer.

It may almost seem like cheating if we add an array while knowing where the hidden value is, only to then search for it; or convert a number into phase information, only to use an algorithm to reveal it from the phase information. We should also note that this process requires *loading* all the data or information in advance of running our algorithm. To some extent, the very act of loading the information means that you know all the information. However, that is the situation currently. In code, I can just use the db variable to store the initial value or circuit – this will be our Oracle. Hopefully, in the future, we will have a quantum database that we can point to and perform our operations on, but for now, this Oracle or database will need to be set up in the circuit initially.

We will use this Oracle in our first algorithm.

Observing the effect of amplitude amplification

We have already learned that, in a quantum system, we can have 2^n states, where n is the number of qubits. One of the advantages of a quantum computer is that you can control those variables. For example, let's say that we want to embed a number, such as 2, in a quantum computer so that when we measure the quantum system, the variable 2 (or 10 in binary) shows up with the highest probability possible. How could we selectively add these desired numbers to a quantum circuit?

Let's work through this example, which is a slightly different way to approach amplitude amplification, though I hope it will make the whole process clearer.

Our goal is to measure the desired numbers in the output with high probability; the remaining numbers should have a low probability. One way to do this would be by creating a matrix that stores our numbers and then running an operator that will amplify the amplitude of those numbers.

We will represent the position of the value(s) we want to embed along the diagonal, as follows:

$$\begin{bmatrix} [00] & 0 & 0 & 0 \\ 0 & [01] & 0 & 0 \\ 0 & 0 & [10] & 0 \\ 0 & 0 & 0 & [11] \end{bmatrix} \quad eq.\,7.1$$

The value that we want to store will become a -1, while the rest of the diagonal elements will be 1s. The non-diagonal values will remain as zeros. So, if we want to embed the number 2 (or 10 in binary), then the matrix must look like this:

$$\begin{bmatrix} 1 & 0 & 0 & 0 \\ 0 & 1 & 0 & 0 \\ 0 & 0 & -1 & 0 \\ 0 & 0 & 0 & 1 \end{bmatrix} \quad eq.\,7.2$$

If we create a circuit that represents this and then measure the qubits, we won't see 10 as the predominant probability, so we need a circuit that can bring the number out or find it if it is stored in the Oracle. Some of the quantum circuits that represent these matrices are more difficult to create than others, and this is an active area of research. A simple circuit to create the number 3 can be created using a new two-qubit gate called the CZ gate. The matrix representation of the number 3 (or 11 in binary), also known as the CZ gate, is shown here:

$$\begin{bmatrix} 1 & 0 & 0 & 0 \\ 0 & 1 & 0 & 0 \\ 0 & 0 & 1 & 0 \\ 0 & 0 & 0 & -1 \end{bmatrix} \quad eq.\,7.3$$

We will store this number in the Oracle so that it will be represented as the db database in terms of code.

The operator that will be applied to this matrix is called the **Grover operator** and it will increase the amplitude or probability of finding the $|11\rangle$ state. In this experiment, we won't worry about the actual process in which amplitude amplification works. Fortunately, it has been covered in many books, so some references to them have been provided at the end of this chapter in the *Further reading* section.

You have been provided with three functions:

- `init_db(n)`: This function allows you to initialize the quantum register using n as the number of qubits. This also limits the range of numbers you can store from 0 to 2^n. The return values include the db database and the maximum value, which is 2^n.

- `insert_db(values, db)`: This function will allow you to save a range of values in the Oracle or db. Note that `values` is a list, so if we want to store 0 and 3, we must pass [0,3].

- `query_db(db, n, m, limit=0, local=True, device_name="")`: This will apply the Grover operator to the Oracle and increase the amplitude of the value(s) we have stored.

Grover's operator using unitary matrices

In this section, we will show the validity of this concept using only unitary matrices for both the database and Grover's operator. This allows us to have complete flexibility over the values that have been embedded and use as many qubits as allowed by the simulator.

Let's try out the Grover operator in terms of code:

1. First, we will create and initialize a circuit of two qubits using `init_db()` and print out the matrix:

```
Qubits=2
db, dim=init_db(Qubits)
print(db)
```

Output:

```
range= 0 to  3
[[1. 0. 0. 0.]
 [0. 1. 0. 0.]
 [0. 0. 1. 0.]
 [0. 0. 0. 1.]]
```

This is just an initialized matrix and contains 1s in the diagonal.

2. Now, let's insert 3 using `insert_db`, as shown here:

```
db, m = insert_db([3],db)
print(db)
```

Output:

```
3 added to db
[[ 1.  0.  0.   0.]
 [ 0.  1.  0.   0.]
 [ 0.  0.  1.   0.]
 [ 0.  0.  0. -1.]]
```

The last diagonal has a -1 in it now. We are ready to send this to the Grover operator.

3. The `query_db` function will apply the Grover operator, measure the qubits on the local simulator, and provide the results:

```
result=query_db(db, Qubits, m ,1)
```

Output:

```
total size 4
qubits 2
db reads 1
{3: 1000}
```

The following bar chart shows that only the number 3 has been measured:

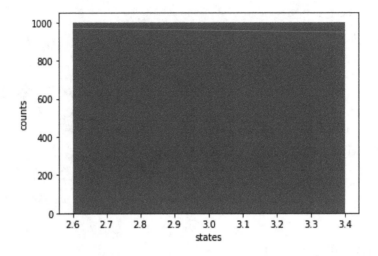

Figure 7.1 – Measuring the value of 3 after storing it in the database and using the Grover operator

4. Now, let's repeat this process and store 0, 15, 16, 41, 140, 200, 255 in an 8-qubit register. We must start with the following code:

```
Qubits=8
db, dim=init_db(Qubits)
db, m = insert_db([0, 15, 16, 41, 140, 200, 255], db)
print('total hidden values',m)
```

Output:

```
range= 0 to   255
0 added to db
15 added to db
16 added to db
41 added to db
140 added to db
200 added to db
255 added to db
total hidden values 7
```

5. Now, let's query the database and reveal the values that have been measured in the bar chart:

```
result=query_db(db, Qubits, m ,1)
```

The following chart shows the numbers that we had initially embedded in the database showing up with high counts:

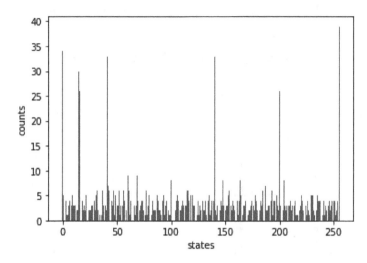

Figure 7.2 – Embedded values revealed after applying the Grover operator and measuring them

6. Now, let's send a 7-qubit database to an Amazon Braket simulator. As you may recall from the previous chapter, TN1 cannot process a unitary matrix, while SV1 can process up to a 7-qubit matrix as a unitary. Therefore, let's embed the same numbers in a 7-qubit system and then send it to SV1:

```
Qubits=7
db, dim=init_db(Qubits)
db, m = insert_db([0, 15, 16, 41, 140, 200, 255], db)
print('total hidden values',m)
```

Output:

```
range= 0 to  127
0 added to db
15 added to db
16 added to db
41 added to db
```

```
140 is too large, ignored
200 is too large, ignored
255 is too large, ignored
total hidden values 4
```

Notice that some of the values were not stored because our database is not large enough. In the next line, we will get the results.

7. Let's query the database by passing it to the SV1 simulator using the following code:

```
result=query_db(db, Qubits, m, 0, False, 'SV1' )
```

The following chart shows the results of the values that were saved in the database:

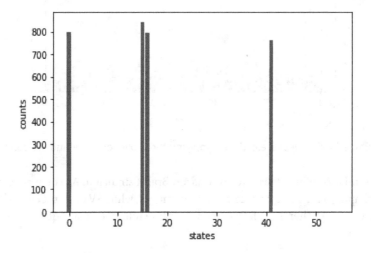

Figure 7.3 – Result of using the Grover operator on SV1

So far, we have tried embedding different values in a database represented by a matrix and showed that, using a unitary simulator, the Grover operator can ensure that the stored numbers are converted into higher probability amplitudes for those states. In the next section, we will do the same process on a gate quantum device.

Grover's search algorithm using quantum circuits

Now, let's attempt to do the same process that we followed in the previous section, only now using quantum gates and a quantum circuit that represent both the number that is being embedded and the Grover operation. We can also run this on a gate quantum computer. Since we are not using a matrix, there are limitations in terms of building the Grover operator as the key component is a multiple control Z gate. For our purposes, the CCX, which is a 3-qubit gate, and the CCCX, which is a 4-qubit gate, have been defined within the `query_circuit_db()` function. This will allow us to use the Grover operator with a database using up to 4 qubits. We can demonstrate this using a simple circuit and embed six numbers in the 4-qubit database.

Let's start with the simple example of embedding 3 in a 2-qubit database:

1. 3 has already been embedded in a 2-qubit database using the CZ gate. This gate can be seen in *Figure 7.3*. As shown there, the last diagonal value is -1. The first part of the circuit is shown here:

    ```
    db=Circuit().cz(0,1)
    print(db)
    ```

    Output:

    ```
    T   :  |0|

    q0 :  -C-
           |
    q1 :  -Z-
    T   :  |0|
    ```

    The circuit shows the CZ gate between qubit 0 and qubit 1. This represents how to create the Oracle. Now, let's add the Grover operation.

2. Let's run the circuit using the `query_circuit_db()` function. Notice that we add the database, the number of qubits, and the number of values stored in the database as parameters:

    ```
    result=query_circuit_db(db, 2, 1)
    ```

    Output:

    ```
    T   :  |0|1|2|3|4|5|6|

    q0 :  -H-C-H-X-C-X-H-
             |     |
    q1 :  -H-Z-H-X-Z-X-H-
    T   :  |0|1|2|3|4|5|6|
    ```

The following chart shows that we can reveal a value of 3 from the database. This run was made on a local simulator:

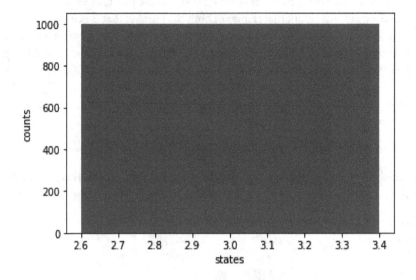

Figure 7.4 – A value of 3 has been revealed from the Grover search using a quantum circuit (there is only one bar at 3; please ignore the fractional values on the x-axis)

3. Next, we will create a 3-qubit Oracle and store two numbers – that is, 5 and 6. If we visualize the matrix, it will have eight diagonal elements. We want to have the diagonal elements that represent the numbers 5 and 6 have a value of -1. We can do this by using two CZ gates – one between qubit 0 and 1 and the other between qubit 0 and 2. We can do this using the following circuit:

```
db=Circuit().cz(0,1).cz(0,2)
print(db)
```

Output:

```
T   : |0|1|
q0  : -C-C-
         | |
q1  : -Z-|-
           |
q2  : ---Z-
T   : |0|1|
```

4. Again, let's use the `query_circuit_db()` function to reveal the circuit and the values stored in the Oracle. Notice that the circuit that's been implemented is much longer. The following code is creating the 3-qubit CCZ gate out of the allowed gates:

```
result=query_circuit_db(db, 3, 2)
```

Output:

```
T  : |0|1| 2 |3|4|5|6 |7|8|9|10|11|12|13|14|15|16|
q0 : -H-C-C---H-X------C--------C--C--T--C--X--H--
        | |            |        |  |     |
q1 : -H-Z-|-H-X---C----|---C-T--|--X--Ti-X--X--H--
          |       |        |  | |
q2 : -H---Z---H-X-X-Ti-X-T-X-Ti-X--T--X--H--------
T  : |0|1| 2 |3|4|5|6 |7|8|9|10|11|12|13|14|15|16|
```

5. Finally, let's create a 4-qubit Oracle and store six numbers in it. It turns out that adding two CX gates – one from qubit 0 to qubit 1 and the other from qubit 2 to qubit 3 – creates this effect. This Oracle can be created like so:

```
db=Circuit().cz(0,1).cz(2,3)
print(db)
```

Output:

```
T  : |0|
q0 : -C-
      |
q1 : -Z-
q2 : -C-
      |
q3 : -Z-
T  : |0|
```

6. To ensure that we have the desired circuit, let's quickly check it using a matrix representation of the gates and tensor product. In this step and the next, we will take a detour to build the matrix from CZ gates and confirm it has the -1 values in six positions on the diagonal. The matrix representation of the CZ gate is shown here:

$$\#CZ=|0\rangle\langle0|\otimes I+|1\rangle\langle1|\otimes Z$$

```
arr_cz=np.kron([[1,0],[0,0]],arr_i)+np.kron([[0,0],
               [0,1]], arr_z)
print(arr_cz)
```

Output:

```
[[ 1  0  0  0]
 [ 0  1  0  0]
 [ 0  0  1  0]
 [ 0  0  0 -1]]
```

Let's perform a tensor product on two CZ gates (**CZ** ⊗ **CZ**) to produce the matrix representation:

```
arr_czcz=np.kron(arr_cz,arr_cz)
print(arr_czcz)
```

Output:

```
[[ 1  0  0  0  0  0  0  0  0  0  0  0  0  0  0  0]
 [ 0  1  0  0  0  0  0  0  0  0  0  0  0  0  0  0]
 [ 0  0  1  0  0  0  0  0  0  0  0  0  0  0  0  0]
 [ 0  0  0 -1  0  0  0  0  0  0  0  0  0  0  0  0]
 [ 0  0  0  0  1  0  0  0  0  0  0  0  0  0  0  0]
 [ 0  0  0  0  0  1  0  0  0  0  0  0  0  0  0  0]
 [ 0  0  0  0  0  0  1  0  0  0  0  0  0  0  0  0]
 [ 0  0  0  0  0  0  0 -1  0  0  0  0  0  0  0  0]
 [ 0  0  0  0  0  0  0  0  1  0  0  0  0  0  0  0]
 [ 0  0  0  0  0  0  0  0  0  1  0  0  0  0  0  0]
 [ 0  0  0  0  0  0  0  0  0  0  1  0  0  0  0  0]
 [ 0  0  0  0  0  0  0  0  0  0  0 -1  0  0  0  0]
 [ 0  0  0  0  0  0  0  0  0  0  0  0 -1  0  0  0]
 [ 0  0  0  0  0  0  0  0  0  0  0  0  0 -1  0  0]]
```

```
[ 0   0   0   0   0   0   0   0   0   0   0   0   0   0  -1   0]
[ 0   0   0   0   0   0   0   0   0   0   0   0   0   0   0   1]]
```

According to the preceding output, we should expect to get 3, 7, 11, 12, 13 , and 14 as the numbers that are stored in the gate circuit's equivalent version.

7. Now, let's run the Grover search on the gate circuit Oracle with two CZ gates:

    ```
    result=query_circuit_db(db, 4, 6, 3)
    ```

    You will notice quite a large circuit in the output that also states db reads 3. This means that the Grover operator was run on this circuit three times. Why is this necessary? Before we answer this question, we can confirm that the following chart shows the appropriate values (3, 7, 11, 12, 13, and 14) with the higher counts:

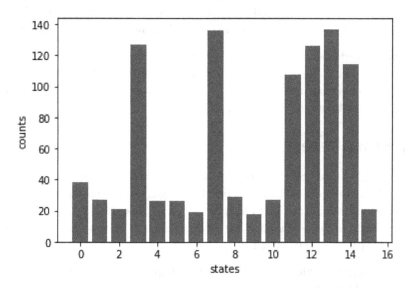

Figure 7.5 – Values detected from using the Grover search on an Oracle with CZ ⊗ CZ

Repetitions of the Grover diffuser operator

In the previous section, we saw db reads 3 in the output. This is the number of times the Grover operator was repeated. The number of times the operator is used can be calculated as follows:

$$r \approx \sqrt{\frac{2^n}{m}} \qquad eq.\,7.4$$

Here, n is the number of qubits, and m is the number of values stored.

In the `query_circuit_db()` function, the fourth parameter allows you to bypass the default calculation and limit or exceed the ideal value of `r`. This allows you to visually see the effect of each Grover operator on the *amplification* of the desired values. You may want to try this out and see what results you get.

Using Grover's algorithm in searches

In the previous subsection, we experimented with a function that implemented Grover's operator. We showed that if we were to store a set of numbers in an Oracle, then Grover's operator would only amplify the probability amplitudes of those numbers. In our case, we already knew the number. However, if the Oracle was part of a larger circuit or, in the future, it represented a quantum database search algorithm, the Grover operator would return the required search results. In addition, conditional clauses can also be created using quantum circuits so that they create the same effect in the Oracle.

In this section, we learned how to embed one or more numbers into a qubit and then use the Grover operator to amply the probability of measuring those specific numbers. This technique can be used to search for hidden values in an unstructured list. In the next section, we will look at another way of storing and transforming information in qubits.

Working with phases

In this section, we will discuss how information is stored in qubits in the measurement axis or the z-axis, also called the Computational basis, and the phase angle, which we will refer to as the Fourier basis. It is possible to store information in the phase angle of the qubits and then translate it into the measurement basis. In the next section, we will learn how to think about numbers and their representation in the phase angle of a qubit.

Let's start with the a variable, which represents a binary number. In our example, we will use a 5-bit number – that is, a=11111. To represent this binary number, we need a register of 5 bits. We can convert this number back into decimal by using the following equation:

$$a = a_4 \times 2^4 + a_3 \times 2^3 + a_2 \times 2^2 + a_1 \times 2^1 + a_0 \times 2^0 \qquad \text{eq. 7.5}$$

This will result in the following equation:

$$a = 16a_4 + 8a_3 + 4a_2 + 2a_1 + 1a_0 \qquad \text{eq. 7.6}$$

In terms of our example, where we are using a=11111, we will get the following equation:

$$a_4 = 1, a_3 = 1, a_2 = 1, a_1 = 1, a_0 = 1 \qquad \text{eq. 7.7}$$

Here, you can see that a4 has a contribution of 16 to a, while a_0 only has a contribution of 1 to a. It is clear that the value of $a = 16+8+4+2+1=31$.

In other words, our values go from 0, where digits a_0 to a_4 are 0 to 31, where all digits are *1*. If we were to represent this as a circle split into 32 sections, then we could fill the contribution of each digit as follows:

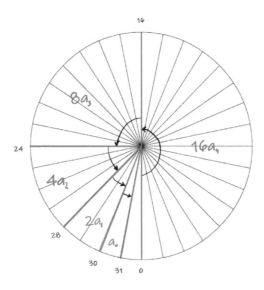

Figure 7.6 – Circle divided into 32 segments to represent 11111

If we only had four right-most bits, then we would have a total of 16 different values. By doing this, we could represent 1111 in the following way, ensuring that we take the contribution of each binary digit:

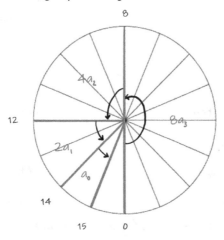

Figure 7.7 – Circle divided into 16 segments to represent 1111

Going further down the number of bits, if we only had 3 bits, then we could create a circle with eight segments. The contribution of each binary digit would be represented in the circle like so:

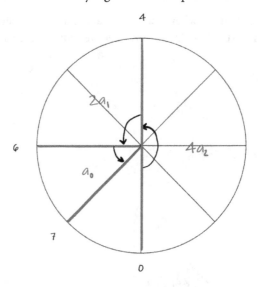

Figure 7.8 – Circle with eight segments to represent 111

We can continue this down to 1 bit. The following diagram shows the contributions of each bit as we move from all 5 bits down to a single bit:

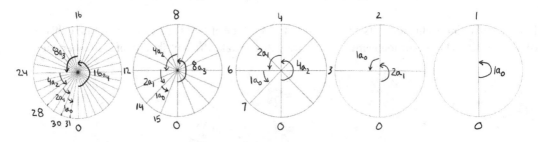

Figure 7.9 – Representation of 11111 on an incrementally smaller number of bits

Now, let's represent a different number to provide context. We can represent $a = 3$ using 5 bits, as follows:

$$a = a_4 a_3 a_2 a_1 a_0 = 00011 \qquad eq.\ 7.8$$

Once again, we get the following equation:

$$a = a_4 \times 2^4 + a_3 \times 2^3 + a_2 \times 2^2 + a_1 \times 2^1 + a_0 \times 2^0 \qquad eq.\ 7.9$$

Thus, we get the following output:

$$a = 0 + 0 + 0 + 1 \times 2 + 1 \times 1 \qquad eq.\,7.10$$

This can be represented like so:

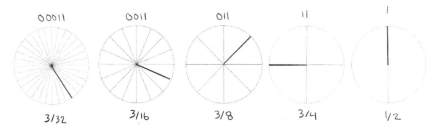

Figure 7.10 – Representation of 3 on incrementally smaller bit circles, starting with 5 bits

Note that on the left-hand side, we are representing the full number, 00011, which is 3 segments out of 32. However, as we reduce the number of bits, we reach a point at 1 bit where we cannot fully represent 3 anymore since it is represented by 11 in binary. The single bit can only hold a value of 1, so we can only represent one out of the two segments.

Repeating the same process for b= 5 with 5 bits, we can use the following equation:

$$b = b_4 b_3 b_2 b_1 b_0 = 00101 \qquad eq.\,7.11$$

In this case, we get the following equation:

$$b = b_4 \times 2^4 + b_3 \times 2^3 + b_2 \times 2^2 + b_1 \times 2^1 + b_0 \times 2^0 \qquad eq.7.12$$

Thus, we get the following output:

$$b = 0 + 0 + 1 \times 4 + 0 + 1 \times 1 \qquad eq.7.13$$

We can represent b with the circle segments, as shown here:

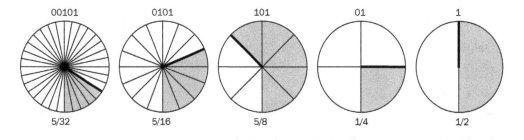

Figure 7.11 – Representation of 5 on incrementally smaller bit circles, starting with 5 bits

Notice that, with the left-most circle, we are moving 5 segments out of 32. The same goes for the 16-segment circle and even the 8-segment circle as the number of bits is reduced. Now, as we reach the 4-segment circle, we are only able to take on the two right-most digits – that is, 01. This is only 1 segment out of the 4. Finally, we end up with the right-most circle, which has the number 1 and thus uses one of the two segments.

We will use the same concept to store a number in the phase of qubits. If you imagine each circle as a view from the top of a Bloch sphere, looking down at the cross-section at the equator, then the rotated line represents how much the vector is rotated in the counterclockwise direction from the bottom, which represents zero degrees.

In the next section, we will review moving the qubit vector between the Computational basis and the phase angle, also known as the Fourier basis.

> **Note – Drawing Circuits and the Bloch Sphere**
>
> We are going to be using the `draw_circuit()` function, which was introduced and created in the previous chapter. Please refer back to the initial part of that chapter and the relevant GitHub code before proceeding. This function can only be used for one qubit circuit since the Bloch sphere can only represent one qubit.

Translating between the Computational basis and the Fourier basis

We have frequently used the Hadamard gate to move a qubit from the z-axis to the equator of the Bloch sphere. Let's repeat this process and add a small phase using the T gate. Then, we will use the Hadamard gate again and see what happens:

1. First, let's create a circuit and apply the Hadamard gate and the T gate to a single qubit, as shown here:

    ```
    circ=Circuit().h(0).t(0)
    draw_circuit(circ)
    ```

    Output:

    ```
    T  : |0|1|

    q0 : -H-T-

    T  : |0|1|

    Additional result types: StateVector

    Matrix:

    [[0.70710678+0.j ]
    ```

```
    [0.5          +0.5j]]
State Vector: |psi> = sqrt( [0.5] ) |0> + ( sqrt( [0.5] ))
e^i [0.25] pi |1>
```

The following diagram shows the direction of the qubit vector. The Hadamard gate brings the qubit vector to the |+⟩ state on the equator, and then the T gate rotates the vector along the equator by an angle of π/4 from the |+⟩ state:

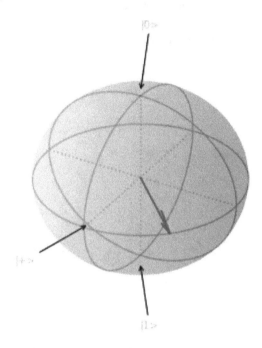

Figure 7.12 – Qubit state with a phase angle of π/4 degrees

2. Now, let's reapply the Hadamard gate:

    ```
    draw_circuit(circ.h(0))
    ```

    Output:

    ```
    T   : |0|1|2|

    q0  : -H-T-H-

    T   : |0|1|2|


    Additional result types: StateVector

    Matrix:
    ```

```
[[0.85355339+0.35355339j]
 [0.14644661-0.35355339j]]
```

```
State Vector: |psi> = sqrt( [0.85355339] ) |0> + ( sqrt(
[0.14644661] )) e^i [-0.5] pi |1>
```

The following diagram shows the vector moving back up, but not exactly at the |0⟩ state. The phase information is carried over to the measurement basis. Here, we can see that the probability of measuring a 0 has reduced to 0.85, while the probability of measuring a 1 has increased to 0.14:

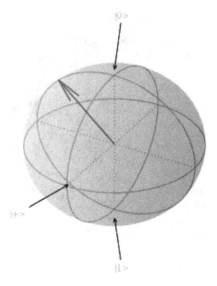

Figure 7.13 – Bloch sphere showing the resulting qubit state

In this section, we saw that we can treat adding phase information and measurement along the z-axis as a way to convert or translate from one type of information storage into another. In the next section, we will look at more examples of adding phase information to a qubit.

Adding phase information to a qubit

So far, we have learned how a number can be represented as phase angles on a series of circles, as well as how there might be some equivalence between the phase angle and the measurement of the qubit along the z-axis if the information is transferred from one basis to the other. In this section, we will take one qubit and incrementally add a π rotation, then $\pi/2$, and then $\pi/4$. This is similar to what we did in *Figure 7.8*. There, with a circle that had been divided into 8 segments, a π rotation represented a value of $4a_2$, the $\pi/2$ rotation represented $2a_1$, and, finally, the $\pi/4$ rotation represented a_0. Please refer to that figure to check this.

Now, we will add this same information to a qubit. We will use the `phaseshift()` function to add the phase to the qubit:

1. First, let's add a π rotation after applying the Hadamard gate to qubit 0:

    ```
    circ=Circuit().h(0).phaseshift(0,np.pi)
    draw_circuit(circ)
    ```

    Output:

    ```
    T  : |0|      1      |

    q0 : -H-PHASE(3.14)-

    T  : |0|      1      |


    Additional result types: StateVector
    Matrix:
    [[ 0.70710678+0.00000000e+00j]
     [-0.70710678+8.65956056e-17j]]


    State Vector: |psi> = sqrt( [0.5] ) |0> + ( sqrt( [0.5] ))
    e^i [1.] pi |1>
    ```

    The following chart shows that the qubit is pointing to the | -) state with a phase angle of `1.0 pi` (this is printed in the last line of the preceding output – that is, `e^i [1.] pi`):

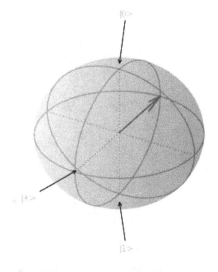

Figure 7.14 – Qubit state at |-) with π rotation

2. Now, let's add a phase angle of π/2:

```
circ=circ.phaseshift(0,np.pi/2)
draw_circuit(circ)
```

Output:

```
T   : |0|      1      |      2      |
q0  : -H-PHASE(3.14)-PHASE(1.57)-
T   : |0|      1      |      2      |


Additional result types: StateVector
Matrix:
[[ 7.07106781e-01+0.j            ]
 [-1.29893408e-16-0.70710678j]]


State Vector: |psi> = sqrt( [0.5] ) |0> + ( sqrt( [0.5] ))
e^i [-0.5] pi |1>
```

The following diagram shows the state of the qubit. As you can see, it has rotated counterclockwise by another half of the previous angle. This location is also known as the | - i⟩ state:

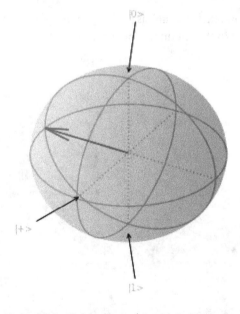

Figure 7.15 – Qubit state at |-i⟩ with 3π/4 rotation

3. Finally, let's rotate the qubit further by adding a phase angle of π/4:

```
circ=circ.phaseshift(0,np.pi/4)
draw_circuit(circ)
```

Output:

```
T  : |0|    1     |    2     |    3     |
q0 : -H-PHASE(3.14)-PHASE(1.57)-PHASE(0.785)-
T  : |0|    1     |    2     |    3     |


Additional result types: StateVector
Matrix:
[[0.70710678+0.j ]
 [0.5        -0.5j]]


State Vector: |psi> = sqrt( [0.5] ) |0> + ( sqrt( [0.5] ))
e^i [-0.25] pi |1>
```

We have arrived at the location we wanted with a phase angle of 7π/8 (the same as - π /4), as shown here:

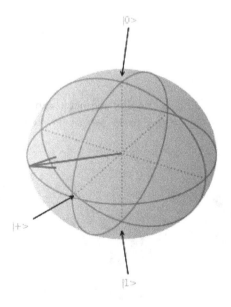

Figure 7.16 – Qubit state with 7π/8 rotation

With that, we've learned how to incrementally add phase information in a way that's similar to adding binary number information to the circles. In the next subsection, we will add a number to the phase information of multiple qubits using the method we have just discussed.

How the phase adder circuit is used in quantum circuits

The phase adder circuit will allow us to add phase information to a set of qubits in the same way as adding a phase to multiple circles. So far, we've learned how to move between the measurement x-axis (or the Computational basis) to the Fourier basis, where we can add phase information. Now, we will use the same method to add 3 to the phase angles of 5 qubits. We will add the binary number 00011, as shown in *Equation 7.8* to *Equation 7.10*. In the end, the qubit angles should look similar to those shown in *Figure 7.10*. The function to set up the desired quantity of qubits and embed the phase rotation based on the number (in decimal) is draw_multi_qubit_phase().

Let's add the phase information, review how that information would be represented if we were to measure the qubits, and then perform the phase estimation function to convert the phase information into amplitudes that can be measured to reveal the number:

1. When we execute the draw_multi_qubit_phase() function, we will get a series of Bloch spheres. The first represents the qubit or bit, 0, associated with a_0; the next is qubit 1 associated with a_1; and so on. Remember that qubit 0 has two segments, qubit 1 has four, and that qubit 4 has 32 segments:

    ```
    Qubits=5
    Number=3
    qc=draw_multi_qubit_phase(Qubits,Number)
    ```

    Output:

    ```
    Qubits: 5 Number: 3 binary: 00011
    ```

    The output also draws the five qubits one after another as can be seen in the GitHub code. The five Bloch spheres have been copied in the figure below to summarize the results.

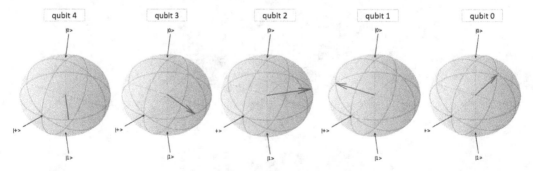

Figure 7.17 – Qubits representing the number 3 in the Fourier basis through phase angles

2. Now, let's review the circuit:

```
print(qc)
```

Output:

```
T   : |0|       1       |       2       |
q0  : -H-PHASE(3.14)---------------
q1  : -H-PHASE(3.14)--PHASE(1.57)--
q2  : -H-PHASE(1.57)--PHASE(0.785)-
q3  : -H-PHASE(0.785)-PHASE(0.393)-
q4  : -H-PHASE(0.393)-PHASE(0.196)-
T   : |0|       1       |       2       |
```

Please note that the preceding code just adds the appropriate angles to the qubits. Each qubit is separate and not entangled.

3. All the information is in the phase angles. If we were to measure this circuit, which has 5 qubits and therefore 32 possible values from 00000 to 11111, we would have an equal probability of getting each value. We can try this out by running the following code:

```
device = LocalSimulator()
result = device.run(qc, shots=10000).result()
counts = result.measurement_counts
print(counts)
# plot using Counter
plt.bar(counts.keys(), counts.values());
plt.xlabel('value');
plt.ylabel('counts');
```

The output is as follows. Notice that no specific information is available in the z-axis, nor the Computational basis that we measured in:

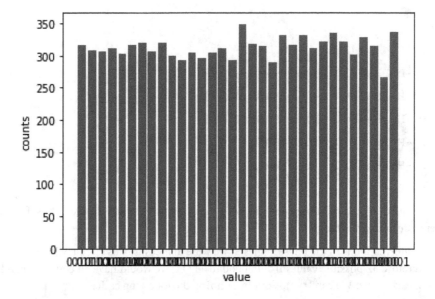

Figure 7.18 – Measurement of the qubits with information on the Fourier basis

4. Now, let's apply another function that will convert the information in the qubit phases into the z-axis. This function contains a series of phase gates based on the inverse quantum Fourier transform. We will use this function to transform the information on the Fourier basis into the Computational basis, where it can be measured. The code for the inverse QFT function, qft_inv_gate(), will be provided. This function represents the phase estimation algorithm. Detailed treatment of both QFT and its inverse has been provided in the *Further reading* section.

> **More Details on the Quantum Fourier Transform and Quantum Phase Estimation Algorithms**
>
> For our purposes, a detailed treatment of QFT or QPE is not necessary. If you are not familiar with QFT and inverse QFT/QPE or would like to understand these algorithms in more detail, please review the resources in the *Further reading* section.

To proceed, let's make a copy of our circuit and run the function on the copy. This way, we can use the original circuit again when needed:

```
qc_copy=qc.copy()
phase_circuit=qft_inv_gate(qc_copy,Qubits)
```

5. Now that we have transformed the phase information into the measurement basis, let's measure it using the following code:

```
device = LocalSimulator()
result = device.run(phase_circuit,
                    shots=1000).result()
counts = result.measurement_counts
print(counts)
# plot using Counter
plt.bar(counts.keys(), counts.values());
plt.xlabel('value');
plt.ylabel('counts');
```

Output:

```
Counter({'00011': 1000})
```

The preceding output shows 3 in binary, which we originally put in the phase information. The following bar chart also shows this value:

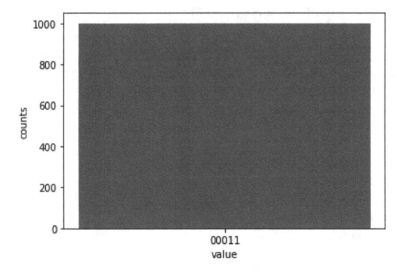

Figure 7.19 – A value of 3 measured after applying the inverse QFT function

With that, we've learned how phase information can be converted into measurement information using a function called the inverse QFT. This is a very useful function in many quantum algorithms, including Shor's algorithm.

In the next section, we will compare the circuit and add phase information with QFT.

Using Quantum Fourier Transform and its inverse

Now that we have learned how to code a binary number into phase information, you will find that the standard way of converting binary information in a quantum circuit into phase information follows the same process. Let's run the two functions and compare their circuits:

1. First, let's run the function that adds the phase information for the number 3 on only 3 qubits and prints the circuit:

```
Qubits=3
Number=3
qc=draw_multi_qubit_phase(Qubits,Number)
print(qc)
```

Output:

```
T   : |0|       1       |       2       |

q0  : -H-PHASE(3.14)--------------

q1  : -H-PHASE(3.14)-PHASE(1.57)-

q2  : -H-PHASE(1.57)-PHASE(0.785)-

T   : |0|       1       |       2       |
```

2. Now, let's run the function that will add the number in the circuit using X gates. In other words, it will move the default |0⟩ state to a |1⟩ state, where we have a 1 in the number. Thus, to create 011, we will apply an X gate to the first two qubits. Then, this function will perform a quantum Fourier transform on the qubits to transform the information into the Fourier basis:

```
device = LocalSimulator()
Qubits=3
num=3

qc=qc_num(num,Qubits)
qc=qft_gate(qc,Qubits)
print(qc)
```

Output:

```
T   : |0|       1       |       2       |       3       |4|

q0  : -X--------------C--------------C-----------H-
                      |              |
q1  : -X-C-----------|-----------H-PHASE(1.57)---
         |           |
```

```
q2 : -H-PHASE(1.57)-PHASE(0.785)-----------------
T  : |0|     1      |     2      |     3     |4|
```

Here, you can see that the X gate is in qubit 0 and qubit 1, which changes the initial state from $|000\rangle$ to $|011\rangle$). Next, the QFT circuit adds Hadamard gates to the qubit so that phase information will be added. Then, it uses several controlled phase gates to apply the appropriate phase rotations to the required qubit, just like when we applied phase rotations to store the number 3 earlier. One thing to note is that since the circuit only needs to add a Hadamard gate to move a qubit from the $|1\rangle$ state to the $|-\rangle$ state, a π rotation automatically occurs and that rotation does not need to be added to the QFT circuit in qubit 0 and qubit 1, as shown in the circuit in *step 1*. The rest of the phase angles are the same and the circuits are equivalent. Now, we have two ways to transform a number into a Fourier basis.

3. Now, if we do the inverse of the QFT, we should be able to move the phase information to the Computational basis and recover the same number from both circuits:

```
qc=qft_inv_gate(qc,Qubits)
print(qc)
device = LocalSimulator()
result = device.run(qc, shots=10000).result()
counts = result.measurement_counts
print(counts)
plt.bar(counts.keys(), counts.values());
plt.xlabel('value');
plt.ylabel('counts');
```

Output:

```
Counter({'011': 10000})
```

The preceding output shows the number 3 or 011 in binary, as we expected.

Here, we learned that we can convert a binary number into the phase information of qubits programmatically by adding incremental phase rotations, or that we can add the number to a quantum circuit and apply QFT. We also saw that a number in the Fourier basis does not show up when measured. We must use the inverse QFT circuit to move the information to the Computational basis; then, we can measure it.

In the final section, you will learn how to add numbers by adding the phases, thus giving us a circuit that is a phase adder.

Adding numbers using the phase adder

In this section, we will apply the tools we have gained from this chapter to add a number in the phase information of qubits:

1. First, let's create a circuit with the number 3 embedded in the phase of 5 qubits:

    ```
    Qubits=5
    Number=3
    qc_3=draw_multi_qubit_phase(Qubits,Number)
    print(qc_3)
    ```

    Output:

    ```
    Qubits: 5 Number: 3 binary: 00011
    ```

2. Next, let's create a circuit with the number 5 embedded in the phase of 5 qubits:

    ```
    Qubits=5
    Number=5
    qc_5=draw_multi_qubit_phase(Qubits,Number,False)
    print(qc_5)
    ```

    Output:

    ```
    Qubits: 5 Number: 5 binary: 00101
    ```

    Please note that in this case, the function's third parameter is set to False. This will prevent Hadamard gates from being added to the circuit again.

3. Now, let's use the add method from Amazon Braket to add the two circuits together:

    ```
    qc_total=qc_3.add(qc_5)
    print(qc_total)
    ```

    Output:

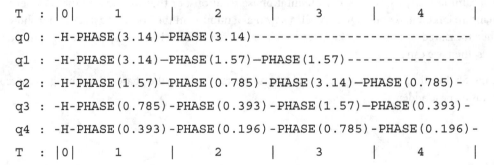

```
T  : |0|     1       |    2      |    3      |    4      |
q0 : -H-PHASE(3.14)-PHASE(3.14)--------------------------
q1 : -H-PHASE(3.14)-PHASE(1.57)-PHASE(1.57)-------------
q2 : -H-PHASE(1.57)-PHASE(0.785)-PHASE(3.14)-PHASE(0.785)-
q3 : -H-PHASE(0.785)-PHASE(0.393)-PHASE(1.57)-PHASE(0.393)-
q4 : -H-PHASE(0.393)-PHASE(0.196)-PHASE(0.785)-PHASE(0.196)-
T  : |0|     1       |    2      |    3      |    4      |
```

Here, the two sets of instructions, which are mainly phase rotations of the two numbers, have been added to the 5 qubits.

4. Now, we just need to perform the inverse of QFT to reveal the added-up phase information:

```
phase_circuit=qft_inv_gate(qc_total,5)
device = LocalSimulator()
result = device.run(phase_circuit,
                    shots=1000).result()
counts = result.measurement_counts
print(counts)
# plot using Counter
plt.bar(counts.keys(), counts.values());
plt.xlabel('value');
plt.ylabel('counts');
```

Output:

```
Counter({'01000': 1000})
```

As you can see, we can recover the number 8 or 01000 in binary.

With that, we have finished experimenting with quantum phase information. We have shown how phase information is stored in qubits and how it can be created using the QFT function. We also reviewed how this information can be added to the Fourier basis and that it can be measured after running the inverse QFT circuit.

Summary

In this chapter, we experimented with some important concepts in terms of quantum algorithms. We used functions to observe how two famous quantum algorithms work. First, we learned about the concept of an Oracle, which stores information that can then be acted upon by the algorithm we are testing. Next, we learned about Grover's algorithm and how it uses amplitude amplification to increase the probability amplitudes of specific states that represent a hidden number or condition. We saw that this is used by Grover's algorithm to search for numbers in the Oracle. Next, we understood quantum phase information. We started by looking at examples of incrementally adding rotations that represent the equivalent number of slices in a series of circles. Then, we reviewed the concept of moving between the Fourier and Computational bases and adding phase information to qubits. We prepared qubits with phase information similar to the way we added rotations to the circles to represent a number. This phase information did not produce any information when measured. We had to use the inverse QFT circuit to move the information to the Computational basis before it could be measured. It was revealed that adding phase information to the individual qubits followed a process that was similar to the one that's used in the QFT circuit and that the two are equivalent. Then, we learned that numbers can be added in the phase of qubits to reveal the sum at the end once the inverse QFT has been applied.

In the next chapter, we will extend our knowledge of quantum algorithms to useful hybrid algorithms. These are algorithms that use quantum computers and require considerable classical computation. We will make use of the QFT, Quantum Phase Estimation, and Phase adder circuits to show how Shor's algorithm works. In addition, we will investigate more complicated methods to make optimizations using a gate quantum computer.

Further reading

To learn more about the topics that were covered in this chapter, take a look at the following resources:

- Amazon Braket advanced examples showing both QFT and **Quantum Phase Estimation (QPE)** circuits:

  `https://github.com/aws/amazon-braket-examples/tree/main/examples/advanced_circuits_algorithms`

- A detailed explanation of quantum circuits:

  Dancing with Qubits by *Robert S. Sutor*: `https://www.packtpub.com/product/data/9781838827366`

Code deep dive:

Several functions were pre-built and provided in this and the previous chapter. You can find these in the GitHub repository for this chapter. Try reviewing the code to see if it is clear based on the steps described in this chapter. Some of these functions are as follows:

`run_circuit()`

`draw_bloch()`

`draw_circuit()`

`qc_num()`

`draw_multi_qubit_phase()`

`draw_multi_qubit_phase_qc()`

`qft_gate()`

`qft_inv_gate()`

Using Hybrid Algorithms – Optimization Using Gate-Based Quantum Computers

We'll now begin discussing how gate-based quantum computers can be used for optimization. We have already reviewed the fundamental concepts of the qubit, the Bloch Sphere, quantum gates, and simple quantum circuits. We will now understand how phase information is used to make calculations on quantum computers. In *Chapter 7, Using Gate Quantum Computers – Basic Quantum Algorithms*, we introduced the phase adder, which was able to do addition and subtraction by manipulating the phase of the qubits on the Fourier basis; then, inverse QFT was used to reveal the value that had been stored.

In this chapter, we will continue developing an intuition behind optimization using this phase information. We covered optimization in *Chapter 5, Using a Quantum Annealer – Developing a QUBO Function and Applying Constraints*, where we took a **Binary Quadratic Model** (BQM) and found its minimum using the D-Wave annealer. We will cover the same type of **Quadratic Unconstrained Binary Optimization** (QUBO) problems in this chapter.

First, you will learn how, by using the phase adder, we can create a binary quadratic function. Next, you will learn how phase information, along with specific qubit rotations, can be used to increase the probability of specific answers and reduce the probability of others. We will also introduce the **Quantum Approximate Optimization Algorithm** (QAOA) and show how this method leverages RZ and ZZ gates to add phase information, and then RX gates to move that information into the measurement basis. As we develop the optimization program, you will learn how it needs to be classically modified using specific parameters to get to the lowest value and thus produce the optimal result.

In this chapter, we will cover the following main topics:

- Representing a binary quadratic function using a phase adder
- Introduction to QAOA concepts
- Experimentally validating QAOA concepts
- Fine-tuning parameters for QAOA
- Implementing QAOA for optimization

Technical requirements

The source code for this chapter is available in this book's GitHub repository at https://github.com/PacktPublishing/Quantum-Computing-Experimentation-with-Amazon-Braket/tree/main/Chapter08.

Representing a binary quadratic function using a phase adder

In *Chapter 5, Using a Quantum Annealer – Developing a QUBO Function and Applying Constraints*, we showed how D-Wave solves QUBO problems. If the problem is set up as a matrix, then we can use the diagonal terms as the linear values and the non-diagonal terms as the quadratic terms in a BQM, where the independent variables have only binary values, {0, 1}. The optimized solution is then found using D-Wave and other QUBO solvers, which produce a binary string with the lowest energy.

A binary quadratic model can be represented by the following equation:

$$y = \sum_{i<j}^{n} c_{i,j} x_i x_j \qquad x \in \{0,1\} \qquad eq.\,(8.1)$$

As mentioned previously, x_i and x_j are binary variables, while $c_{i,j}$ is a floating-point coefficient. By saying $i<j$, we are stating that we are working with an upper-triangular matrix. Note that for simplicity, *since x is binary, we can treat x^2 as x*. We will refer to c_{00} or c_{11} as just c_0 and c_1.

Let's say we had the matrix representing the coefficients as follows:

$$\begin{pmatrix} c_0 & c_{01} \\ 0 & c_1 \end{pmatrix} = \begin{pmatrix} -1 & -1 \\ 0 & 2 \end{pmatrix} \qquad eq.\,(8.2)$$

This can be represented by the following equation:

$$y = -1x_0^2 + 2x_1^2 - x_0 x_1 \qquad eq.\,(8.3)$$

Now, we can find the possible values of y for all values of x_0 and x_1 and then find the minimum value of y. The following table shows a summary of these results:

x_0	x_1	y	
0	0	0	
0	1	2	Maximum
1	0	-1	Minimum
1	1	0	

Table 8.1 – Values of y based on all possible combinations of x0 and x1

Also, notice that the contribution of linear term x_0 is -1, while that of x_1 is 2 when either of them has a value of 1. However, the contribution when both x_0 and x_1 are 1 is the quadratic term -1. We can create a quantum circuit that adds these contributions using a conditional phase adder. This will allow us to get all the possible values of y if all the input values, x_0 and x_1, are in a superposition of the $|1\rangle$ and $|0\rangle$ states:

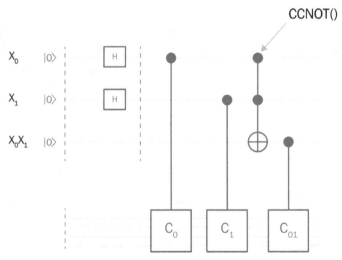

Figure 8.1 – Simplified circuit for the conditional phase adder

In *Figure 8.1*, notice that the first qubit represents x_0, while the second qubit represents x_1. If the first qubit is 1, this will activate the control phase adder, c_0, causing the circuit to add a phase representing c_0, and if x_1 is 1, then it will activate the phase adder, c_1, with the contribution of the value of c_1. The third qubit represents the quadratic term $x_0 x_1$. If x_0 and x_1 are both 1, then because of the CCNOT gate (also called the CCX or Toffoli gate), the value of the third qubit will become 1. The CCNOT gate is a doubly controlled NOT gate. Therefore, the first two dots represent the control part of the circuit, and the final NOT symbol, $\oplus$, represents the target. When both control qubits are 1, then the target state flips from $|0\rangle$ to $|1\rangle$ or from $|1\rangle$ to $|0\rangle$. The square boxes represent the same phase addition or subtraction circuit we implemented in *Chapter 7, Using Gate Quantum Computers – Basic Quantum Algorithms*, with the only difference being that we are now going to control every rotation by adding a control to it. Thus, an RZ gate that's being used in the phase addition or phase subtraction circuit will be replaced with a CRZ gate.

Note that in the following code, we will refer to *equation 8.3* as the objective and the result will be referred to as the cost.

With that, you've learned how to represent a binary quadratic model as a matrix and how controlled gates can be used to add phase information based on the values of the matrix. Now, let's work through an example of this using the sample code provided in this book's GitHub repository:

1. First, we want to enter the matrix of the coefficients. Qubits will be used to represent the phase circuit, so the number of qubits needs to be large enough to hold the largest cost value, considering both positive and negative values. We know that with n qubits, we can store 2^n different values. If we use three qubits, we can represent $2^3=8$ different values. To handle negative numbers, we will divide the available qubit states, as shown in the following table:

Cost	-3	-2	-1	0	1	2	3
Qubit States	101	110	111	000	001	010	011

Table 8.2 – Range of cost mapped to possible qubit values

If the cost can be >=4 or <=-4, we need to use more qubits for the phase adder to store the cost.

Here, we will use `Qubits=3` and create the objective matrix:

```
# Define the objective
Qubits=3
objective=np.array([[-1,-1],[0,2]])
```

2. This next part of the circuit will convert the matrix into an equation that represents the BQM. This step is not necessary, but it allows us to visualize the `objective` function from the matrix:

```
eq=''
SUB = str.maketrans("0123456789", "₀₁₂₃₄₅₆₇₈₉")
```

```
SUP = str.maketrans("0123456789", "0123456789")
len_r1=len(objective)


extra_qubits={}
r2=len_r1
ex_qu=0
```

This section of the code formats the diagonal element of the matrix into the linear terms of the BQM:

```
for i in range (len_r1):
    if objective[i,i]<0:
        eq=eq+str(objective[i,i])+'x'+
            str(i).translate(SUB)+'2'.translate(SUP)
    elif objective[i,i]>0:
        eq=eq+'+'+str(objective[i,i])+'x'+
            str(i).translate(SUB)+'2'.translate(SUP)
```

This section of the code formats the non-diagonal elements of the matrix into the quadratic elements of the BQM:

```
for i in range (len_r1):
    for j in range (len_r1):
        if i<j:

            if objective[i,j]<0:
                extra_qubits[(i,j)]=r2
                r2+=1
                eq=eq+str(objective[i,j])+'x'+
                    str(i).translate(SUB)+
                    'x'+str(j).translate(SUB)
            elif objective[i,j]>0:
                extra_qubits[(i,j)]=r2
                r2+=1
                eq=eq+'+'+str(objective[i,j])+
                    'x'+str(i).translate(SUB)+
                    'x'+str(j).translate(SUB)
print(eq)
# starting qubit for register 2
```

```
q_start=r2
print(q_start)
```

Output:

$$-1x_0^2+2x_1^2-1x_0x_1$$

3

The preceding output shows the correct equation and also prints out the qubit number, which will be used as the first qubit of the phase adder.

3. Now, we can start the quantum circuit and add Hadamard gates to the first two qubits that represent x0 and x1. This step will put both qubits in superposition. We will also continue to add Hadamard gates to the qubits that will be used for phase addition and subtraction:

```
qc=Circuit()
qc=qc.h([0,1])

for q in range(Qubits):
    qc=qc.h(q+q_start)
```

4. We have already provided two functions, subtract_coefficient() and add_coefficient(), which will place the appropriate amount of phase, depending on the coefficients in the objective matrix:

```
for i in range (len_r1):
    if objective[i,i]<0:
        qc=subtract_coefficient(qc, q_start, Qubits,
                            i, objective[i,i])
    elif objective[i,i]>0:
        qc=add_coefficient(qc, q_start, Qubits, i,
                            objective[i,i])
print(qc)
```

The output of this circuit is quite large and has not been shown here. Please refer to this book's GitHub repository to review the output and other code elements that are not shown here. The output shows the circuit and includes phase subtraction, representing the -1 coefficient for x_0, and phase addition, representing the +2 coefficient for x_1.

5. Next, we will add the contribution of the quadratic term from x_0x_1. This requires adding the CCNOT gate first to an extra qubit. The `extra_qubits[]` array stores the qubit values. Then, phase subtraction is implemented, which represents the -1 coefficient:

```
#adding contribution between x0 and x1 (coupling term)

for i in range (len_r1):
    for j in range (len_r1):
        if i<j:
            if objective[i,j]<0:
                qc=qc.ccnot(i,j,extra_qubits[i,j])
                qc=subtract_coefficient(qc, q_start,
                    Qubits, extra_qubits[i,j],
                    objective[i,j])
            elif objective[i,j]>0:
                qc=qc.ccnot(i,j,extra_qubits[i,j])
                qc=add_coefficient(qc, q_start,
                    Qubits, extra_qubits[i,j],
                    objective[I,j])

qc=qft_inv_gate(qc, Qubits, q_start )
print(qc)
```

The output is not shown here; please refer to the code for this chapter in this book's GitHub repository.

The output will be the full circuit. Now, we are ready to execute this circuit to see the results.

6. We will execute the circuit on `LocalSimulator()`. We are using another function, `plot_results_mc()`, to correctly plot the results with the probability of each x_0 and x_1 combination, along with the value of the `objective` function in parenthesis:

```
device = LocalSimulator()
result = device.run(qc, shots=1000).result()
counts = result.measurement_counts
print(counts)
# plot using Counter
plot_results_mc(counts,Qubits)
```

Output:

```
Counter(''00000'': 264,''10011'': 252,''11100'':
242,''01001'': 242})
valid values -3.0 to 3.0
from lowest to highest value
input (cost) count
-----   ----- -----
10(-1) 252
00(0) 264
11(0) 242
01(2) 242
```

The output shows all combinations of x_0x_1 values, their associated cost in parenthesis, and the count. As we can see, all the values have approximately the same probability. Also, the cost that was produced by the `objective` function matches what was shown in *Table 8.1*.

This has been plotted in the following figure:

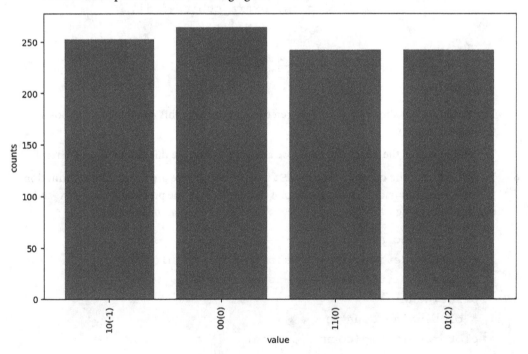

Figure 8.2 – Probability of all costs (in parenthesis) produced by the objective function

It is interesting to note that since we used the Hadamard gates to put both independent variables, x_0 and x_1, in superposition in *Step 3*, the quantum circuit samples all possible answers from this equation. Thus, it reveals both the minimum and maximum values, which means this method could be used to find all the solutions, along with the minimum cost of the `objective` function. The disadvantage is that as the number of variables increases, the quantum circuit will become quite large and the sampling that will be necessary to find the minimum cost will also increase. This, in effect, is a way for quantum computers to sample answers such as the Monte Carlo method, or Solver in Microsoft Excel, which randomly samples the input variables to determine the probability profile of the output results.

7. We can now try a different and larger `objective` function to observe the results that will be produced. To help with this, the preceding steps have been simplified with an additional function, `multi_qubit_polynomial()`. We will define the number of qubits to store the costs, the `objective` function in the form of a matrix, and then run the `multi_qubit_polynomial()` function. Next, the circuit is run on `LocalSimulator()` and the results are plotted using `plot_results_mc()`:

```
Qubits=6
objective=np.array([[1,-2,1,-1,-3,5],[0,2,-1,-1,2,-1],
                    [0,0,3,3,-3,-3],  [0,0,0,1,-2,2],
                    [0,0,0,0,1,3],[0,0,0,0,0,2]])

print(objective)
qc, len_r1, q_start=multi_qubit_polynomial(Qubits,
                                            objective)
device = LocalSimulator()
result = device.run(qc, shots=10000).result()
counts = result.measurement_counts
plot_results_mc(counts, Qubits)
```

Output:

```
[[ 1 -2  1 -1 -3  5]
 [ 0  2 -1 -1  2 -1]
 [ 0  0  3  3 -3 -3]
 [ 0  0  0  1 -2  2]
 [ 0  0  0  0  1  3]
 [ 0  0  0  0  0  2]]
```

$+1x_0^2+2x_1^2+3x_2^2+1x_3^2+1x_4^2+2x_5^2-2x_0x_1+1x_0x_2-1x_0x_3-3x_0x_4+5x_0x_5-1x_1x_2-1x_1x_3+2x_1x_4-1x_1x_5+3x_2x_3-3x_2x_4-3x_2x_5-2x_3x_4+2x_3x_5+3x_4x_5$

This first part of the output will show the matrix and the equation. Due to the size of the circuit, it may take up to 5 minutes before all the possible answers are revealed. Here, the truncated values are shown from the lowest to highest (in terms of cost), as sampled by the simulator:

```
from lowest to highest value
input (cost) count
-----  -----  -----
100110(-3) 152
110110(-2) 171
100010(-1) 166
000110(0) 176

...

101111(10) 159
100101(10) 158
111101(11) 144
101101(14) 168
```

Based on the preceding output, the solution, 100110, will produce the lowest value of -3 from this objective function. Note that the solution represents the binary value of x_0, x_1, x_2, x_3, x_4, and x_5. Thus, the minimum value is produced when x_0, x_3, and x_4 are all 1 and when x_1, x_2, and x_5 are all 0.

A plot showing the same values can be seen here:

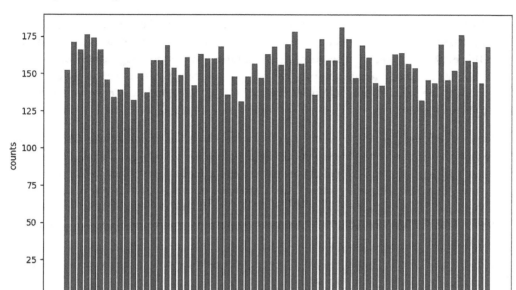

Figure 8.3 – All possible solutions for the objective function

In the output, all the possible values appear to fluctuate around some mean number of shots. However, it should be noted that, theoretically, all the probabilities are the same. If the circuit is printed, you will see that it uses 27 qubits and has a gate depth of 51.

With this, we've seen that a simple extension of the phase adder circuit can be used to sample all the values of a binary quadratic function. If we were looking for the minimum of this function, we could use this method, but this is never efficient.

For now, we want to consider whether there is a way for a quantum circuit to take a similar equation and *increase* the probability of finding the minimum value. Thus, we are looking for a quantum circuit for a QUBO solver that finds the minimum value of the binary quadratic model as efficiently as possible. In this case, we want to reduce the number of samples (shots) and still find the minimum value solution with a high probability. This method will be introduced in the next section.

Introduction to QAOA concepts

The standard method of finding the minimum of a binary quadratic model on a gate-based quantum computer is based on a method introduced by Edward Farhi, Jeffrey Goldstone, and Sam Gutmann in 2014. This method is called the **Quantum Approximate Optimization Algorithm (QAOA)**. It is a hybrid algorithm since it requires its parameters to be classically tuned, as we will see later. We will proceed with the key steps in QAOA by discussing how to handle the linear terms, and then the quadratic terms of the BQM:

1. First, let's focus on how the linear coefficients can be mapped onto qubit rotations so that the variables with negative coefficients have a higher probability of getting a $|1\rangle$ state. This makes use of rotating the qubit vector along the equator of the Bloch sphere using the RZ gate, and then rotating the qubit vector toward the measurement basis using the RX gate in such a way that the probability of the $|1\rangle$ state increases for the qubits (and variables) that contribute to a lower value. Similarly, we rotate the qubits that contribute to positive (or higher) values toward the $|0\rangle$ state.

2. Initially, the qubits are initialized to the $|-\rangle$ state. *Figure 8.4* shows the first step. The qubit is rotated in the positive Z direction $(+\theta)$ if the variable has a negative coefficient, and the qubit is rotated in the negative Z direction $(-\theta)$ if the variable has a positive coefficient. The reason will become obvious in the next step. However, it should be noted that the probability of measuring the qubit in either the $|0\rangle$ or $|1\rangle$ state is 50% at this point. A Bloch Sphere simulator link has been added to the *Further reading* section in case you would like to try these rotations out yourself:

1. RZ rotation

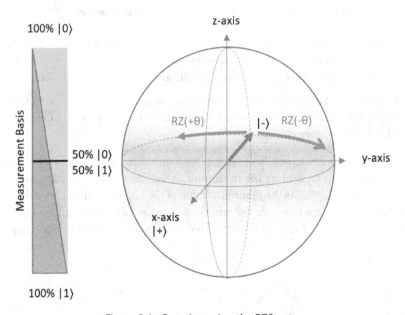

Figure 8.4 – Rotation using the RZ() gate

3. The next step is to apply the RX() gate. This will rotate the qubit vector that is on the right side up toward a higher probability of the $|0\rangle$ state, and those that are on the left side down toward a higher probability of the $|1\rangle$ state, as shown in the following diagram:

2. RX rotation

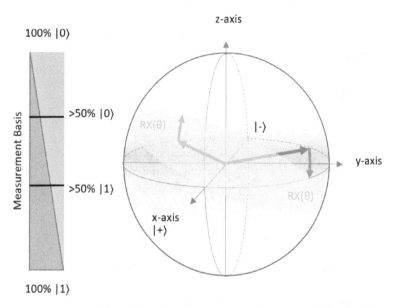

Figure 8.5 – Rotation using the RX() gate

As can be seen, this method changes the probability of specific states when applied to all the linear coefficients. However, a question arises: what are the correct rotation angles for the RZ and RX rotations? This is controlled by parameters that we will refer to as param1 and param2 in the code. One other caveat is that the accuracy of the results increases if the qubit vector is moved up in a series of RZ-RX steps with varying angles, rather than a single set of RZ-RX gates. This can be seen in the following diagram:

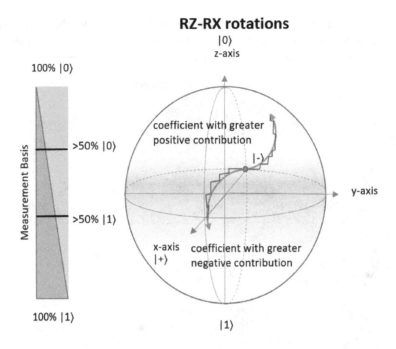

Figure 8.6 – Step-wise evolution of qubit vectors towards using RZ-RX rotations with varying parameters.

4. Now, we will address how to handle the quadratic term. In this case, we can use the ZZ gate on the pair of qubits representing the quadratic pair of variables. This makes use of the ability of quantum computers to entangle qubits. Therefore, if two variables, x_0 and x_1, have a negative coefficient, we want the probability of picking x_0 and x_1 together to increase. Thus, either we will select both x_0 and x_1 or not select them at all. For this, we want the probability of $x_0, x_1 = 11$ and 00 to increase, and the probability of $x_0, x_1 = 01$ and 10 to decrease. However, if x_0 and x_1 have a large positive coefficient, we want the opposite effect and the probability of $x_0, x_1 = 01$ and 10 to increase and the probability of $x_0, x_1 = 11$ and 00 to decrease. We can control the level of this effect by changing the angle of the ZZ gate. The RX gates will then be applied to rotate this information into the measurement basis. There is no clear way to show this effect on a Bloch sphere, so we will measure the state vector as it changes with varying coupling terms. The coupling term is the coefficient between the two variables:

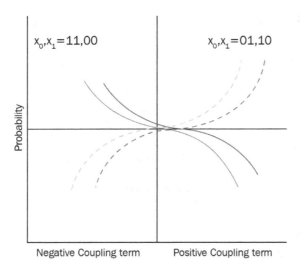

Figure 8.7 – Effect of using ZZ gates on changing the probability of qubit pairs

The formal mathematical treatment of QAOA is outside the scope of this book, but we will show you how this process is implemented in code. The following diagram shows one cycle of the RZ-ZZ-RX gates for two variables, x_0 and x_1. Note that the RZ gates are applied to each qubit representing the linear terms, as discussed in *Step 1*. Then, the two-qubit ZZ gate is applied between the two qubits to represent the quadratic term, as discussed in *Step 3*. Finally, the RX gates are applied to each of the qubits:

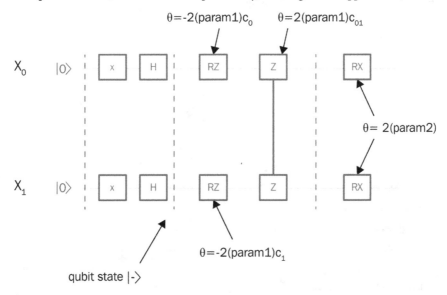

Figure 8.8 – Implementing QAOA for two variables and one cycle. The rotation angle for each gate is identified based on param1, param2, and the coefficients from the objective matrix

Now that we have reviewed the main concepts behind QAOA, let's validate them.

Experimentally validating QAOA concepts

So far, we have seen how specific gate rotations can be used to increase the probability of the qubit states that produce the lowest cost. We have also seen that we apply the X gate first and then the Hadamard gate to all the qubits to bring them to the |-) state. From there, we apply RZ and ZZ rotations to individual qubits and pairs of qubits, respectively. Finally, we apply the RX gates to bring the information into the measurement basis. Let's implement this in code:

1. First, let's look at the effect that RZ rotations have on the linear terms. We will begin by defining the objective function, as follows:

```
objective=np.array([[-1,-1],[0,2]])
eq=matrix_to_polynomial(objective)
```

Output:

$-1x_0^2+2x_1^2-1x_0x_1$

2. We want to see the effect of the coefficient on x_0, which is -1, and on x_1, which is 2 on the qubit vectors. In the following code, we will create a combined circuit, qc, and separate circuits, qc1 and qc2, to observe the effect on a single qubit using the Bloch sphere. We can use the draw_circuit() function to do this. Note that the parameters are defined here and can be adjusted to observe the effect on the qubits:

```
#single circuit
qc=Circuit()
qc=qc.x([0,1]).h([0,1])

param1=0.2
param2=0.4

#separate qubit circuits
qc1=Circuit()
qc2=Circuit()
qc1=qc1.x(0).h(0)
qc2=qc2.x(0).h(0)

print('full circuit')
print(qc)
print('Now print individual qubits circuit')
```

```
    print('qubit 1')
    draw_circuit(qc1)
    print('qubit 2')
    draw_circuit(qc2)
```

Output (reduced):

```
T   : |0|1|

q0  : -X-H-

q1  : -X-H-
```

The Bloch sphere from both qubits is shown in the following diagram:

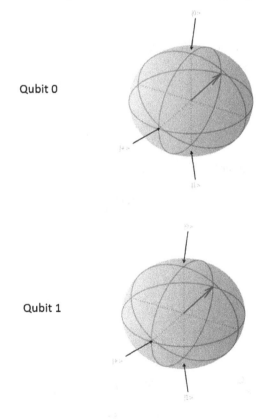

Figure 8.9 – Qubits 0 and 1 initialized to the |-) state

3. Now, we will apply the RZ rotations that equal `-2*param1*coefficient` to the variable:

```
    #single circuit
    qc=qc.rz(0,2*-param1*objective[0,0]).rz(1,2*-
```

```
                param1*objective[1,1])
    #separate qubit circuits
    qc1=qc1.rz(0,2*-param1*objective[0,0])
    qc2=qc2.rz(0,2*-param1*objective[1,1])
    print(qc)
    draw_circuit(qc1)
    draw_circuit(qc2)
```

Output (reduced):

```
T   : |0|1|    2     |
q0  : -X-H-Rz(0.4)--
q1  : -X-H-Rz(-0.8)-
```

The individual qubits are shown in the following diagram:

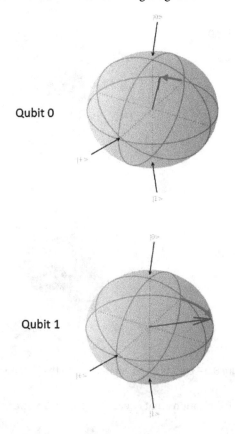

Figure 8.10 – Qubits after adding RZ rotations (blue arc added for clarity)

Notice that qubit 0 has moved toward the left and that qubit 1 has moved almost twice the angle to the right.

4.   For this exercise, we are only focusing on the effect of the linear coefficients, so we will apply the RX gates to see the change in probabilities for the final values. Notice that we use the 2*param2 value in the rotations:

```
qc=qc.rx(0,2*param2).rx(1,2*param2)
qc1=qc1.rx(0,2*param2)
qc2=qc2.rx(0,2*param2)
print(qc)
draw_circuit(qc1)
draw_circuit(qc2)
```

Output (reduced):

```
T   : |0|1|    2     |   3   |
q0  : -X-H-Rz(0.4)--Rx(0.8)-
q1  : -X-H-Rz(-0.8)-Rx(0.8)-
```

The two qubits after this step are shown in the following diagram:

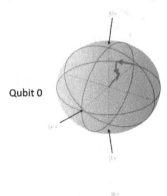

Qubit 0

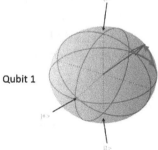

Qubit 1

Figure 8.11 – Qubits after RX gates (blue arcs added for clarity)

5. Now, we can measure the qubits to determine whether the probability of the correct variable has increased. Note that we did not use the coupling term, so this would be the cost with only the linear terms:

```
device = LocalSimulator()
result = device.run(qc, shots=1000).result()
counts = result.measurement_counts
plt.bar(counts.keys(), counts.values());
plt.xlabel('value');
plt.ylabel('counts');
plt.show()
```

The output is shown in the following diagram:

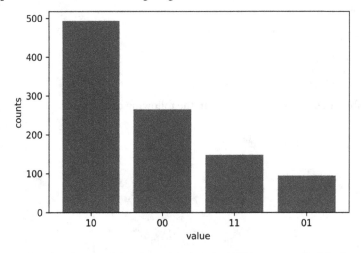

Figure 8.12 – Results of measuring the qubits with the RZ and RX gates applied for linear terms only

Here, we can see that the optimal solution is 10, which means $x_0=1$ and $x_1=0$. If we only had linear terms, this method would increase the probability of finding the minimum. You can also check whether the relative probabilities match the lowest to highest cost. However, we now need to see the effect of the coefficient, c_{01}, or the coupling between x_0 and x_1.

6. Let's rebuild the circuit so that it includes the coupling term:

```
qc=Circuit()
qc=qc.x([0,1]).h([0,1])
param1=0.3
param2=0.3
qc=qc.rz(0,-2*param1*objective[0,0])
```

```
qc=qc.rz(1,-2*param1*objective[1,1])
qc=qc.zz(0,1,2*param1*objective[0,1])
qc=qc.rx(0,2*param2).rx(1,2*param2)
print(qc)
```

Output:

```
T   : |0|1|    2     |   3     |    4     |


q0  : -X-H-Rz(0.6)--ZZ(-0.6)-Rx(0.6)-
                        |
q1  : -X-H-Rz(-1.2)-ZZ(-0.6)-Rx(0.6)-
```

Notice that both parameters are set to 0.3 to increase their effect; however, this does not mean the accuracy will increase.

7. Now, let's execute the circuit and print out the probabilities:

```
device = LocalSimulator()
result = device.run(qc, shots=10000).result()
counts = result.measurement_counts
plt.bar(counts.keys(), counts.values());
plt.xlabel('value');
plt.ylabel('counts');
plt.show()
```

The output is shown in the following diagram:

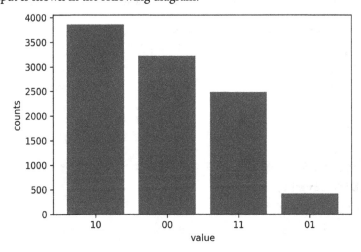

Figure 8.13 – Results of measuring the qubits with the RZ, ZZ,
and RX gates (both linear and quadratic terms)

The result shows that the probability of 11 and 00 went up at the expense of the probability for 01, which is the highest cost. Ideally, 00 and 11 should have the same probability since the cost is the same; however, this hasn't been achieved. Nonetheless, the probabilities appear to be useful in finding the optimal minimum, which is 10. Could we improve the results if we had more accurate parameters and used more cycles?

With that, we've seen how the basic QAOA concepts are implemented. A more appropriate way is to use smaller angles and repeat the RZ-ZZ-RX steps a few times. Each time, the parameters have to be determined classically. The parameters are problem-dependent and, as shown in *Figure 8.6*, we do not want the total rotation to be more than pi degrees. Thus, based on the values of the coefficients, and the number of iterations, the parameters will change to give optimal results. In this book, we will only cover one cycle and determine one set of parameters. In actual QAOA implementations, a classical optimization application (for example, scipy.optimize.minimize) is used to repeatedly find the optimal parameters and improve the results. A more detailed example of this full implementation can also be found in the Amazon Braket examples provided in the *Further reading* section. Now that we have a basic understanding of how QAOA works, let's dive deeper into optimizing the parameters.

Fine-tuning parameters for QAOA

In the previous sections, we developed the concepts for how QAOA works and used a set of parameters that scale the rotations of the RZ, ZZ, and RX gates. It should also be apparent that rotating the angle too far will only cause it to start moving in the opposite direction of where we want it. Thus, the parameters depend on having an understanding of the problem, the size of the coefficients, and the number of times the RZ, ZZ, and RX gates are repeated. We will continue with our objective function to see whether we can improve on the parameters and get a better result:

1. In this first example, we will set param2 to 0.1 and vary param1 using x2 while plotting the probabilities of the four possible answers. The code for this is as follows:

```
x2=np.arange(0,1.5,.1)# set x
x=x2
prob_00=[]
prob_01=[]
prob_10=[]
prob_11=[]

c_0=objective[0,0]
c_1=objective[1,1]
c_01=objective[0,1]
param2=0.1
```

2. he following code uses the `param_tuning_example()` function, which determines the minimum cost of the objective function, $-1x_0^2 + 2x_1^2 - 1x_0 x_1$, as we vary `param1` and store the values for plotting:

```
for param1 in(x):
    result, counts=param_tuning_example(c_0, c_1,
                                         c_01, param1,
                                         param2)

    prob_00.append(abs(result.values[0][0])**2)
    prob_01.append(abs(result.values[0][1])**2)
    prob_10.append(abs(result.values[0][2])**2)
    prob_11.append(abs(result.values[0][3])**2)

plt.plot(x,prob_01,'-.',label='01',linewidth=3.0)
plt.plot(x,prob_11,'--',label='11',linewidth=3.0)
plt.plot(x,prob_00,'--',label='00')
plt.plot(x,prob_10,'-.',label='10')

plt.title("Varying param1")
plt.xlabel("param1")
plt.ylabel("probability")
plt.legend()
plt.show()
```

The key part of this code, which is highlighted in the preceding block, will be used in the other examples to change the parameters (`param1` and `param2`) or even the effect of the coupling coefficient, `c_01`. The rest of the code stores the probabilities, as the parameter is varied, and then plots the result.

The output is shown in the following diagram:

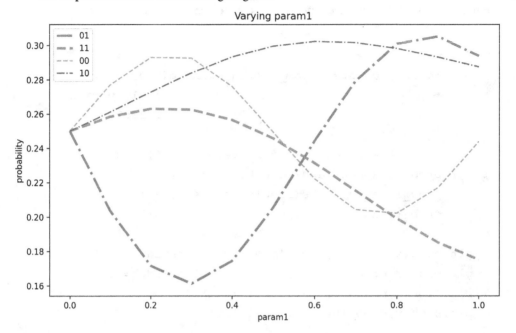

Figure 8.14 – Effect of varying param1 with param2 = 0.1

As you may recall, in our solution, `10` should have the highest probability while `11` and `00` should have the same but lower probabilities, and `01` should have the lowest probability. This seems to be applicable around `param1=0.5`. We will use this value in the next step and vary `param2`.

3. Now, let's fix `param1=0.5` and vary `param2` to view the probabilities. Only the relevant portion of the code is shown here:

```
x2=np.arange(0,1.1,.1)
x=x2

...

param1=0.5
for param2 in(x):
    result, counts=param_tuning_example(c_0, c_1,
                                        c_01, param1,
                                        param2)
```

The results are shown in the following diagram:

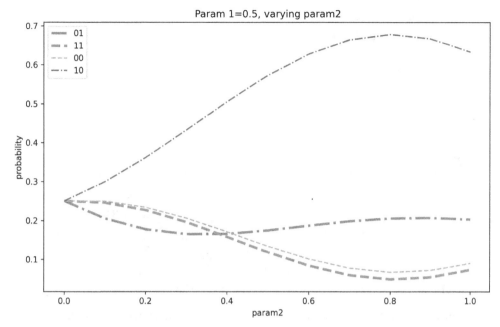

Figure 8.15 – Effect of varying param2 with param1 = 0.5

The results are quite interesting. As `param2` is increased, the probability of `10` increases, the probability of `01` decreases, and the probability of `11` and `00` remains about equal between the other two values, so long as `param2` is less than `0.4`. Thus, we can pick a value of `0.2` for `param2`.

4. The next part of the code includes an example where a series of plots with fixed values of `param1` are plotted along with varying `param2`. You can use this code to look at the effect of varying the parameters. Here is the relevant part of the code:

```
x1=np.arange(-6,6.5,.5)
x2=np.arange(0,1.1,.1)
figure(figsize=(10, 6), dpi=100)
# set x
x=x2


prob_00=[]
prob_01=[]
prob_10=[]
prob_11=[]


#coefficients from the objective matrix
```

```
c_0=objective[0,0]
c_1=objective[1,1]
c_01=objective[0,1]

param1=0.5


for param2 in(x):
    result, counts=param_tuning_example(c_0, c_1,
                                        c_01, param1,
                                        param2)
prob_00.append(abs(result.values[0][0])**2)
prob_01.append(abs(result.values[0][1])**2)
prob_10.append(abs(result.values[0][2])**2)
prob_11.append(abs(result.values[0][3])**2)
```

You can scan the different plots and find the one where the parameters produce the most accurate and desired probabilities. This is the plot where param1 is fixed at 0.5. Note that when param2 is 0.2, the probability of 00 and 11 are approximately equal and between 10 and 01. This plot is shown in *Figure 8.16*:

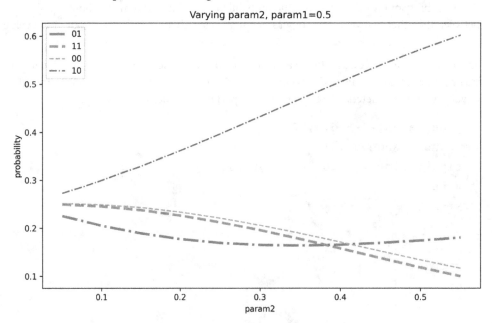

Figure 8.16 – Ideal parameter profile for the desired results

5. Now, we can use our ideal `param1=0.5` and `param2=0.2` to repeat the QAOA steps that we performed in the previous section:

```
qc=Circuit()
qc=qc.x([0,1]).h([0,1])


param1=0.5
param2=0.2


qc=qc.rz(0,-2*param1*objective[0,0])
qc=qc.rz(1,-2*param1*objective[1,1])
qc=qc.zz(0,1,2*param1*objective[0,1])


qc=qc.rx(0,2*param2).rx(1,2*param2)
print(qc)
```

Output:

```
T   : |0|1|  2   |  3  |   4   |
q0  : -X-H-Rz(1)—ZZ(-1)-Rx(0.4)-
                  |
q1  : -X-H-Rz(-2)-ZZ(-1)-Rx(0.4)-
T   : |0|1|  2   |  3  |   4   |
```

After using the appropriate parameters, we will find the following resulting probabilities as shown in *Figure 8.17*:

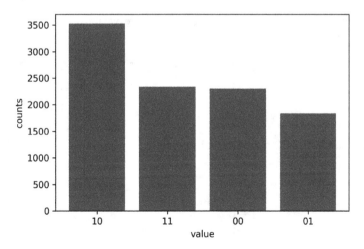

Figure 8.17 – Results of the QAOA steps after using fine-tuned parameters

The results show the desired high probability for 10 (lowest cost), equal probabilities for 00 and 11 (equal cost of 0), and the lowest probability for 01 (highest cost).

With that, we've explained how to set up a QAOA circuit and how to manually fine-tune its parameters. In an ideal circuit, this parameter tuning would be performed by an optimization algorithm. However, for our purposes, we will find another method that rapidly finds the parameters that can be used to fine-tune QAOA. This implementation will be discussed in the next section.

Implementing QAOA for optimization

So far, we've learned how to create a binary quadratic objective function and then create a quantum circuit that will evolve by increasing the probability of the state that produces the minimum cost. We also showed how QAOA depends on parameters that must be evaluated classically. In this section, we will create a simple QAOA implementation where we can visually and efficiently determine the parameters and optimize the objective function.

In the first section of this chapter, *Representing a binary quadratic function using a phase adder,* we started by defining an objective function and showed that a quantum computer could sample all the values of that function while determining the minimum value with the same probability as every other value. This requires a considerable number of measurements, and the last example in that section took a while to execute. The results were shown in *Figure 8.3*. Now, we will use our implementation of QAOA to increase the probability of the minimum cost, which was -3 with the 100110 solution. For this purpose, two functions are provided. The first is the param_optimizer() function, which will use varying sets of param1 and param2 and display the minimum cost that was found during the sampling with each set of parameters using only one QAOA cycle. The second function, optimize_bqm(), uses the set of parameters that found the lowest cost, reruns the single QAOA cycle using that set of parameters, and then plots the probabilities of the costs found. The goal of this is to increase the probability of the lower cost values. Let's get started:

1. To use our new QAOA method on the original objective, we must redefine the objective function, as shown here:

```
objective=np.array([[1,-2,1,-1,-3,5],[0,2,-1,-1,2,-1],
                    [0,0,3,3,-3,-3], [0,0,0,1,-2,2],
                    [0,0,0,0,1,3],[0,0,0,0,0,2]])
print(objective)
eq=matrix_to_polynomial(objective)
```

Output:

```
[[ 1 -2  1 -1 -3  5]
 [ 0  2 -1 -1  2 -1]
 [ 0  0  3  3 -3 -3]
 [ 0  0  0  1 -2  2]
 [ 0  0  0  0  1  3]
 [ 0  0  0  0  0  2]]
```

$+1x_0^2+2x_1^2+3x_2^2+1x_3^2+1x_4^2+2x_5^2-2x_0x_1+1x_0x_2-1x_0x_3-3x_0x_4+5x_0x_5-1x_1x_2-1x_1x_3+2x_1x_4-1x_1x_5+3x_2x_3-3x_2x_4-3x_2x_5-2x_3x_4+2x_3x_5+3x_4x_5$

2. Now, we are ready to run `param_optimizer()`. The last argument in the function is the number of shots used each time a parameter combination is executed. Thus, this number should be kept low for efficiency at 50. However, larger values will increase the chance of finding the global minimum. By using QAOA and only one cycle, we find the minimum cost of -3 multiple times, even if we were to use a sampling of only 10 to 20:

```
param1=np.arange(0,0.4,.05)
print(param1)
param2=np.arange(0.1,0.9,.1)
print(param2)ideal_param1, ideal_param2, lowest_
energy, lowest_count=param_optimizer(param1, param2,
objective,50)
print(ideal_param1, ideal_param2, lowest_energy, lowest_
count)
```

Output:

```
[0.   0.05 0.1  0.15 0.2  0.25 0.3  0.35]
[0.1 0.2 0.3 0.4 0.5 0.6 0.7 0.8]
0.1 0.4 -3 8
```

The preceding output shows the *parameters* 0.1 and 0.4 that produced the lowest cost with the highest occurrence or probability. *Figure 8.18* shows a grid of the parameter search area and the lowest cost that was found in each of the grid elements:

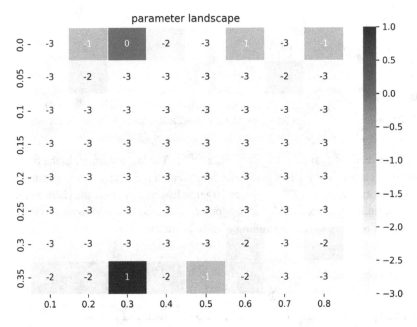

Figure 8.18 – Grid showing the minimum cost found in the parameter search area

Interestingly, QAOA finds the minimum at many different locations on the parameter landscape. The code tracks the number of times the lowest value is found so we can refine the parameters. With this low sampling of 50 per grid item, the lowest cost of -3 was found 8 times, where param1=0.1 and param2=0.4. This is probabilistic and will change if the measurements are increased.

3. Now, we can use these fine-tuned parameters to execute the optimize_bqm() function:

```
solution,energy,quantity=optimize_bqm([ideal_param1],
                                       [ideal_param2],
                                       objective,
                                       10000)
print('Solution:',solution, 'Energy:',energy, 'Qty
      Sampled',quantity)
```

Output:

```
Solution: 100110 Energy: -3 Qty Sampled 702
```

This provides the correct solution, and the minimum energy is sampled 702 times. The following figure shows the probability of measuring the different cost values:

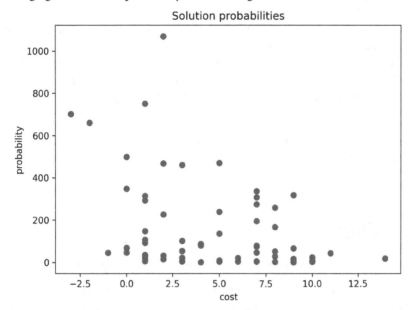

Figure 8.19 – The solution probabilities show that the lowest costs have a high probability of being measured while the higher costs have a low probability of being measured

As we can see, QAOA has increased the probability of the lower costs, and reduced the probability of finding higher costs. We were able to show that with a quantum simulator, QAOA works and can provide optimal solutions to an objective function. This gives us a strong tool that we will apply in *Section 3, Real-World Optimization Use Cases*.

In this section, we applied the concept of QAOA to a function that sampled a parameter landscape to optimize the parameters that are used for the RZ/ZZ gates and the RX gates, which are required to increase the probability of measuring the minimum (optimal) solution of an objective function. Then, we applied these parameters and displayed the increased probability of sampling the minimum cost. Even though we did not cycle through multiple times, this method produced good results and provided the minimum required.

Summary

In this chapter, we focused on implementing the **Quantum Approximate Optimization Algorithm (QAOA)**, a hybrid algorithm. We started by using the phase adder circuit from *Chapter 7, Using Gate Quantum Computers – Basic Quantum Algorithms*, which has been modified for addition and subtraction. We used this to create a circuit that can sample all the possible solutions of an objective function. We found that this method provides equal probabilities of the different solutions and required a substantially large number of qubits and gate depth. To find the minimum value more efficiently, for optimization applications, it is necessary to be able to efficiently sample the lowest cost. We went over the concepts of how QAOA works and how its parameters impact the performance of the algorithm. We discussed that, in practice, the algorithm uses a classical optimization application to find the optimal parameters, and that this process is repeated in a few cycles to find the optimal value. Then, we implemented this algorithm with a single cycle approach. We used a binary quadratic `objective` function with six variables and found the optimal parameters from the possible parameter landscape. Then, we used the parameters that produced the most likelihood of seeing the lowest cost to run the final optimization function. This resulted in us finding the lowest expected cost with an increased probability.

In the next chapter, we will experiment with the tools we have gathered in this section and benchmark them on Amazon Braket simulators and real quantum devices. This will expose us to not only the nuances of QPU architecture and the need to optimize our algorithms, but also provide us with an awareness of the capabilities and limitations of current quantum hardware and simulators.

Further reading

To learn more about the topics that were covered in this chapter, take a look at the following resources:

- The full implementation of QAOA can be found in the Amazon Braket examples at `https://github.com/aws/amazon-braket-examples/tree/main/examples/hybrid_quantum_algorithms/QAOA`.

- The initial paper titled *A Quantum Approximate Optimization Algorithm* by Edward Farhi, Jeffrey Goldstone, and Sam Gutmann, introducing QAOA, can be found here: `https://arxiv.org/abs/1411.4028`.

- Bloch Sphere simulator: `https://javafxpert.github.io/grok-bloch/`.

- **Code Deep Dive**: Please review the code in the following functions, all of which were provided as part of the discussion in this chapter. These can be found in this book's GitHub repository:

  - `qft_inv_gate()`

  - `plot_results_mc()`

  - `matrix_to_polynomial()`

  - `param_tuning_example()`

  - `param_optimizer()`

  - `optimize_bqm()`

Running QAOA on Simulators and Amazon Braket Devices

We have now reached the last chapter of *Section 2, Building Blocks for Real World Use Cases,* of this book. We started this section with *Chapter 5, Using a Quantum Annealer – Developing a QUBO Function and Applying Constraints,* where we showed how **Quadratic Binary Optimization** (**QUBO**) problems can be solved using D-Wave's quantum annealer. Then, from *Chapter 6, Using Gate-Based Quantum Computers – Qubits and Quantum Circuits,* to *Chapter 8, Using Hybrid Algorithms – Optimization Using Gate-Based Quantum Computers,* we incrementally developed the concepts of gate-based quantum circuits, which led to the hybrid **Quantum Approximate Optimization Algorithm** (**QAOA**). We showed that this algorithm also solves QUBO problems by increasing the probability of detecting values that have a lower cost. However, this algorithm requires a set of parameters that must be tuned through classical means. We ended *Chapter 8, Using Hybrid Algorithms – Optimization Using Gate-Based Quantum Computers,* with a binary quadratic model where a very small number of measurements helped in identifying a landscape of possible parameters. With specific parameters, the lowest cost was found.

We do not want to manually observe the whole landscape every time; instead, we would prefer to have an algorithm that, with the least number of trials and sampling, rapidly finds the minimum value by incrementally moving toward the ideal parameters. Therefore, in this chapter, we will develop a full QAOA hybrid algorithm that uses a classical optimization function to fine-tune the parameters. We also stated that the ideal QAOA does not use only one set of parameters for its RX and RZ rotations, but multiple smaller incremental steps with varying parameter values that profoundly increase the optimum solution. We will also use this technique in this chapter. The rest of this chapter will compare the various QUBO solvers that are available to us through Amazon Braket. We will represent the QUBO problem as an upper-triangular matrix. We will find the limits of what can be solved and the level of accuracy that can be achieved by quantum devices compared to the classical algorithms and quantum simulators that are available in Amazon Braket.

In this chapter, we will cover the following topics:

- Further QAOA considerations

- Benchmarking QAOA on Amazon Braket devices

- Summary of results

By the end of this chapter, you will have a firm understanding of QAOA, how it works, and how it can be applied to various quantum devices. This will create a solid foundation for when you're using out-of-the-box QAOA libraries and applications or diving deeper into the mathematics behind developing QAOA. This will give you a nuanced view of how a variational hybrid algorithm works, which will be a starting point for other such variational algorithms.

Technical requirements

The source code for this chapter is available in this book's GitHub repository at `https://github.com/PacktPublishing/Quantum-Computing-Experimentation-with-Amazon-Braket/tree/main/Chapter09`.

Further QAOA considerations

In the previous chapter, the QAOA implementation moved through a range of parameter values, including `param1` and `param2`. We found that, in the parameter *landscape*, varying costs were returned and certain pairs of parameters sometimes yielded the lowest cost. Can we use an optimizer to move toward the lowest cost more efficiently than mapping the whole parameter landscape? This will be the first area we will investigate. In addition, in the previous chapter, we stated that by repeatedly applying a combination of Z and X rotations with appropriate parameters, the probability profile can be modified more effectively so that we see the minimum cost. We will review this as well.

Full QAOA hybrid algorithm using a classical parameter optimizer

Classical optimization algorithms have various ways of evaluating the landscape for a lower cost value and continuing to move towards a minima. However, we know that sometimes these algorithms can get stuck in a local minima. In the previous chapter, we saw that in the parameter landscape, we can find some lower-cost values. However, there is a considerable challenge with this method. Since the results from quantum measurement are probabilistic, this creates a very noisy way for the optimization algorithm to determine which way to move to optimize. Our goal has been to use the least amount of measurements (shots) to find the minimum cost. In addition, by changing the parameters, we are only changing the "probability" of measuring the lowest cost. Therefore, we can observe the lowest cost even when the probability profile is not optimal. Alternatively, we may have the best probability profile and may not detect the lowest cost if there are too few measurements.

> **Caution: Substantial Quantum Device Costs**
>
> As we go further, we will continue to do a large number of quantum device executions and sometimes with large number of shots when evaluating the parameter landscape. Please always be aware of the costs associated with running on quantum devices, especially IonQ, as they can be quite high. You should always run the `estimate_cost()` function in advance with the device name and number of shots to get a per execution price. Then you should multiply the price with the number of times the device will be called to develop the full parameter landscape in this chapter and future chapters where QAOA is used.

In this section, we want to gain an intuition for how QAOA and its parameters work. To do this, we will develop the probability profile for each set of parameters in a landscape by using 100,000 shots. This will allow us to *see* how the probability profiles change with the change in parameters, and whether the lowest cost has an increased probability compared to all the other costs.

We will use the `optimize_bqm()` function, as we did in the previous chapter. In this case however, we will plot the *probability profiles of the costs* for various set of parameters in a range between 0.1 and 0.7. Let's get started:

1. First, let's create a range of values from 0.1 to 0.7 with an interval of 0.15 using the `arange()` function. We will use the same values for both parameters that were used in QAOA – `param1` and `param2`:

    ```
    param1=np.arange(0.1,0.8,0.15,dtype=float)
    param2=np.arange(0.1,0.8,0.15,dtype=float)
    print(param1)
    print(param2)
    ```

    Output:

    ```
    [0.1  0.25 0.4  0.55 0.7 ]
    [0.1  0.25 0.4  0.55 0.7 ]
    ```

2. Now, we will load the matrix from the `IonQ_matrix.csv` file. This contains an 11x11 matrix that we will use later with the Ion Trap:

    ```
    file = open("IonQ_matrix.csv")
    Q = np.loadtxt(file, delimiter=",")
    file.close()
    print(Q)
    ```

Output:

```
[[ 1.3   -0.63 -0.34 -0.3    0.22  0.1    0.03 -0.5    0.28 -0.8
 -0.1 ]
 [ 0.    0.51 -0.25  0.42   0.45  0.89   0.09 -0.8   -0.74 -0.68
 -0.2 ]
 [ 0.    0.    0.84   0.03 -0.3    0.5   -0.22  0.7   -0.3    0.6
 0.3 ]
 [ 0.    0.    0.     0.75   0.51 -0.2    0.25  0.3   -0.03  0.03
 0.4 ]
 [ 0.    0.    0.     0.     0.27 -0.65  -0.4   0.2   -0.46  0.54
 -0.2 ]
 [ 0.    0.    0.     0.     0.     0.15  -0.95  0.51   0.67 -0.22
 -0.4 ]
 [ 0.    0.    0.     0.     0.     0.     0.35 -0.6    0.63  0.2
 0.25]
 [ 0.    0.    0.     0.     0.     0.     0.     0.25 -0.81 -0.59
 -0.4 ]
 [ 0.    0.    0.     0.     0.     0.     0.     0.     0.5   0.01
 0.3 ]
 [ 0.    0.    0.     0.     0.     0.     0.     0.     0.     0.6
 -0.1 ]
 [ 0.    0.    0.     0.     0.     0.     0.     0.     0.     0.
 0.1 ]]
```

3. Now, we can iterate through the `parameter` landscape. The values that are generated have been summarized in *Figure 9.1*:

```
for p1 in param1:
    for p2 in param2:
        solution,energy,quantity=optimize_bqm([p1],
            [p2], Q, 100000)
        print('Parameters', p1, p2, 'Solution:',
            solution, 'Energy:',energy,
            'Qty Sampled',quantity)
```

Summarized output:

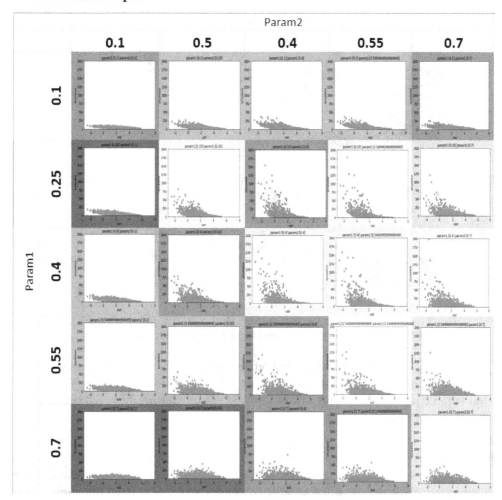

Figure 9.1 – The effect the parameter values have on the probability distribution in the QAOA algorithm

In *Figure 9.1*, for each sub-plot, the *X*-axis is the cost and the *Y*-axis is the occurrences. The highest occurrence of the lowest cost, `-2.5`, was found at `param1=0.4` and `param2=0.55`. The individual plots are available in the code output which can be found in this book's GitHub repository.

4. The same process is repeated, only this time, each parameter is only sampled 10 times using the `param_optimizer()` function, and the lowest value that's found for each set is plotted:

```
ideal_param1, ideal_param2, lowest_energy=
    param_optimizer(param1, param2, Q, 10)
```

Output:

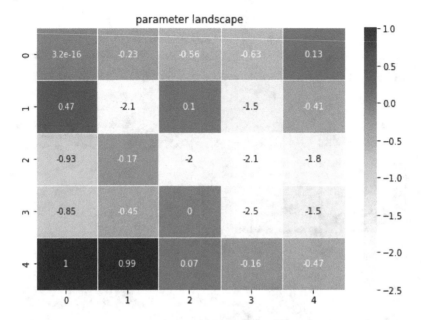

Figure 9.2 – Lowest costs found in the parameter landscape

Since we only sample a few times, it is not certain whether we will see the lowest cost where the optimal probability profile is created. In *Step 3*, the largest occurrence of the lowest cost was found at `param1=0.4` and `param 2=0.55`. However, here, the lowest cost of `-2.5` was found at `param1=0.55` and `param2=0.55`.

With that, we understand how the parameters affect the probability of finding the minimum value. However, what if we don't know the minimum value, the ideal parameters, or the probability profiles? In a typical scenario, we would get a function and would have to run it through an algorithm that finds the minimum cost. To do this, we will use the `scipy.optimize.minimze()` optimizer. This takes an `objective` function with input parameters and will move to the minimum cost by trying out different parameter values. In other words, rather than creating the full parameter landscape, as we have done previously, we will let the optimizer fine-tune the parameters toward lower costs. Keep in mind that since we have a noisy objective function, it presents a considerable challenge for the optimizer. An objective function called `func_bqm()` has been created that produces the QAOA quantum circuit, similar to `optimize_bqm()`, but it can be used by the optimizer.

Let's see how this works with the same `IonQ_matrix` file, where we know the minimum cost is -2.5:

1. First, we will create global variables that will be used to collect the cost values as the optimizer runs. We are limiting the measurements to only 10 shots and giving initial starting values of 0.3 to each parameter. Notice that we are using the *Nelder-Mead* method, which will try different parameter values to move toward the lowest cost. However, we already realize that the output of `func_bqm()` is going to be noisy, which will prevent `minimize()` from converging rapidly:

```
shots=10
SV=False
Q=Q
param1_list=[]
param2_list=[]
min_value_list=[]
solution_list=[]
quantity_list=[]
params=[0.3,0.3]
res = minimize(func_bqm, params, method='Nelder-Mead',
               tol=0.001)
print(res)
```

Output:

```
final_simplex: (array([[0.31335937, 0.30210938],
       [0.31336539, 0.30210349],
       [0.31336547, 0.30210334]]), array([-2.5, -2.5, -2.5]))
           fun: -2.5000000000000004
       message: 'Optimization terminated successfully.'
          nfev: 69
           nit: 28
        status: 0
       success: True
             x: array([0.31335937, 0.30210938])
```

The preceding output shows that the function found the minimum value of -2.5 in 69 iterations. The final fine-tuned parameters were 0.31335937 and 0.30210938.

2. Let's plot the different parameter values that the optimizer used:

```
plt.plot(param1_list)
plt.plot(param2_list)
plt.show()
```

Output:

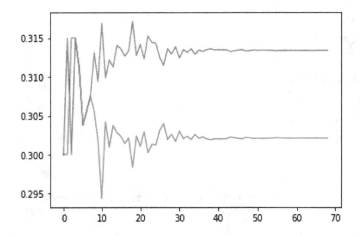

Figure 9.3 – Parameter tuning with an optimizer using Nelder-Mead

You may want to try running these scenarios multiple times to get more familiar with the optimizer.

3. We can also plot the values of the cost that were picked up by the optimizer:

```
plt.plot(min_value_list)
plt.show()
```

Output:

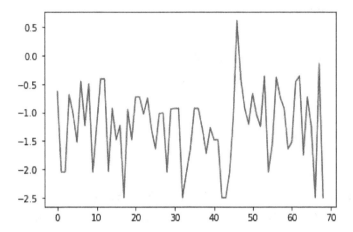

Figure 9.4 – Cost values during iterations within the optimizer using Nelder-Mead

Ideally, these values should gradually approach the lowest cost. However, due to the noisy nature of the quantum objective function, even when the parameters are not changing much, the cost values fluctuate dramatically, especially since we are using only 10 measurements per iteration. In this example, the lowest cost was found before 20 iterations; however, the optimizer continues to try out different values with the expectation that the cost should stabilize toward a minimum.

4. Now, let's try a different optimizer method called **Powell**. One advantage of this method is that we can set bounds on the parameters and let the optimizer vary the parameters within those bounds. We will reset the list variables that will be used for plotting the results and give an initial starting point for the parameters. The bounds on param1 and param2 will be added:

```
shots=10
SV=False
Q=Q
param1_list=[]
param2_list=[]
min_value_list=[]
solution_list=[]
quantity_list=[]
params=[0.3,0.3]
res = minimize(func_bqm, params, bounds=((0.1, 0.8),
            (0.1, 0.8)), method='Powell', tol=0.01)
print(res)
```

Output:

```
direc: array([[1., 0.],
       [0., 1.]])
  fun: -2.5000000000000004
message: 'Optimization terminated successfully.'
 nfev: 35
  nit: 2
status: 0
success: True
    x: array([0.26858092, 0.58975883])
```

The function also found ideal parameters, 0.26858092 and 0.58975883, that are very close to the values we determined earlier after plotting all the probability profiles in *Figure 9.1*.

5. Now, let's plot the parameters since the optimizer varied them:

```
plt.plot(param1_list)
plt.plot(param2_list)
plt.show()
```

Output:

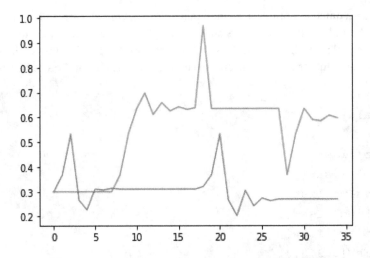

Figure 9.5 – Parameter tuning by optimizer using Powell

6. Next, we will plot the cost since it varied through the 35 iterations:

```
plt.plot(min_value_list)
plt.show()
```

Output:

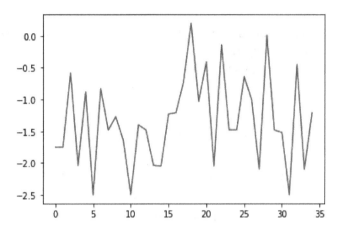

Figure 9.6 – Cost values during iterations within the optimizer using Powell

The optimizer found the lowest value within five iterations but continued to run to find other locations where there might be a better value. In addition, we can see the impact that the probabilistic nature of the quantum circuit has.

With that, we have reviewed how QAOA can give a better optimum by adding a classical optimizer and allowing it to fine-tune the parameters. In the next section, we will look at the other critical component in getting better results, which is using small incremental rotation steps while building the QAOA algorithm.

Multiple-step parameter optimization in QAOA

While discussing QAOA, we have only been using one cycle of the RZ and RX gate rotations. However, in the previous chapter, as shown in *Figure 8.6*, we realized that QAOA can be improved by small incremental steps and repeatedly applying the RZ and RX gate rotations and their parameters. In this section, we will review the improvement we get in the results while using this method. We will fix the first set of parameters from the previous section's exercise and then vary the second set of `param1` and `param2` to view the effect. Let's get started:

1. First, we must prepare the second cycle parameter range:

```
param1=np.arange(0.1,0.8,0.15,dtype=float)
param2=np.arange(0.1,0.8,0.15,dtype=float)
```

```
print(param1)
print(param2)
```

Output:

```
[0.1   0.25 0.4   0.55 0.7 ]
[0.1   0.25 0.4   0.55 0.7 ]
```

2. Now, we must run the optimization function and pass in the param values for both cycles. The first set of values are arbitrarily fixed to 0.25 and 0.35, respectively, while the values for the second cycle are varied through the parameter landscape:

```
for p1 in param1:
    for p2 in param2:
        solution,energy,quantity=optimize_bqm([0.25,
            p1], [0.35, p2], Q, 100000)
        print('Parameters', p1, p2, 'Solution:',
            solution, 'Energy:',energy,
            'Qty Sampled',quantity)
```

Output (only one plot shown):

```
Parameters 0.4 0.4 Solution: 11000001111 Energy:
-2.5000000000000004 Qty Sampled 2707
```

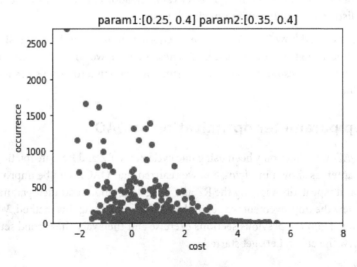

Figure 9.7 – Improved probability of the optimum value found using
two cycles of Z and X rotations in the QAOA algorithm

The results show that we can get a dramatic improvement in finding the minimum cost with parameters that have been fine-tuned through repeated RZ and RX gate operations.

In the end, an ideal QAOA implementation will make appropriate use of low sampling, multiple cycles of RZ and RX gates, and an efficient classical optimizer model that can rapidly find the optimal parameters.

Now that we have reviewed the two additional components of QAOA, we are better equipped to run this hybrid algorithm on various quantum devices. In the next section, we will review considerations for implementing QAOA on various devices, its limitations, and review the performance of the algorithm.

Benchmarking QAOA on Amazon Braket devices

In this section, we will use what we have learned with QAOA to compare the performance of Amazon Braket devices. This includes the SV1 and TN1 quantum simulators, IonQ's 11-qubit Ion Trap quantum computer, Rigetti's new Aspen-11 38-qubit superconducting quantum processor, D-Wave's quantum annealer, and the classical simulated annealer, which is also available through D-Wave. We will start with an 11x11 matrix that represents our problem and work our way up to a 100x100 matrix. Along the way, we will discover the strategies that are needed to solve these types of matrices on different quantum devices and the limits of each device.

Optimizing an 11x11 matrix

We will continue to use the `IonQ_matrix.csv` file in this section. The IonQ device that's available on Amazon Braket has 11 qubits, so we cannot solve a matrix larger than this with the available device. However, in the IonQ device, every qubit can be entangled with every other qubit, so we do not have to worry about mapping our problem to the QPU architecture. We have already run this matrix with the local simulator. Therefore, we will continue with the Amazon Braket **SV1** and **TN1** simulators and then the other Amazon Braket devices. Let's get started:

1. First, we will prepare the range for the parameters. We are using the same matrix Q that was loaded from the `IonQ_matrix.csv` file:

    ```
    param=np.arange(0.1,0.5,0.1,dtype=float)
    print(param)
    ```

    Output:

    ```
    [0.1 0.2 0.3 0.4]
    ```

    We will use the same range for both parameters. Note that running each set of parameter trials takes time and has a charge on Amazon Braket, so we have limited the number of possible trials.

2. To use Amazon Braket devices, we can use the `param_optimizer_device()` function. This can be used with the IonQ and Rigetti Amazon Braket quantum computer devices and the SV1 and TN1 simulators:

```
ideal_param1, ideal_param2, lowest_energy=
    param_optimizer_device(param, param, Q, 100,'SV1')
print(ideal_param1, ideal_param2, lowest_energy)
```

Output:

```
0.1 0.4 -2.5000000000000004
```

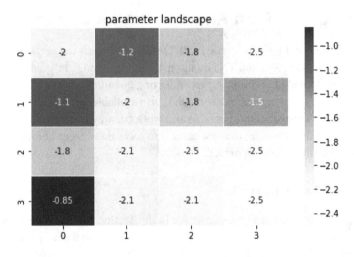

Figure 9.8 – Lowest costs found in the parameter landscape when using SV1

The lowest costs that were found match what we saw previously. Since we are using a simulator and the price of using the simulator is less, we have increased the number of shots from 10 to 100, so we see the lowest cost more often throughout the landscape. Our output reads out one of the parameters where the lowest cost is found at `param1=0.1` and `param2=0.4`.

3. Now, let's run the same matrix on TN1:

```
ideal_param1, ideal_param2, lowest_energy=
    param_optimizer_device(param, param, Q, 100,'TN1')
print(ideal_param1, ideal_param2, lowest_energy)
```

Output:

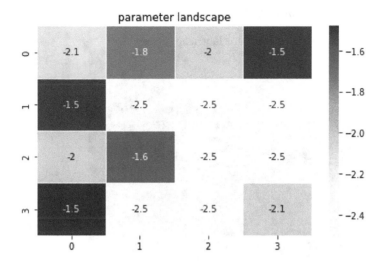

Figure 9.9 – Lowest costs found in the parameter landscape when using TN1

TN1 also provides a similar pattern for this specific problem, but the minimum is found more often due to the probabilistic nature. Notice we have use the same number of shots, the matrix Q, and parameter ranges. Please run this function a few times to see how the minimum cost values change on the paramater landscape.

4. Finally, we want to use this matrix to tune parameters on IonQ. We will reduce the range of parameters that will be tested to reduce the charge of using the Ion Trap multiple times:

```
param=np.arange(0.2,0.5,0.1,dtype=float)
print(param)
```

Output:

```
[0.2 0.3 0.4]
```

5. The following code submits the matrix to the IonQ device nine times. Since we are submitting these tasks individually, the execution waits in the queue nine times and takes considerable time to run. Since we are going to a real quantum computer with only 100 shots, the chance of seeing the lowest value is slim:

```
ideal_param1, ideal_param2, lowest_energy=
    param_optimizer_device(param, param, Q, 100,'IonQ
                    Device')
print(ideal_param1, ideal_param2, lowest_energy)
```

Output:

```
0.2 0.2 -2.0500000000000003
```

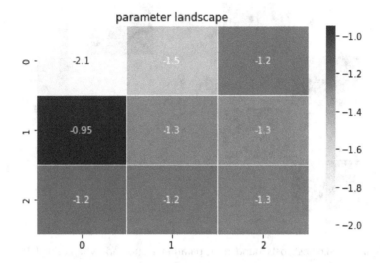

Figure 9.10 – Lowest costs found in the parameter landscape when using IonQ

As expected, we do not see the lowest cost of -2.5 and the lowest cost of -2.05 is reached when both parameters are 0.2.

6. Since we have some idea of the parameters to use to find the lowest cost, several trials were done using IonQ. These can be found in the code for this chapter. Here, we will show one example where IonQ was able to find the lowest cost. To use IonQ, a new function, `schedule_optimize_bqm_task()`, has been provided that schedules the task to the Amazon Braket device and returns `task_id`. Since the tasks may take a while to work their way through the queue before they are executed on the IonQ device, it is useful to use this function. In this case, the following parameters were used:

```
param1=[0.27723358]
param2=[0.28702843]
shots=1000
```

7. Next, we must set `device` to the IonQ device:

```
device=set_device('IonQ Device')
```

Output:

```
Device('name': IonQ Device, 'arn': arn:aws:braket:::device/
qpu/ionq/ionQdevice)
```

8. We can also estimate the cost of running this job on IonQ:

```
estimate_cost(device,num_shots=shots)
```

Output:

```
device cost per  shot : $ 0.01

total cost for 1000 shots is $10.30
```

9. The following code submits the QAOA circuit on the IonQ device with the fixed parameters:

```
task_id=schedule_optimize_bqm_task(param1, param2, Q,
                                   shots, device)
results, metadata, counts=recover_task(task_id)
solution=[]
quantity=[]
energy=[]
for keys,values in zip(counts.keys(),counts.values()):
    solution.append(keys)
    quantity.append(values)
    energy.append(sum_energy(Q,keys))
energy_np=np.array(energy)
index=np.argsort(energy)
plt.scatter(energy,quantity)
plt.show()
print('minimum found', energy[index[0]])
```

Output:

```
minimum found -2.5000000000000004
```

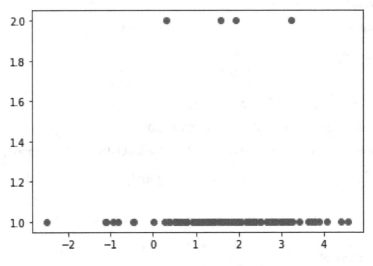

Figure 9.11 – Probability result from IonQ

As can be seen in *Figure 9.11*, even though quantum computers are still noisy, we can see that the lowest solution was found. However, this was not the case on every run. The code provided with this chapter includes some additional runs, including two and three cycles of the RZ and RX rotations.

Now, let's learn how to run a problem represented by a larger matrix.

Optimizing a 34x34 matrix

We will now attempt to solve a 34x34 full upper triangular matrix. This matrix is too large to be run on the local simulator. In addition, this cannot be solved on TN1 since TN1 requires a problem that has been defined by a sparse matrix, which is a matrix that has mostly zero values. TN1 will return a message stating *Predicted runtime based on the best contraction path found exceeds the TN1 limit.* This is the largest matrix that can be solved on SV1. Just one run with carefully chosen parameters took approximately 1 hour to run and even with 100 samples, it did not produce a result even close to the minimum cost.

Now, we must use the D-Wave quantum annealer. We can use the run_dwave() function here, which only requires an upper triangular matrix and creates the binary quadratic model to solve on the D-Wave annealer.

Note that this method does not create a quantum circuit and does not involve QAOA. However, it optimizes the energy landscape using quantum annealers, as we discussed in *Chapter 5, Using Quantum Annealers – Developing a QUBO Function and Using Constraints*.

Follow these steps to create the matrix and find the optimum cost for the various simulators and quantum devices. We will also discover which devices will optimize this QUBO efficiently:

1. First, we must generate the 34x34 matrix using the `generate_matrix()` function. This function reads a file that already has a random set of integer values in a 100x100 matrix. By entering the number of qubits, the function returns a matrix of the desired size for testing purposes:

    ```
    Qubits=34
    Q34=generate_matrix(Qubits)
    print(Q34)
    ```

    Output:

    ```
    [[-5.   1.   1.  ...   1.   1.   2.]
     [ 0.  -4.   2.  ...   2.   1.   1.]
     [ 0.   0.  -5.  ...   1.   2.   2.]

     ...

     [ 0.   0.   0.  ...  -3.   2.   1.]
     [ 0.   0.   0.  ...   0.  -3.   3.]
     [ 0.   0.   0.  ...   0.   0.  -3.]]
    ```

2. Now, we must pass the matrix to the function that has been provided with `run_dwave()`. This function will convert the matrix into a BQM, send the BQM to the D-Wave Annealer device, and print the results:

    ```
    response=run_dwave(Q34)
    ```

    Output:

    ```
    Number of qubits:   5760
    Number of couplers 40279
    Shots max 10,000
    429496729600
    Recommended shots 10000
    Estimated cost $2.20
             0  1  2  3  4  5 ... 33 energy num_oc. ...
    0        1  0  0  0  0  0 ...  0   -9.0       1 ...
    ```

    Only the first row of the list of possible results is shown here. As we can see, the minimum energy found was -9.

3. Next, we must send the matrix to the classical simulated annealer (NEAL) using the `run_neal()` function:

```
response=run_neal(Q34)
```

Output:

```
Sample(sample={0: 1, 1: 0, 2: 1, 3: 0, 4: 0, 5: 0, 6: 0, 7:
0, 8: 0, 9: 0, 10: 0, 11: 0, 12: 0, 13: 0, 14: 0, 15: 0, 16:
0, 17: 0, 18: 0, 19: 0, 20: 1, 21: 0, 22: 0, 23: 0, 24: 0,
25: 0, 26: 0, 27: 1, 28: 0, 29: 0, 30: 0, 31: 0, 32: 0, 33:
0}, energy=-12.0, num_occurrences=1)
```

```
1010000000000000000010000001000000
```

This result is generated relatively quickly and we get the minimum energy at -12. The long string of zeros and ones is the actual solution of the 34 bits, which produces a cost of -12. Notice that it only has four *ones* in it which represents the index values of 0, 2, 20 and 27. The probabilistic sampler, which we will run in the next step, looks for all possible solutions with 1 index with a value of 1, then two indexes with a value of 1 and so on. Thus it is looking for smaller to larger number of 1 values in the solution.

4. We can also try the `ProbabilisticSampler()` function, which we used in *Chapter 5, Using Quantum Annealers – Developing a QUBO Function and Using Constraints*. The following solver example has been set up with a maximum of 20,000 samples per iteration within a range from 1 to 10. This range starts with a solution containing only single ones, then two ones, and so on:

```
ProbabilisticSampler(Q34,20000,0,1,10)
```

Output:

```
Best found: [0, 2, 20, 27]
```

```
count: 4
```

```
Energy: -12.0
```

```
Solutions Sampled: 146579
```

```
[34,
  561,
  5984,
  46376,
  278256,
  1344904,
  5379616,
  18156204,
```

```
52451256,

131128140]
```

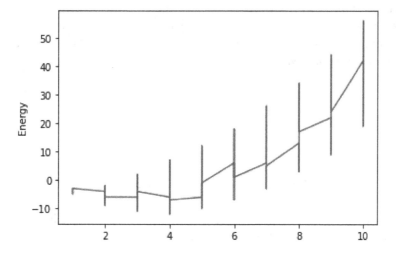

Figure 9.12 – Result of the probabilistic sampler with a limited range of solutions

Interestingly, in *Figure 9.12* we can see that this sampler can find the minimum value by randomly sampling the solution space in a sequence of the number of ones found in the solution. This was successful because the optimal solution only had four ones in the solution, and the total possible combinations with four ones is 46,376. The output above also displays an array of numbers, [34,561,5984,46376,...,131128140], which indicates the total possible combinations in each step. There are only 46,376 combinations (the fourth number in the array) with four ones in the solution, so it is easier to find the minimum value.

The observation, in this case, is that with a fully connected upper triangular matrix, getting a solution becomes somewhat challenging when using quantum methods and simulators. The SV1 result took too long to execute and produced a solution that was not close to the minimum cost. TN1 did not produce a result either. D-Wave's result was close to the minimum, but the maximum allowed shots of 10,000 may not be sufficient to find a solution in a landscape of 2^{34} or approximately 17 billion different solutions. To find the actual solution, we had to rely on the classical simulated annealer and the probabilistic sampler.

Optimizing a 38x38 sparse matrix

The next size we will review is a 38x38 problem matrix. However, we will use a very specific matrix that has the same graph as the Rigetti Aspen-11 quantum computer. Thus, it is intended to be the ideal shape for the Rigetti Aspen-11 QPU topology. The same process can be used for the Rigetti Aspen M-1 device. Please note that the Aspen M-1 topology was covered in *Chapter 2, Braket Devices Explained*, and you can review it in *Figure 2.9*. In this chapter, we will use the Aspen-11:

Figure 9.13 – Rigetti Aspen-11 topology

The reason for this is to minimize any swapping and errors and therefore produce the best results possible. For actual problems, this will not be the case.

We will use the already existing matrix file; that is, `Aspen_matrix.csv`. If you wish to create a new file with randomly generated values, you can use the `create_aspen_11__matrix()` and `create_aspen_M1_matrix()` functions provided. You can uncomment the appropriate line in the code with the `create_aspen...()` functions and create a new matrix:

1. First, we will load the sparse matrix:

```
file = open("Aspen_matrix.csv")
A = np.loadtxt(file, delimiter=",")
file.close()
print(A)
```

Output:

```
[[-2.    0.1   0.    ...   0.    0.    0. ]
 [ 0.   -2.    0.7 ...   0.    0.    0. ]
 [ 0.    0.   -4.    ...   0.    0.    0. ]

 ...

 [ 0.    0.    0.    ...  -2.    0.2   0. ]
 [ 0.    0.    0.    ...   0.   -4.    1.3]
 [ 0.    0.    0.    ...   0.    0.   -4. ]]
```

As we can see, because of the qubit numbers, the 38-qubit device is represented by the matrix file with a shape of (48,48). It contains mostly zero values except in the diagonals and the locations that represent the connections between the qubits in the Aspen-11 topology. Also, note that some diagonal values are also zero. This is because, in the Aspen-11 topology, those qubit numbers do not exist (for example, 8, 9, and so on). Positive values are in red, while negative values are in blue. The Excel file containing the conditional color on the values is included in this book's GitHub repository. The GitHub repository for this chapter also contains the `Aspen-M-1_matrix.csv` and the color coded `fig 9.14 Aspen-M-1_matrix.xlxs` file which shows the same information as that of Apsen 11 shown in *Figure 9.14* below:

Figure 9.14 – The 48x48 matrix file representing the 38-qubit Aspen-11 device

2. We will find the optimal parameters to solve this matrix, as we did previously, using the `param_optimizer_device()` function. Please note that this function generates a task for the quantum device for each parameter combination and waits in the queue for that task to finish before sending the next task. Thus, it will tie up the notebook for a considerable amount of time. For this reason, the parameter values that have been sampled has been reduced:

```
param=np.arange(0.2,0.7,0.3,dtype=float)
print(param)
ideal_param1, ideal_param2, lowest_energy=
    param_optimizer_device(param, param, A,
```

```
                                    100,'Aspen-11')
   print(ideal_param1, ideal_param2, lowest_energy)
```

Output:

```
[0.2  0.5]
0.5  0.2  -49.8
```

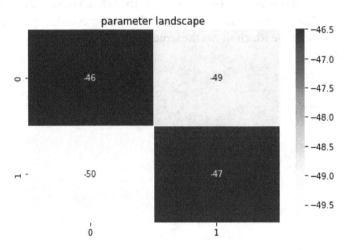

Figure 9.15 – The lowest cost values found on the parameter landscape using Aspen-11

The values that were found represent the few parameter combinations and the low number of shots. The minimum value of -49.8 was found at 0.5 and 0.2. In the next section, we will learn about Amazon Braket Jobs, where we can combine multiple tasks into one job for the quantum processor, making the process more efficient and increasing the effectiveness of the QAOA algorithm.

3. Now, let's run the matrix on the Amazon Braket TN1 simulator. TN1 does not allow blank qubit numbers (or qubits that are not used), so to run the 48x48 matrix on TN1, we need to remove the blank diagonal values. The convert_aspen_to_tn1() function converts the A matrix of size (48x48) into a TN matrix of size (38x38) so that it can be run on TN1:

```
    TN=convert_aspen_to_tn1(A)
```

Output:

```
{0: 0, 1: 1, 2: 2, 3: 3, 4: 4, 5: 5, 6: 6, 7: 7, 10: 8, 11:
9, 12: 10, 13: 11, 14: 12, 15: 13, 16: 14, 17: 15, 20: 16,
21: 17, 22: 18, 23: 19, 24: 20, 25: 21, 26: 22, 27: 23, 30:
24, 31: 25, 32: 26, 33: 27, 34: 28, 35: 29, 36: 30, 37: 31,
42: 32, 43: 33, 44: 34, 45: 35, 46: 36, 47: 37}

[[-2.    0.1  0.   ...  0.    0.    0. ]
```

```
[ 0.   -2.    0.7 ...  0.    0.    0. ]
[ 0.    0.   -4.   ...  0.    0.    0. ]

...

[ 0.    0.    0.  ... -2.    0.2   0. ]
[ 0.    0.    0.  ...  0.   -4.    1.3]
[ 0.    0.    0.  ...  0.    0.   -4. ]]
(38, 38)
```

The preceding output shows how the original 48 qubit numbers can be mapped to 38 qubits and that the modified matrix now has a shape of (38,38).

4. Now, let's process this matrix with TN1 while keeping the number of shots low at 100:

```
param=np.arange(0.2,0.7,0.1,dtype=float)
print(param)
ideal_param1, ideal_param2, lowest_energy=
    param_optimizer_device(param, param, TN,
                       100,'TN1')
print(ideal_param1, ideal_param2, lowest_energy)
```

Output:

```
[0.2 0.5]
0.2 0.5 -62.5
```

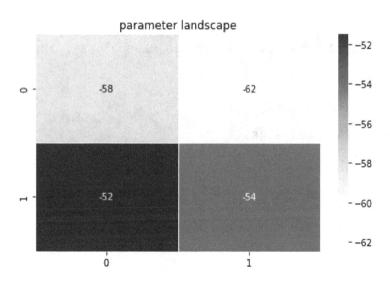

Figure 9.16 – The lowest cost values found on the parameter landscape when using TN1

The lowest cost of -62.5 was found at 0.2 and 0.5.

5.   Now, let's run the matrix on D-Wave's annealer:

```
response=run_dwave(TN)
```

Output:

```
Number of qubits:   5760

Number of couplers 40279

Shots max 10,000

Estimated cost $2.20
          0  1  2  3  4  5  6   ... 37 energy num_oc. ...
0         1  1  1  0  1  0  1   ...  1  -67.8       71 ...
11101011101101011111011011011111100111
decimal equivalent: 253092542439
Validate energy -67.8
```

D-Wave finds the lowest cost of -67.8 with the 10,000 shots. The 38-bit representation of the solution is 11101011101101011111011011011111100111.

6.   Now, let's run the matrix through the probabilistic sampler, which will give us an overall view of the energy landscape sorted by the number of qubits that have a value of one:

```
ProbabilisticSampler(TN,2000)
```

Output:

```
Best found: [0, 1, 2, 3, 4, 6, 7, 8, 10, 11, 12, 13, 15, 16,
17, 18, 20, 22, 23, 24, 25, 27, 28, 29, 30, 31, 32, 34, 35,
36, 37]

count: 31

Energy: -62.79999999999999

Solutions Sampled: 67483
```

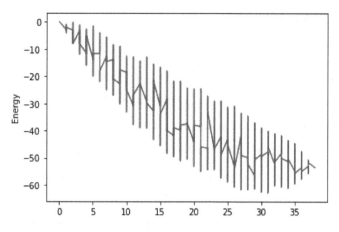

Figure 9.17 – Energy landscape from the probabilistic sampler

The probabilistic sampler is a good way to sample the matrix and see where the minimum value is likely. In this case, we can see that the minimum value is -62.8. This is pretty close to the actual minimum. We can also see that the best solution has 31 ones in its 38-bit value.

7. Finally, let's use the classical simulated annealer to find the minimum value:

```
response=run_neal(TN)
```

Output:

```
Sample(sample={0: 1, 1: 1, 2: 1, 3: 0, 4: 1, 5: 0, 6: 1, 7:
1, 8: 1, 9: 0, 10: 1, 11: 1, 12: 0, 13: 1, 14: 0, 15: 1, 16:
1, 17: 1, 18: 1, 19: 1, 20: 0, 21: 1, 22: 1, 23: 0, 24: 1,
25: 1, 26: 0, 27: 1, 28: 1, 29: 1, 30: 1, 31: 1, 32: 1, 33:
0, 34: 0, 35: 1, 36: 1, 37: 1}, energy=-67.80000000000001,
num_occurrences=1)
```

```
11101011101101011110110110111111100111
```

```
253092542439
```

We can now see the minimum cost of -67.8 for the 38-bit solution of 11101011101101 01111011011011111100111.

The code provided for this chapter includes additional matrix runs, including 14x14, 50x50, and 100x100. Now, let's summarize what we have learned from these experiments and see what intuition we can gain when solving QUBO problems using QAOA on gate-based quantum computers and BQM on annealers.

Summary of results

You must consider the following when deciding which QPU can be used for calculations:

- The number of qubits needed for the problem and the qubit limit of the device
- The speed of execution (processing time and the time in the queue)
- The minimum number of shots required for accurate results versus the shot limit of the device
- The quality of the results that's expected based on the errors of the device
- The quadratic terms in the matrix (full versus sparse matrix) and the qubit's interconnectivity
- The cost of execution that was evaluated based on the execution time or the number of shots
- The probabilistic versus exact result requirement to decide between measurements (shots) versus state vector results or a classical solver
- Gate-based versus quantum annealing (also known as gate-based simulator versus simulated annealer)
- The availability of the device (review the schedule when certain quantum devices are available)

All these factors can be complicated when deciding which device to use in solving specific problems. To simplify this, the following diagram shows the limit on the number of variables that can be used on the different devices and where the device may not be able to solve a fully connected matrix:

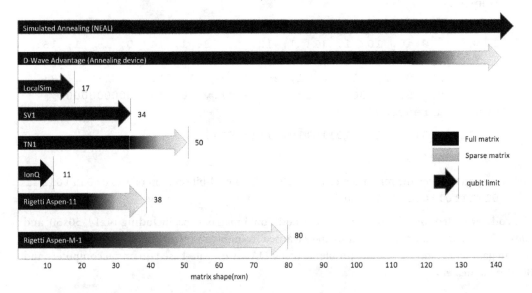

Figure 9.18 – Relative performance of various devices available in Amazon Braket

You should also try out different size matrices to form an opinion on the quality of the results and the limits of each device. The vertical axis is loosely associated with the quality of the results. The top devices provide accurate results, while the lower ones have more inherent errors.

Summary

In this chapter, we discussed the practical considerations of QAOA while fine-tuning the parameters further to get the lowest cost. This allows us to use not only the quantum annealer to solve optimization problems, but also gate-based quantum annealers. Then, we used various BQM matrices to evaluate the performance and limitations of the devices available in Amazon Braket. We looked at various considerations when deciding which solver to use and summarized the capabilities and limitations of the various devices available in Amazon Braket. The goal of this chapter was not to benchmark the devices, but to show how each system can be used and some of the nuances you should consider. I encourage you to create inputs and try to experiment with the different devices or make some code modifications if needed to try out new methods or devices that may have been added to Amazon Braket. With this, we have also ended *Section 2, Building Blocks for Real World Use Cases* of this book.

In *Chapter 10, Amazon Braket Hybrid Jobs, PennyLane, and Other Braket features*, we will look at Amazon Braket Hybrid Jobs, which allows multiple calls to a quantum device to be run as one Job. This can be very helpful as you have seen in this chapter when we utilized a quantum device many times with slightly modified quantum circuits. These variational algorithms can be more efficiently run using Amazon Braket Hybrid Jobs. We will also quickly review some of the additional features that have been added to Amazon Braket including leveraging the PennyLane library, Qiskit, and Xanadu.

Further reading

- To gain more insights into the concepts that were covered in this chapter, please refer to the following Amazon Braket resources and example on QAOA:

  - `https://docs.aws.amazon.com/braket/latest/developerguide/braket-devices.html`

  - `https://aws.amazon.com/braket/quantum-computers/`

  - `https://github.com/aws/amazon-braket-examples/tree/main/examples/hybrid_quantum_algorithms/QAOA`

- For information on the *Chain Strength* of D-Wave, please refer to `https://www.dwavesys.com/media/kjtlcemb/14-1054a-a_advantage_system_performance_update.pdf`.

Code Deep Dive:

Please review the code in the following new functions that were introduced in this chapter and were provided as part of this chapter's discussion. They can be found in the GitHub repository for this chapter:

- `run_dwave()`
- `run_neal()`
- `create_aspen_11_matrix()`
- `create_aspen_M-1_matrix()`
- `generate_matrix()`
- `generate_sparse_matrix()`
- `convert_aspen_to_tn1()`

Concluding section 2

This section showed you the possibilities and limitations in this new field of quantum computing. We started by learning about quantum annealing and were introduced to the D-Wave advantage device, which can be used to find the minimum of a QUBO problem. Then, we slowly worked our way through understanding how quantum computers work. We started with qubits, then quantum gates, and eventually more elaborate quantum circuits that can add, subtract, and reveal numbers that are stored in the phase information of the qubits. We showed you how to use a quantum phase adder to determine all possible values of a function. This led to us creating a way to amplify the probability of the minimum cost using the QAOA hybrid algorithm, which requires classical parameter tuning. Finally, we evaluated the practical implementation of this algorithm on various devices.

In the current evolution of quantum computers, there are considerable challenges when it comes to getting results that are faster or better than classical solvers. Some of these are as follows:

- A limited number of qubits.
- Low connectivity between qubits in some cases.
- The probabilistic nature of measuring qubit states.
- Limits on the number of measurements.
- Gate operations have a limited length.
- Rapid time to qubit decoherence.
- There are limited quantum algorithms with proven advantages.
- Loading and storing data.

The quantum computing industry is rapidly bringing better and more sophisticated devices to the cloud. Amazon Braket allows us to experiment with a commonly used optimization model both classically, on quantum simulators, and with gate-based quantum computing and quantum annealing devices. Amazon Braket also allows us to use Xanadu's **PennyLane** library, which is constantly being improved and includes many efficient algorithms for practical use cases. The library contains the latest advancements in efficient and easy-to-use hybrid quantum algorithms. We will leverage Amazon Braket Jobs to submit our full variational algorithm as one job in *Chapter 10, Amazon Braket Hybrid Jobs, PennyLane, and Other Braket Features*.

In *Section 3, Real World Use Cases,* we will use pre-built libraries to tackle real-world problems in optimization, molecule simulations, and machine learning and execute them on the Amazon Braket platform. We will execute our use cases on quantum simulators and look at how to experiment with current quantum computers wherever possible based on their size and capabilities.

Section 3:
Real-World
Use Cases

In this section, you will see how today's quantum computers can begin to be used to solve real-world problems. You will use the very basic tools, techniques, and mathematics that are fundamental for formulating real-world problems for quantum computers. After this, you should have an idea of the limitations but also the opportunities for how your organization can use this new technology as it matures.

This section contains the following chapters:

- *Chapter 10, Amazon Braket Hybrid Jobs, PennyLane, and Other Braket Features*
- *Chapter 11, Single-Objective Optimization Use Case*
- *Chapter 12, Multi-Objective Optimization Use Case*

10
Amazon Braket Hybrid Jobs, PennyLane, and other Braket Features

Amazon Braket includes a set of features that dramatically expands the user's ability to evaluate and test various quantum algorithms in the most efficient manner. First, we will discuss Amazon Braket Hybrid Jobs, which provides a default environment where users can efficiently run hybrid algorithms such as **Quantum Approximate Optimization Algorithm** (**QAOA**) and **Variational Quantum Eigensolver** (**VQE**). In this chapter, we will use our previous implementation of QAOA within the Amazon Braket framework.

Amazon Braket also provides additional environments where users of the PennyLane libraries can run their hybrid algorithms using AWS and Amazon Braket resources. There are many additional features to explore in Amazon Braket and within Amazon Braket Hybrid Jobs. However, the major coverage in this chapter will be around Amazon Braket Hybrid Jobs, while the other add-on devices and features will be mentioned briefly in this chapter along with links to find more information.

The following items will be covered:

- Amazon Braket Hybrid Jobs
- A QAOA example using Amazon Braket Hybrid Jobs
- PennyLane jobs using Amazon Braket
- Xanadu Borealis
- IBM Qiskit
- Other Braket features

Technical requirement

The source code for this chapter is available in the following GitHub repository:

https://github.com/PacktPublishing/Quantum-Computing-Experimentation-with-Amazon-Braket/tree/main/Chapter10.

Utilizing Amazon Braket Hybrid Jobs

Amazon Braket Hybrid Jobs allows users to run a hybrid algorithm such as QAOA as a single job to a quantum processor. This way, when the **Quantum Processing Unit (QPU)** becomes available, it is dedicated to the job until all the quantum circuit requests are processed and then the QPU is released.

To accomplish this, we will need to split the code written in the last section on QAOA into the **job control code**, which will be the Jupyter Notebook, and the **job source module**, which is stored as a python (QAOA.py) file. This is executed by the Amazon Braket Hybrid Jobs instance after it is created.

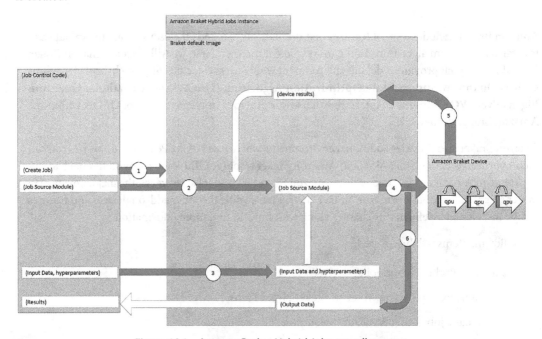

Figure 10.1 – Amazon Braket Hybrid Jobs overall process

Figure 10.1 shows the overall process at a high level. The steps in the figure are explained here:

1. The AwsQuantumJob.create() method initiates the Amazon Braket Hybrid Jobs instance, which will execute the Python script and execute tasks on the Amazon Braket devices.

2. The source module or the Python script is moved to the instance in the script directory.

3. Any data input is moved to the input directory for access to the source module, and hyperparameters become available to the source module through an environment.

4. The source module is executed along with any calls to quantum devices. When a device becomes available, the job retains priority until it exits.

5. Results from the quantum device tasks are stored in the task folder and can be accessed from within the source module for the hybrid quantum algorithm.

6. Final results from the source module can be saved using the save_job_results() function and later picked up by the job control code.

Permissions

Since Amazon Braket Hybrid Jobs requires resources to create the instance, build directories in S3 storage, and execute jobs, adequate permission needs to be given to the user. To ensure the user has permission to utilize Amazon Braket Hybrid Jobs functionality, the appropriate policy needs to be added to the user profile. The following steps are an example of adding the policy to a user account:

1. From Amazon Braket Hybrid Jobs, select the **Permissions** item and then click on the **Verify existing roles** button:

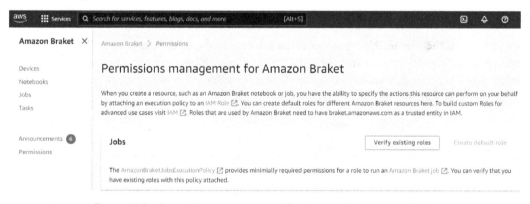

Figure 10.2 – Permissions management for Amazon Braket Hybrid Jobs

2. Next, click on the **Create default role** button:

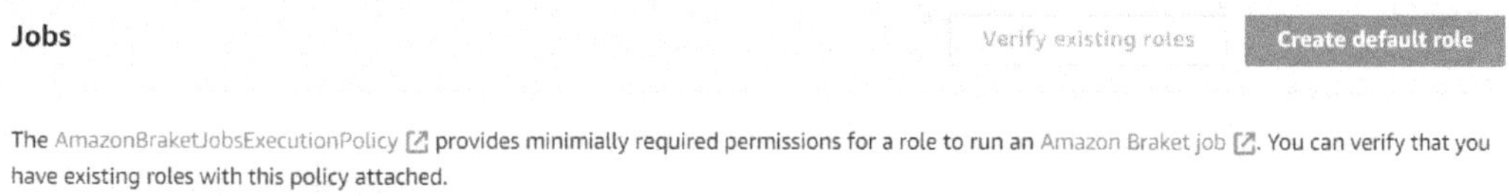

Jobs

        Verify existing roles   **Create default role**

The AmazonBraketJobsExecutionPolicy ⧉ provides minimially required permissions for a role to run an Amazon Braket job ⧉. You can verify that you have existing roles with this policy attached.

Figure 10.3 – Create default role for Amazon Braket Hybrid Jobs

3.   After the policy is created, you should see the following message, and the user can use the Amazon Braket Hybrid Jobs functions:

Figure 10.4 – Confirmation of Amazon Braket Hybrid Jobs role creation

Now that we have the permissions set up to use Amazon Braket Hybrid Jobs, we will review the basic code structure, function, and parameters to make it work.

Using Amazon Braket Hybrid Jobs

We use the `AwsQuantumJob.create()` function to initiate the creation of the Amazon Braket Job instance. The following section will detail the structure of the code and the required parameters.

Basic code structure for Amazon Braket Hybrid Jobs

We will refer to the Jupyter Notebook code as **Job Control Code**. This code will include the `AwsQuantumJob.create()` function. The `source_module` parameter points to **Job Source Module**. This is the code that will be executed on the Amazon Braket Job instance, and `entry_point` is the name of the function where the execution will begin.

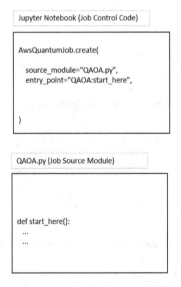

Figure 10.5 – Code structure for Amazon Braket Hybrid Jobs

The Python (QAOA.py) file identified in the source_module parameter is copied to the Amazon Braket Hybrid Jobs script folder. In addition, any file identified in the input_data parameter is copied to the data/input folder.

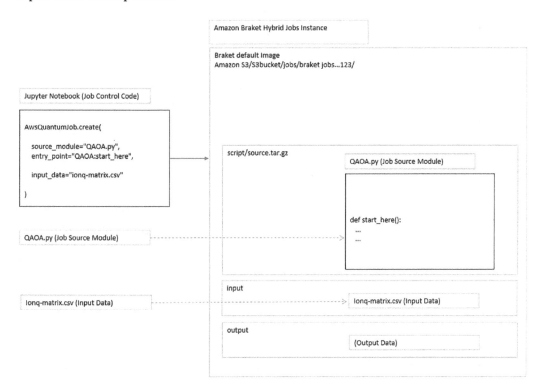

Figure 10.6 – Amazon Braket Hybrid Jobs instance and folder structure

Passing parameters and data to the Amazon Braket Hybrid Jobs instance

After the Amazon Braket Hybrid Jobs instance is created, the **Job Source Module** will be run from the function identified as entry_point. In the case of this example, this is start_here(). To retrieve the necessary information from within the new instance, a set of environment variables are used:

- The device_arn string is required for the device on which the job will be run. The location of the device determines where the instance is created. The device_arn string is passed to the os.environ["AMZN_BRAKET_DEVICE_ARN"] environment variable in **Job Source Module**.

- A set of input parameters can be saved as a Python dictionary and passed using hyperparameters. This information is saved in a file, and the file path is captured from the os.environ["AMZN_BRAKET_HP_FILE"] environment variable.

- If an input data file is required, the name of the file is passed to the input_data parameter. When the Amazon Braket Hybrid Jobs instance is created, this file will be copied to the data/input folder and the path can be retrieved in **Job Source Module** using the os.environ["AMZN_BRAKET_INPUT_DIR"] environment variable. It is necessary to construct the full file path and name string before the file can be opened.

The following figure shows how **Job Control Code** and **Job Source Module** interact:

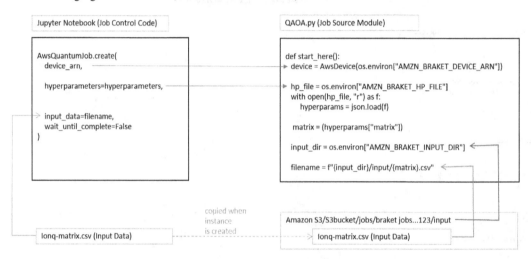

Figure 10.7 – Environment variables used by Job Source Module

Next, we will discuss how to pass information from **Job Source Module** back to **Job Control Code**.

Sending results back to Job Control Code

After the processing is complete, the final results are saved in a Python dictionary and passed back to **Job Control Code** using the save_job_result() function. The dictionary is retrieved using the job.result() method, as shown here:

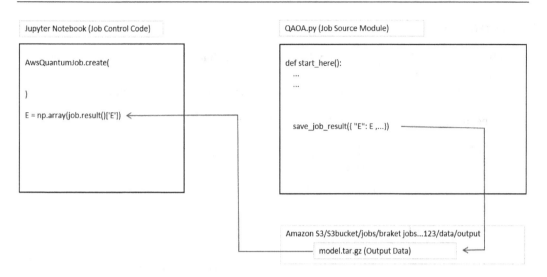

Figure 10.8 – Passing results back to Job Control Code

> **Note**
> The results are saved as individual dictionary items including 1D arrays.

This is the basic structure required to use Amazon Braket Hybrid Jobs. We will review this in more detail as we work through the sample code in this chapter and split the QAOA code in order to leverage Amazon Braket Hybrid Jobs.

A QAOA example using Amazon Braket Hybrid Jobs

In this example, we want to execute the QAOA code on the ionq-matrix.csv input file. Remember that this file contains **Binary Quadratic Model** (**BQM**) data in an 11x11 matrix. We have already found the optimal value of this input as -2.5. In this section, we will split the code used before, into the structure needed for Amazon Braket Hybrid Jobs. We will review **Job Control Code** first in its entirety and then review the **Job Source Module** code.

> **Note on Charges**
> Please carefully consider the potential charges of executing the following job. The code will execute multiple runs to an Amazon Braket device. If p is the number of QAOA parameter trial values, then the code will execute p^2 tasks with the base number of shots, and then one extra task with 10 times the base number of shots. In addition, there is a charge for the time the Amazon Braket Hybrid Jobs instance is active. More information on pricing can be found at https://aws.amazon.com/braket/pricing/.

Job Control Code

Job Control Code is in the Jupyter Notebook. Let's run through it. The key steps include preparing the required hyperparameter data and input file, passing this information to the `AwsQuantumJob.create()` method, capturing the results, and displaying them. Let's walk through the code line by line:

1. In the first code block, we import the required libraries:

```
import seaborn as sns
import matplotlib.pyplot as plt
from matplotlib.pyplot import figure
import numpy as np
import time
%matplotlib inline
from braket.aws import AwsQuantumJob,  AwsSession
import time
```

2. Next, we define the name of the file that contains the matrix data. This file will be copied from the local directory to the new job instance that is created by Amazon Braket Hybrid Jobs:

```
matrix="ionq-matrix"
filename=matrix+".csv"
```

3. We need to define variables that will create the parameter array. These values will be passed to the Python code later using hyperparameters. These are required in the form of a list:

```
start=0.1
end=0.7
step=0.1
shots=10
param=np.round(np.arange(start,end,step,dtype=float),
              2).tolist()
```

4. We can also define the job name that will show up in the job list in Amazon Braket. Using the `time()` function is helpful to ensure a unique string is created every time. If this function is not used, Amazon Braket will create its own default job name:

```
job_name="QAOA-ionqmatrix-SV1"+str(int(time.time()))
```

5.   The following dictionary is used to store the hyperparameters. Note that all values must be converted to a string:

```
#Define hyperparameters
#need to be strings
hyperparameters = {
    "start": str(start),
    "end":str(end),
    "step":str(step),
    "shots":str(shots),
    "matrix":matrix
}
```

6.   We initiate the creation of the Amazon Braket Hybrid Jobs instance using the AwsQuantumJob. create() method. Notice that we have discussed the different input parameters that are passed through this function call to the Python environment variables. After the instance is created using the default environment, the execution will move into the start_here() function in the QAOA.py code. We have typed in the device ARN string for the SV1 simulator, which will be passed to the Python code as well. The input_data string is used to pass the matrix filename, which will be moved to a default directory when the Amazon Braket Hybrid Jobs instance is created. Since we are not specifying an environment, the default environment with the Amazon Braket and other commonly used libraries is created. We also set wait_ until_complete=False so that the Jupyter Notebook execution is freed up at this point:

```
job = AwsQuantumJob.create(
    "arn:aws:braket:::device/quantum-simulator/amazon/
sv1",
    source_module="QAOA.py",
    entry_point="QAOA:start_here",
    job_name=job_name,
    hyperparameters=hyperparameters,
    input_data=filename,
    wait_until_complete=False
)
```

7. We can verify the Amazon Braket Hybrid Jobs job was created through the AWS console by clicking on the **Jobs** item in Amazon Braket. If the job was created properly, you should see the job name and the status of **RUNNING**. To check the status of the job, press the **Refresh** button:

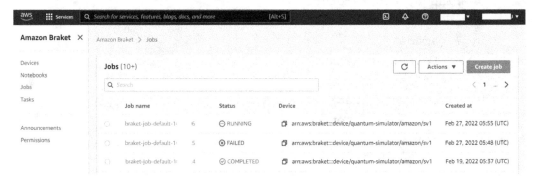

Figure 10.9 – Amazon Braket Hybrid Jobs listing

8. This code block will be run to check whether the Amazon Braket Hybrid Jobs job has completed. The job name and status are also available in the Amazon Braket Hybrid Jobs list. Click the **Refresh** button to verify the job status. More details about the job can be found by uncommenting `#print(job.metadata())`. After the job is complete, the following code will pick up the job results:

```
status=job.state()
print(status)
if status=='COMPLETED':
    #print(job.metadata())
    print(job.result())
```

9. The energy values for the parameter landscape are returned as a one-dimensional array that has to be reshaped into a two-dimensional matrix:

```
E = np.array(job.result()['E'])
D= E.reshape(len(param), len(param))
```

10. The following code block will draw the parameter landscape with the minimum energy found at each set of parameter values:

```
plt.figure(1, figsize=[7, 5])
sns.heatmap(D, annot=True,xticklabels=param,
            yticklabels=param,  linewidths=.5,
            cmap="YlGnBu", annot_kws = {'alpha': 1})
```

```
plt.title('parameter landscape');
plt.tight_layout();
```

The output plot is shown here:

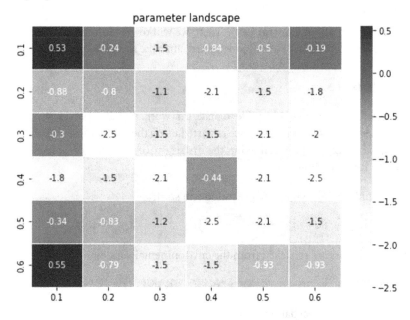

Figure 10.10 – Parameter landscape with lowest energy values found on SV1

As we have seen in the previous chapter, we run QAOA with varying parameters and look for where the lowest energy is found. We will use those parameters as the ideal parameters in the next step.

11. We now pull out the remaining output variables that are returned in the results:

```
ideal_param1=job.result()['ideal_param1']
ideal_param2=job.result()['ideal_param2']
lowest_energy=job.result()['lowest_energy']
best_energy=job.result()['best_energy']
best_solution=job.result()['best_solution']
print('ideal_param1:',ideal_param1,'ideal_param2:',
        ideal_param2,'lowest_energy:',lowest_energy)
print('best_energy:',best_energy,'best_solution:',
        best_solution)
```

Output:

```
ideal_param1: 0.30000000000000004 ideal_param2: 0.2 lowest_
energy: -2.5000000000000004
```

```
best_energy: -2.5000000000000004 best_solution: 11000001111
```

This was the full execution of **Job Control Code**. Next, we will review **Job Source Module**, which is executed within the Amazon Braket Hybrid Jobs service after the instance is created.

Job Source Module

Now we will review what is in the QAOA.py file to make this work. As stated previously, the Python file is executed after the Amazon Braket job instance is started using the AwsQuantumJob.create() method. The code execution starts as defined in the entry_point input parameter. We will now go over the start_here() function:

1. This is the definition line where the execution will start:

    ```
    def start_here():
    ```

2. The hyperparameters are retrieved from the environmental variable:

    ```
    hp_file = os.environ["AMZN_BRAKET_HP_FILE"]
    ```

3. The code extracts the hyperparameters:

    ```
    with open(hp_file, "r") as f:
        hyperparams = json.load(f)
    start = float(hyperparams["start"])
    end = float(hyperparams["end"])
    step = float(hyperparams["step"])
    shots = int(hyperparams["shots"])
    matrix = (hyperparams["matrix"])
    ```

4. The parameter range array is created using the values passed through the hyperparameters:

    ```
    param=np.arange(start,end,step,dtype=float)
    ```

5. The input directory is retrieved for the file, which is transferred to the new Amazon job environment instance. Note that this directory is created automatically since we let Amazon Braket automatically copy the file:

    ```
    input_dir = os.environ["AMZN_BRAKET_INPUT_DIR"]
    ```

6. The filename with path is constructed for the input matrix file:

```
filename = f"{input_dir}/input/{matrix}.csv"
```

7. The code loads the matrix:

```
file = open(filename)
Q = np.loadtxt(file, delimiter=",")
file.close()
```

8. The Amazon Braket device name is retrieved by the following code:

```
device = AwsDevice(
        os.environ["AMZN_BRAKET_DEVICE_ARN"])
```

9. The code now executes the `param_optimizer_device()` function, which has been slightly adjusted to run in this environment. This code still creates the QAOA circuit as before and executes it multiple times for different parameter combinations. The parameter landscape variable is passed back into the E variable as a one-dimensional array:

```
E, ideal_param1, ideal_param2, lowest_energy =
        param_optimizer_device (param, param, Q,
                                        shots, device)
```

10. As we learned in *Chapter 9, Running QAOA on Simulators and Amazon Braket Devices*, we can improve our chances of seeing the lowest value by increasing the number of shots and also cycling through the QAOA circuit multiple times. In this case, the code is set up to repeat the best parameter values twice and increase the number of shots by a factor of 10. You may try different strategies, or replace this with a different `Optimize` function. However, this is a simple method that allows us to better control the total charge incurred:

```
best_energy, best_solution = optimize_bqm_device
    ([ideal_param1,ideal_param1],
    [ideal_param2,ideal_param2],
    Q, shots*10, device)
```

11. Now, all the various output variables are passed out of the Amazon Braket Hybrid Jobs instance and stored as result data in Amazon S3 storage:

```
save_job_result({ "E": E ,
                    "ideal_param1": ideal_param1,
                    "ideal_param2": ideal_param2,
                    "lowest_energy": lowest_energy,
```

```
                                   "best_energy": best_energy,
                                   "best_solution": best_solution})
```

These results can be retrieved by the Jupyter Notebook after the execution on Amazon Braket Hybrid Jobs completes.

We have reviewed the structure and use of Amazon Braket Hybrid Jobs on the QAOA code developed in the last chapter. This functionality allows us to execute hybrid quantum computing jobs more effectively where multiple calls to a quantum device and intermediate classical tuning are needed. Running the same process on other backends, such as the IonQ or Rigetti Aspen devices, is also possible; however, please be cautious of the price as this QAOA implementation will create a large number of tasks on the QPU. I encourage you to experiment with actual quantum devices when you are confident that the values from the simulator are accurate.

In the next sections, we will briefly go over PennyLane and other Amazon Braket features that will be useful to you. The goal here is to only make you aware of these features and to encourage you to explore further using the links in the *Further reading* section.

Xanadu PennyLane

PennyLane is a vast library of quantum computing tools developed by Xanadu. This library contains many functions that help with optimization, chemistry, and quantum machine learning use cases. You can explore the many well-written tutorials directly on the PennyLane website at `https://pennylane.ai/`.

Calling Amazon Braket devices from PennyLane

Amazon provides a plugin for PennyLane users to run their algorithms on Amazon Braket devices. The setup for this can be found at `https://amazon-braket-pennylane-plugin-python.readthedocs.io/en/latest/`.

To use this, you will have to install the PennyLane library using the following command line:

```
pip3 install pennylane
```

And then also add the following:

```
pip3 install amazon-braket-pennylane-plugin
```

Using PennyLane within Amazon Braket Hybrid Jobs

Amazon Braket Hybrid Jobs allows the creation of a PennyLane instance that has all the PennyLane libraries installed. To make use of this, pass the appropriate value from the following to the `image_uri` parameter in the `AwsQuantumJob.create()` function:

```
image_uri_tf = retrieve_image(Framework.PL_TENSORFLOW, "us-west-2")
```

```
image_uri_pytorch = retrieve_image(Framework.PL_PYTORCH, "us-west-2")
```

For example, if we want to create the Amazon Braket Hybrid Jobs instance in the us-west-2 region, with the PennyLane `TENSORFLOW` library, then we can define `image_uri_tf` as just mentioned, and then add the following extra line as one of the parameters:

```
Image_uri=image_uri_tf
```

Xanadu Borealis

Amazon Braket has included the **Xanadu Borealis** photonic quantum computer. This device can be used to demonstrate the ability to create **Gaussian Boson Sampling (GBS)** on a quantum computer. More information about this device can be obtained at the following links:

- `https://aws.amazon.com/braket/quantum-computers/xanadu/`
- `https://xanadu.ai/products/borealis/`
- `https://strawberryfields.readthedocs.io/en/stable/introduction/photonic_hardware.html`

I would suggest running the demos as provided in these links if you are interested in learning more about how this photonic quantum computer can create computational advantage.

IBM Qiskit

The **Qiskit** community has added a backend provider for Qiskit users that can access Amazon Braket devices. It is now possible to create your circuit in Qiskit and execute it on an Amazon Braket device. For more information on this, please review the following:

```
https://aws.amazon.com/blogs/quantum-computing/introducing-the-qiskit-provider-for-amazon-braket/
```

In order to install the libraries in your Qiskit environment, please use the following:

```
pip install qiskit_braket_provider
```

Other Amazon Braket Hybrid Jobs features

In this section, we will look at some additional features of Amazon Braket Hybrid Jobs that make it user-friendly.

Controlling the region of the environment

If it is desired to create the image in a different region than that of the device, the `retrieve_image()` function can be used to specify where the Amazon Hybrid Jobs instance will be created, as shown here:

```
image_uri_base = retrieve_image(Framework.BASE,
                                "us-west-2")
```

This value is then passed to the `image_uri` parameter.

Hardware configuration

The `instance_config` parameter can be used to create a different hardware configuration where the image created has more memory. More information can be found at the following:

https://docs.aws.amazon.com/braket/latest/developerguide/braket-jobs-configure-job-instance-for-script.html

Multiple parallel device execution

It is possible to submit tasks concurrently to reduce execution time. For more information on limits on quantum devices and quotas for concurrent execution, please review the information available here:

- https://docs.aws.amazon.com/braket/latest/developerguide/braket-devices.html
- https://docs.aws.amazon.com/braket/latest/developerguide/braket-quotas.html

Debugging failed jobs

If the Amazon Hybrid Job fails, it is possible to find the cause of the failure and view the results of any print statements using the **CloudWatch** service.

More information on **CloudWatch** can be found at the following:

https://docs.aws.amazon.com/braket/latest/developerguide/braket-monitor-metrics.html

After a job fails, click on the job link in the Amazon Braket Hybrid Jobs list. This will give more details on the job and a link to CloudWatch:

Figure 10.11 – Braket Jobs status

Click on the **View in CloudWatch** link. This will open the **CloudWatch** window where the debugging and print information can be found.

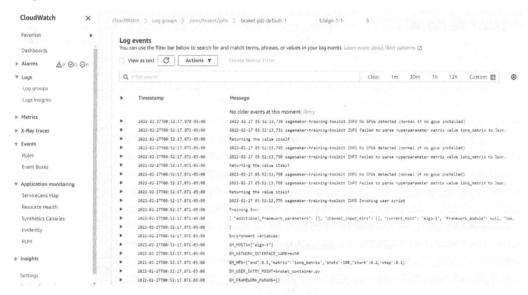

Figure 10.12 – CloudWatch window

Containers

In the QAOA example, we did not specify an image for `AwsQuantJob.create()`, and a default image was used. The `retrieve_image()` function can be used to modify the image region or to create an instance with PennyLane libraries already loaded. If you need to create a unique environment with different libraries, then Amazon Braket allows this through the use of Docker and containers.

Information on this can be found in the following:

`https://docs.aws.amazon.com/braket/latest/developerguide/braket-jobs-byoc.html`

Summary

In this chapter, we have reviewed the practical implementation of QAOA on Amazon Braket Hybrid Jobs. We reviewed how the code needs to be restructured for this purpose and how information is passed between **Job Control Code** and **Job Source Module**. Amazon Braket Hybrid Jobs allows us to efficiently use the Amazon Braket quantum devices when they become available. The ability to run PennyLane through Amazon Braket or create unique environments through containers expands the ability of the user to create unique products and services for their specific needs.

In the next chapter, we will look at a real-world use case where a single objective optimization is needed. We will identify the appropriate solvers and quantum devices available to us to solve the optimization problem using real quantum computer resources and then validate with classical resources.

Further reading

- Information on Amazon Braket:

  - `https://docs.aws.amazon.com/braket/latest/developerguide/braket-how-it-works.html`

  - `https://docs.aws.amazon.com/braket/latest/developerguide/braket-jobs.html`

  - `https://aws.amazon.com/braket/pricing/`

- Amazon Braket GitHub library and examples:

  `https://github.com/aws/amazon-braket-sdk-python`

- Some more information on pricing and free tiers:

  `https://aws.amazon.com/braket/pricing/#:~:text=AWS%20Free%20Tier%20gives%20you,through%20the%20Hybrid%20Jobs%20feature`

- Information on cross-region setup in Amazon Braket:

  - `https://aws.amazon.com/blogs/quantum-computing/setting-up-a-cross-region-private-environment-in-amazon-braket/`

  - `https://docs.aws.amazon.com/braket/latest/developerguide/braket-jobs-script-environment.html`

- PennyLane examples:

  - https://docs.aws.amazon.com/braket/latest/developerguide/hybrid.html

  - https://github.com/aws/amazon-braket-examples/tree/df98ae92898cbef81070f6815d63902f51db09d3/examples/hybrid_jobs

- Borealis computational advantage:

  https://www.nature.com/articles/s41586-022-04725-x

Code deep dive:

Please review the code in the following Python file, which includes the core components and functions of QAOA that are run by Amazon Braket Hybrid Jobs in this chapter:

QAOA.py.

11
Single-Objective Optimization Use Case

There are many classical tools available to solve optimization problems. For example, we can use genetic and simulated annealing algorithms directly on the problem. In addition, we can use **linear programming** or **mixed integer linear programming** methods, along with applications such as Gurobi and IBM C-Plex. In our case, we want to use quantum computers to solve optimization problems. To do this, we must convert our problem into a **Quadratic Unconstrained Binary Optimization (QUBO)** problem. Most real-world problems have integers and floating-point numbers, so this becomes a challenge because we must find a way to convert those into a series of binary variables that span our number range.

To show the process of optimization on both quantum annealers and quantum computers, we will go over a simple example of solving the knapsack problem. This is a common example and well documented.

You are already familiar with some QUBO formulations from *Chapter 5, Using a Quantum Annealer – Developing a QUBO Function and Applying Constraints*, and later in *Chapter 9, Running QAOA on Simulators and Amazon Braket Devices*, and *Chapter 10, Amazon Braket Hybrid Jobs, PennyLane, and Other Braket Features*, where we created **Binary Quadratic Models (BQMs)** to run on gate-based quantum simulators and quantum devices. Remember that the BQM is the upper triangular matrix. We will start with the mathematical definition of the knapsack problem and then visualize solving this problem classically using a probabilistic method. Next, we will convert the problem into a QUBO and solve it classically using our probabilistic QUBO solver. This will help ensure we have understood the problem and created the QUBO correctly. Finally, we will solve the QUBO using Amazon Braket simulators and the Aspen M-1 quantum computer. Note that to solve an optimization problem on a quantum computer, we will use the Define solver we created in *Chapter 8, Using Hybrid Algorithms – Optimization Using Gate-Based Quantum Computers*, and evaluated on various devices in *Chapter 9, Running QAOA on Simulators and Amazon Braket Devices*.

The following main topics will be covered in this chapter:

- Introduction to the knapsack problem
- Visualizing the knapsack problem
- QUBO formulation for the knapsack problem:

  - Implementing the knapsack problem in code
  - Solving the knapsack problem using the probabilistic sampler

- Getting results from different QUBO samplers:

  - D-Wave 2000Q
  - Amazon Braket Simulator SV1 using QAOA
  - Rigetti Aspen 11 and M-1 using QAOA

- A process for solving constrained optimization problems

Technical requirements

The source code for this chapter is available in this book's GitHub repository: `https://github.com/PacktPublishing/Quantum-Computing-Experimentation-with-Amazon-Braket/tree/main/Chapter11`.

Introduction to the knapsack problem

The knapsack problem is a good place to start when learning how to solve real-world combinatorial optimization problems that have constraints.

There are many types of knapsack problems, but we will only focus on the 0/1 knapsack problem with integer weights. In this case, we have a certain number of items with given weights and values, and our objective is to fit as many items in the knapsack as possible to maximize the value. The items that are not added to the knapsack have a value of 0, while those that fit in the knapsack have a value of 1. Of course, this means we would want to add all the items; however, we have a constraint on the total weight that we can place in the knapsack. This makes the problem considerably harder to solve, even though many solvers can solve this efficiently.

Each item in the knapsack is represented by x_i, and each has a value, v_i. The objective is to maximize the total value, V, of items, x_i, placed inside the knapsack:

$$V = \sum_{i}^{N} v_i x_i \qquad x \in \{0,1\} \qquad eq.\,(11.1)$$

We also want to introduce a constraint – that is, the maximum weight, W_c, that the knapsack can hold. If the weight of each item is w_i, then we have the following relationship:

$$W = \sum_{i}^{N} w_i x_i \leq W_c \qquad x \in \{0,1\} \qquad eq.\,(11.2)$$

Note that x_i is a binary variable that is either 0 or 1 and indicates whether the item is in the knapsack or not.

Now, let's create a simple program with sample data to see how this works.

Visualizing the knapsack problem

The code for the knapsack problem has been provided in this book's GitHub repository. This initial part of the code sets up a sample knapsack problem and then solves it using a probabilistic method. Other classical methods are available and have been mentioned in the *Further reading* section.

First, let's explain how the `plot_knapsack()` function works. This function tries adding the items in a variety of ways, starting with one-item combinations, then two-item combinations, and then tracks the maximum value and weight found. It will do this until it reaches the total number of items. While sampling, it will print the solution (items, value, and weight) if the value exceeds the previously stored maximum value. The plots show all the combinations it finds. The X-axis is the sample number (not the number of items in the solution).

Now, let's set up and run through a sample knapsack problem. The data of the value and the weight of each item are provided in the `knapsack_data.txt` file. Next, we will run this data through a probabilistic method to find the solution using the `plot_knapsack()` function. This will allow us to visualize the problem landscape. Let's get started:

1. The knapsack data is provided in the `knapsack_data.txt` file. The following code will import and display the knapsack data, which includes the values and weights of 10 items:

    ```
    import pandas as pd
    data_file_name="knapsack_data.txt"
    # parse input data
    df = pd.read_csv(data_file_name, header=None)
    df.columns = ['value', 'weight']
    print(df)
    ```

    Output:

    ```
         value  weight
    0      2       2
    1      4       3
    ```

2	6	2
3	8	3
4	10	3
5	12	5
6	14	6
7	16	5
8	18	8
9	20	9

Note that if all the items were in the knapsack, the total value would be 110 and the total weight would be 46.

2. Now, let's store the values and weights in arrays:

```
value=[]
weight=[]
for i in (df.values.tolist()):
    value.append(i[0])
    weight.append(i[1])
```

3. Next, we will set the weight capacity to 10:

```
weight_capacity=10
```

4. We will use the plot_knapsack() function that has been provided to solve this knapsack problem and find the items that can fit in the knapsack. This will provide the maximum value while staying at or under a total weight of 10. This function is a modification of the probabilistic_solver() function, so it will use the same method of trying one-item solutions, then two-item solutions, and so on. This method should help you build intuition when solving similar problems for the first time. Let's proceed:

```
plot_knapsack(data_file_name,weight_capacity)
```

Output ([Items] value weight):

[0] 2 2

[1] 4 3

[2] 6 2

[3] 8 3

[4] 10 3

[5] 12 5

```
[6]  14 6
[7]  16 5
[8]  18 8
[9]  20 9
[2,  7]  22 7
[2,  8]  24 10
[4,  7]  26 8
[5,  7]  28 10
[2,  3,  7]  30 10
[2,  4,  7]  32 10
```

The preceding output shows different item combinations that successively have a higher value than the preceding combination. It shows that items 2, 4, and 7 have the highest possible value of 32 and use up all the weight capacity, that is, 10.

The following diagrams show the effect of adding more and more items to the knapsack. Each data point in the plot, from left to right, represents a combination of items starting with one-item combinations, then two-item combinations, and so on. *Figure 11.1* contains two plots that show how the value and weight increases without any weight constraint:

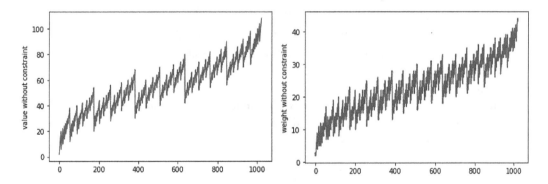

Figure 11.1 – Value and weight of item combinations in the knapsack without constraints

To understand these plots, let's now look at *Figure 11.2*. The number of items selected in the solution is identified between the dashed lines. There are 10 one-item solutions on the right, while there is only one 10-item solution on the right. Note that the maximum value of all 10 items is 110, while the weight of all items is 46:

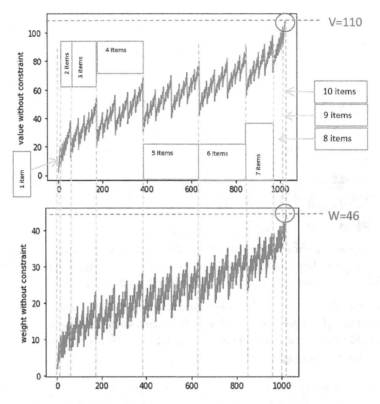

Figure 11.2 – Interpreting the plot results for item combinations in
the knapsack without weight and value constraints

Figure 11.3 includes two plots showing the effect of adding the weight constraint. The combination of items added to the knapsack and their value is now limited to a maximum weight of 10. We are looking for the combination of items that gives the largest value under this condition:

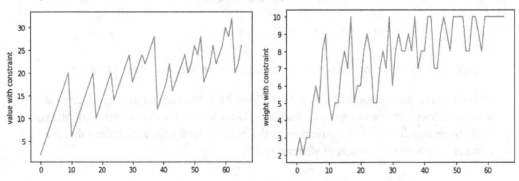

Figure 11.3 – Value and weight of item combinations in the knapsack with the weight constraint

Based on this information, as shown in *Figure 11.4*, the maximum value is based on the [2, 4, 7] item combination with a value of 32 and a maxed-out weight of 10:

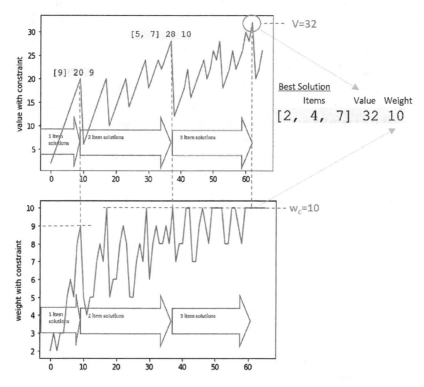

Figure 11.4 – Interpreting the plot results for item combinations in the knapsack with the weight constraint

With that, you've seen how the knapsack problem can be solved classically. The plot_knapsack() function simply tried out different combinations based on the data that was provided and kept track of the value and weights, ensuring only better value solutions within the weight constraint were stored. Classical solvers use various methods, including dynamic programming, to rapidly solve this type of problem. In the next section, we will look at what is involved in creating a QUBO formulation of this problem so that we can solve it on Amazon Braket devices.

QUBO formulation for the knapsack problem

Converting a constraint problem into a QUBO (or an unconstrained) model requires the matrix to include all the constraint information. In *Chapter 5, Using the Quantum Annealer – Developing a QUBO Function and Using Constraints*, we developed the constraint for the number of employees. That constraint was relatively easy to implement as we were able to add terms right on top of the original matrix. Please review that chapter and its *Simple penalty function to implement the constraint* section before proceeding. As you will see, we must convert the "constrained" problem into a QUBO, which is a matrix where we do not have any constraints; the solver must be able to track the total weight of the items selected in the knapsack. How will it do this when we are simply giving a matrix? One way to think about this is that the QUBO matrix must include data for scenarios already mapped out for the QUBO solver. Alternatively, you could think of the QUBO as a partially solved set of key relationships that the QUBO solver can then take to solve the rest of the combinatorial optimization problem.

This will get mathematically intensive; however, we will only focus on the key learning here, and the detailed mathematics are provided in the *Appendix*.

In the case of the knapsack, the constraint in *eq. (11.2)* can be implemented using the following relationship:

$$\left(\sum_{i}^{N} w_i x_i - Wc \right)^2 = 0 \qquad x \in \{0,1\} \qquad eq.\,(11.3)$$

Notice that this creates a parabola where the lowest point on the parabola is where the sum of the weights of the items selected is equal to W_c. We will have to add this term to the objective in *eq. (11.1)*.

To implement *eq. (11.3)* in the QUBO, we need binary variables to represent (and track) the weight based on the items that are selected. We will use a binary variable, y_n, that will represent the integer weight from 1 to W_c. Notice that we now have N number of binary item variables, x_i, and W_c number of binary weight variables, y_n. We have converted the integer problem into a binary problem. However, we now also need to make sure that only one weight, yn, is selected, so we must introduce another constraint:

$$\left(\sum_{n}^{W_c} y_n - 1 \right)^2 = 0 \qquad y \in \{0,1\} \qquad eq.\,(11.4)$$

This constraint, if implemented correctly, should influence the QUBO to have the minimum solution, where only one weight variable, y_n, is selected.

Now that we have two sets of variables, we also need to associate the total weight of the items, x_i, in the knapsack with ny_n, which represents the weight we are tracking using the binary variables, y_n. This requires yet another constraint, which can be written as follows:

$$\left(\sum_i^N w_i x_i - \sum_n^{W_c} ny_n \right)^2 = 0 \qquad y \in \{0,1\} \qquad eq.\,(11.5)$$

Even though this looks complicated, notice that this is a general form of *eq. (11.3)* due to the following:

$$\sum_n^{W_c} ny_n = Wc \text{ if there is only one } y_n \text{ and } n = Wc \qquad eq.\,(11.6)$$

Here, *eq. (11.5)* is required to make sure the weight represented by the items that are selected is equal to the weight that is tracked. Imagine if these were not the same – our solution would not make any sense. *Later, you will see that we must validate that these constraints are not violated in the solutions.*

We now have *eq. (11.1)*, which represents the original objective function, and *eq. (11.4)* and *eq. (11.5)*, which together represent the weight constraint.

The derivation of this method was introduced by *Andrew Lucas*, along with other QUBO formulations in https://www.frontiersin.org/articles/10.3389/fphy.2014.00005/full. Andrew introduced a log trick that reduces the number of y_n variables needed and results in forcing the solution to not exceed the weight constraint. To keep things simple, we will not use the log trick and our implementation will retain the integer weights.

Now that we have the required constraints, we can expand the terms to determine the final equation for our BQM, which will be represented as an upper triangular matrix.

We will write out the full equation here along with the A, B, and C multipliers, which we can use to tweak the strength of the different components of our formulation:

$$minimize \left[A\left(\sum_n^{W_c} y_n - 1 \right)^2 + B\left(\sum_i^N w_i x_i - \sum_n^{W_c} ny_n \right)^2 + C\left(\sum_i^N -v_i x_i \right) \right] \qquad eq.\,(11.7)$$

The two terms for multipliers A and B, when combined, will enforce the weight constraint. The last term, with the C multiplier, represents the objective that we are minimizing. Notice that we are using $-v_i$ here since our QUBO solvers are programmed for minimization. *When our objective is to maximize the values, we must change the sign to make it a minimization problem for the QUBO solvers.*

The derivation of the final BQM is outside the scope of this chapter. However, since converting real-world problems into a BQM is a precursor to solving these problems on annealers and quantum computers, the full derivation is provided in the *Appendix*. The following matrices are the result of expanding *eq. (11.7)*:

$$M_v = \sum_i^N -v_i x_i \qquad eq.\,(11.8)$$

$$M_x = \sum_i^N w_i^2 x_i + \sum_{i<j}^N 2 w_i w_j\, x_i\, x_j \qquad eq.\,(11.9)$$

$$M_{xy} = \sum_{i,n}^{N,W_c} -2 w_i n\, x_i y_n \qquad eq.\,(11.10)$$

$$M_{yc} = \sum_n^{W_c} -1\, y_n + \sum_{n<m}^{W_c} 2\, y_n y_m \qquad eq.\,(11.11)$$

$$M_y = \sum_n^{W_c} n^2\, y_n + \sum_{n,m}^{W_c} 2nm\, y_n y_m \qquad eq.\,(11.12)$$

The following relationships are useful as we combine the matrices to create the final matrix, M_f:

$$M_{xf} = BM_x + CM_v \qquad eq.\,(11.13)$$

$$BM_{xy} \qquad eq.\,(11.14)$$

$$M_{yf} = AM_{yc} + BM_y \qquad eq.\,(11.15)$$

The following diagram may help you visualize each of the component matrices and how they stitch together to create the final matrix, M_f:

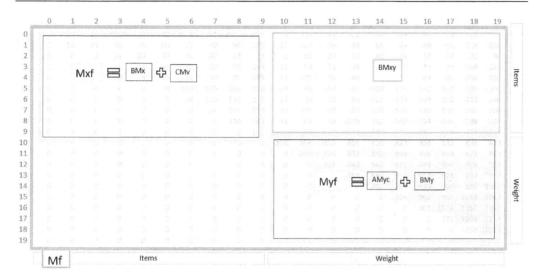

Figure 11.5 – Matrix combinations and stitching them together to create the final matrix, M_f

With that, we have derived the QUBO formulation for the constrained 0/1 knapsack problem with integer weights. We have also learned how the integer weight constraint needs to be converted into a new binary variable and that the constraint gets converted into two new constraints. The first constraint ensures that only one weight value is selected in the QUBO solution, while the other ensures that the weight of the items matches the weight value. We also realize that if these constraints are not fully enforced by the solver, we will end up with infeasible solutions that will have to be discarded. In the next section, we will take our sample knapsack problem and create the representative QUBO matrix, M_f, using code.

Implementing the knapsack QUBO in code

In this section, we will create the QUBO matrix from *eq. (11.8)* through *eq. (11.15)*. First, we will create the individual matrices and then stitch them together to create a combined upper triangular matrix:

1. Let's start by creating the M_v matrix from *eq. (11.8)*. This is an *NxN* matrix and the diagonal values are $-v_i$. There are no non-diagonal terms:

    ```
    N=len(value)
    Mv = np.zeros([N,N],dtype=float)
    for i in range(N):
        Mv[i][i] =-value[i]
    print(Mv)
    ```

Output:

```
[[ -2.    0.    0.    0.    0.    0.    0.    0.    0.    0.]
 [  0.   -4.    0.    0.    0.    0.    0.    0.    0.    0.]
 [  0.    0.   -6.    0.    0.    0.    0.    0.    0.    0.]
 [  0.    0.    0.   -8.    0.    0.    0.    0.    0.    0.]
 [  0.    0.    0.    0.  -10.    0.    0.    0.    0.    0.]
 [  0.    0.    0.    0.    0.  -12.    0.    0.    0.    0.]
 [  0.    0.    0.    0.    0.    0.  -14.    0.    0.    0.]
 [  0.    0.    0.    0.    0.    0.    0.  -16.    0.    0.]
 [  0.    0.    0.    0.    0.    0.    0.    0.  -18.    0.]
 [  0.    0.    0.    0.    0.    0.    0.    0.    0.  -20.]]
```

2. Let's sample this matrix using `ProbabilisticSampler()`:

```
    ProbabilisticSampler(Mv,1000)
```

Output:

Best found: [0, 1, 2, 3, 4, 5, 6, 7, 8, 9]

count: 10

Energy: -110.0

Solutions Sampled: 1024

The output shows that by itself, the optimal solution of the M_v matrix is all 10 items and a total minimal energy of -110. If there were not constraints, this would be the case. *Figure 11.6* also shows this. As the number of items in the solution increases, we find lower energy values. The optimal is when all 10 items are in the solution (x-axis) with an energy of -110.

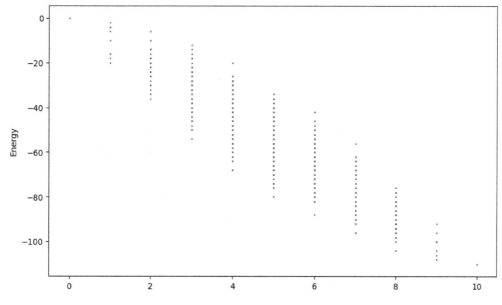

Figure 11.6 – Energy mapping of M$_v$

Note

The X axis of the probabilistic sampler plot represents the count or the sum of the variables with a value of 1 returned in the solutions. It is easy to tell that this matrix has a minimum energy of -110 with all 10 items selected (bottom-right point). The energy of -110 is the sum of the value of all 10 items. This is the case if there is no weight constraint, as we saw in *Figure 11.1* (only the sign is reversed). Seeing this energy landscape is a good way to find out whether you are sending the correct matrix to your QUBO solver. For example, if we erroneously send M$_v$ to the D-Wave annealer, we will keep getting the solution that all 10 items are in the knapsack. This plot helps us see why the solver keeps selecting all the values.

In our problem, we have a weight constraint that we need to implement.

---

3. Now, we will start creating the first component of the constraint. This will be the matrix, M$_x$, from *eq. (11.9)*:

```
N=len(value)
Mx = np.zeros([N,N],dtype=float)
for i in range(N):
    for j in range(N):
        if i==j:
            Mx[i][i] =weight[i]**2
        elif i<j:
```

```
                    Mx[i][j]=2*weight[i]*weight[j]
    print(Mx)
```

Output:

```
[[  4.  12.   8.  12.  12.  20.  24.  20.  32.  36.]
 [  0.   9.  12.  18.  18.  30.  36.  30.  48.  54.]
 [  0.   0.   4.  12.  12.  20.  24.  20.  32.  36.]
 [  0.   0.   0.   9.  18.  30.  36.  30.  48.  54.]
 [  0.   0.   0.   0.   9.  30.  36.  30.  48.  54.]
 [  0.   0.   0.   0.   0.  25.  60.  50.  80.  90.]
 [  0.   0.   0.   0.   0.   0.  36.  60.  96. 108.]
 [  0.   0.   0.   0.   0.   0.   0.  25.  80.  90.]
 [  0.   0.   0.   0.   0.   0.   0.   0.  64. 144.]
 [  0.   0.   0.   0.   0.   0.   0.   0.   0.  81.]]
```

We have not reviewed this using the probabilistic solver, but just looking at the matrix, we can tell it will be 0 when no item is selected and the sum of all the terms when all the items are selected. The fact that all the values are positive indicates that the QUBO is enforcing a higher and higher penalty (a product of the weights) as more items are added to the knapsack.

4. Now, we will implement the M_{yc} matrix from *eq. (11.11)*. This constraint ensures only one weight is selected:

```
wc=weight_capacity
Myc = np.zeros([wc,wc],dtype=float)
for i in range(wc):
    for j in range(wc):
        if i==j:
            Myc[i][i] =-1
        elif i<j:
            Myc[i][j]=2
print(Myc)
# offset = 1
```

Output:

```
[[-1.  2.  2.  2.  2.  2.  2.  2.  2.  2.]
 [ 0. -1.  2.  2.  2.  2.  2.  2.  2.  2.]
```

```
[ 0.   0.  -1.   2.   2.   2.   2.   2.   2.   2.]
[ 0.   0.   0.  -1.   2.   2.   2.   2.   2.   2.]
[ 0.   0.   0.   0.  -1.   2.   2.   2.   2.   2.]
[ 0.   0.   0.   0.   0.  -1.   2.   2.   2.   2.]
[ 0.   0.   0.   0.   0.   0.  -1.   2.   2.   2.]
[ 0.   0.   0.   0.   0.   0.   0.  -1.   2.   2.]
[ 0.   0.   0.   0.   0.   0.   0.   0.  -1.   2.]
[ 0.   0.   0.   0.   0.   0.   0.   0.   0.  -1.]]
```

Notice that all the diagonal terms are -1 and that all the upper right terms are 2.

5. We can check the effect of this matrix using `ProbabilisticSampler()`:

> `ProbabilisticSampler(Myc,1000,1, 0,10)`

Output:

```
Best found: [7]
count: 1
Energy: 0.0
Solutions Sampled: 1024
```

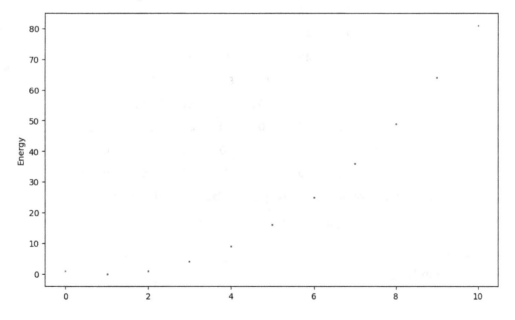

Figure 11.7 – Energy mapping of M_{yc}

The preceding diagram shows that the minimum is at 1 and that the positive values grow as the number of weights selected grows. If implemented correctly, it should penalize the overall energy if more than one y_n value is selected, $(\Sigma y_n > 1)$. The energy values in this matrix do not seem to be very large, so to make sure this critical constraint is enforced, we will have to use a large value for C – that is, the multiplier on this matrix.

6. Now, we will implement the next matrix, M_y, from *eq. (11.12)*:

```
wc=weight_capacity
My = np.zeros([wc,wc],dtype=float)
for n in range(1,wc+1):
    for m in range(1,wc+1):
        if n==m:
            My[n-1][m-1] =n**2
        elif n<m:
            My[n-1][m-1] =2*(n*m)
print(My)
```

Output:

```
[[  1.    4.    6.    8.   10.   12.   14.   16.   18.   20.]
 [  0.    4.   12.   16.   20.   24.   28.   32.   36.   40.]
 [  0.    0.    9.   24.   30.   36.   42.   48.   54.   60.]
 [  0.    0.    0.   16.   40.   48.   56.   64.   72.   80.]
 [  0.    0.    0.    0.   25.   60.   70.   80.   90.  100.]
 [  0.    0.    0.    0.    0.   36.   84.   96.  108.  120.]
 [  0.    0.    0.    0.    0.    0.   49.  112.  126.  140.]
 [  0.    0.    0.    0.    0.    0.    0.   64.  144.  160.]
 [  0.    0.    0.    0.    0.    0.    0.    0.   81.  180.]
 [  0.    0.    0.    0.    0.    0.    0.    0.    0.  100.]]
```

7. We can review the effect of this matrix using `ProbabilisticSampler()`:

```
ProbabilisticSampler(My,1000)
```

Output:

Best found: []

count: 0

Energy: 0

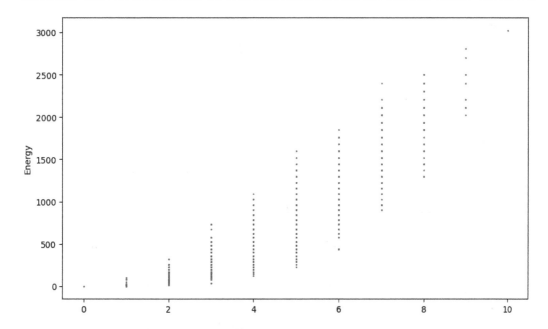

Figure 11.8 – Energy mapping of M_y

In the preceding diagram, the X-axis represents the number of weights selected, $(\Sigma y_n = 1)$. As expected, there is a minimum penalty for selecting one weight. However, more than one weight, y_n, would be an infeasible solution and is heavily penalized (with large positive numbers). If all 10 weights were selected, we would have a penalty of 3000.

8. The next matrix, M_{xy}, from *eq. (11.10)* ties the items, x_i, with the weights, y_n. This matrix is different. It does not have to be a square matrix, as one side has a size of N and the other side has a size of W_c. It will be the "filler" in the larger and final upper triangular matrix, which fits between the M_{xy} and M_{yf} matrices:

```
wc=weight_capacity
Mxy = np.zeros([N,wc],dtype=float)
for i in range(N):
    for n in range(1,wc+1):

            Mxy[i][n-1] =-2*weight[i]*n
print(Mxy)
```

Output:

```
[[  -4.    -8.  -12.  -16.  -20.  -24.  -28.  -32.  -36.
-40.]
 [  -6.  -12.  -18.  -24.  -30.  -36.  -42.  -48.  -54.
-60.]
 [  -4.    -8.  -12.  -16.  -20.  -24.  -28.  -32.  -36.
-40.]
 [  -6.  -12.  -18.  -24.  -30.  -36.  -42.  -48.  -54.
-60.]
 [  -6.  -12.  -18.  -24.  -30.  -36.  -42.  -48.  -54.
-60.]
 [ -10.  -20.  -30.  -40.  -50.  -60.  -70.  -80.  -90.
-100.]
 [ -12.  -24.  -36.  -48.  -60.  -72.  -84.  -96. -108.
-120.]
 [ -10.  -20.  -30.  -40.  -50.  -60.  -70.  -80.  -90.
-100.]
 [ -16.  -32.  -48.  -64.  -80.  -96. -112. -128. -144.
-160.]
 [ -18.  -36.  -54.  -72.  -90. -108. -126. -144. -162.
-180.]]
```

> **Note**
>
> The probabilistic sampler will not be able to plot this. However, we can tell that it contains all negative values, which implies that this part of the matrix is attempting to enforce the connection between the items selected and their weights.

9. Now, we can finally stitch the matrices together into the final QUBO matrix, M_f, which we will use for the remainder of this chapter. The following diagram shows how the pieces are put together and the intermediate matrix that's used to store those pieces:

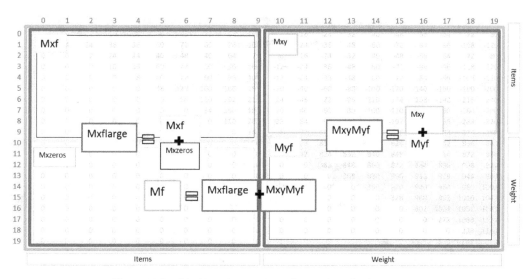

Figure 11.9 – Stitching the matrix to the produce final matrix, M_f

Stitching the QUBO matrices together

Now, we will combine or stitch the matrices together to create a larger matrix that represents the QUBO formulation of the knapsack problem.

Please review *Figure 11.9*, which shows how the various smaller matrices will be stitched together to create the full matrix, M_f. Each time the matrix is added, we will use a multiplier to ensure the size of the matrix is appropriately scaled. In the following code, there are three multipliers: – A, which ensures only one weight is selected, B, which ensures the weight matches the total weight, and C, which ensures the correct items are selected. In this first example, we will use a value of 1 for all the multipliers:

1. The following code adds specific matrix values on top of each other using the + sign. Then, it connects or stitches the different resulting matrices together in the desired axis (or direction) using the np.append() function:

```
A=1 #ensure only one weight is selected
B=1 # ensure weight matches total weight
C=1   # ensure correct items are selected

Mxf=C*np.array(Mv)+B*np.array(Mx)
print('Mxf',np.shape(Mxf))
Myf=A*np.array(Myc)+B*np.array(My)
print('Myf',np.shape(Myf))
#stitch the two matrices Mxy and Myf into MxyMyf
```

```
MxyMyf=np.append(B*Mxy, Myf , axis=0)
print('MxyMyf',np.shape(MxyMyf))
# create the Mxzeros matrix (all zeros)
Mxzeros=np.zeros([wc,N],dtype=float)
print('Mxzeros',np.shape(Mxzeros))
# stitch the Mxzeros with Mxf to create Mxflarge
Mxflarge=np.append(Mxf, Mxzeros, axis=0)
print('Mxflarge',np.shape(Mxflarge))
# Finally crate Mf by stitching MxyMyf and Mxflarge
Mf=np.append(Mxflarge,MxyMyf, axis=1)
print('Mf',np.shape(Mf))
print(Mf)
np.savetxt('Mf.csv', Mf, delimiter=',')
```

Output:

Mxf (10, 10)

Myf (10, 10)

MxyMyf (20, 10)

Mxzeros (10, 10)

Mxflarge (20, 10)

Mf (20, 20)

The preceding output shows the shape of the different matrices so that we can validate them.

2. Now, let's create the M_f matrix with the multipliers scaled to a larger number. In this case, A=400, B=2, and C=1. Later, we will find that this level of scaling is needed for the individual matrices to have enough influence and enforce their conditions:

```
A=400 #ensure only one weight is selected
B=2 # ensure weight matches total weight
C=1  # ensure correct items are selected
Mxf=C*np.array(Mv)+B*np.array(Mx)
print('Mxf',np.shape(Mxf))
Myf=A*np.array(Myc)+B*np.array(My)
print('Myf',np.shape(Myf))
MxyMyf=np.append(B*Mxy, Myf , axis=0)
print('MxyMyf',np.shape(MxyMyf))
Mxzeros=np.zeros([wc,N],dtype=float)
```

```
print('Mxzeros',np.shape(Mxzeros))
Mxflarge=np.append(Mxf, Mxzeros, axis=0)
print('Mxflarge',np.shape(Mxflarge))
Mf=np.append(Mxflarge,MxyMyf, axis=1)
print('Mf',np.shape(Mf))
print(Mf)
np.savetxt('Mf.csv', Mf, delimiter=',')
```

Output:

```
Mxf (10, 10)

Myf (10, 10)

MxyMyf (20, 10)

Mxzeros (10, 10)

Mxflarge (20, 10)

Mf (20, 20)
```

Again, we can see the correct size of the matrices, but in this case, the values of the final M_f matrix are different.

The following diagram shows the complete matrix with the values conditionally colored to make it easier to see the magnitude of the penalties. Notice that we now have a new index for the full matrix going from 0 to 19 (highlighted in yellow):

	0	1	2	3	4	5	6	7	8	9	10	11	12	13	14	15	16	17	18	19
0	6	24	16	24	24	40	48	40	64	72	-8	-16	-24	-32	-40	-48	-56	-64	-72	-80
1	0	14	24	36	36	60	72	60	96	108	-12	-24	-36	-48	-60	-72	-84	-96	-108	-120
2	0	0	2	24	24	40	48	40	64	72	-8	-16	-24	-32	-40	-48	-56	-64	-72	-80
3	0	0	0	10	36	60	72	60	96	108	-12	-24	-36	-48	-60	-72	-84	-96	-108	-120
4	0	0	0	0	8	60	72	60	96	108	-12	-24	-36	-48	-60	-72	-84	-96	-108	-120
5	0	0	0	0	0	38	120	100	160	180	-20	-40	-60	-80	-100	-120	-140	-160	-180	-200
6	0	0	0	0	0	0	58	120	192	216	-24	-48	-72	-96	-120	-144	-168	-192	-216	-240
7	0	0	0	0	0	0	0	34	160	180	-20	-40	-60	-80	-100	-120	-140	-160	-180	-200
8	0	0	0	0	0	0	0	0	110	288	-32	-64	-96	-128	-160	-192	-224	-256	-288	-320
9	0	0	0	0	0	0	0	0	0	142	-36	-72	-108	-144	-180	-216	-252	-288	-324	-360
10	0	0	0	0	0	0	0	0	0	0	-398	808	812	816	820	824	828	832	836	840
11	0	0	0	0	0	0	0	0	0	0	0	-392	824	832	840	848	856	864	872	880
12	0	0	0	0	0	0	0	0	0	0	0	0	-382	848	860	872	884	896	908	920
13	0	0	0	0	0	0	0	0	0	0	0	0	0	-368	880	896	912	928	944	960
14	0	0	0	0	0	0	0	0	0	0	0	0	0	0	-350	920	940	960	980	1000
15	0	0	0	0	0	0	0	0	0	0	0	0	0	0	0	-328	968	992	1016	1040
16	0	0	0	0	0	0	0	0	0	0	0	0	0	0	0	0	-302	1024	1052	1080
17	0	0	0	0	0	0	0	0	0	0	0	0	0	0	0	0	0	-272	1088	1120
18	0	0	0	0	0	0	0	0	0	0	0	0	0	0	0	0	0	0	-238	1160
19	0	0	0	0	0	0	0	0	0	0	0	0	0	0	0	0	0	0	0	-200

Figure 11.10 – The final M_f matrix

With that, we have created the full QUBO formulation or the BQM for our specific knapsack problem. Admittedly, there were a considerable number of mathematical steps and coding to get to this point. However, we are now ready to let the classical QUBO solvers, the D-Wave annealer, and quantum devices find the solution. Once you have derived the math and code for the QUBO for your real-world use case, it can be used repeatedly. In the next section, we will use the Mf matrix as we evaluate various QUBO solvers.

Getting results from different QUBO samplers

One advantage of using the QUBO method is that once the matrix has been created, any QUBO solver can be used to find the minimum energy solution. However, there are some nuances that you must be aware of. In the case of D-Wave, the function we will use converts the matrix into the BQM and then sends it to the Amazon Braket D-Wave device. In the case of sending the QUBO to Rigetti, the function must create the quantum circuit and then optimize the QAOA parameters. Also, the circuit for Rigetti is slightly different because it does not utilize ZZ gates; instead, it uses a combination of CX and CZ gates. For now, it is only necessary to know that these differences exist and have been encapsulated within the solver functions we will use here. If you are interested in diving into how to prepare each matrix for the specific solver, as well as how to interpret the results, please review the various functions.

Now, let's solve the Knapsack problem, which has been converted into a QUBO matrix whose shape is `20x20`. First, we will use the `ProbabilisticSampler()` function. To ensure we can correctly interpret the plots from the probabilistic sampler, it is important to know what the X axis on the plot will represent. In this problem, the X axis represents the sum of the x_i and y_n values that are returned. We will refer to it as the total count in the solution or S_{tc}:

$$S_{tc} = \sum_{i}^{N} x_i + \sum_{n}^{W_c} y_n \qquad eq.\,(11.16)$$

The probabilistic solver looks for all combinations of $S_{tc}=1$, then $S_{tc}=2$, then $S_{tc}=3$, and so on. In our case, the final value is $S_{tc}=20$, when all 10 items, x_i, and 10 weights, y_n, are selected. However, since our constraint should only select one weight, we should not get more than 10 items and one weight in the solution. Therefore, we have the following:

$$S_{tc}<=11 \qquad eq.\,(11.17)$$

This is the kind of awareness we will need before we can evaluate whether the QUBO has been created properly and have confidence that the solvers are going to be successful in providing a feasible result.

In the steps that follow, we will go over the code that was used to run the sampler and then evaluate the feasibility of the results. In the code provided online, each device has slightly different code due to the way the results are returned. I will not be repeating the process for each device in this chapter, but you can review the code if you are curious.

Using the probabilistic sampler

Now, let's run the M_f matrix on the `ProbabilisticSampler()` function to view the energy landscape and determine whether the matrix has been created correctly. If not, we may have to adjust the A, B, and C multipliers to ensure the constraints are working properly. In *Steps 1 to 5* here, the code loops through the sampler several times to determine the best values and stores feasible solutions. Then, *Step 6* prints out the feasible solutions:

1. First, we must set the count to 50, which is the number of times we will look at the best solution that's returned by the `ProbabilisticSampler()` function. We must also define the variables that will be used to store the final feasible or good solutions:

    ```
    cond1_fail=0
    cond2_fail=0
    good_solution=[]
    good_value=[]
    good_weight=[]
    good_energy=[]
    count=50
    for trial in range (count):
    ```

2. The part of the code runs `ProbabilisticSampler()` with the matrix as the first parameter and the maximum number of combinations to try (per the number of items returned in the solution) at 1000:

    ```
    solution=ProbabilisticSampler(Mf,1000)
    print(solution[0],solution[1])
    ```

    Output:

    ```
    Best found: [4, 7, 17]

    count: 3

    Energy: -426.0

    Solutions Sampled: 15422

    [4, 7, 17] -426.0
    ```

    The preceding output shows the first result that was returned. The plot that was returned is shown in *Figure 11.13*. The result indicates that the solution had items 4, 7, and 17 as its variables. In this case, the solution picked items 4 and 7 and selected a weight of 8, which is 17 in the new index.

    Now, we must ensure this is a valid result that meets the two conditions.

3. To extract all the items, x_i, selected, we will look at the M_f matrix's indexes 0 to 9, (i<N), and then evaluate the total value, V_t, and total weight, W_t:

```
item_list=[]
Vt=0
Wt=0
for i in solution[0]:
    if i <N:
        Vt+=value[i]
        Wt+=weight[i]
        print(i, value[i], weight[i])
        item_list.append(i)
print('Items added to Knapsack',item_list)
print('Total value:',Vt)
print('Total weight:',Wt)
```

Output:

```
4 10 3

7 16 5

Items added to Knapsack [4, 7]

Total value: 26

Total weight: 8
```

4 and 7 contribute to a value of 26 and a weight of 8, based on the original information we were provided from the knapsack data. Now, we can do the constraint checks.

4. First, we must ensure that only one weight, y_n, was returned in the solution, ($\Sigma y_n = 1$). For this, we will look at the M_f matrix index and ensure it is greater than N (i>=N) and save the weight values, n=i-N+1, in weight_list[]. Note that i-N+1=n (the weight), as defined in the weight variable, $y_n = 1$. In the following code, we are identifying whether more than one solution was found, check_y>1, or whether exactly one solution was found, check_y==1. If the solution from the solver is infeasible, a FAIL message will be printed:

```
check_y=0
weight_list=[]
for i in solution[0]:
    if i>=N:
        check_y+=1
        weight_list.append(i-N+1)
print('Condition 1 - Only one weight should be
```

```
            selected.')
    if check_y>1:
        print('FAIL: One weight condition not met',
              weight_list)
        cond1_fail+=1
    elif check_y==1:
        print('OK: condition met', weight_list)
```

Output:

```
Condition 1 - Only one weight should be selected.

OK: condition met [8]
```

In our case, only one weight was found in the solution, which was at the index value of 17, or a weight of 8. If more than one weight had been selected by the solver, we would have received a FAIL message.

5. If only one weight is found, then we will have satisfied the first constraint, and we would continue to evaluate the second constraint to ensure the weight of the items, x_i, selected, W_t, is the single weight saved in weight_list[0], ($\Sigma w_i x_i = W_t = n$). If this second condition is not met, then the solution from the solver is infeasible and a FAIL message will be printed. If the weights match, then we must add the solution items, value, weight, and energy to the feasible (or good) solution lists. Finally, if no weight is found in the solution, we will receive a FAIL message:

```
        print('Condition 2 - Total weight should be
              equal to weight selected')
        if Wt==weight_list[0]:
            print('OK: Condition met', Wt)
            good_solution.append(item_list)
            good_value.append(Vt)
            good_weight.append(Wt)
            good_energy.append(solution[1])
        else:
            print('FAIL: Weight match condition not
                met', Wt, weight_list[0])
            cond2_fail+=1
    else:
        print('FAIL: No weight was found')
```

Output:

```
Condition 2 - Total weight should be equal to weight selected
OK: Condition met 8
```

The message acknowledges that the weight that was found by the solver matches what was calculated by the data. This confirms that the solver provided a valid solution.

Since both conditions have been met, the solution will be appended to the good_ solution, good_value, good_weight, and good_energy arrays.

After this process has looped through the ProbabilisticSampler() function 50 times, it will evaluate and print out the final results.

6. Now, we can display all the feasible solutions that pass the two constraints. For real quantum computers, if the A, B, and C multipliers haven't been set correctly, we may not get any feasible solution. Therefore, if no feasible solution is found, you should go back and adjust the A, B, and C multipliers or increase the trials on the ProbabilisticSampler() function. In addition, the reason for developing checks for feasible solutions is that due to the probabilistic nature of quantum computers and the inherent errors that can be introduced, various solutions will just not be feasible when dealing with constrained problems, so those need to be filtered out:

```
good_count=len(good_value)
if good_count==0:
    print('-------FAIL!------------')
    print('No good values found')
    print('Condition 1: One weight condition
            failed',(cond1_fail/count)*100, '%')
    print('Condition 2: Weight match condition
            failed',(cond2_fail/count)*100, '%')
else:
    print('-------Success!------------')
    for i in range(good_count):
        print(i, good_solution[i], 'Value',
                good_value[i],'Wt', good_weight[i],
                'energy', good_energy[i])
```

Output:

```
-------Success!------------
0 [4, 7] Value 26 Wt 8 energy -426.0
1 [0, 4, 7] Value 28 Wt 10 energy -428.0
2 [5, 7] Value 28 Wt 10 energy -428.0
3 [2, 3, 7] Value 30 Wt 10 energy -430.0
4 [5, 7] Value 28 Wt 10 energy -428.0
5 [2, 3, 7] Value 30 Wt 10 energy -430.0
6 [2, 4, 7] Value 32 Wt 10 energy -432.0
```

Based on the output, the best solution contains items 2, 4, and 7, with a total value of 32 and a total weight of 10, which is the maximum allowed weight in the knapsack. The energy that was returned for this solution is -432.

A note about the energy returned

Notice that the energy returned is not the *value* that we were looking for – it is the combination of all the linear and quadratic terms from the M_{xf}, M_{xy}, and M_{yf} matrices. When the binary solution selects certain x_i and y_n variables to be equal to one, then the terms at the intersections are also added up. The best solution has the lowest energy, which is -432, and picked items 2, 4, and 7 for the x_i variables and 19 for the weight (this is equivalent to a weight of 10 or yn=10).

The following diagram shows all the energies that were added up. If this matrix was created properly, with an adequate amount of A, B, and C multipliers, then the correct answer should have the lowest energy. However, this is not the weight or value. Also, keep in mind that the total weight, W_t, and total value, V_t, of the items in the knapsack were *calculated after* we looked at the solution from the solver. Therefore, we can match whether the weight, W_t, from one side of the matrix agrees with the weight, y_n, that was selected from the other side of the matrix.

> **Note**
>
> In most cases, considerable post-processing is required to ensure the final answer is extracted correctly from the string of binary digits that's returned from the QUBO solvers. We will see this when we look at the D-Wave and Rigetti devices.

	0	1	2	3	4	5	6	7	8	9	10	11	12	13	14	15	16	17	18	19
0	6	24	16	24	24	40	48	40	64	72	-8	-16	-24	-32	-40	-48	-56	-64	-72	-80
1	0	14	24	36	36	60	72	60	96	108	-12	-24	-36	-48	-60	-72	-84	-96	-108	-120
2	0	0	2	24	24	40	48	40	64	72	-8	-16	-24	-32	-40	-48	-56	-64	-72	**-80**
3	0	0	0	10	36	60	72	60	96	108	-12	-24	-36	-48	-60	-72	-84	-96	-108	-120
4	0	0	0	0	8	60	72	60	96	108	-12	-24	-36	-48	-60	-72	-84	-96	-108	**-120**
5	0	0	0	0	0	38	120	100	160	180	-20	-40	-60	-80	-100	-120	-140	-160	-180	-200
6	0	0	0	0	0	0	58	120	192	216	-24	-48	-72	-96	-120	-144	-168	-192	-216	-240
7	0	0	0	0	0	0	0	34	160	180	-20	-40	-60	-80	-100	-120	-140	-160	-180	**-200**
8	0	0	0	0	0	0	0	0	110	288	-32	-64	-96	-128	-160	-192	-224	-256	-288	-320
9	0	0	0	0	0	0	0	0	0	142	-36	-72	-108	-144	-180	-216	-252	-288	-324	-360
10	0	0	0	0	0	0	0	0	0	0	-398	808	812	816	820	824	828	832	836	840
11	0	0	0	0	0	0	0	0	0	0	0	-392	824	832	840	848	856	864	872	880
12	0	0	0	0	0	0	0	0	0	0	0	0	-382	848	860	872	884	896	908	920
13	0	0	0	0	0	0	0	0	0	0	0	0	0	-368	880	896	912	928	944	960
14	0	0	0	0	0	0	0	0	0	0	0	0	0	0	-350	920	940	960	980	1000
15	0	0	0	0	0	0	0	0	0	0	0	0	0	0	0	-328	968	992	1016	1040
16	0	0	0	0	0	0	0	0	0	0	0	0	0	0	0	0	-302	1024	1052	1080
17	0	0	0	0	0	0	0	0	0	0	0	0	0	0	0	0	0	-272	1088	1120
18	0	0	0	0	0	0	0	0	0	0	0	0	0	0	0	0	0	0	-238	1160
19	0	0	0	0	0	0	0	0	0	0	0	0	0	0	0	0	0	0	0	**-200**

Figure 11.11 – The terms that have been summed to produce the lowest energy solution

A note on tweaking the multipliers

Previously, we mentioned that the correct multipliers need to be used to ensure we get the correct solutions. Here, we can compare the solutions that were returned when the multipliers are all equal to one, and where A=400.

The following is one of the solution plots that was returned by the probabilistic sampler when A=1:

```
A=1 #ensure only one weight is selected
B=1 # ensure weight matches total weight
C=1  # ensure correct items are selected
```

In the following energy landscape, notice that there are many low-energy solutions (energy <0) where S_{tc} (the sum of the number of x_i and y_n values selected) is greater than 11 (the X-axis). Remember from eq. (11.17) that S_{tc} cannot be greater than 11 for feasible solutions. This implies that one of the constraints is not working. Most likely, it is the M_{yc} matrix with multiplier A (see eq. (11.15) and Figure 11.5). We need to make A larger to enforce the constraint:

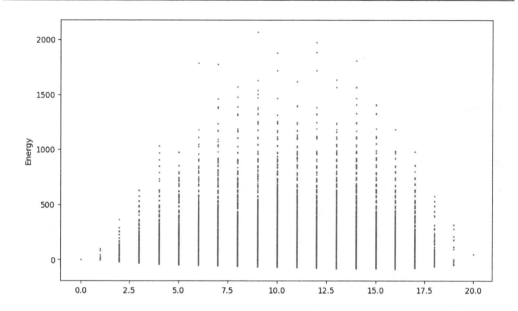

Figure 11.12 – Energy landscape using the probabilistic solver when A=1, B=1, and C=1 (X-axis = S_{ts})

Let's look at the sample output when A=1.

Output:

```
Best found: [0, 1, 2, 3, 4, 5, 6, 7, 8, 9, 14, 15, 16, 17, 18, 19]

count: 16

Energy: -85.0

Solutions Sampled: 15422

[0, 1, 2, 3, 4, 5, 6, 7, 8, 9, 14, 15, 16, 17, 18, 19] -85.0

0 2 2

1 4 3

2 6 2

3 8 3

4 10 3

5 12 5

6 14 6

7 16 5
```

```
8 18 8

9 20 9

Items added to Knapsack [0, 1, 2, 3, 4, 5, 6, 7, 8, 9]

Total value: 110

Total weight: 46

Condition 1 - Only one weight should be selected.

FAIL: One weight condition not met [5, 6, 7, 8, 9, 10]
```

In the preceding output, we can see weights with the 14, 15, 16, 17, 18, and 19 indices selected. This means that multiple weights, yn (5, 6, 7, 8, 9, and 10), were selected in this solution, which is infeasible.

Now, let's look at the energy plot after setting A=400:

```
A=400 #ensure only one weight is selected
B=2 # ensure weight matches total weight
C=1  # ensure correct items are selected
```

In the energy landscape, Stc (X-axis) with values greater than 11 has a high positive energy value and is being penalized correctly:

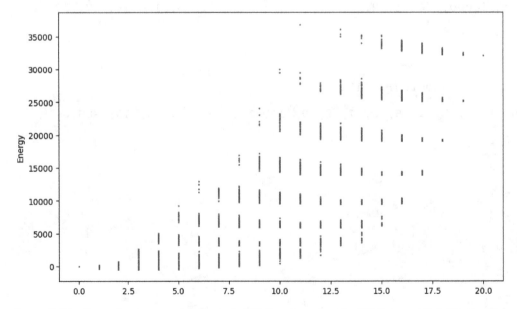

Figure 11.13 – Energy landscape using the probabilistic solver when A=400, B=1, and C=1 (X-axis = Sts)

Now, we can evaluate one of the solutions that was returned from the sampler with A=400.

Output:

```
Best found: [2, 4, 7, 19]

count: 4

Energy: -432.0

Solutions Sampled: 15422

[2, 4, 7, 19] -432.0

2 6 2

4 10 3

7 16 5

Items added to Knapsack [2, 4, 7]

Total value: 32

Total weight: 10

Condition 1 - Only one weight should be selected.

OK: condition met [10]

Condition 2 - Total weight should be equal to weight selected

OK: Condition met 10
```

In this sample output, our solution is [2, 4, 7, 19]. 2, 4, and 7 were selected, while 10 was selected as the weight (19 in the solution). This turns out to be the best solution and all the constraints have been met.

Based on the results of the probabilistic solver (you can confirm this using any classical solver), we now know the best solution. Now, let's see what solutions we get from the various quantum devices on Amazon Braket.

Running the knapsack problem on a D-Wave device

The function to convert a matrix into a BQM for D-Wave and submit the BQM to the D-Wave sampler is `run_dwave()`. This function has been modified in this chapter to bring out `chain_strength` as a parameter. This is necessary because, depending on the number of variables, we want to ensure that D-Wave does not have any chain breaks and provides the correct solutions. For a large number of variables, a higher chain strength might be needed. However, keep in mind that a value that is too high can prevent the annealer from providing correct results. Values may range between 0.1 and 20.0 but for this problem, the D-Wave 2000Q appears to do best at 15 to 25. Second, within the `run_dwave()` function, the D-Wave 2000Q sampler has been set since we only have 20 variables and do not need the Advantage system. Now, let's execute the M_f matrix on the Amazon Braket D-Wave 2000Q device:

1. First, we need to ensure that the `chain_strength` parameter is at an adequate value:

    ```
    chain_strength = 22
    ```

2. Now, we must run the sampler function:

    ```
    response=run_dwave(Mf, chain_strength)
    ```

    Output:

    Number of qubits: 2048

    Number of couplers 5974

    Shots max 10,000

    26214400

    Recommended shots 10000

    Estimated cost $2.20

	0	1	2	3	4	5	6	7	8	9	...	19	energy	num_oc.	...
1616	0	0	0	1	1	0	0	1	0	0	...	1	-432.0	1	...
1686	0	0	0	1	1	0	0	1	0	0	...	1	-432.0	1	...

3. The solutions that have been returned have an index of 0 to 19 for the variables. Remember that we will need to extract the x_n and y_n values and ensure that we have feasible solutions. The process is the same as it is for the probabilistic solver, so the code block has not been repeated here.

4. After evaluating the solutions and ensuring the constraints have been met, we receive an output.

    Output:

    ```
    -------Success!------------
    0 [2, 4, 7] Value 32 Wt 10 energy -432.0
    1 [2, 4, 7] Value 32 Wt 10 energy -432.0
    2 [2, 4, 7] Value 32 Wt 10 energy -432.0
    3 [2, 3, 7] Value 30 Wt 10 energy -430.0
    ```

    As you can see, in this run, we got items 2, 4, and 7, with a total value of 32 and a total weight of 10. This is a valid solution and also provides the best value. If you do not get the best-expected value for the energy, which in our knapsack problem is -432, you can run repeated trials or make further modifications to the chain's strength to find the best solution.

5. We can also use D-Wave's simulated annealer (**NEAL**) to see how often it finds the best solution. We will program the best value bit string and compare the results that are returned from 1000 trials:

    ```
    success=0
    expected='00101001000000000001'
    total=1000
    for i in range(total):
        result=run_neal(Mf)
        if result==expected:
            success+=1
    print('percent success:',100*success/total)
    ```

    Output:

    ```
    percent success:  4.8
    ```

    Surprisingly, for this small problem, the success rate of finding the solution is only 4.8% when using the simulated annealer.

So far, we have tried the problem classically by using a probabilistic method on the knapsack problem; we converted the knapsack problem into a QUBO, solved it using a probabilistic QUBO solver, and ran it on the D-Wave annealer. Now, we will run the problem QUBO matrix, M_p on gate-based methods using QAOA.

Running the knapsack problem on Amazon Braket simulator SV1

Now, we will switch to running the knapsack problem on gate-based devices. Remember that to optimize a function on a quantum computer, we must use the QAOA algorithm. We will use a slightly modified version of the QAOA solver that will return *all* the samples rather than only the minimum value. This is very useful as we can find not only the best solution but also a range of good solutions.

As a reminder, in *Chapter 8, Using Hybrid Algorithms – Optimization Using Gate-Based Quantum Computers*, we learned how to find the minimum energy of an objective function using gate-based quantum computers through QAOA. This method was further developed and used in subsequent chapters.

The following steps summarize the process of using QAOA:

1.   First, we create the quantum circuit, also referred to as the **Ansatz**, which increases the probability of finding the lowest energy value. However, the Ansatz is created using two parameters that need to be adjusted.

2.   Next, we vary the two parameters and display the lowest energy found in the parameter landscape using the param_optimizer() function. We can do *Steps 1* and *2* on a QUBO matrix.

3.   Finally, we take the best parameters found and then run the same quantum circuit with these optimal parameters and a higher number of shots to find the lowest energy. We can do this using the optimize_bqm() function. This function returns the best solution found. However, for this chapter, we will use a modified version of the optimizer function, quantum_device_sampler(). This allows us to specify the device we want to use for the optimizer, and it also adjusts the quantum circuit for the difference between IonQ and Rigetti devices based on the allowed quantum gates. It also returns all of the solutions returned by the multiple sampler runs. This will give us a richer solution set from which to extract our feasible knapsack results. Please review the online code for more details.

Our first test will be on Amazon Braket simulator SV1:

1.   First, we will assign the device and number of shots:

```
device=set_device('SV1')
estimate_cost(device,num_shots=1000)
```

Output:

```
Device('name': SV1, 'arn': arn:aws:braket:::device/quantum-
simulator/amazon/sv1)

simulator cost per  minute : $ 0.075

total cost cannot be estimated
```

2.   Now, we will run the QAOA algorithm to find the optimal parameters:

```
Qubits=len(Mf)
max_val=2**Qubits
param=np.arange(0.1,0.6,0.1,dtype=float)
print(param)
ideal_param1, ideal_param2, lowest_energy=
    param_optimizer_device(param, param, Mf, 1000,'SV1')
print(ideal_param1, ideal_param2, lowest_energy)
```

Output:

`0.30000000000000004 0.2 -430.0`

Here, the optimal parameter values are 0.3 and 0.2 and gave the lowest energy value – that is, -430. Interestingly, this energy is very close to what we got from the probabilistic solver and D-Wave's annealer. However, we can do better:

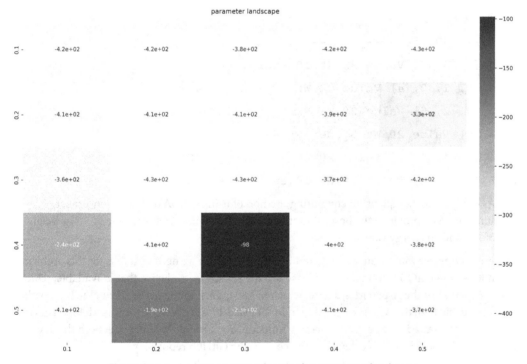

Figure 11.14 – Lowest energy values in the parameter landscape

3. Now, let's use the optimal parameters, 3.0 and 2.0, and increase the number of shots to get more solutions from the QAOA algorithm by using the `quantum_device_sampler()` function:

```
solution, quantity, energy, index=quantum_device_
sampler([ideal_param1], [ideal_param2], Mf, 100000,'SV1')
```

The output from this code block has not been shown here as it includes thousands of results. Also, keep in mind that we only used the optimal parameters, though a range of parameters around the optimal values could also have been sent to sample from a range of more fine-tuned parameters. The results from all the executions are stored in the return variables.

4. Now, let's evaluate the solutions and extract the feasible results where the constraints were met. The code for this has already been explained in the probabilistic sampler run section, so it won't be repeated here. The final portion of the output contains the best feasible solutions that were found.

Output:

```
-------Success!------------
0 [2, 4, 7] Value 32 Wt 10 energy -432.0
1 [0, 1, 2, 4] Value 22 Wt 10 energy -422.0
2 [0, 2, 5] Value 20 Wt 9 energy -420.0
3 [9] Value 20 Wt 9 energy -420.0
4 [0, 1, 2, 3] Value 20 Wt 10 energy -420.0
5 [0, 1, 5] Value 18 Wt 10 energy -418.0
```

As can be seen, the quantum computing method of using QAOA and Amazon Braket simulator SV1 provided the best solution with items 2, 4, and 7 and a value of 32, a weight of 10, and an energy value of -432.

In the next section, we will use an actual quantum computer. Since we need 20 qubits for this problem, we cannot use the IonQ 11 qubit device. Please use the latest Rigetti device that is available, which could be Aspen 11 or the Aspen M-1 device, which has 80 qubits. In the next section, I will show the results from using both the Aspen 11 and Aspen M-1 device. Please check which Rigetti Aspen device you have using the `available_devices()` function. You can follow along with both the devices in the book, and use the available device in the code in the GitHub repository.

Running the knapsack optimization problem on a Rigetti Aspen 11 device

Now, let's run the knapsack optimization problem on the Rigetti Aspen 11 quantum computer. Here, we will estimate the cost for running this job, submit the job, and verify the results:

1. Set up the Rigetti device and estimate the cost for 100000 shots:

    ```
    device=set_device('Aspen-11')
    estimate_cost(device,num_shots=100000)
    ```

    Output:

    ```
    Device('name': Aspen-11, 'arn': arn:aws:braket:::device/qpu/
    rigetti/Aspen-11)

    device cost per  shot : $ 0.00035

    total cost for 100000 shots is $35.30
    ```

2. Now, run the QAOA sampler using the optimal parameters from the SV1 parameter optimization step:

    ```
    solution, quantity, energy, index=quantum_device_
    sampler([ideal_param1], [ideal_param2], Mf,
    100000,'Aspen-11')
    ```

    The output from this code block has not been shown here as it includes thousands of results.

3. Now, let's evaluate the solution and find feasible results that meet the constraints. Note that with Rigetti, the returned bit string is reversed, so the quantum_device_sampler() function returns a reversed bit string for Rigetti devices. The code for this part is not included as it follows the same steps as in the probabilistic sampler example.

    Output:

    ```
    -------Success!------------
    0 [2, 4, 7] Value 32 Wt 10 energy -432.0
    1 [4, 7] Value 26 Wt 8 energy -426.0
    2 [0, 1, 7] Value 22 Wt 10 energy -422.0
    3 [0, 7] Value 18 Wt 7 energy -418.0
    4 [1, 5] Value 16 Wt 8 energy -416.0
    5 [0] Value 2 Wt 2 energy -402.0
    ```

    Here, we also get the best value and a series of other good solutions with slightly higher energy values.

Running on a Rigetti Aspen M-1 device

Now, let's run the knapsack optimization problem on the Rigetti Aspen M-1 quantum computer. Here, we will estimate the cost for running this job, submit the job, and verify the results:

1. Set up the Rigetti device and estimate the cost for 100000 shots:

    ```
    device=set_device('Aspen-M-1')
    estimate_cost(device,num_shots=100000)
    ```

    Output:

    ```
    Device('name': Aspen-M-1, 'arn': arn:aws:braket:us-west-
    1::device/qpu/rigetti/Aspen-M-1)
    ```

    ```
    device cost per  shot : $ 0.00035
    ```

    ```
    total cost for 100000 shots is $35.30
    ```

2. Now, let's run the QAOA sampler using the 0.3 and 0.3 parameters (*note that these parameters were chosen based on various other tests on SV1 and Rigetti*):

    ```
    solution, quantity, energy, index=quantum_device_
    sampler([0.3], [0.3], Mf, 100000,'Aspen-M-1')
    ```

    The output from this code block has not been shown here as it includes thousands of results.

3. Now, let's evaluate the solution and find feasible results that meet the constraints. Note that with Rigetti, the returned bit string is reversed, so the quantum_device_sampler() function returns a reversed bit string for Rigetti devices. The code for this part is not included as it follows the same steps as in the probabilistic sampler example.

    Output:

    ```
    -------Success!------------
    0 [2, 4, 7] Value 32 Wt 10 energy -432.0
    1 [2, 4, 5] Value 28 Wt 10 energy -428.0
    3 [1, 2, 7] Value 26 Wt 10 energy -426.0
    6 [0, 4, 5] Value 24 Wt 10 energy -424.0
    7 [1, 2, 5] Value 22 Wt 10 energy -422.0
    ```

    Here, we also get the best value and a series of other good solutions with slightly higher energy values.

With that, we have finished executing the knapsack problem using various classical and probabilistic tools, QUBO, simulated quantum computing, and an actual quantum computer. We were able to ensure that we knew what the best classical solution was by using `plot_knapsack()`. Then, we created the QUBO formulation and ensured our QUBO matrix, M_f, was adjusted correctly using the A, B, and C multipliers to produce the best results based on the constraints. We sampled this matrix using `ProbabilisticSampler()`. To evaluate the final results and ensure feasible solutions, we had to evaluate that only one weight, ($\Sigma y_n=1$), was in the solution and that the total weight, W_f, that was returned from the items in the solution ($x_i=1$) and the weight selected ($y_n=1$) were equal ($\Sigma w_i x_i=n$). In all subsequent devices, we filtered the results to ensure feasibility and displayed the best results that were found. Then, we used the `run_dwave()` function, which converts the QUBO into a BQM, and ran our problem on Amazon Braket's D-Wave 2000Q device, giving us close to the best answer. Next, to find the solution using gate-quantum computing methods, we converted the QUBO into a quantum circuit and found the optimal parameters using the `param_optimizer_device()` function. Later, we used the optimal parameters on the `quantum_device_sampler()` function to get the final solutions. The final solutions on SV1, Rigetti Aspen 11, and Rigetti Aspen M-1 contained the best solution for the knapsack problem. Some of the lessons you learned in this chapter can be very helpful as you take on various real-world problems with quantum computers. In the next section, we will summarize the key learning and steps in a framework that you can use in the future.

A process for solving constrained optimization problems

Based on various optimization problems I have solved on various classical, QUBO-based solvers, annealers, and gate-quantum computers, it is important to use a step-by-step process where there is a good understanding of the problem classically before moving on to developing the QUBO. When developing the QUBO formulation, it is important to get the constraint strengths right, which may require some trial and error or calculations to get the optimal multipliers. If a QUBO formulation that results in a single matrix is not developed correctly, none of the QUBO solvers, annealers, or gate-quantum computing methods will be able to give the best result. So, it is important to get this formulation and resulting matrix correct. Then, before the matrix can be used by various QUBO solvers, it is important to understand the format the solver requires. For example, for the D-Wave annealers, the QUBO needs to be converted into a BQM before sending it to the sampler; for gate-quantum computing devices, a gate quantum circuit Ansatz (trial) must be created and further tweaked with correct parameters before the results can be captured. Finally, when the answers are probabilistic and can receive errors from actual devices, the solutions must be analyzed and validated for feasibility using the original problem and its constraints. The following diagram summarizes this process and might be helpful as you experiment with real-world problems using Amazon Braket devices:

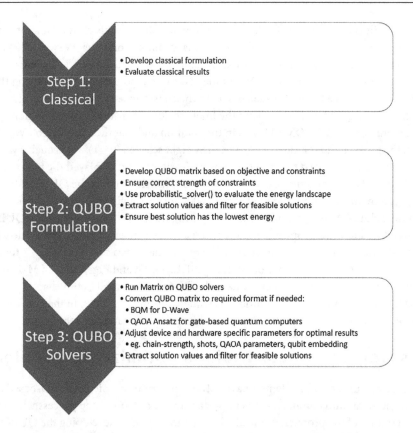

Step 1: Classical
- Develop classical formulation
- Evaluate classical results

Step 2: QUBO Formulation
- Develop QUBO matrix based on objective and constraints
- Ensure correct strength of constraints
- Use probabilistic_solver() to evaluate the energy landscape
- Extract solution values and filter for feasible solutions
- Ensure best solution has the lowest energy

Step 3: QUBO Solvers
- Run Matrix on QUBO solvers
- Convert QUBO matrix to required format if needed:
  - BQM for D-Wave
  - QAOA Ansatz for gate-based quantum computers
- Adjust device and hardware specific parameters for optimal results
  - eg. chain-strength, shots, QAOA parameters, qubit embedding
- Extract solution values and filter for feasible solutions

Figure 11.15 – The suggested process for solving real-world
optimization problems using Amazon Braket devices

Remember that since quantum computers are probabilistic, jumping straight into trying out a formulation on a quantum computer will be considerably disappointing and frustrating. The preceding framework should help you solve real-world problems on quantum computers. By doing this, you will be confident that the solution provided by the quantum computer is correct.

Summary

In this chapter, we solved the knapsack problem, which represents a very simple real-world problem, on various Amazon Braket devices and suggested a process for developing and solving similar problems. Many real-world problems can be mapped to one of many types of knapsack problem formulations and the more elaborate bin packing problems formulations. The 0/1 knapsack formulation, with its binary item variable, single objective, and single integer weight constraint, is a good foundational problem to evaluate how to build a QUBO formulation. This in itself is a mathematically intensive process and requires various device and hardware-specific parameter fine-tuning to ensure the formulation will give the desired results. We tested our formulation classically and then ensured our

QUBO formulation gave the best result. Next, we evaluated the QUBO formulation development on various Amazon Braket devices. We also reviewed a suggested step-by-step framework for solving such problems. This process will help you start solving other such problems on a quantum computer using Amazon Braket.

In the next chapter, we will look at a real-world problem that has multiple objectives and learn how to solve it.

Further reading

To learn more about the topics that were covered in this chapter, take a look at the following resources:

- Various classical knapsack problem solvers: `https://www.geeksforgeeks.org/0-1-knapsack-problem-dp-10/`

- *Ising formulations of many NP problems*, by Andrew Lucas (check out section 5.2. Knapsack with Integer Weights): `https://www.frontiersin.org/articles/10.3389/fphy.2014.00005/full`

Code deep dive:

Please review the code in the following functions. These have been used previously in this book:

- `run_dwave()`

- `ProbabilisticSampler()`

Please review the code in the following new functions; these were introduced in this chapter and were provided as part of the discussion. They can be found in the GitHub repository for this chapter:

- `plot_knapsack()`

- `param_optimizer_device()`

- `quantum_device_sampler()`

12
Multi-Objective Optimization Use Case

By now, you have gained the confidence to try various types of circuits, tests, and small problems on quantum computing and simulator devices available on Amazon Braket. You have learned how the annealer differs from gate quantum computers and the limits of each device. You have seen how to convert a constrained problem into a **Quadratic Unconstrained Binary Optimization** (QUBO) format. You have also learned how to develop a **Binary Quadratic Model** (BQM) to optimize the D-Wave annealer; the same BQM was used to create the quantum circuit for the QAOA algorithm for gate-based quantum computers. We used various matrices to represent a BQM and developed the BQM for the knapsack problem in the previous chapter.

In this final chapter, we will go over a scenario with two competing objectives. This will help you learn how to address real-world problems that have multiple and frequently conflicting objectives. We will look at a mock example of a retail store with two managers who have turned adversarial due to misaligned objectives and incentives based on their area performance.

First, we will develop the problem and then work through two scenarios. In one of the scenarios, a procurement manager is in control of prioritizing the objective and decides on which suppliers the company should work with. In the other scenario, an inventory manager, who works with marketing and the store managers, gets to decide which products are purchased. We will run these scenarios classically, then use the D-Wave annealer to analyze the current conflict. Then, we will find an optimal strategy that will benefit the whole store.

The following topics will be covered in this chapter:

- Looking into a mock inventory management problem
- Determining the conflict based on the opposing objectives
- Determining a better global solution

Technical requirements

The source code for this chapter is available in this book's GitHub repository: `https://github.com/PacktPublishing/Quantum-Computing-Experimentation-with-Amazon-Braket/tree/main/Chapter12`.

Looking into a mock inventory management problem

We will start with a mock example to show how multiple and conflicting objectives can be evaluated and resolved using a simple method. We will follow these steps:

1. First, we will set up the multi-objective problem.

2. Then, we will show the two competing scenarios, A and B, in code.

3. Next, we will use the probabilistic solver we used in the previous chapter and find the optimal values using D-Wave through Amazon Braket.

4. Finally, we will find a method that finds the maximum benefit for both objectives.

Setting up the multi-objective problem

Let's set up the problem. In this hypothetical scenario of a retail store, the inventory manager is accountable for stocking products that are in demand and generating the most revenue for the company by ensuring enough products are in stock. The procurement manager is responsible for ensuring that the products are procured with the least amount of risk and cost from reliable suppliers. The procurement manager wants to implement plans to reduce the overall risk. They wish to sign up the optimal number of key and reliable suppliers and factories without increasing any overhead and the additional risk of dealing with too many suppliers. This seems like a losing proposition when the product's needs require signing up risky and high-cost suppliers.

The inventory manager has been trying to stock the right amount of products to meet the trends and demands of the customers, also ensuring complementary products are available and products with the least profit margin are not stocked. However, it seems like a losing battle, especially when the procurement manager cannot keep up with the product trends, and items that are not selling are bundled in with the shipments. The following diagram shows the current situation: we have product shortages and items that are not in demand stacking up in the inventory, as well as risky suppliers or others that seem to be fulfilling demand on schedule. Here, both the inventory and procurement managers are not achieving their target performance:

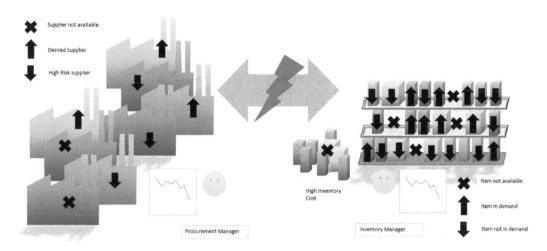

Figure 12.1 – Current situation between inventory and procurement

You have been assigned to help figure out how to resolve this situation. How can you help each manager optimize their area and, more importantly, can you find a solution to these competing objectives?

Let's look at this problem systematically.

In *Scenario A*, we will do the following:

1. Optimize the suppliers based on the procurement manager's data, which is stored in the *Ms* matrix.

2. Find the available items from those suppliers based on the availability matrix, *Ma*.

3. Create a new BQM for these new items and optimize the items for the inventory manager to place in the store.

In *Scenario B*, we will do the following:

1. Optimize the items based on the inventory manager's data, which is stored in the *Mi* BQM matrix.

2. Find the minimum number of suppliers that can meet the item demand using the *Ma* matrix.

The following diagram shows a summary of how we want to optimize each scenario:

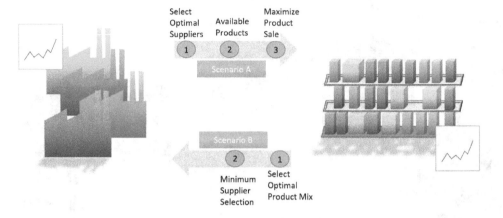

Figure 12.2 – Steps to evaluate the best solutions for scenarios A and B

In this mock example, we will assume that Ms is a matrix that represents the combined risk function of selecting a set of suppliers. We want to minimize the energy of this matrix for the procurement manager. A second matrix, Mi, represents the inventory energy function of the combination of items or products that are stocked. It has already been multiplied by -1, so we need to minimize the energy of this matrix. A third matrix, Ma, shows which products are available from each supplier. This matrix will be used in scenario A to find all the products available from the selected suppliers. It will also be used in scenario B to find the minimum suppliers that provide or *cover* the required items.

The following diagram shows the data in the availability matrix, Ma, and summarizes how it is used to achieve the goals of scenarios A and B:

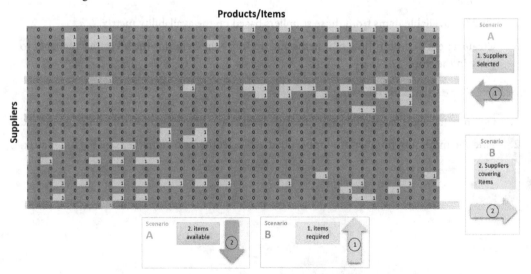

Figure 12.3 – The availability matrix, Ma, and its use in scenarios A and B

The key equations are given here:

$$using\ Ms, minimize \left\{ supplier\ energy = \sum_{i \leq j}^{n} Ms_{i,j} s_i s_j \right\} \quad s \in \{0,1\} \qquad eq.\,(12.1)$$

$$using\ Mi, minimize \left\{ inventory\ energy = \sum_{i \leq j}^{n} Mi_{i,j} i_i i_j \right\} \quad i \in \{0,1\} \qquad eq.\,(12.2)$$

These equations have the constraint that all items selected must be available at the selected suppliers.

Evaluating the best product mix based on scenario A

Now that we have set up the problem and know the two objectives and the constraint, let's start reviewing the code to find the results of scenario A. In this case, we want to optimize using the supplier matrix, *Ms*, and then determine which products can be sold for maximum profit:

1. First, let's import the three matrices that represent our problem – that is, `Mi`, `Ms`, and `Ma`:

    ```
    from numpy import genfromtxt
    Mi = genfromtxt('items.csv', delimiter=',')
    Ms = genfromtxt('supplier.csv', delimiter=',')
    Ma = genfromtxt('availability.csv', delimiter=',')
    ```

2. Next, we can review the shape and values of the three matrices. 80 items are represented in `Mi`:

    ```
    print(np.shape(Mi))
    print(Mi)
    ```

    Output:

    ```
    (80, 80)
    [[-0.6    0.7    0.03 ...  0.02   0.01   0.03]
     [ 0.    -0.91   0.02 ...  0.03   0.04   0.  ]
     [ 0.     0.    -0.92 ...  0.01   0.02   0.04]
     ...
     [ 0.     0.     0.   ... -0.39   0.7    0.02]
     [ 0.     0.     0.   ...  0.     0.2   -0.9 ]
     [ 0.     0.     0.   ...  0.     0.    -0.34]]
    ```

This matrix is the standard upper triangular matrix we have used to represent a BQM. Negative values on the diagonal represent desired products and any negative non-diagonal terms represent complementary products that we want to select together. You may want to open and view the `items.csv` file for more details.

3. Let's review the Ms matrix using the following code:

```
print(np.shape(Ms))
print(Ms)
```

Output:

```
(30, 30)
[[-1.30e+00   3.35e-02   4.91e-02   2.83e-02   1.03e-01   6.93e-02
7.03e-02

   3.57e-03   7.35e-02   1.19e-02   2.40e-02   1.14e-01   5.54e-02
8.98e-02

   1.08e-01   8.33e-02   1.99e-02   5.05e-03   3.46e-02   2.63e-02
1.90e-02

   7.09e-02   6.71e-02   1.02e-01   1.21e-01   7.46e-02   1.22e-01
8.05e-02

   2.03e-02   3.35e-02]

 ...

 [ 0.00e+00   0.00e+00   0.00e+00   0.00e+00   0.00e+00   0.00e+00
0.00e+00

   0.00e+00   0.00e+00   0.00e+00   0.00e+00   0.00e+00   0.00e+00
0.00e+00

   0.00e+00   0.00e+00   0.00e+00   0.00e+00   0.00e+00   0.00e+00
0.00e+00

   0.00e+00   0.00e+00   0.00e+00   0.00e+00   0.00e+00   0.00e+00
0.00e+00

   0.00e+00  -4.06e-01]]
```

The Ms matrix is also a BQM that represents 30 suppliers.

4. Now, let's review the Ma matrix, which contains the item availability information:

```
print(np.shape(Ma))
print(Ma)
```

Output:

```
(30, 80)
[[0. 0. 0. ... 0. 0. 0.]
 [0. 1. 0. ... 1. 0. 0.]
 [0. 0. 0. ... 0. 0. 0.]

 ...

 [1. 0. 0. ... 0. 0. 0.]
 [1. 0. 1. ... 0. 0. 0.]
 [0. 0. 0. ... 0. 0. 0.]]
```

The Ma matrix represents item availability and is displayed in the preceding output. Notice that the matrix is not the standard BQM. This matrix is a 30x80 matrix. The 30 rows represent the 30 suppliers, while the 80 rows represent the 80 items. A 1 indicates that the item is available at the supplier.

5. We can quickly visualize the Ms matrix by using the probabilisticsampler() function:

```
sup_list=ProbabilisticSampler(Ms,100)
```

Output:

Best found: [0, 1, 5, 6, 10, 12, 14, 20, 26, 29]

count: 10

Energy: -8.9079

Solutions Sampled: 2762

With only 100 samples per number of suppliers in the solution, we find that the best supplier combination is [0, 1, 5, 6, 10, 12, 14, 20, 26, 29]. This is 10 suppliers with the lowest energy of -8.9079. This would recommend that the procurement manager only signs contracts with these suppliers. Since this is a probabilistic result, your execution may produce slightly different values. The following plot shows that there are other likely minimum values between 10 and 14 suppliers. It also shows that there is a broad range of energy values for those supplier numbers, indicating that picking the wrong 10 suppliers could have a large impact on the risk of supplier selection:

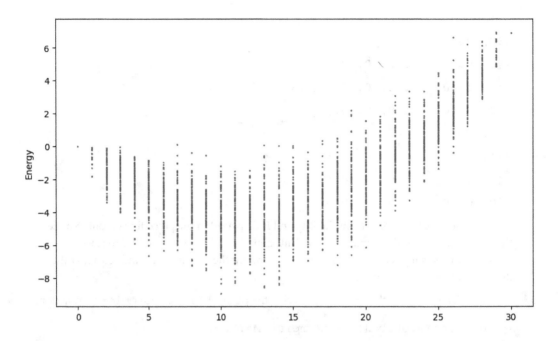

Figure 12.4 – Supplier BQM matrix, Ms, energy landscape visualization

6. Now, we want to see which items are available through these suppliers. Let's use the `availability()` function to get a list of available items for a list of suppliers while using the Ma matrix:

```
a=availability(sup_list[0],Ma)
```

7. We can review the list of available items, a, from all these suppliers using the following command:

```
print(len(a),a)
```

Output:

```
43 [ 0  1  2  3  5  9 14 16 17 22 24 25 28 29 32 35 36 38 39
41 42 44 45 46
```

```
 47 48 50 51 52 53 54 55 57 58 60 63 65 66 69 70 74 76 77]
```

Based on the selected suppliers, the output shows that there are 43 available items that the inventory manager can now decide to stock in the store. Since this is a probabilistic result, your execution may produce slightly different values.

8. The inventory manager does not want to stock all items; they would prefer to optimize within the available items to see which would be the most optimal in reducing costs and maximizing profit. To do this, we need to provide the inventory manager with a new BQM matrix that represents these items only. The `item_m()` function has been provided for this. In this case, the list, a, represents the items available based on the optimal suppliers, and Mi is the inventory BQM for all items. The resulting m_i is a smaller subset BQM matrix of the new items available to the inventory manager:

```
m_i=item_m(a, Mi)
print(np.shape(m_i))
print(m_i)
```

Output:

```
(43, 43)
[[-0.6    0.7    0.03 ...  0.     0.02  0.02]
 [ 0.    -0.91   0.02 ...  0.04   0.    0.03]
 [ 0.     0.    -0.92 ...  0.03   0.02  0.01]

 ...

 [ 0.     0.     0.    ... -0.93   0.03  0.02]
 [ 0.     0.     0.    ...  0.     0.02 -0.9 ]
 [ 0.     0.     0.    ...  0.     0.   -0.39]]
```

The preceding matrix represents the BQM for the 43 items that are now available to the inventory manager. Now, we can simply optimize this matrix to find the optimal items to stock.

9. Let's use the `ProbabilisticSampler()` function once more to evaluate the optimal products:

```
p_items=ProbabilisticSampler(m_i,100)
```

Output:

```
Best found: [1, 2, 4, 5, 6, 7, 8, 10, 11, 12, 13, 15, 16, 18,
20, 21, 23, 28, 29, 31, 32, 33, 35, 36, 37, 38, 39, 40]

count: 28

Energy: -14.850000000000051

Solutions Sampled: 4088
```

Out of the 43 items, the inventory manager will now stock only 28 items, as shown in the preceding output. Keep in mind that the index values for these 28 items are based on the new m_i matrix and that to retrieve the actual product number, we will have to refer to the original indexes in the Mi matrix. This is not necessary right now and will be shown in the next section. The main point so far is that this gives a minimum energy value of -14.85 for the inventory. The visualization of the m_i matrix is given in the following plot. Would the inventory manager be happy with this option?

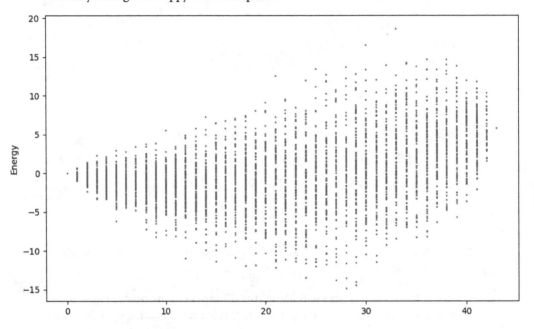

Figure 12.5 – Available inventory BQM matrix, m_i, energy landscape visualization

So far, we have looked at the initial steps and process of how to optimize the suppliers and then the inventory. With our classical probabilistic sampler and with just a few shots, we found that the procurement manager could get an energy value of -8.9079 with 10 suppliers. Then, we evaluated the available items from these combined sets of suppliers to determine that the optimal set of products to be stocked was 28 with an energy value of -14.85. However, this was just the beginning; we want to find better values for both managers, run through scenario A, and then work backward from the inventory to the supplier optimization in scenario B. We will go over this next.

Determining the conflict based on the opposing objectives

Now, we want to loop through the steps in the previous section to find better results for scenario A and then work backward to find reasonably good values for scenario B. Please refer to *Figure 12.2*, which summarizes these steps. First, we will do this with the classical probabilistic solver and then use D-Wave.

Evaluating the results with the probabilistic solver

We can quickly visualize and then evaluate the conflict by looping through the steps multiple times and plotting the results of each scenario. Here, we will continue to use the probabilistic solver:

1. The following code is for scenario A and accumulates supplier and inventory energy values for plotting. We will repeat the process 20 times, as set in the `total` variable. The code lines should be familiar from the previous section. At the end of the code, we will convert the item values from the `m_i` matrix into actual product numbers that are stored in `i_item`. The energy values from the supplier list are stored in `plot_sup1`, while the energy values from the resulting inventory in `p_items` are stored in `plot_prod1`. We will start by finding the optimal suppliers and then finding the items that are available from those suppliers. We will only show the results of the first iteration:

```
plot_sup1=[]
plot_prod1=[]
total=20
for trials in range(total):
    sup_list=ProbabilisticSampler(Ms,100)
    print('Ideal suppliers:',sup_list[0])
    print('Supplier energy', sup_list[1])
# save the energy of the best suppliers for plotting
    plot_sup1.append(sup_list[1])
# calculate list of available items
    a=availability(sup_list[0],Ma)
    print('Items available:',len(a),a)
# build new BQM of the available items
    m_i=item_m(a, Mi)
    print(np.shape(m_i))
```

Output:

```
Best found: [0, 5, 10, 11, 12, 14, 15, 20, 21]
count: 9
Energy: -9.184190000000001
Solutions Sampled: 2762
Ideal suppliers: [0, 5, 10, 11, 12, 14, 15, 20, 21]
Supplier energy -9.184190000000001
Items available: 40 [ 0  2  3  5  8  9 13 15 18 20 22 23 24
25 27 29 32 35 36 38 39 41 42 44
 45 46 47 48 50 51 52 53 54 55 66 69 70 74 77 79]
(40, 40)
```

The preceding output is only for the first output of 20. The plots of the energy landscape are available in this book's GitHub repository for this chapter and have not been shown here. These plots of the energy landscape of the Ms matrix will be similar to those in *Figure 12.4*. This output shows that 9 suppliers were selected, which resulted in a total of 40 items becoming available to the inventory manager. The supplier energy value was -9.18.

2. Next, we will optimize the items that should be stocked in the store by the inventory manager:

```
# find optimal items to stock in store
    p_items=ProbabilisticSampler(m_i,100)
# refer back to original item numbers in Mi
    i_item=np.zeros(len(p_items[0]))
    for I in range(len(p_items[0])):
        i_item[i]=a[p_items[0][i]]
    print('Items in solution:',i_item)
    print('Item Energy', p_items[1])
# store the energy of the optimal items for plotting
    plot_prod1.append(p_items[1])
```

Output:

```
Best found: [1, 2, 3, 5, 6, 7, 9, 10, 11, 12, 13, 14, 19, 20,
23, 25, 27, 29, 30, 31, 32, 33, 34, 35, 36, 37, 38, 39]
count: 28
Energy: -17.940000000000083
Solutions Sampled: 3781
```

```
Items in solution: [ 2.   3.   5.   9. 13. 15. 20. 22. 23. 24.
25. 27. 38. 39. 44. 46. 48. 51.
 52. 53. 54. 55. 66. 69. 70. 74. 77. 79.]
Item Energy -17.940000000000083
```

In this case, we have 28 optimal items, with an energy value of -17.94. The plot of the energy landscape for the m_i matrix has not been shown here but it will be similar to what's shown in *Figure 12.5*. Also, note that we converted the item numbers from the optimized list back into the original index of the items in the Mi matrix.

3. The following code is for scenario B and accumulates supplier and inventory energy values for plotting. We will perform the steps for scenario B 20 times as well. Please refer to *Figure 12.2* for the key steps in scenario B. In this case, we will find the optimal items from all 80 items in the Mi BQM matrix. Next, we will use a new function, SetCoverSampler(), to find the minimum suppliers that provide those items. This new function is a modification of the probabilistic sampler so that we can visualize the energy landscape. More efficient code can be created for this purpose as well if desired. A plot of the first iteration is shown in *Figure 12.6*. Then, we will find the energy value of these suppliers from the Ms BQM matrix. We won't need to optimize any further since the set cover means that the minimum suppliers have been found. Finally, all the energy values will be stored for plotting.

Let's proceed with the code for these two steps for scenario B. First, we will find the optimal items using the Mi BQM matrix:

```
plot_sup2=[]
plot_prod2=[]
total=20
for trials in range(total):
# optimize and print energy landscape for Mi
    p_items=ProbabilisticSampler(Mi,100)
    print('Ideal items:', p_items[0])
    print('Items energy:', p_items[1])
# store energy of items for plotting
    plot_prod2.append(p_items[1])
```

Output:

```
Best found: [1, 4, 5, 7, 9, 10, 11, 13, 15, 24, 26, 27, 33,
34, 37, 38, 39, 40, 44, 45, 47, 49, 50, 52, 56, 57, 58, 63,
64, 65, 66, 69, 71, 72, 73, 75, 77, 78, 79]
count: 39
Energy: -36.94999999999979
```

```
Solutions Sampled: 7862
Ideal items: [1, 4, 5, 7, 9, 10, 11, 13, 15, 24, 26, 27, 33,
34, 37, 38, 39, 40, 44, 45, 47, 49, 50, 52, 56, 57, 58, 63,
64, 65, 66, 69, 71, 72, 73, 75, 77, 78, 79]
Items energy: -36.94999999999979
```

Please review the output in the code in this chapter's GitHub repository. The output shows that 39 optimum items were found from the total of 80 items for stocking in the store. The energy value of these items is -36.94 and has been saved for plotting.

4. Next, we will use the `SetCoverSampler()` function to find the minimum suppliers that provide those items. This new function is a modification of the probabilistic sampler so that we can visualize the energy landscape. More efficient code can be created for this purpose as well if desired:

```
# find energy landscape for set cover and minimum
# suppliers to cover required items
    sup_list=SetCoverSampler(Ma,p_items[0],100)
    print('Min Suppliers to cover items:',sup_list[0])
```

Output:

```
Best found: [0, 1, 2, 4, 8, 9, 10, 12, 14, 15, 17, 18, 20,
21, 22, 23, 24, 25, 26, 27, 28]
count: 21
Energy: -39.0
Solutions Sampled: 2762
Min Suppliers to cover items: [0, 1, 2, 4, 8, 9, 10, 12, 14,
15, 17, 18, 20, 21, 22, 23, 24, 25, 26, 27, 28]
```

In the output, we find 21 suppliers that cover the 39 required items.

A plot of the first iteration is shown here. You can see that the energy drops as the number of suppliers increases. This shows that more items are being covered by the increasing number of suppliers. At 21 suppliers (X-axis), the minimum energy is found and all the items are covered. This energy value of -39 represents the solution covering the 39 items. As we increase the suppliers, the value is not improved. We only need to return the lowest number of suppliers where the lowest energy is found:

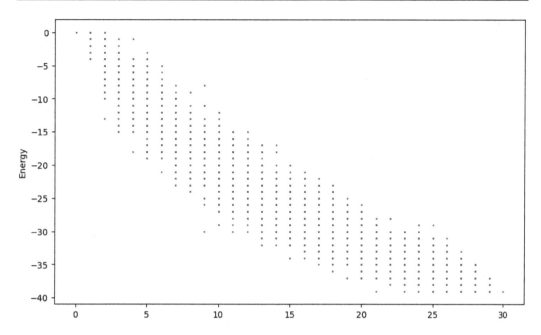

Figure 12.6 – Supplier energy landscape from the SetCoverSampler() function

5.   Now, we must simply find the energy of the suppliers based on the data in the Ms matrix and also store the energy for plotting:

```
# Find the minimum suppliers that cover required items
    sup_list=SetCoverSampler(Ma,p_items[0],100)
    sup_energy=0
    for i in sup_list[0]:
        for j in sup_list[0]:
            if i<=j:
                sup_energy+=Ms[i,j]
    print('Supplier Energy',sup_energy)
# save minimum supplier energy for plotting
    plot_sup2.append(sup_energy)
```

Output:

Supplier Energy -0.3361099999999987

6. Now, we can plot the results:

```
plt.scatter(plot_sup1,plot_prod1,color='green')
plt.scatter(plot_sup2,plot_prod2,color='red')
plt.xlabel('supplier')
plt.ylabel('product')
plt.title('Find optimal supplier and product')
```

The resulting plot is as follows:

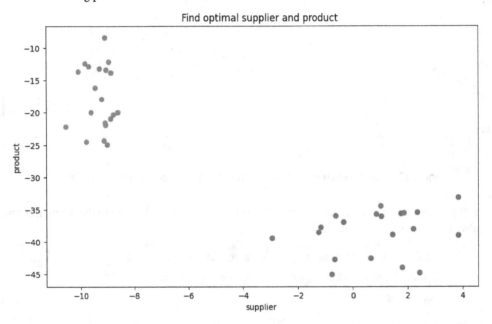

Figure 12.7 – Results from sampling scenario A (top left green dots) and scenario B (bottom right red dots)

As you can see, with these quick classical results, the two objectives – supplier optimization and product optimization – conflict. In the plot data for scenario A (top left green dots), the supplier energy value is low, making the procurement manager happy. However, the product energy value is not optimized based on the available items. On the other hand, as shown in the plot data for scenario B (bottom right red dots), the inventory manager will get good results due to the low product energy value. However, the supplier energy value is not optimized. In the latter case, the procurement manager, by providing the required items, is not able to optimize the suppliers.

If the corporation is evaluating each manager for their specific performance and compensating them for optimizing their area, this will result in an internal conflict. These misaligned objectives will cause an adversarial relationship between the managers and the haphazard scenario shown in *Figure 12.1*.

We now have a general picture of the situation. Since the classical method requires a considerable amount of time to visualize the landscape, we sampled a limited number of times, so we did not get the best value for each scenario. In the next section, we will use D-Wave to find the optimal (or close to optimal) values for both scenarios.

Evaluating the optimal values using the D-Wave annealer

The plots in the previous section showed considerable variance. Depending on the suppliers selected, many item combinations are possible and depending on the items selected, many different supplier combinations are possible. Now, let's turn to the D-Wave annealer to give us the best energy values possible for the two scenarios:

1. Starting with scenario A, we will optimize the suppliers using the Ms **BQM** matrix. We will use the `run_dwave()` function to find the optimal value for this matrix. We will use a value of 0.5 for the chain strength as a starting point. This can be changed to find possibly better solutions considering the number of variables. The `run_dwave()` function is set up to use the D-Wave Advantage system, which can embed a fully connected matrix whose size does not exceed 134. Since our matrix size was 110, we cannot use D-Wave 2000Q, which only has a capacity for embedding a fully connected matrix that's 65 in size. Let's proceed:

    ```
    dwave_plot_sup1=[]
    dwave_plot_prod1=[]
    sup_result=run_dwave(Ms,0.5)
    ```

Output:

```
Number of qubits:   5760

Number of couplers 40135

Shots max 10,000

26843545600

Recommended shots 10000

Estimated cost $2.20
```

	0	1	2	3	4	5	6	...	29	energy	num_oc.	...
0	1	0	0	0	0	1	1	...	0	-11.68817	68	...
1492	1	0	0	0	0	1	1	...	0	-11.68817	1	...

```
['BINARY', 5022 rows, 10000 samples, 30 variables]
{0: 1, 1: 0, 2: 0, 3: 0, 4: 0, 5: 1, 6: 1, 7: 1, 8: 1, 9: 1,
10: 1, 11: 1, 12: 0, 13: 0, 14: 1, 15: 0, 16: 0, 17: 0, 18:
0, 19: 0, 20: 1, 21: 1, 22: 0, 23: 0, 24: 0, 25: 0, 26: 0,
27: 0, 28: 1, 29: 0}
```

100001111111001000001100000010

decimal equivalent: 570196738

Validate energy -11.688170000000005

We will process this data and clean it up in the next line.

2. Now, let's process the output to get the suppliers and energy values:

```
first_sup=sup_result.first
sup_list=[]
for s in range(len(Ms)):
    if first_sup.sample[s]==1:
        sup_list.append(s)
print(sup_list)
print('Supplier energy', first_sup[1])
dwave_plot_sup1.append(first_sup[1])
```

Output:

[0, 5, 6, 7, 8, 9, 10, 11, 14, 20, 21, 28]

Supplier energy -11.688170000000003

Already, we can see that this energy value is the lowest we have seen for the suppliers.

3. Now, we need to find the items that are available based on this reduced supplier list:

```
a=availability(sup_list,Ma)
print('Items available:',len(a),a)
```

Output:

Items available: 54 [0 1 2 3 5 8 9 13 15 16 17 18 20
22 23 24 25 27 29 30 31 32 33 34 35 36 37 38 39 40 41 42 44
45 46 47 48 49 50 51 52 53 55 57 58 66 69 70 74 75 76 77 78
79]

4. Now, we must optimize these items since we've created a BQM matrix for them:

```
m_i=item_m(a, Mi)
print(np.shape(m_i))
item_result=run_dwave(m_i,0.5)
```

Output:

```
(54, 54)
```

```
Number of qubits:   5760
```

```
Number of couplers 40279
```

```
Shots max 10,000
```

```
450359962737049600
```

```
Recommended shots 10000
```

```
Estimated cost $2.20
```

```
        0  1  2  3  4  5  6  7  ... 53 energy num_oc. ...

0       0  1  1  1  1  1  1  1  ...  1 -38.97      36 ...

2       0  1  1  1  1  1  1  1  ...  1 -38.97      31 ...
```

5. Now, we must extract the items from the D-Wave solution, calculate the energy of these items based on the new m_i matrix, and remap them to their original index:

```
first_item=item_result.first
itm_list=[]
for s in range(len(m_i)):
    if first_item.sample[s]==1:
        itm_list.append(s)
i_item=np.zeros(len(itm_list))
for i in range(len(itm_list)):
    i_item[i]=a[itm_list[i]]
print('Items in solution:',i_item)
print('Item Energy:', first_item[1])
dwave_plot_prod1.append(first_item[1])
```

Output:

```
Items in solution: [ 1.   2.   3.   5.   8.   9. 13. 15. 23. 25.
34. 37. 38. 39. 40. 42. 44. 53. 57. 58. 69. 70. 74. 75. 77.
78. 79.]
```

```
Item Energy: -38.969999999999885
```

Interestingly, this energy value is the best we have seen for the inventory. Should the inventory manager accept this solution? Let's continue to find out.

6.   Here is the code for plotting this new result (purple) on the previous plot:

```
plt.scatter(dwave_plot_sup1,dwave_plot_prod1,
            color='purple')
plt.scatter(plot_sup1,plot_prod1,color='green')
plt.scatter(plot_sup2,plot_prod2,color='red')
plt.xlabel('supplier')
plt.ylabel('product')
plt.title('Find optimal supplier and product')
```

This results in the following output:

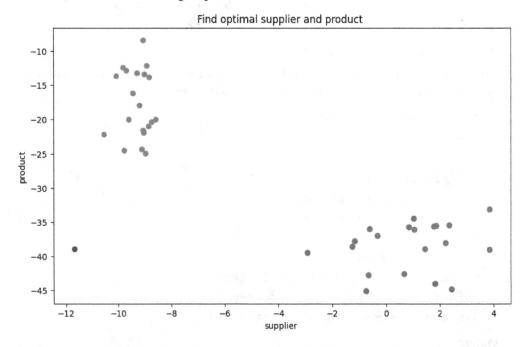

Figure 12.8 – Additional plot of the D-Wave results for scenario A (a single purple dot at the bottom left)

These are excellent results for the procurement manager, and to some extent, they are not too bad for the inventory manager. However, we have not seen how much better the inventory manager can do if using D-Wave to find the optimal results from scenario B.

7.   We will now reverse the process for scenario B. In this case, we will start by optimizing the inventory using D-Wave:

```
dwave_plot_sup2=[]
dwave_plot_prod2=[]
item_results=run_dwave(Mi,0.5)
```

Output:

```
Shots max 10,000

3022314549036572936765440 0

Recommended shots 10000

Estimated cost $2.20
```

```
        0  1  2  3  4  5  6  7  ...  79 energy num_oc. ...
13      0  0  1  1  1  1  1  1  ...   1 -90.39        8 ...
```

This is quite an unexpected result. The inventory manager has the option of getting an energy value of -90.39 based on the correct selection of items based on the Mi **BQM** matrix.

8. Now, we need to extract the item values and then process them to see which suppliers provide these items:

```
first_item=item_results.first
itm_list=[]
for s in range(len(Mi)):
    if first_item.sample[s]==1:
        itm_list.append(s)
print('items:',itm_list)
print('Supplier energy', first_item[1])
dwave_plot_prod2.append(first_item[1])
```

Output:

```
items: [2, 3, 4, 5, 6, 7, 8, 9, 10, 11, 12, 13, 14, 15, 19,
25, 26, 34, 37, 38, 39, 40, 41, 42, 43, 44, 46, 50, 52, 53,
55, 56, 57, 58, 59, 62, 63, 69, 70, 71, 72, 73, 74, 75, 76,
77, 78, 79]
```

```
Supplier energy -90.38999999999956
```

9. We will still use the probabilistic SetCoverSampler() function to determine the minimum suppliers needed to cover these items:

```
sup_list=SetCoverSampler(Ma,itm_list,50)
```

Output:

```
Best found: [0, 1, 2, 3, 4, 6, 7, 8, 9, 13, 14, 15, 16, 17,
18, 20, 21, 23, 24, 26, 27, 29]

count: 22

Energy: -47.0

Solutions Sampled: 141
```

10. Now, we need to find the actual supplier energy for this mix of 22 suppliers:

```
print('Min Suppliers to cover items:',sup_list[0])
sup_energy=0
for i in sup_list[0]:
    for j in sup_list[0]:
        if i<=j:
            sup_energy+=Ms[i,j]
print('Supplier Energy',sup_energy)
dwave_plot_sup2.append(sup_energy)
```

Output:

```
Min Suppliers to cover items: [0, 1, 2, 3, 4, 6, 7, 8, 9, 13,
14, 15, 16, 17, 18, 20, 21, 23, 24, 26, 27, 29]

Supplier Energy -0.16731999999999692
```

This energy value for the suppliers is quite poor. The considerable improvement in the product energy value has resulted in a very poor outcome for the supplier risks energy value. This result is not going to please the procurement manager.

11. Now, let's plot these results and relook at the energy value comparison of the two scenarios:

```
plt.scatter(dwave_plot_sup1,dwave_plot_
prod1,color='black')
plt.scatter(dwave_plot_sup2,dwave_plot_prod2,color='red')
plt.scatter(plot_sup1,plot_prod1,color='gray')
plt.scatter(plot_sup2,plot_prod2,color='pink')

plt.xlabel('supplier')
plt.ylabel('product')
plt.title('Find optimal supplier and product')
```

The results are shown in the following plot:

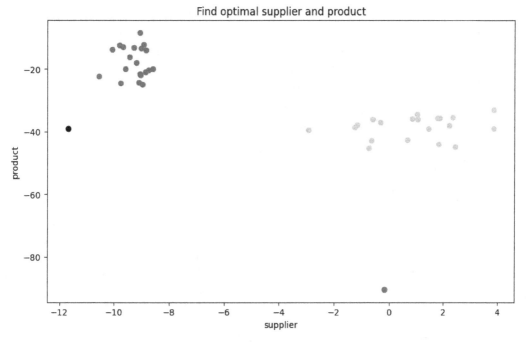

Figure 12.9 – Classical and D-Wave results for scenario A (left) and B (right)

The ideal scenarios for each area are detrimental to the other area. The procurement manager has been working toward pushing the risks lower toward the D-Wave result (the single purple dot on the left of the plot), while the inventory manager has been driving toward the best overall inventory outcome, as shown by the D-Wave result (the single red dot at the bottom right of the plot). Both these efforts hurt the other area and if compensation is misaligned, the conflict will remain.

With that, we have seen how the two objectives force the company in two different directions. These types of multi-objective scenarios exist when the dynamics within a company aren't understood completely. Now, it's time to determine how our quantum annealing method can find a resolution to this dilemma.

Determining a better global solution

How can we address both objectives and find a global solution? A mathematical treatment of creating a QUBO that represents both objectives and includes the appropriate constraint with a set cover formulation is outside the scope of this book. Please check out the *Further reading* section for examples and more details regarding this area. However, we can use a simple method with the techniques we have developed to find an answer.

Here are the high-level steps we will go over:

1. Create a combined BQM matrix, Mf, with both the Ms and Mi matrices and find an appropriate way to "connect" the items to the suppliers using Ma. We are looking for a way where, if an item is picked in the solution, there is a large negative coupling value that will also cause the optimization to pick the appropriate supplier of that item (and vice versa). We will use a multiplier, A, that is large enough to ensure this condition is enforced:

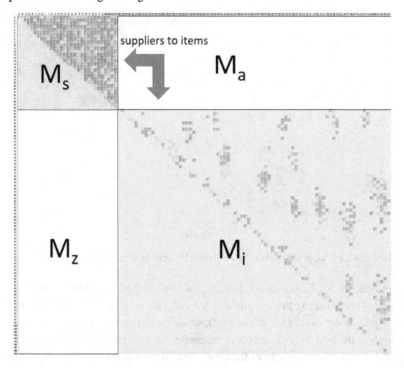

Figure 12.10 – Combined BQM matrix, Mf

2. Since the supplier units are not the same as the item units, we will combine them into one objective, along with the I and S multipliers, which we can use to change the relative strength of the values of Mi and Ms, respectively.

3. This method is not guaranteed to ensure valid solutions are found. We will have to extract the values of the suppliers and items and then validate if the solution is feasible based on the Ma availability matrix. We can only influence that the correct items and supplier combinations are picked by adjusting the value of A.

4. We will plot both the *infeasible* and *feasible* solutions that are found on the same plot.

5. We will also span through various multiplier values – A, I, and S – to find where the best feasible solutions are found. We will save various feasible solutions from different trials and then plot the results.

6. Finally, we will plot the values found with the highest product of the supplier and inventory energy values. This will give us a final set of the most optimal solutions.

With that, we have summarized the steps needed to find the global solution to the two conflicting objectives. In the next section, we will implement this in code.

Evaluating with the classical probabilistic solver

Let's get started and learn how to implement the high-level steps mentioned earlier using the classical probabilistic solver method:

1. First, we will set the multipliers and create the modified Ma matrix, Ma2. Here, if an item is provided by a supplier, we will replace 1 in the matrix with -A. This way, we can change the strength of A to enforce this constraint:

```
A=0.5
S=2.5
I=0.5
Ma2=Ma.copy()
Ma2 = np.where(Ma2==1, -A, 0)
print(Ma2)
print(np.shape(Ma2))
```

Output:

```
[[ 0.    0.    0.   ...  0.    0.    0. ]
 [ 0.   -0.5  0.   ... -0.5  0.    0. ]
 [ 0.    0.    0.   ...  0.    0.    0. ]

 ...

 [-0.5  0.    0.   ...  0.    0.    0. ]
 [-0.5  0.   -0.5  ...  0.    0.    0. ]
 [ 0.    0.    0.   ...  0.    0.    0. ]]
(30, 80)
```

If A is too large, it will overshadow the effects of the Mf and Mi matrices, while if A=0, the optimization will lead to all items and suppliers, which is not feasible.

2. Now, we can stitch together the Mf matrix, as shown in *Figure 12.10*:

```
Mz=np.zeros([len(Mi),len(Ms)],dtype=float)
print('Mz',np.shape(Mz))
Msz=np.append(S*Ms, Mz, axis=0)
print('Msz',np.shape(Msz))
Mai=np.append(Ma2, I*Mi, axis=0)
print('Mai',np.shape(Mai))
Mf=np.append(Msz,Mai, axis=1)
print('Mf',np.shape(Mf))
print(Mf)
np.savetxt('Mf.csv', Mf, delimiter=',')
```

Output:

```
Mz (80, 30)

Msz (110, 30)

Mai (110, 80)

Mf (110, 110)

[[-3.25      0.08375  0.12275 ...  0.        0.        0.      ]
 [ 0.       -0.415    0.23575 ... -0.5       0.        0.      ]
 [ 0.        0.       -0.365   ...  0.        0.        0.      ]

 ...

 [ 0.        0.        0.       ... -0.195     0.35      0.01    ]
 [ 0.        0.        0.       ...  0.        0.1      -0.45    ]
 [ 0.        0.        0.       ...  0.        0.       -0.17    ]]
```

The shape of the new Mf matrix is 110x110 and has been saved to the Mf.csv file.

3. Since this is a valid **BQM** matrix, we can quickly check it using the probabilistic solver:

```
result=ProbabilisticSampler(Mf,100)
```

Output:

```
Best found:  [0, 1, 4, 5, 6, 7, 8, 9, 10, 11, 13, 14, 15, 16,
17, 18, 20, 21, 22, 23, 24, 26, 27, 28, 29, 30, 32, 33, 34,
35, 36, 37, 38, 39, 40, 41, 42, 43, 44, 45, 47, 48, 49, 50,
51, 52, 53, 54, 55, 58, 60, 61, 62, 63, 64, 66, 67, 68, 69,
70, 71, 72, 73, 75, 76, 77, 78, 79, 80, 82, 83, 84, 85, 86,
87, 88, 89, 90, 91, 92, 93, 94, 95, 97, 98, 99, 100, 101,
103, 104, 105, 106, 107, 108, 109]
```

```
count: 95
```

```
Energy: -80.00992500000018
```

```
Solutions Sampled: 10902
```

What do all these values mean? The resulting index values represent both the supplier and item values. The values from 0 to 29 represent the 30 suppliers, while the values from 30 to 109 represent the 80 items. The energy value of -80.00 does not correspond to the supplier or item energy, but that of the overall optimal for the full Mf matrix. Thus, we have to ensure that this is a feasible solution and then separately calculate the supplier and inventory energy values.

4.   We can extract the supplier and item values using the following code:

```
sup_list=[]
item_list=[]
for i in (result[0]):
    if i<len(Ms):
        sup_list.append(i)
    else:
        item_list.append(i-len(Ms))
```

5.   Now, let's print the lists and calculate the supplier and item energies:

```
print(sup_list)
sup_energy=0
for i in sup_list:
    for j in sup_list:
        if i<=j:
            sup_energy+=Ms[i,j]
print('Supplier Energy',sup_energy)
print(item_list)
item_energy=0
```

```
    for i in item_list:
        for j in item_list:
            if i<=j:
                item_energy+=Mi[i,j]
    print('Item Energy',item_energy)
```

Output:

[0, 1, 4, 5, 6, 7, 8, 9, 10, 11, 13, 14, 15, 16, 17, 18, 20, 21, 22, 23, 24, 26, 27, 28, 29]

Supplier Energy -1.1539699999999968

[0, 2, 3, 4, 5, 6, 7, 8, 9, 10, 11, 12, 13, 14, 15, 17, 18, 19, 20, 21, 22, 23, 24, 25, 28, 30, 31, 32, 33, 34, 36, 37, 38, 39, 40, 41, 42, 43, 45, 46, 47, 48, 49, 50, 52, 53, 54, 55, 56, 57, 58, 59, 60, 61, 62, 63, 64, 65, 67, 68, 69, 70, 71, 73, 74, 75, 76, 77, 78, 79]

Item Energy -10.249999999999492

6. The following code checks if a feasible solution has been found. First, we will extract the available items, a, based on the suppliers in the solution. Next, we will check if each of the items in the solution are included in the available item list. If all the selected items are found in the selected supplier, then the condition is met, and we have a feasible solution. On the other hand, if even one item in the solution is not found in the available item list, this means the solution cannot be feasible. Let's print out the condition array so that you can check the status of each item:

```
a=availability(sup_list,Ma)
print('all items available',a)
# Is this feasible:
if(np.isin(False,(np.isin(item_list,a)))):
    print('Not feasible')
# print result of each condition
    print(np.isin(item_list,a))
else:
    print('Feasible')
```

Output:

all items available [0 1 2 3 4 5 6 7 8 9 10 11 12 13 14 15 16 17 18 19 20 21 22 23
 24 25 27 28 29 30 31 32 33 34 35 36 37 38 39 40 41 42 44 45 46 47 48 49

```
    50 51 52 53 55 56 57 58 59 60 62 63 64 65 66 68 69 70 71 72
    73 74 75 76

    77 78 79]
```

Not feasible

```
[ True    True    True    True    True    True    True    True    True True
  True    True    True    True    True    True    True    True    True    True
  True    True    True    True    True    True    True    True    True    True
  True    True    True    True    True    True    True False    True    True
  True    True    True    True    True    True False    True    True    True
  True    True    True False    True    True    True    True False    True
  True    True    True    True    True    True    True    True    True    True]
```

In this example, we found an infeasible solution because a few of the items in the solution were not in the available item list. We want to repeat this process many times so that we can accumulate several optimal solutions and separate the feasible solutions from the infeasible ones. Rather than using the probabilistic sampler, we will use the strength of the D-Wave device and its ability to find many good solutions.

Evaluating the best solution using D-Wave

In the previous section, we used fixed values of S, I, and A. It turns out that we did not get a feasible solution. How can we find more feasible solutions? We can change the multipliers or span a range of values that will help us look for solutions in different regions between the two conflicting objectives. First, we will set up the code to run this process using D-Wave and show the results with a fixed set of values for S, I, and A. Then, we will repeat the code with ranges of values of S, I, and A.

Let's start by repeating the same steps as in the previous section but use D-Wave for more sampling and better results:

1. The initial part of the code for building the Mf matrix is the same as in the previous section. Please also check out *Figure 12.10* to see how the matrix is visually stitched together. Once the Mf BQM matrix has been created, we execute it on D-Wave using the following code:

```
A=0.5
S=2.5
I=0.5
# add a -A value in Ma2 for available items
Ma2=Ma.copy()
Ma2 = np.where(Ma2==1, -A, 0)
print('Ma2',Ma2)
print(np.shape(Ma2))
Mz=np.zeros([len(Mi),len(Ms)],dtype=float)
```

```
print('Mz',np.shape(Mz))
Msz=np.append(S*Ms, Mz, axis=0)
print('Msz',np.shape(Msz))

Mai=np.append(Ma2, I*Mi, axis=0)
print('Mai',np.shape(Mai))

Mf=np.append(Msz,Mai, axis=1)
print('Mf',np.shape(Mf))
print(Mf)
np.savetxt('Mf.csv', Mf, delimiter=',')
result=run_dwave(Mf,0.5)
```

Output:

```
[[ 0.    0.    0.   ...  0.    0.    0.  ]
 [ 0.   -0.5   0.   ... -0.5   0.    0.  ]
 [ 0.    0.    0.   ...  0.    0.    0.  ]
 ...
 [-0.5   0.    0.   ...  0.    0.    0.  ]
 [-0.5   0.   -0.5  ...  0.    0.    0.  ]
 [ 0.    0.    0.   ...  0.    0.    0.  ]]
Ma2 (30, 80)
Mz (80, 30)
Msz (110, 30)
Mai (110, 80)
Mf (110, 110)
[[-3.25  0.08375  0.12275 ...  0.      0.      0.     ]
 [ 0.   -0.415    0.23575 ... -0.5     0.      0.     ]
 [ 0.    0.      -0.365   ...  0.      0.      0.     ]
 ...
 [ 0.    0.       0.      ... -0.195   0.35    0.01   ]
 [ 0.    0.       0.      ...  0.      0.1    -0.45   ]
 [ 0.    0.       0.      ...  0.      0.     -0.17   ]]
```

```
Number of qubits:   5760

Number of couplers 40135

Shots max 10,000

32451855365842672678315602057625600

Recommended shots 10000

Estimated cost $2.20
        0  1  2  3  4  5  6  7  8  9 10 11 12 13 ... 109
energy num_oc. ...

327   1  1  1  0  0  1  1  1  1  1  1  1  0  0 ...  1
-113.747975         1 ...

43    1  1  1  0  0  1  1  1  1  1  1  1  0  0 ...  1
-113.737975         1 ...
```

2. The item and supplier values have been extracted from the D-Wave results and the feasible and infeasible solutions have been stored for plotting. The code hasn't been reproduced here, but it follows the same method shown in the previous section.

The following is the result of the only feasible solutions found and the resulting plot.

Output:

```
Feasible

suppliers: -6.1589599999999995 [0, 1, 2, 5, 6, 7, 8, 9, 10,
11, 14, 17, 18, 20, 21, 23, 24, 26, 27, 28]

products: -72.45999999999951 [0, 1, 2, 3, 4, 5, 6, 7, 8, 9,
10, 11, 12, 13, 14, 15, 16, 17, 20, 24, 25, 26, 32, 34, 37,
38, 39, 40, 41, 42, 44, 46, 48, 50, 53, 55, 56, 57, 58, 63,
66, 69, 70, 71, 72, 73, 74, 75, 76, 77, 78, 79]

Feasible

suppliers: -5.34476 [0, 1, 2, 5, 6, 7, 8, 9, 10, 11, 14, 17,
18, 20, 21, 23, 24, 26, 27, 28, 29]

products: -73.86999999999946 [0, 1, 2, 3, 4, 5, 6, 7, 8, 9,
10, 11, 12, 13, 14, 15, 16, 17, 23, 25, 26, 27, 32, 34, 37,
38, 39, 40, 42, 44, 46, 48, 50, 52, 55, 56, 57, 58, 63, 65,
66, 69, 70, 71, 72, 73, 74, 75, 76, 77, 78, 79]

Feasible

suppliers: -5.34476 [0, 1, 2, 5, 6, 7, 8, 9, 10, 11, 14, 17,
18, 20, 21, 23, 24, 26, 27, 28, 29]
```

```
products: -67.44999999999938 [0, 1, 2, 3, 4, 5, 6, 7, 8, 9,
10, 11, 12, 13, 14, 15, 16, 17, 22, 23, 25, 26, 32, 33, 34,
37, 38, 39, 40, 41, 42, 44, 45, 46, 48, 50, 52, 55, 56, 57,
58, 63, 65, 66, 69, 70, 71, 72, 73, 74, 75, 76, 77, 78]
```

The following plot shows the three feasible solutions, as indicated by the arrows in the middle of the region of infeasible solutions:

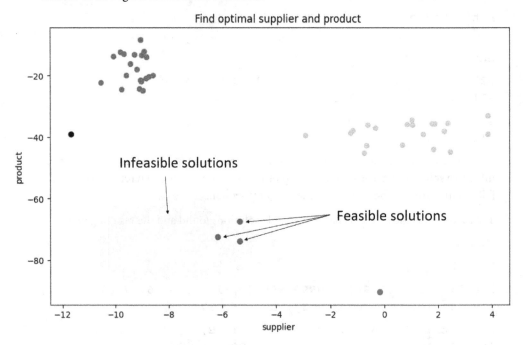

Figure 12.11 – Searching for the global optimum using D-Wave

3. Next, we will take a range of values for each of the multipliers – S, I, and A – to find other feasible solutions. The following plot shows the effect of varying the multipliers. Note that as I approaches 0 (I →0), we will have no influence from Mi. However, as S approches 0, (S→0), we have no influence from the values of Ms. On the other hand, if A approaches 0, (A→0), then the solutions end up in the bottom-left corner but are all infeasible because the effect of the availability matrix, Ma, has been removed. On the other hand, larger values of A, (A ≫ 0), pull the solutions toward the top right and start enforcing the item availability constraint. If A is too strong, the effect of the supplier and item matrices is overshadowed:

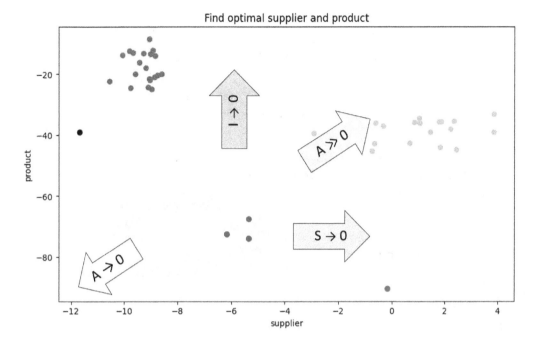

Figure 12.12 – Effect of multipliers on the region where the solutions are evaluated

4. By spanning the values, we can see a landscape of solutions that will include feasible and infeasible solutions between the extremes. The results from the various range of multiplier values that were used with D-Wave are shown here:

```
dwave_plot_sup3=[]
dwave_plot_prod3=[]
dwave_plot_sup4=[]
dwave_plot_prod4=[]

save_sup_list=[]
save_sup_energy=[]
save_item_list=[]
save_item_energy=[]

# Vary the range of multipliers A, S and I
for A in np.arange(0.5, 1.0, 0.2):
    for S in np.arange (2.0, 3.5, 0.5):
        for I in np.arange (0.5, 1.0, 0.2):
```

```
            print('Starting:',A,S,I)
            Ma2=Ma.copy()
            Ma2 = np.where(Ma2==1, -A, 0)
            Mz=np.zeros([len(Mi),len(Ms)],dtype=float)
            Msz=np.append(S*Ms, Mz, axis=0)
            Mai=np.append(Ma2, I*Mi, axis=0)
            Mf=np.append(Msz,Mai, axis=1)
    # Find solutions using D-Wave.
    # Solutions may be improved using different Chain
    # strength values.
            result=run_dwave(Mf,0.5)
  ...
    (remaining code is not shown)
```

Output:

Starting: 0.5 2.0 0.5

Number of qubits: 5760

Number of couplers 40135

Shots max 10,000

324518553658426726783156020557625600

Recommended shots 10000

Estimated cost $2.20

```
        0  1  2  3  4  ... 109      energy num_oc. ...
20      1  1  1  0  0  ...   1   -110.7085        1 ...
3       1  1  0  0  0  ...   1   -110.65112       1 ...
```
(remaining output is not shown)

The preceding output only shows a portion of the first iteration's output. The many D-Wave iterations are accumulated to extract all infeasible and feasible solutions. All the data has been plotted in the following plot:

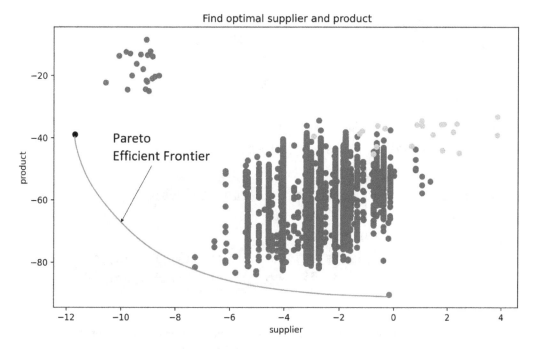

Figure 12.13 – Various D-Wave trials with a range of values for the A, S, and I multipliers

Varying the multipliers gives us many solutions between scenarios A and B. The lower-left boundary of the feasible solutions forms a Pareto efficient frontier, as shown in the preceding plot. This is because any solution "above" this boundary will be less ideal or efficient for the company. In the next step, we will remove the values we don't consider to be on this Pareto efficient frontier. How we move on this frontier depends on how much the store prioritizes one area's contribution over the other using the S and I multipliers. In our problem, S=10 and I=1.

5. Now, let's calculate the global score of each of the feasible solutions by multiplying the inventory and supplier energies. Then, we will sort this list by the lowest to largest energy values:

```
S=10
I=1
global_score=[]
for i in range(len(save_sup_energy)):
    global_score.append(S*save_sup_energy[i]*I*save_item_
energy[i])
#sort values with based on global score
index=np.argsort(global_score)
# print from highest score first (reverse order)
```

```
print(index,global_score[index[-1]])
print('supplier',save_sup_energy[index[-1]])
print(save_sup_list[index[-1]])
print('product',save_item_energy[index[-1]])
print(save_item_list[index[-1]])
```

The largest resulting ideal solution is shown here:

```
[4408 4701 4521 ...   83   65   87] 5934.441512999961

supplier -7.280629999999997

[0, 2, 5, 6, 7, 8, 9, 10, 11, 14, 17, 18, 20, 21, 23, 24, 26,
27, 28]

product -81.5099999999995

[0, 2, 3, 4, 5, 6, 7, 8, 9, 10, 11, 12, 13, 14, 15, 16, 17,
23, 25, 26, 34, 37, 38, 39, 40, 41, 42, 44, 46, 48, 50, 52,
53, 55, 56, 57, 58, 63, 66, 69, 70, 71, 72, 73, 74, 76, 77,
78, 79]
```

The preceding output shows the supplier and product mix that provides this optimal solution. The supplier energy value is -7.28, while the inventory energy value is -81.5 for this solution. The output shows that the largest score is 5934.44.

6. From the saved values in the previous step, we can select several solutions and display them on the Pareto efficient frontier. In this case, we will limit the top solutions to 20:

```
ef_sup_energy=[]
ef_item_energy=[]
N=20
n=0
for i in reversed(index):
    if n<N:
        print(global_score[i])
        print(' supplier',save_sup_energy[i])
        print('',save_sup_list[i])
        print(' product',save_item_energy[i])
        print('',save_item_list[i])
        ef_sup_energy.append(save_sup_energy[i])
        ef_item_energy.append(save_item_energy[i])

    n+=1
```

Output:

```
5934.441512999961
 supplier -7.280629999999997
 [0, 2, 5, 6, 7, 8, 9, 10, 11, 14, 17, 18, 20, 21, 23, 24,
26, 27, 28]
 product -81.5099999999995
 [0, 2, 3, 4, 5, 6, 7, 8, 9, 10, 11, 12, 13, 14, 15, 16, 17,
23, 25, 26, 34, 37, 38, 39, 40, 41, 42, 44, 46, 48, 50, 52,
53, 55, 56, 57, 58, 63, 66, 69, 70, 71, 72, 73, 74, 76, 77,
78, 79]
5700.733289999959
 supplier -7.280629999999997
 [0, 2, 5, 6, 7, 8, 9, 10, 11, 14, 17, 18, 20, 21, 23, 24,
26, 27, 28]
 product -78.29999999999947
 [0, 1, 2, 3, 4, 5, 6, 7, 8, 9, 10, 11, 12, 13, 14, 15, 16,
17, 25, 26, 34, 37, 38, 39, 40, 41, 42, 44, 45, 46, 48, 50,
52, 53, 55, 56, 57, 58, 63, 69, 70, 71, 72, 73, 74, 75, 76,
77, 78, 79]
```

Only the first two of the best scores are shown in the output here. The energy values and the item and supplier arrays have also been printed.

7. Finally, we will only display the top 20 scores and show how they relate to the past plots we have generated using the probabilistic solver and the best values from scenario A and scenario B using D-Wave. We will also look at the Pareto efficient frontier curve:

```
plt.scatter(ef_sup_energy,ef_item_energy,color='blue')
plt.scatter(plot_sup1,plot_prod1,color='gray')
plt.scatter(plot_sup2,plot_prod2,color='pink')
plt.scatter(dwave_plot_sup1,dwave_plot_prod1,
        color='black')
plt.scatter(dwave_plot_sup2,dwave_plot_prod2,
        color='red')
plt.xlabel('supplier')
plt.ylabel('product')
plt.title('Find optimal supplier and product')
plt.show()
```

The following plot shows the top 20 values found. The optimal solution with the largest score has been identified on the Pareto efficient frontier between the limits of the best solutions for scenario A and scenario B:

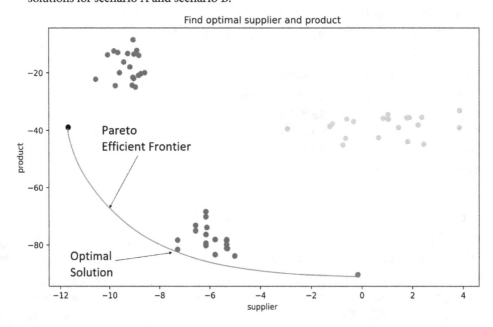

Figure 12.14 – Optimal solution found by selecting the highest energy global score from feasible solutions

The ideal solution is to find a compromise for both the inventory and procurement managers. However, they cannot do better than this if they are to take the global benefit of the store into account. The managers and store leadership can now align their objectives and compensation the structure toward a global strategy. This strategy, if implemented as a global objective, will result in managers cooperating and streamlining operations, as shown in the following diagram:

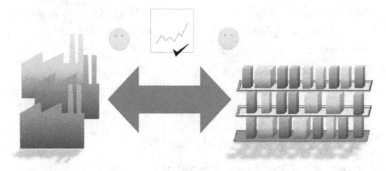

Figure 12.15 – Global optimization of multiple objectives resulting in better performance

We have now concluded the multi-objective optimization exercise using D-Wave through Amazon Braket. Due to a large number of variables in this example, it was not possible to run this model on the currently available gate-based quantum devices. However, as soon as new devices that can handle 110 or more variables are added to Amazon Braket, the same Mf matrix that we sent to the D-Wave annealer can be sent to the `quantum_device_sampler()` function to get solutions from gate-based quantum computers.

Summary

In this chapter, we extended our use of Amazon Braket devices to a mock multi-objective optimization problem. We showed the process it would take to map real-world problems to quantum devices on Amazon Braket. Without a rigorous mathematical derivation, we were able to leverage D-Wave to provide an optimal global solution. This type of technique may become important as system and business analysts start using Amazon Braket to solve optimization problems, as well as start re-analyzing their business processes in terms of quadratic relationships and global objectives that may not have been considered or ignored in the past due to classical solver limitations.

Further reading

To learn more about the topics that were covered in this chapter, take a look at the following resources:

- For a rigorous list of mathematical derivations of QUBOs, including set cover, please check out the following links:

  - `https://www.researchgate.net/publication/235702677_Ising_formulations_of_many_NP_problems`

  - `https://arxiv.org/abs/1811.11538`

- The following CDL hackathon code might be helpful if you wish to do a more rigorous mathematical evaluation with a problem similar to the one that was presented in this chapter: `https://github.com/CDL-Quantum/Hackathon2021/tree/main/ZebraKet`.

- The techniques you've learned about in this chapter can be used to solve slightly more complex problems, including portfolio optimization, which is also a multi-objective problem with constraints on the number of assets and the need to find feasible solutions. You are encouraged to read the following papers:

  - `https://www.researchgate.net/publication/342706781_Portfolio_Optimization_of_40_Stocks_Using_the_DWave_Quantum_Annealer`

  - `https://www.researchgate.net/publication/343786420_Portfolio_Optimization_of_60_Stocks_Using_Classical_and_Quantum_Algorithms`

- The knapsack formulation was used to solve a COVID optimization problem. First, we developed the disease evolution model (SEIRD) and then optimized it to find if a region should be locked down or kept open based on the amount of hospital capacity. The starter code for a basic (SIR) model can be found here, along with the final paper:

  - `https://github.com/AlignedIT/SIR-Model`

  - `https://www.medrxiv.org/content/10.1101/2021.06.14.21258907v1.full`

- More samples and further learning opportunities can be found by reviewing the following Amazon Braket and D-Wave examples:

  - `https://github.com/aws/amazon-braket-examples`

  - `https://github.com/dwave-examples`

- Please reference the Amazon Braket documentation for any code changes: `https://docs.aws.amazon.com/braket/latest/developerguide/what-is-braket.html`.

Code Deep Dive

Please review the code in the following functions, which have been used previously in this book:

- `run_dwave()`
- `ProbabilisticSampler()`

Please review the code in the following new functions, which were introduced in this chapter and were provided as part of the discussion. They can be found in the code for this chapter in this book's GitHub repository:

- `item_m()`
- `availability()`
- `SetCoverSampler()`

The following are links to some commonly used quantum computing libraries and platforms:

- `https://quantum-computing.ibm.com/`
- `https://qiskit.org/textbook/preface.html`
- `https://docs.rigetti.com/qcs/`
- `https://grove-docs.readthedocs.io/en/latest/index.html`
- `https://xanadu.ai/`

- `https://pennylane.readthedocs.io/en/stable/`
- `https://www.dwavesys.com/`
- `https://cqcl.github.io/tket/pytket/api/index.html`
- `https://quantumai.google/`
- `https://ionq.com/`
- `https://developer.nvidia.com/cuquantum-sdk`
- `https://cqcl.github.io/lambeq/index.html`
- `https://quantumai.google/openfermion`
- `https://qiskit.org/documentation/nature/`

The following are books I highly recommend to dive deeper into quantum computing:

- `https://www.amazon.com/Quantum-Programming-Illustrated-Aleksandar-Radovanovic-ebook/dp/B08B3MVXHB`
- `https://www.amazon.com/Essential-Mathematics-Quantum-Computing-complexities/dp/1801073147`
- `https://www.amazon.com/Dancing-Qubits-quantum-computing-change/dp/1838827366`
- `https://www.amazon.com/Quantum-Chemistry-Computing-Curious-Illustrated/dp/1803243902`
- `https://www.amazon.com/Quantum-Computing_-An-Applied-Approach/dp/3030832732`

Concluding section 3

This section was intended to show you a few examples of how real-world problems can be mapped to quantum computers and D-Wave's quantum annealer. We leveraged Amazon Braket Jobs, which allows users to run many quantum tasks within one job. We also showed how a QUBO is required to rigorously map a real-world optimization problem to a quantum computer or quantum annealer. Then, we saw how a multi-objective optimization problem can be quickly set up without rigorous mathematics.

With this, we have concluded this chapter and also this book. Some examples are included in the *Further reading* sections at the end of every chapter, and I would consider these good next steps to investigate. It would also be a good idea to dig into the code and functions that we have covered at a high level in this book. This will make it easy for you to make adjustments as new devices are added and new features become available in Amazon Braket. More importantly, I hope that you will create unique libraries for how you utilize Amazon Braket and add more use cases.

Even though this book focused mostly on optimization, many other use cases can be explored, including other basic quantum algorithms, simulation problems, natural language processing, and quantum machine learning. This was intended to be a starting point and to quickly get you comfortable with some basic concepts that lead to useful applications of quantum computing. Ongoing research and improvements are being to all quantum algorithms and you can try refining them. In most cases, please keep in mind that there is considerable mathematics and quantum mechanics rigor, research, and theory behind all the ideas I presented in a simplified manner in this book.

Finally, Amazon Braket was never intended to be an isolated platform. I structured this book so that you can write code and functions while using minimal additional libraries. This gives you the option to add the full capacity of other quantum computing libraries and other AWS services. I have added a few commonly used quantum computing platforms to the *Further reading* section.

I hope that the experiments in this book have helped accelerate your understanding of quantum computing. I wish you all the best on your continued growth and journey in this exciting area!

Appendix – Knapsack BQM Derivation

This appendix will show a sample expansion of the **quadratic unconstrained binary optimization (QUBO)** for the Knapsack problem, which we covered in *Chapter 11, Single Objective Optimization Use Case*. We will start with *equation 11.7* (reproduced here for clarity). In this equation, we described the objective and the two constraints in a mathematical form representing a QUBO. Many real-world problems also include objectives and constraints and can be defined in a similar QUBO format. The reason for showing this derivation is to give you an appreciation of how we go from the initial mathematical version to the **binary quadratic model (BQM)** matrix M_f.

Getting started with the derivation

Here, we will detail the QUBO formulation of the 0/1 knapsack formulation with integer weight constraint taken from *Chapter 11*:

$$A\left(\sum_n^{W_c} y_n - 1\right)^2 + B\left(\sum_i^N w_i x_i - \sum_n^{W_c} n y_n\right)^2 - C\left(\sum_i^N v_i x_i\right) \qquad eq.(11.7)$$

Splitting the preceding equation into the three equations gives us the following:

$$A\left(\sum_n^{W_c} y_n - 1\right)^2 \qquad eq.(A.1)$$

$$B\left(\sum_i^N w_i x_i - \sum_n^{W_c} n y_n\right)^2 \qquad eq.(A.2)$$

$$-C\left(\sum_i^N v_i x_i\right) \qquad eq.(A.3)$$

We know that x_i and y_n are binary.

Before we continue, let's review the expansion of the square of a sum:

$$\left(\sum_i^n a_i x_i\right)^2 = (a_1 x_1 + a_2 x_2 \ldots + a_n x_n) \times (a_1 x_1 + a_2 x_2 \ldots + a_n x_n) \quad eq.(A.4)$$

Here, a_i is a constant:

$$= \sum_{i}^{n} a_i^2 x_i^2 + 2\sum_{i<j}^{n} a_i a_j x_i x_j \qquad eq.\,(A.5)$$

Since x_i is binary,

$$x_i^2 = x_i \qquad eq.\,(A.6)$$

Thus,

$$\left(\sum_{i}^{n} ax_i\right)^2 = \sum_{i}^{n} a^2 x_i + \sum_{i<j}^{n} 2a_i a_j x_i x_j \qquad eq.\,(A.7)$$

The first sum on the right side of the equation represents the linear terms or the terms on the diagonal of the matrix, while the second sum on the right side is the upper-right quadratic terms.

Now, expanding equation A. 1:

$$A\left(\sum_{n}^{W_c} y_n - 1\right)^2 = A\left[\left(\sum_{n}^{W_c} y_n\right)^2 - 2\sum_{n}^{W_c} y_n + 1\right] \qquad eq.\,(A.8)$$

Using *equation A. 7*, we can expand the first term:

$$= A\left[\left(\sum_{n}^{W_c} y_n + 2\sum_{n<m}^{W_c} y_n y_m\right) - 2\sum_{n}^{W_c} y_n + 1\right] \qquad eq.\,(A.9)$$

$$= A\left[\sum_{n}^{W_c} -y_n + \sum_{n<m}^{W_c} 2y_n y_m\right] + A \qquad eq.\,(A.10)$$

Next, we can expand *equation A. 2*:

$$B\left(\sum_{i}^{N} w_i x_i - \sum_{n}^{W_c} ny_n\right)^2 = B\left[\left(\sum_{i}^{N} w_i x_i\right)^2 - 2\sum_{i}^{N} w_i x_i \sum_{n}^{W_c} ny_n + \left(\sum_{n}^{W_c} ny_n\right)^2\right] \qquad eq.\,(A.11)$$

We will now expand each of the three terms on the right side of *equation A.11*.

The first term in *equation A. 11* can be expanded as follows:

$$\left(\sum_i^N w_i x_i\right)^2 = \sum_i^N w_i^2 x_i + \sum_{i<j}^N 2w_i w_j \, x_i \, x_j \qquad eq. (A. 12)$$

The second term in *equation A.11* can be simplified to the following:

$$-2\sum_i^N w_i x_i \sum_n^{W_c} n y_n = \sum_{i,n}^{N,W_c} -2w_i n \, x_i y_n \qquad eq. (A. 13)$$

Note this is going to connect the x_i terms with the y_n terms.

The last term in *equation A. 11* is expanded to the following:

$$\left(\sum_n^{W_c} n y_n\right)^2 = \sum_n^{W_c} n^2 y_n + \sum_{n,m}^{W_c} 2nm \, y_n y_m \qquad eq. (A. 14)$$

Creating the required matrices

Now that we have expanded the equations, we can look at how each of the expanded terms relates to a portion of the final matrix.

Equation A. 3 does not need expansion. We can create our first matrix M_v from *equation A. 3*:

$$CM_v = C\left[\sum_i^N -v_i x_i\right] \qquad eq. (A. 15)$$

Here, we can use C to control the effect of the value of each item if needed.

We will represent the next matrix M_{yc} from *equation A. 10* as follows:

$$AM_{yc} = A\left[\sum_n^{W_c} -1 \, y_n + \sum_{n<m}^{W_c} 2 \, y_n y_m\right] \qquad eq. (A. 16)$$

Note that basically, this matrix has *-1* on the diagonal terms and *2* on the upper right. This matrix implements the constraint that there is only one weight in the solution. We will use the multiplier *A* to control the effect of this matrix, which will be to penalize any solutions with more than one weight and ensure the constraint is being applied. The constant *A* in *equation A. 10* is going to be ignored since it cannot be implemented in the matrix and becomes an offset to add to the final energy value.

The next three matrices will come from the results of expanding *equation A. 2*.

First, we represent the matrix BM_x from *equation A. 12*:

$$BM_x = B\left[\sum_i^N w_i^2 x_i + \sum_{i<j}^N 2w_i w_j \, x_i \, x_j\right] \qquad eq.\,(A.17)$$

We represent the next matrix BM_{xy} from *equation A. 13*:

$$BM_{xy} = B\left[\sum_{i,n}^{N,W_c} -2w_i n \, x_i y_n\right] \qquad eq.\,(A.18)$$

And, we represent the final matrix BM_y from *equation A. 14*:

$$BM_y = B\left[\sum_n^{W_c} n^2 y_n + \sum_{n,m}^{W_c} 2nm \, y_n y_m\right] \qquad eq.\,(A.19)$$

These three matrices ensure that the weight of the items selected in the knapsack equals the weight represented by y_n. The value of the multiplier *B* can be used to ensure this constraint is working properly.

Keep in mind the following:

- We also have an offset of *A*, which came from *equation A. 10*.
- M_v and M_x use the same variable x_i.
- M_{xy} uses both x_i and y_n variables.
- M_{yc} and M_y use the same variable y_n.

This results in the primary BQM matrix equations along with their multipliers as used in the code for *Chapter 11*:

$$M_{xf} = BM_x + CM_v = B\left[\sum_i^N w_i^2 x_i + \sum_{i<j}^N 2w_i w_j\, x_i\, x_j\right] + C\left[\sum_i^N -v_i x_i\right] \quad eq.(A.20)$$

$$BM_{xy} = B\left[\sum_{i,n}^{N,W_c} -2w_i n\, x_i y_n\right] \quad eq.(A.21)$$

$$M_{yf} = AM_{yc} + BM_y = A\left[\sum_n^{W_c} -1\, y_n + \sum_{n<m}^{W_c} 2\, y_n y_m\right] + B\left[\sum_n^{W_c} n^2\, y_n + \sum_{n,m}^{W_c} 2nm\, y_n y_m\right] eq.(A.22)$$

Equations A. 20, A. 21, and *A. 22* can be further consolidated based on the binary variables if desired, as shown here:

$$Minimize\left[\begin{array}{c} \sum_i^N (Bw_i^2 - Cv_i)\, x_i + \sum_{i<j}^N 2Bw_i w_j\, x_i\, x_j \\[2mm] + \sum_{i,n}^{N,W_c} -2Bw_i n\, x_i y_n \\[2mm] + \sum_n^{W_c} (Bn^2 - A)\, y_n + \sum_{n<m}^{W_c} (2A + 2Bnm)\, y_n y_m \end{array}\right] \quad eq.(A.23)$$

Conclusion

We have shown how we take a QUBO formulation of a real-world problem, in this case, a Knapsack problem, and expand the terms to derive our BQM matrix. The matrix can then be sent to the quantum annealer or to a gate-based quantum computer for optimization. You may now return to *Chapter 11, Single-Objective Optimization Use Cases* and continue to review how matrix M_f is used in finding the solutions for the Knapsack problem.

Index

Symbols

11x11 matrix
  optimizing 253-258
34x34 full upper triangular matrix
  optimizing 258-261
38x38 sparse matrix
  optimizing 262-267

A

active devices
  finding 62, 63
Amazon Braket
  about 3
  changes 4
  circuit implementation 154-156
  components 4
  landscape 4
  pricing, reference link 281
  quotas, reference link 290
  reference link 22
  remote access, providing with Boto3 19-21
  SDK installation, validating 22
  simulators 36
  starting 8-11
  supported devices, reference link 290

Amazon Braket devices
  calling, from PennyLane 288
  QAOA, benchmarking 253
  relative performance 268, 269
Amazon Braket Hybrid Jobs
  code structure 278, 279
  containers 291
  data, passing 279, 280
  failed jobs, debugging 290, 291
  hardware configuration 290
  Job Control Code 282-285
  Job Source Module 286-288
  multiple parallel device execution 290
  parameters, passing 279, 280
  PennyLane, using 289
  permissions 277, 278
  QAOA example 281
  region of environment, controlling 290
  results, sending back to Job
    Control Code 280, 281
  utilizing 276, 277
Amazon Braket simulator SV1
  knapsack problem, running on 328-330
Amazon simulator
  cost, of executing simple quantum circuit 80
  simple quantum circuit, running on 77-79

amplitude amplification effect
    Grover diffuser operator repetitions 189
    Grover's algorithm, using in searches 190
    observing 179, 180
    quantum circuits, using for Grover's
        search algorithm 185-189
    unitary matrices, using for Grover's
        operator 180-184
Anaconda
    download link 20
analog quantum computers 31
annealers 27
annealing 87
annealing-based quantum devices 26
annealing cycle 87
Ansatz 328
AWS account
    signing in 22
AWS Braket account
    creating 5-7
AWS S3 service
    configuring 12, 13

B

billing service
    utilizing 58, 59
binary quadratic function
    representing, with phase adder 210-219
Binary Quadratic Model (BQM) 100, 281
Bloch Clock
    about 138
    hour of day, representing 139
    minutes and seconds, representing 139, 140
Boto3
    used, for providing remote access
        to Amazon Braket 19-21

Bring your own container (BYOC)
    reference link 292

C

CCNOT gate 212
classical parameter optimizer
    using, for full QAOA hybrid
        algorithm 242-251
combinatorial optimization problems 89
Computational basis 190
conflict, determining on opposing objectives
    about 347
    optimal values, evaluating with
        D-Wave annealer 353-359
    results, evaluating with probabilistic
        solver 347-352
constrained optimization problems
    suggested process, for solving 333, 334
controlled-NOT (cNOT) operation 32

D

density matrix simulator (DM1) 37
depolarizing errors 37
derivation 379-381
device
    Amazon simulators, assigning 65
    assigning 64
    local simulator, assigning 64
    quantum devices, assigning 65
device costs
    about 55
    charges, viewing 58, 59
    estimating 66-71
    QPU devices, versus simulator
        devices 56, 57

D-Wave
  simple conceptual model 90, 91
  URL 31
D-Wave 2000Q
  about 28, 29
  qubit architecture 29
D-Wave Advantage 30
D-Wave annealer
  three-variable problem, running 94-98
D-Wave device
  knapsack problem, running on 326, 327
D-Wave quantum devices 27, 28

F

Fourier basis 190, 194
full QAOA hybrid algorithm
  classical parameter optimizer, using 242-251

G

gate-based quantum devices
  about 31
  properties 31
Gaussian Boson Sampling (GBS) 289
genetic algorithms 86
global minimum
  versus local minimum 86
global solution, to conflicting objectives
  best solution, evaluating with
    D-Wave 365-374
  determining 359-361
  evaluation, with classical
    probabilistic solver 361-365
Google experiment 153, 154
Google Supremacy experiment 153

gradient descent
  about 86
  versus simulated annealing 88
Grover diffuser operator
  repetitions 189
Grover operator
  about 180
  unitary matrices, using for 180-184
Grover's search algorithm
  quantum circuits, using for 185-189
  using 190

H

Heisenberg's uncertainty principle 88

I

inner products 37
IonQ Hardware, best practices
  reference link 33
IonQ qubit connectivity graph 33
IonQ's quantum device 32, 33
Ising 26
Ising states 89

J

Job Control Code 282-285
Job Source Module 286-288
Josephson junction 27

K

knapsack optimization problem
  running, on Rigetti Aspen 11 device 331
  running, on Rigetti Aspen
    M-1 device 332, 333

knapsack problem
    about 296, 297
    QUBO formulation 302-305
    running, on Amazon Braket
        simulator SV1 328-330
    running, on D-Wave device 326, 327
    visualizing 297-301
knapsack QUBO
    implementing, in code 305-312

L

linear ion trap 32
local density matrix simulator 37
local minimum
    versus global minimum 86
local state vector simulator 37

M

matrices
    creating 381-383
matrix mathematics
    using 126
    using, to represent
        single-qubit gates 127-133
mock inventory management problem
    about 338
    best product mix, evaluating based
        on scenario A 341-346
    multi-objective problem, setting up 338-341
monitoring, Amazon Braket with
    Amazon CloudWatch
    reference link 290
Monte Carlo method 90
multiple qubit quantum circuits
    building 141, 142

multiple-step parameter optimization
    in Quantum Approximate Optimization
        Algorithm (QAOA) 251-253

N

National Bureau of Standards 32
National Institute of Standards and
    Technology (NIST) 32
notebooks
    using 15-18
notebook service
    shutting down 18, 19
    starting 13-15
    working with 13

O

objective function 86
optimization problems
    solving 86
Oracle 178
orthogonality 124
Oxford Quantum Circuits (OQC)
    about 35
    URL 35

P

parameters
    fine-tuning, for QAOA 230-236
party optimization
    example 98-101
Pauli gate 37
PennyLane
    about 288
    Amazon Braket devices, calling from 288
    reference link 288

using, within Amazon Braket
Hybrid Jobs 289
PennyLane-Braket Plugin
reference link 288
phase adder circuit
about 200
used, for representing binary
quadratic function 210-219
phase angle, of qubit
about 190
numbers, adding with phase adder 206, 207
phase adder circuit, adding 200-203
phase information, adding 196-200
Quantum Fourier Transform
inverse, using 205
Quantum Fourier Transform, using 204, 205
translation, between Computational
basis and Fourier basis 194-196
working with 190-194
policy, for users
creating 45-48
Powell 249
probabilistic sampler
energy returned 321
multipliers, tweaking 322-325
using 317-321

Q

Qiskit
about 289
reference link 289
QPU devices
cost estimation 56, 57
Quadratic Unconstrained Binary
Optimization (QUBO)
about 26, 379
conceptual model, for D-Wave 90, 91

example, with ExactSolver() 92-94
example, with three variables 92-94
formulation, for knapsack problem 302-305
problems 89, 90
three-variable problem, running
on D-Wave annealer 94-98
quantum annealing 26, 88, 89
Quantum Approximate Optimization
Algorithm (QAOA)
benchmarking, on Amazon
Braket devices 253
concepts 220-224
concepts, validating experimentally 224-230
considerations 242
example, with Amazon Braket
Hybrid Jobs 281
implementing, for optimization 236-239
multiple-step parameter
optimization 251-253
parameters, fine-tuning 230-236
quantum circuit 122
quantum device costs 243
Quantum Fourier Transform (QFT)
about 38, 178
inverse, using 205
using 204, 205
quantum gates
using, in quantum circuit 134-138
quantum Oracle 178
Quantum Processing Unit (QPU) 276
quantum tunneling 28, 88
qubit
about 27
as Bloch sphere 124, 125
basics 123
QUBO matrices
combining 313-316

QUBO samplers
  results, obtaining from 316

R

Rigetti Aspen 11 device
  knapsack optimization problem,
      running on 331
Rigetti Aspen-M-1
  architecture 34, 35
  knapsack optimization problem,
      running on 332, 333
Rigetti Computing 34
Rigetti quantum devices 34, 35
Rigetti Systems
  URL 35

S

sampling 28
shots 28
simple quantum circuit
  binary value, representing 74-76
  cost, of executing on Amazon simulator 80
  creating 72, 73
  example 73, 74
  running, on Amazon simulator 77-79
simulated annealing
  about 86-88
  versus gradient descent 88
simulator devices
  cost estimation 56, 57
single 7x2 circuit, execution results
  about 156
  on Amazon Braket simulators 163-166
  on local device 156-162
  on quantum devices 166-173

single-qubit gate rotation
  example 138
single-qubit gates
  representing, by using matrix
      mathematics 127-133
spin states 89
state vector simulator (SV1) 37, 253
Strawberry Fields
  reference link 289
superconducting quantum interference
    device (SQUID) 28

T

tasks
  results, viewing 52-54
  viewing 51, 52
team selection example
  about 101, 102
  data, reviewing 103
  energy landscape, visualizing with
      probabilistic solver 108-110
  penalty function, to implement
      constraint 111-114
  problem, representing in graph form 104
  problem, running on classical and
      quantum solvers 115-119
  problem, summarizing 104
  QUBO problems, solving on D-Wave 102
  traditional formulation 105-108
tensor network simulator (TN1) 38, 253
tensor products 37
test code
  executing 49, 50
three-qubit circuit
  example 143-153
three-variable problem
  running, on D-Wave annealer 94-98

U

Unitary Operator 126
Universal Quantum Computer 121
user groups
    creating 41, 42
    policy, creating 45-48
    setting up 40
users
    adding, to user groups 44
    setting up 40, 43

X

Xanadu Borealis
    about 289
    reference link 289

`Packt.com`

Subscribe to our online digital library for full access to over 7,000 books and videos, as well as industry leading tools to help you plan your personal development and advance your career. For more information, please visit our website.

Why subscribe?

- Spend less time learning and more time coding with practical eBooks and Videos from over 4,000 industry professionals

- Improve your learning with Skill Plans built especially for you

- Get a free eBook or video every month

- Fully searchable for easy access to vital information

- Copy and paste, print, and bookmark content

Did you know that Packt offers eBook versions of every book published, with PDF and ePub files available? You can upgrade to the eBook version at `packt.com` and as a print book customer, you are entitled to a discount on the eBook copy. Get in touch with us at `customercare@packtpub.com` for more details.

At `www.packt.com`, you can also read a collection of free technical articles, sign up for a range of free newsletters, and receive exclusive discounts and offers on Packt books and eBooks.

Other Books You May Enjoy

If you enjoyed this book, you may be interested in these other books by Packt:

Quantum Computing in Practice with Qiskit® and IBM Quantum Experience®

Hassi Norlén

ISBN: 978-1-83882-844-8

- Visualize a qubit in Python and understand the concept of superposition
- Install a local Qiskit® simulator and connect to actual quantum hardware
- Compose quantum programs at the level of circuits using Qiskit® Terra
- Compare and contrast Noisy Intermediate-Scale Quantum computing (NISQ) and Universal Fault-Tolerant quantum computing using simulators and IBM Quantum® hardware
- Mitigate noise in quantum circuits and systems using Qiskit® Ignis
- Understand the difference between classical and quantum algorithms by implementing Grover's algorithm in Qiskit®

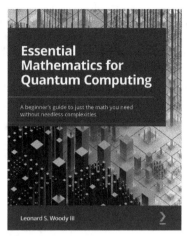

Essential Mathematics for Quantum Computing

Leonard S. Woody III

ISBN: 978-1-80107-314-1

- Operate on vectors (qubits) with matrices (gates)

- Define linear combinations and linear independence

- Understand vector spaces and their basis sets

- Rotate, reflect, and project vectors with matrices

- Realize the connection between complex numbers and the Bloch sphere

- Determine whether a matrix is invertible and find its eigenvalues

- Probabilistically determine the measurement of a qubit

- Tie it all together with bra-ket notation

Packt is searching for authors like you

If you're interested in becoming an author for Packt, please visit authors.packtpub.com and apply today. We have worked with thousands of developers and tech professionals, just like you, to help them share their insight with the global tech community. You can make a general application, apply for a specific hot topic that we are recruiting an author for, or submit your own idea.

Hi!

I am Alex Khan, author of *Quantum Computing Experimentation with Amazon Braket*. I really hope you enjoyed reading this book and found it useful for increasing your productivity and efficiency in using Amazon Braket, understanding the basics of quantum computation, and leveraging quantum computers for optimization problems.

It would really help me (and other potential readers!) if you could leave a review on Amazon sharing your thoughts on *Quantum Computing Experimentation with Amazon Braket*.

Go to the link below or scan the QR code to leave your review:

`https://packt.link/r/1800565267`

Your review will help me to understand what's worked well in this book, and what could be improved upon for future editions, so it really is appreciated.

Best Wishes,

Alex Khan